FUNCTIONAL INTEGRATION
Theory and Applications

FUNCTIONAL INTEGRATION
Theory and Applications

Edited by Jean-Pierre Antoine and Enrique Tirapegui
Institut de Physique Théorique, Université Catholique de Louvain, Louvain-la-Neuve, Belgium

PLENUM PRESS · NEW YORK AND LONDON

Library of Congress Cataloging in Publication Data

Colloquium on Functional Integration Theory and Applications, Louvain-la-Neuve, Belgium, 1979. Functional integration theory and applications.

Includes index.
1. Integration, Functional–Congresses. I. Antoine, Jean-Pierre. II. Tirapegui, Enrique. III. Title.
QC20.7.F85C64 1979 530.1'554 80-21935
ISBN 0-306 40573 3

Proceedings of the Colloquium on
Functional Integration: Theory and Applications,
held in Louvain-la-Neuve, Belgium, November 6–9, 1979.

A Division of Plenum Publishing Corporation
227 West 17th Street, New York, N.Y. 10011

Printed in the United States of America

"Dick was also a profoundly original scientist. He refused to take anybody's word for anything. This meant that he was forced to rediscover or reinvent for himself almost the whole of physics. It took him five years of concentrated work to reinvent quantum mechanics. He said that he couldn't understand the official version of quantum mechanics that was taught in textbooks, and so he had to begin afresh from the beginning. This was a heroic enterprise. He worked harder during those years than anybody else I ever knew. At the end he had a version of quantum mechanics that he could understand."

Quotation from F. Dyson,
"Disturbing the Universe",
Harper & Row, New York, 1979.
Cited by permission of the
publishers.

PREFACE

The idea of the workshop on Functional Integration, Theory and Applications, held in Louvain-la-Neuve from November 6 to 9 1979, was to put in close and informal contact, during a few days, active workers in the field.

There is no doubt now that functional integration is a tool that is being applied in all branches of modern physics. Since the earlier works of Dirac and Feynman enormous progress has been made, but unfortunately we lack still a unifying and rigorous mathematical framework to account for all the situations in which one is interested. We are then in presence of a rapidly changing field in which new achievements, proposals, and points of view are the normal pattern.

Considering this state of affairs we have decided to order the articles starting from the more fundamental and ambitious from the point of view of mathematical rigour, followed by articles in which the main interest is the application to concrete physical situations. It is obvious that this ordering should not be taken too seriously since in many cases there will be an interplay of both objects.

We would like to express our gratitude to all the people that have helped in the preparation of the Conference and in the practical realization of these Proceedings. We are especially indebted to J. DONEUX, O. JANSSENS DE BISTHOVEN and M. VAUSE (U.C.Louvain), F. LANGOUCHE and D. ROEKAERTS (K.U.Leuven) for their valuable help. We are also most grateful to Ms. C. DETROIJE and Ms.L. DUBOIS for their assistance in the organization of the meeting and for their kind cooperation in the material realization of this book. Finally we want to express our genuine thanks to Dr. Ken DERHAM and the Plenum Publishing Company Ltd. for their efficient collaboration.

J.P. Antoine
E. Tirapegui

CONTENTS

ANTICOMMUTATIVE INTEGRATION

Paul Krée

Département de Mathématiques
Université Pierre et Marie Curie
4, Place Jussieu
75230 - Paris

Let ν be the canonical Gaussian promeasure on a real and separable Hilbert space X. The symmetric Fock space of X is denoted $Fock^-(X)$. N. Wiener has constructed an isometry

$$L^2(X,\nu) \overset{W}{\rightarrow} Fock^-(X) . \qquad (0.1)$$

For any choice of orthonormal coordinates $q_1, q_2 \dots$ in X, for any multi-index $k = (k_1,\dots,k_n)$ of length $|k| = \Sigma k_i$, W maps the Hermite function $H_k(q) = \Pi_{i=1}^n H_{k_i}(q_i)$ onto $|k| q^k = |k| q_1^{k_n} \dots q_n^{k_n}$. This isometry is useful in commutative dimension-free analysis, hence in the theory of boson fields. The theory of Dirac fields use anticommutative dimension-free analysis ; hence a free index ε with two values $\pm$ is used below. The expression " ε-symmetric" means symmetric for $\varepsilon = -$, anti-symmetric for $\varepsilon = +$. The scope of this lecture is to construct an isometry of the type (0.1) for $\varepsilon = +$, using identical mathematical formalisms for $\varepsilon = +$ or $-$. For $\varepsilon = +$, the new space L^2 on some complex space $E = \overline{Z} \times Z$, is the completion of ΛE for a scalar product defined by a Grassmann integral

$$(f,g) = \int g \wedge f^+ \quad \nu'$$

where $f \rightarrow f^+$ is some semi-linear bijection of ΛE, where ν' is a coform[1]. Our general result gives in particular for $\varepsilon = -$, a new proof of the explicit form of W. For $\varepsilon = +$, our results are new, even in the finite-dimensional case. The antisymmetric forms corresponding for $\varepsilon = +$ to the Hermite polynomials were introduced in Ref. 1.

§ 1 - FORMAL POWER SERIES AND GRASSMANN ALGEBRAS

Let X be a vector space on the field $\mathbb{K} = \mathbb{R}$ or $\mathbb{C}$. We need a reformulation and a completion of the algebraic study of polynomials, formal series and Grassmann algebras on X.

1.1 The ε-symmetric tensor algebra $T^{\varepsilon}(X)$ of X

We set $T_o(X) = \mathbb{K}$, $T_k(X) = \otimes_k X$ for $k>0$. In the tensor algebra $T(X) = \bigoplus_{k=o}^{\infty} T_k(X)$, the operator Sym of ε-symmetrization is a projector. The range $T^{\varepsilon}(X)$ of this projector is the space of all ε-symmetric tensors on X . This is an associative algebra for the ε-symmetrized tensor product $tt' = \mathrm{Sym}\,(t \otimes t')$. More specifically $tt' = t \wedge t'$ for $\varepsilon = +$, $= t \circ t'$ for $\varepsilon = -$.
If $\{f_i\ , i \in I\}$ is an algebraic basis of X , we describe below the corresponding algebraic basis $\{f^{\alpha}, \alpha \in J(\varepsilon,I)\}$ of $T^{\varepsilon}(X)$. The set of all (non-ordered) finite subsets $\alpha = (i_1, i_2, \ldots, i_{\ell})$ of I is denoted $J(+,I)$. We set $|\alpha| = \ell$, $f^{\alpha} = f_{i_1} \wedge f_{i_2} \wedge \ldots f_{i_{\ell}}$, $\alpha! = 1$, $f^{\phi} = 1$. If $J(-,I)$ denotes the set of all maps $\beta : I \to \mathbb{N}$ with finite support,we use the conventions $(f_i)^{o} = 1, 0! = 1$,
$f^{\beta} = \Pi f_i^{\beta(i)}$; $|\beta| = \Sigma_i \beta(i)$; $\beta! = \Pi_i\, \beta(i)!$.

Setting $J^k(\varepsilon,I) = \{\gamma \in J(\varepsilon,I)\ ,\ |\gamma| = k\}$ the set $\{f^{\gamma}, \gamma \in J(\varepsilon,I)\}$ is an algebraic basis of $T_k^{\varepsilon}(X)$.

Any point $x \in X$ can be written in a unique way $x = \Sigma x_i f_i$. The linear form $x \to x_i$ giving the ith coordinate x_i , is also denoted x_i .

1.2 The algebra $F^{\varepsilon}(X)$ of all ε-symmetric form on X

Let $F_o^{\varepsilon}(X) = \mathbb{K}$. For $k>0$, the space $F_k^{\varepsilon}(X)$ of all ε-symmetric homogeneous forms of degree k on X , is the space of all ε-symmetric and k-linear forms on X^k . For $f_k \in F_k^{\varepsilon}(X)$, $g_{\ell} \in F^{\varepsilon}(X)$, we have a product $f_k\, g_{\ell} = \mathrm{Sym}\ (f_k \otimes g_{\ell}) \in F_{k+\ell}^{\varepsilon}(X)$.
This defines by linear extension a structure of associative algebra on $F^{\varepsilon}(X) = \Pi_{k=o}^{\infty} F_k^{\varepsilon}(X)$. In order to distinguish forms defined on different vector spaces, a form $f = \Sigma f_k \in F_k^{\varepsilon}(X)$ is denoted $f(x) = \Sigma_{k=o}^{\infty} f_k(x)$, even if the value of an ε-symmetric form at a point of X , cannot be defined in general. We note that the algebra $F^{-}(X)$ is isomorphic with the algebra of formal power series on X : the symmetric and k-homogeneous form f_k on X

defines the homogeneous polynomial of degree k : $x \mapsto f_k(x,\ldots,x) = f_k(x^k)$. Sometimes these algebras are identified.

1.3 Natural duality ; twisted duality

The natural duality between $T^\varepsilon(X)$ and its algebraic dual $F^\varepsilon(X)$ is defined by

$$\langle f,t\rangle_{nat} = \Sigma_{k=o}^{\infty} k!\, \langle f_k, t_k\rangle_{k,nat} \tag{1.1}$$

with $\langle f_k, x_1 x_2 \ldots x_k\rangle_{k,nat} = f_k(x_1,x_2,\ldots x_k)$. (1.2)

The involution $t = x_1 \ldots x_k \mapsto t^\vee = x_k x_{k-1} \ldots x_1$ in $T^\varepsilon(X)$ and the corresponding involution $f \to f^\vee$ are called "twist". The twisted duality on $T^\varepsilon(X) \times F^\varepsilon(X)$ is the following bilinear form

$$\langle f,t\rangle = \Sigma k!\, \langle f,t\rangle_k = \langle f^\vee, t\rangle_{nat} = \langle f, t^\vee\rangle_{nat} \tag{1.3}$$

If $\ell : X \to Y$ is a linear map, the corresponding map $T^\varepsilon(X) \to T^\varepsilon(Y)$ is denoted by L . The transposed map : $F^\varepsilon(Y) \to F^\varepsilon(X)$ is $g(y) \mapsto g(\ell x)$; the form $x \mapsto g(\ell x)$ is the inverse image of $y \mapsto g(y)$ by ℓ. For any fixed $t \in T^\varepsilon(X)$, the left derivation $g \to \partial_t g$ in $F^\varepsilon(X)$ is defined by transposition of the right product by t in $T^\varepsilon(X)$. We have for arbitrary $\ell \in F^\varepsilon(Y)$ and ℓ linear $X \to Y$

$$(\partial_{L(t)} h)(\ell x) = \partial_t (h(\ell x)) \tag{1.4}$$

For $\alpha \in J(\varepsilon, I)$ we set $\partial^\alpha g = \partial_{f^\alpha} g$. The right derivative $g\,\partial^\alpha$ is defined in a similar way. For $\varepsilon = +$, $\alpha = (i_1,\ldots,i_\ell) \in J(+,I)$ we set $x^\alpha = x_{i_1} \wedge x_{i_2} \ldots \wedge x_{i_\ell}$. For $\varepsilon = -$, $\beta \in J(-,I)$, we set $x^\beta = \Pi\, x_i^{\beta(i)}$. For arbitrary γ and $\gamma' \in J(\varepsilon, I)$

$$\langle x^\gamma, f^{\gamma'\vee}\rangle = \gamma!\,\delta_{\gamma,\gamma'} \tag{1.5}$$

For any form $g \in F^\varepsilon(X)$, there exists a unique family (g_γ) of scalars such that g is the limit for the weak topology of finite sums $\Sigma_{J'} g_\gamma x^\gamma$, J' finite $\subset J(\varepsilon, I)$. Hence $\{x^\gamma, \gamma \in J(\varepsilon,I)\}$ is a topological basis of $F^\varepsilon(X)$, endowed with the weak topology. We write $g = \Sigma g_\gamma x^\gamma$.

If Z is the product of two vector spaces X and Y , the canonical injections of X and Y in Z are denoted i_1 and

i_2, respectively. The vector space $T^{\varepsilon}(X) \otimes T^{\varepsilon}(Y)$ is identified with $T^{\varepsilon}(Z)$ by the map $t \otimes u \mapsto I_2(u)\, I_1(t)$. This last tensor is denoted simply by ut.

For example, let X and X' be two vector spaces in duality. The ε-canonical two-form on $Y = X \times X'$ is the bilinear form

$$y = (x\,;\xi)\ ;\ y_1 = (x_1;\xi_1) \overset{x.\xi}{\longmapsto} (\langle x, \xi_1\rangle - \varepsilon\langle x_1, \xi\rangle)/2 \qquad (1.6)$$

The exponential of this form $x.\xi$ in the algebra $F^{\varepsilon}(X \times X')$ is denoted $\exp(x.\xi)$.

We suppose that there exists an algebraic basis (1.7)
$\{\varphi_i, i \in I\}$ of X' such that $\langle f_i, \varphi_{i'}\rangle = \delta_{i,i'}$ for arbitrary $i, i' \in I$. Any point $\xi \in X'$ is written $\xi = \Sigma\, \xi_i \varphi_i$. Then

$$\exp x.\xi = \Sigma_{\alpha \in J(\varepsilon, I)}\ \alpha!^{-1}\ x^{\alpha\vee}\ \xi^{\alpha} \ . \qquad (1.8)$$

1.4 Cylindrical forms

If X and X' are two vector spaces in duality, the twisted duality $\langle t,u\rangle = \Sigma\, k!\, \langle t_k, u_k\rangle_k$ is defined on $T^{\varepsilon}(X) \times T^{\varepsilon}(X')$, where $\langle\ ,\ \rangle_k$ is defined in the following way on $T^{\varepsilon}_k(X) \times T^{\varepsilon}_K(X')$

$$\langle t_k, u_k\rangle_k = \langle t_k, u_k^{\vee}\rangle_{k,nat} \qquad (1.9)$$

$$\langle x_1 \ldots x_k, \xi_1 \ldots \xi_k\rangle_{k,nat} = \qquad (1.10)$$
$$= k!^{-1}\ \Sigma_{\alpha \in G(k)}\, sg_{\varepsilon}(\alpha) \langle x_{\alpha(1)}, \xi_1\rangle \ldots \langle x_{\alpha(k)}, \xi_k\rangle$$

Hence $T^{\varepsilon}(X')$ is canonically imbedded into $F^{\varepsilon}(X)$. The image of this injection is by definition the space $F^{\varepsilon}_{cyl}(X)$ of all cylindrical ε-symmetric forms on X. Hence any $u \in T^{\varepsilon}(X')$ is sometimes denoted $u(x)$; for $g \in F^{\varepsilon}(X')$ the scalar $\langle g,u\rangle$ is sometimes denoted $\langle g(\xi), t(x)\rangle$. Now let Y, Y' be two vector spaces in duality, let ℓ be linear : $X \to Y$ with transpose $\ell' : Y' \to X'$. Then for any $g \in F^{\varepsilon}_{cyl}(Y)$

$$g(\ell x) = (L'(g))(x) \qquad (1.11)$$

1.5 Contraction of forms on dual arguments

If X and Y are two vector spaces, we set $E = T^{\varepsilon}(Y)$, $G = T^{\varepsilon}(X)$, hence $G^{\star} = F^{\varepsilon}(X)$. The vector space $Op = L(E, G^{\star})$ of all linear operators $E \to G^{\star}$ is isomorphic to $(G \otimes E)^{\star} \simeq F^{\varepsilon}(X \times Y)$.

If Op is endowed with the weak topology defined by its duality with $G \otimes E$, then this isomorphism, denoted $\hat{Q} \to \tilde{Q}$, is an homeomorphism. For $u \in T^{\varepsilon}(X)$ we set

$$< \tilde{Q}(x,y) , u(\eta) > = \hat{Q}(u) \qquad (1.12)$$

The left hand side is called the <u>right</u> contraction of the right kernel $\tilde{Q}$ of $\hat{Q}$ with u, on their dual arguments y and η. Hence for arbitrary $t \in G$, we have

$$< \tilde{Q}(x,y) , u(\eta)\, t(\xi) > = << \tilde{Q}(x,y) , u(\eta) >, t(\xi) > \qquad (1.13)$$

But $\hat{Q}$ admits a transposed operator $\hat{Q}' \in L(G,E^{\star}) \simeq (G \otimes E)^{\star}$. The left contraction of $\tilde{Q}$ with t on their dual arguments x and ξ is defined by

$$< t(\xi) , \tilde{Q}(x,y) > = \hat{Q}'(t) \qquad (1.14)$$

The form $\tilde{Q}$ is also called the left kernel of $\hat{Q}$.

In the anticommutative case, left and right contractions are not identical even if $X = Y$. If $\{f_i, i \in I\}$ and $\{g_i, i \in I'\}$ are algebraic bases of X and Y, using the corresponding coordinates x_i and y_i', we have for arbitrary $\alpha, \alpha' \in J(\varepsilon,I)$; $\beta, \beta' \in J(\varepsilon,I)$

$$< x^{\alpha} y^{\beta} , g^{\beta'}(\eta) > = x^{\alpha} < y^{\beta} , g^{\beta'} > \qquad (1.15)$$

$$< f^{\alpha}(\xi) , x^{\alpha'} y^{\beta} > = < f^{\alpha} , x^{\alpha'} > y^{\beta} \qquad (1.16)$$

This permits explicit computations. We explain now how $< \tilde{Q}(x,y) , \varphi(\eta) >$ can be sometimes defined, if φ denotes a form on a space Y' in duality with Y. If the range of Q' is contained in $T^{\varepsilon}(Y')$, $\hat{Q}'$ defines a linear operator $T^{\varepsilon}(X) \to T^{\varepsilon}(Y')$; hence $\hat{Q}$ is extended by the bitransposed map $(\hat{Q}')'$: $F^{\varepsilon}(Y') \to F^{\varepsilon}(X)$. Denoting $\hat{Q}$ this extension we set

$$< \tilde{Q}(x,y) , \varphi(\eta) > = \hat{Q}(\varphi) . \qquad (1.17)$$

In the same way, we can set for some form $\tilde{Q}$, for all forms ψ on a space X' in duality with X

$$< \psi(\xi) , \tilde{Q}(x,y) > = \hat{Q}'(\psi) . \qquad (1.18)$$

For example, if X and X' are vector spaces in duality, the kernel of the identity map of $T^{\varepsilon}(X')$ is $\exp x.\xi$. Hence we have

for arbitrary $f \in F^{\varepsilon}(X)$, $\varphi \in F^{\varepsilon}(X')$

$$< \exp x'.\xi \ , \ f(x) > \ = f(x') \ , \qquad (1.19)$$

$$< \varphi(\xi) \ , \ \exp x.\xi' > \ = \varphi(\xi') \ . \qquad (1.20)$$

§ 2 - LEFT CONVOLUTION OPERATORS AND BASIC QUARTETS

2.1 Lemma - Let g be a fixed ε-symmetric form on a vector space X'. Then the operator A of left product by g in $F^{\varepsilon}(X')$ admits a transposed operator in $T^{\varepsilon}(X')$. This operator denoted $u \to \partial_g u$ is called a left convolution operator in $T^{\varepsilon}(X')$.

Principle of the proof. We have $g = g_k + g_{k+1} + \ldots$ with $g_k \neq 0$. For $t = \xi_\ell \xi_{\ell-1} \ldots \xi_1, \in T^{\varepsilon}(X')$ $A'(t)$ is a linear form on $F^{\varepsilon}(X')$ such that for arbitrary j , $h_j \in F^{\varepsilon}(X')$

$$< A'(t) \ , h_j > \ = \ < t, h_j \, g > .$$

Hence $A'(t) = 0$ for $\ell < k$. For $\ell \geqslant k$

$< A'(t), h_j > \ = 0$ for $j > \ell$. But for $j \leqslant \ell$

$< A'(t), h_j > \ = \ell ! \ < \xi_1 \otimes \ldots \otimes \xi_\ell \ , \ f_j \, g_{\ell - j} >_{\ell, nat}$. Using (1.3) a computation gives $A'(t) \in T^{\varepsilon}(X')$.

2.2 Corollary

a) The space Conv (X',ε) of all left convolution operators in $T^{\varepsilon}(X')$ is a subalgebra of End $T^{\varepsilon}(X')$, isomorphic with $F^{\varepsilon}(X')$: $\partial_g \partial_{g'} = \partial_{gg'}$. The form $g(\xi)$ is called the symbol of $u \mapsto \partial_g u$. Hence this operator is invertible in Conv iff the constant term g_o of g does not vanish.

b) If ℓ denotes a linear map $X' \to Y'$:

$$L(\partial_{g(\ell x)} u) = \partial_g (L u) .$$

c) The notation $X'_\alpha \Subset X'$ means that X'_α is a finite dimensional linear subspace of X' . In particular, let $W \in$ Conv (X',ε) with symbol W , $u \in T^{\varepsilon}(X'_\alpha)$ for some $X'_\alpha \overset{i_\alpha}{\Subset} X'$. Then $\hat{W} u = \hat{W}_\alpha u$ where $\hat{W}_\alpha$ denotes the left convolution operator in $T^{\varepsilon}(X_\alpha)$

with Symbol $W_\alpha(\xi) = W(i_\alpha x)$.

d) The space $T^\varepsilon(X')$ is imbedded in $F^\varepsilon(X'^\star)$. Then for g of the type $g = t \in T^\varepsilon(X'^\star)$, the map $u \to \partial_t u$ in $T^\varepsilon(X')$ is induced by the derivation $h \to \partial_t h$ in $F^\varepsilon(X'^\star)$.

Now for any vector space X' , the linear map $\xi \to (\xi;\xi)$: $X' \to X' \times X'$ is denoted by n . The image of $u \in T^\varepsilon(X')$ by N: $T^\varepsilon(X') \to T^\varepsilon(X' \times X')$ is denoted $u(x + x')$. In fact by (1.11), for any vector space X in duality with X', $u(x + x')$ is also the inverse image by $(x,x') \to x + x'$, of the cylindrical form defined by u .

2.3 Proposition

For arbitrary $\hat{W} \in \mathrm{Conv}\,(X',\varepsilon)$, $u \in T^\varepsilon(X')$

$$(\hat{W}\, u)\ (x) \quad = \quad < W(\xi')\ ,\ u(x' + x) > \tag{2.1}$$

Principle of the proof.

An algebraic basis $\{\varphi_i\ ,\ i \in I\}$ is chosen in X' , hence $\xi = \Sigma\, \xi_i\, \varphi_i$ and $W = \Sigma\, W_\alpha\, \xi'^\alpha$.

By the generalized Taylor formula[2]

$$u(x' + x) \quad = \quad \Sigma_\beta\ \beta!^{-1}\ x'^{\beta\vee}\ (\partial^\beta u)\ (x) \tag{2.2}$$

we have using (1.5)

$$< W(\xi')\ ,\ u(x' + x) > \quad = \quad \Sigma_{\alpha,\beta} \beta!^{-1}\ W_\alpha < \xi'^\alpha\ ,\ x'^\beta > (\partial^\beta u)\ (x)$$

$$= \quad \Sigma_\beta\ \ W_\beta (\partial^\beta\ u)\ (x) \ = \ \partial_W\ u \ \ = \hat{W}\ (u)\ .$$

2.4 Definition of a basic quartet

A basic quartet $(\varepsilon,\ X,\ X',\ \ell\ ,b)$ consists of $\varepsilon = \pm$, of two vector spaces X and X' in duality, of a linear bijection $\ell : X \to X'$, and of an homogeneous ε-symmetric two-form $b = b(\xi)$ on X', such that

i) Any $X'_\beta \subset X'$ is contained in some $X'_\alpha \subset X'$ such that

$$X = \ell\ (X'_\alpha) \oplus X'^{\perp}_\alpha \tag{2.3}$$

ii) The following equality holds in $F^\varepsilon(X \times X')$

$$b(\ell^{-1}\ x + \xi) \quad = \quad b(\ell^{-1}\ x) + b(\xi) + x.\xi \tag{2.4}$$

2.5 Lemma

Let (X,X',ℓ,b) be a basic quartet. For any $i_\alpha : X'_\alpha \subset X'$ satisfying (2.3) the dual space $X_\alpha = X / X'^{\perp}_\alpha$ is identified with $\ell(X'_\alpha)$. The bijection $X'_\alpha \to X_\alpha$ induced by ℓ is denoted by ℓ_α. If we set $b_\alpha = b(i_\alpha \xi)$, then $(X_\alpha, X'_\alpha, \ell_\alpha, b_\alpha)$ is a basic quartet.

Proof - In view of (2.3), the restriction to $\ell(X'_\alpha) \times X'_\alpha$ of the bilinear form of duality $< x,\xi >$ on $X \times X'$, is a bilinear form of duality. Because $\dim (X_\alpha)$ is finite, we prove only the following equality of forms on $X_\alpha \times X'_\alpha$

$$b_\alpha(\ell_\alpha^{-1} x\ \xi) = b_\alpha(\ell_\alpha^{-1} x) + b_\alpha(\xi) + x.\xi . \qquad (\star)$$

Denoting by j_α the canonical injection of $\ell(X'_\alpha)$ in X, $(\star)$ follows from (2.4), considering the inverse image of forms on $X \times X'$ by the linear map $j_\alpha \times i_\alpha : \ell(X'_\alpha) \times X'_\alpha \to X \times X'$. For example $j_\alpha \circ \ell^{-1} = \ell_\alpha^{-1} \circ i_\alpha$ implies

$$(b(\ell^{-1}x))(j_\alpha x) = (b(i_\alpha \xi))(\ell_\alpha^{-1} x) = b_\alpha(\ell_\alpha^{-1} x)$$

2.6 Properties of a basic quartet $(\varepsilon, X,X',\ell,b)$

a) For arbitrary ξ and $\xi' \in X'$

$$< \ell\xi, \xi' > = - \varepsilon < \ell\xi', \xi > \qquad (2.5)$$

i.e., the map $\ell : X' \to X$ admits a transposed map $\ell' : X' \to X$; moreover $\ell' = -\varepsilon\ell$. The corresponding map : $T^\varepsilon(X') \to T^\varepsilon(X)$ is denoted by L'.

b) If W denotes the left convolution operator in $T^\varepsilon(X')$ with symbol $W(\xi) = \exp b$, then

$$\forall\, u \in T^\varepsilon(X') \qquad e^b\, \partial_u = e^{b(\xi)}(W\,u)(\ell\,\xi) = e^b(L'W)(\xi) \quad (2.6)$$

c) For arbitrary u and $u' \in T^\varepsilon(X')$

$$< u'(x)\, u(x) \,,\, e^{b(\xi)} > = < Wu(x), (Wu')(\ell\xi) > \qquad (2.7)$$

Proof

a) By (2.4)

$$\ell(\xi+\xi') - b(\xi) - b(\xi') = \ell(\xi).\xi' .$$

The LHS is a form on $Y = X' \times X'$, invariant by the permutation of the arguments ξ and $\xi' \in X'$. Hence the RHS $R = \ell(\xi).\xi'$

has the same property. Hence for arbitrary (ξ,ξ') and $(\xi_1,\xi_1') \in Y$

$$< \ell\, \xi,\xi_1' > - \varepsilon < \ell\, \xi_1,\xi' > = < \ell\, \xi',\xi_1 > - \varepsilon < \ell\, \xi_1' , \xi >$$

b) The proof of (2.6) uses the following identity, true for any form f on X' and any $u \in T^{\varepsilon}(X')$:

$$< f(\xi') , e^{x.\xi} u(x') > = < f(\xi' + \xi) , u(x') > . \qquad (2.8)$$

Note that the L H S I has a meaning because $e^{x.\xi} u(x')$ is the left kernel of the map $f \mapsto f\, \partial_u$ of $T^{\varepsilon}(X)$, or $F^{\varepsilon}(X')$. Moreover for any $X'_\alpha \subset\subset X$ with $u \in T^{\varepsilon}(X'_\alpha)$, the restriction of I and of the R H S of (2.8) to X'_α depends only on the restriction of f . This reduces the proof of (2.8) to the finite-dimensional case. Then (2.8) follows from (2.2). Now the following equalities prove (2.6)

$$e^{b}\, \partial_u = < (e^{b}\, \partial_u)(\xi') , e^{x'.\xi} >$$

$$= < (e^{b})(\xi') , u(x')\, e^{x'.\xi} >$$

$$= < (\exp b)(\xi' + \xi), \hat{W}^{-1} \hat{W} u(x') >$$

$$= < \exp[b(\xi' + \xi) - b(\xi')] , (\hat{W} u)(x') >$$

$$= < \exp[b(\xi) + \ell(\xi).\xi'] , (\hat{W} u)(x') >$$

$$= (\exp b)(\xi)\, (\hat{W} u)(\ell\, \xi)$$

c) Finally, using b) , we have

$$< W u(x) , Wu'(\ell\, \xi) > = < (\partial_W u)(x) , e^{b(\xi)} (W u')(\ell\, \xi) e^{-b(\xi)} >$$

$$= < u(x) , e^{b(\xi)} (W u')(\ell\, \xi) >$$

$$= < u(x) , (e^{b} \partial_{u'})(\xi) > = < u'(x)\, u(x), e^{b(\xi)} >$$

2.7 Left integrals - Right integrals

So far, the bracket formalism was developped only for forms. We introduce now dual objects called "coforms" and the bracket formalism will be extended in this context. More specifically, if X and X' are vector spaces in duality, the space $F^{\varepsilon'}_{cyl}(X)$ of (ε-symmetric and cylindrical) coforms on X is the dual of

$F^{\varepsilon}_{cyl}(X)$. The action of the coform M on the cylindrical form φ is denoted :

$$< M , \varphi > = < \varphi , M > = \int \varphi(x)\, M(x) = \int M(x)\, \varphi(x) \; . \qquad (2.9)$$

In view of § 1.4, $F^{\varepsilon\,'}_{cyl}(X) \simeq F^{\varepsilon}(X')$. This isomorphism $M \longrightarrow \mathcal{L} M$ is called the Laplace transform. The inverse Laplace transform $g = g(\xi) \longrightarrow \mathcal{L}^{-1} g = \delta g$, permits to write left and right contractions on dual arguments as left and right integrals. For example (1.12) and (1.14) can be written

$$\int \tilde{Q}(x,y)\; \delta\varphi(y) \;=\; < \tilde{Q}(x,y) \,,\, \varphi(\eta) > \qquad (2.10)$$

$$\int \delta\psi(x)\; \tilde{Q}(x,y) \;=\; < \psi(\xi) \,,\, \tilde{Q}(x,y) > \qquad (2.11)$$

As another example, we have for an arbitrary coform M on X

$$\int e^{\xi . x}\, M(x) \;=\; \int M(x)\; e^{x . \xi} \;=\; (\mathcal{L} M)(\xi) \qquad (2.12)$$

2.8 Operations on cylindrical coforms

a) If X , X' and Y , Y' are two pairs of vector spaces in duality, ℓ denotes a linear map $X \to Y$ admitting a transposed map $\ell' : Y' \longrightarrow X'$. Hence the coform $\ell(M)$ on Y is defined by.

$$\forall\, u \in T^{\varepsilon}(Y') \qquad < \ell(M) \,,\, u > \;=\; < M \,,\, u(\ell x) >$$

$$\text{Hence} \qquad (\mathcal{L}(\ell M))(\eta) \;=\; (\mathcal{L} M)(\ell'\eta) \qquad (2.13)$$

b) For any coform M on X , this can be applied to the injection $i_\alpha : X'_\alpha \subset X'$, and to the transposed maps $\sigma_\alpha : X \longrightarrow X_\alpha$. Hence M is characterized by a coherent family (M_α) of coforms on the quotient spaces $X_\alpha = X / X'^{\perp}_\alpha$. Moreover $(\mathcal{L} M_\alpha)(\xi) = (\mathcal{L} M)(i_\alpha \xi)$.

c) For a fixed $t \in T^{\varepsilon}(X')$ the coform $M t$ in defined by

$$\forall\, u \in T^{\varepsilon}(Y') \qquad < M t \,,\, u > \;=\; < M \,,\, t u > \qquad (2.14)$$

$$\text{Hence} = < \mathcal{L} M \,,\, t u > \;=\; < (\mathcal{L} M)\, \partial_t \,,\, u > \text{ . Therefore}$$

$$\mathcal{L}(M t) \;=\; (\mathcal{L} M)\, \partial_t \qquad (2.15)$$

The image of the map $m : t \longrightarrow M t : T^{\varepsilon}(X') \longrightarrow F^{\varepsilon\,'}_{cyl}(X)$ is denoted $M\, T^{\varepsilon}(X')$. For example if $Q = (\varepsilon \ldots)$ is a basic quartet, the corresponding normal coform μ on X is defined by its Laplace transform $\mathcal{L}\mu = \exp b$. A combination of (2.6) and (2.15) shows that the map $t \longrightarrow \mu t$: is injective. The problem, now, is to use μ in order to define a scalar product on $T^{\varepsilon}(X') \simeq \mu\, T^{\varepsilon}(X')$.

For example :

$$\underline{\text{Real quartet } (-, E, E, Id(E), \|\xi\|^2/2) = Q_R} \tag{2.16}$$

The scalar product of a real separable Hilbert space X induces a bilinear form of duality on $E \times E$, for an arbitrary dense subspace E of X. Then Q_R in a basic quartet. The corresponding normal coform ν on E is characterized by the coherent family of all reduced Gaussian measures ν_α on all $X_\alpha \Subset E$. Moreover $L^2(X,\nu)$ is the completion of $T^-(E)$ for the trivial scalar product $\int f\, g\, d\nu$.

<u>The two quartets Q_ε , $\varepsilon = \pm$</u> (2.17)

Let G be a dense subspace of a complex separable Hilbert space Z. The antispace of G (resp$Z$) is denoted $\overline{G}$ (resp $\overline{Z}$). The identity map of G defines a semi-linear bijection $G \to \overline{G}$ denoted $z \to \overline{z}$ or $z^\star$. The scalar product of Z defines a duality on $\overline{G} \times G$ denoted $(z,z') = <\overline{z},z'>$ or simply $\overline{z}\, z'$. If X' denotes a second copy of $X = \overline{G} \times G$, the generic point on X' is denoted $\xi = (\overline{\zeta};\zeta')$ or simply $(\overline{\zeta};\zeta)$; see Ref.1. For $\varepsilon = \pm$, the following duality is defined on $X \times X'$:

$$x = (\overline{z};z)\ ;\ \xi = (\overline{\zeta};\zeta) \longmapsto <x,\xi> = \overline{z}\,\zeta - \varepsilon\,\overline{\zeta}\, z\ . \tag{2.18}$$

Then [1] , $Q_\varepsilon = (\varepsilon, X - X', \ell, b)$ is a basic quartet with ℓ = Identity map, $b = b(\xi) = \overline{\zeta}.\zeta$. Moreover the following equality holds in $F^\varepsilon(X \times X')$

$$x.\,\xi = z.\zeta + \overline{\zeta}.z\ . \tag{2.19}$$

The coform on X with Laplace transform exp b is denoted ν'. This is a cylindrical Gaussian measure for $\varepsilon = -$. For $\varepsilon = +$ the cylindrical representation of ν' is given in Ref.1.

§ 3 - TRIPLETS OF SPACES OF FORMS

By convention, the external space of a triplet is endowed with the weak topology. The theorem of bosons fields use Gelfand triplets ($E \subset X \subset {}'E$) where the sesquilinear form of semi-duality between the complex spaces E and $'E$ extends the scalar product of the central Hilbert space X. New triplets are introduced below.

3.1 Definition

A complex triplet $A = (E \xrightarrow{j} E', m)$ consists of two complex spaces E and E' in duality, such that all Cauchy sequences of E' converge, of a linear map $j : E \to E'$, and of a semi-linear bijection m of E onto itself such that

i) $s(x;y) = < m(x), j(y) >$ is a scalar product on E .

ii) There exists a semi-linear map $\tilde{m}$: $E' \to E$ with $< mx, \xi >$ $= < x, \tilde{m}\xi >$ for any $(x;\xi) \in E \times E'$.

iii) The scalar product space (E,s) is separable. Hence j is injective, j has a dense range.

3.2 Proposition

a) The map $j : (E,s) \to E'$ is continuous.

b) The canonical injection of (E,s) into its completion X is denoted k. Then the continuous extension $\hat{i}: X \to E'$ of i is injective.

The triplet A can also be written

$$A = (E \xrightarrow{k} X \xrightarrow{\hat{j}} E') . \tag{3.1}$$

Principle of the proof. We have

$$\forall x , x' \in E \qquad s(m^{-1}x ; x') = < x, j(x') >$$

Hence $(x'_n)_n \to 0$ in (E,s) implies $(x'_n)_n \to 0$ in E' : i is continuous. By continuous extension

$$\forall x \in E \quad \forall x' \in X \quad s(m^{-1}x ; x') = < x, \hat{j}(x') >$$

This implies that $\hat{j}$ is injective.

Now, let (E_α) be an increasingly directed family of vector subspaces of E, invariant with respect to b, such that $\bigcup E_\alpha$ is dense in the scalar product space (E,s). For arbitrary E_α, the transpose of the injection $i_\alpha : E_\alpha \to E$ is the canonical surjection σ_α of E' on $E'_\alpha = E'/E_\alpha^\perp$. If we denote by b_α the map induced by b, s_α the restriction of s to $E_\alpha \times E_\alpha$, $j_\alpha = \sigma_\alpha \, j \, i_\alpha$, then $(E_\alpha \xrightarrow{j_\alpha} E'_\alpha , b_\alpha)$ is a complex triplet. Introducing the completion X_α of (E_α , s_α) we have a commuting diagram and the "semi-transposed" diagram

$$\begin{array}{ccc} X_\alpha & \xrightarrow{k_\alpha} & X \\ \uparrow & & \uparrow k \\ E_\alpha & \xrightarrow{i_\alpha} & E \end{array} \qquad\qquad \begin{array}{ccc} E'_\alpha & \xleftarrow{\sigma_1} & E' \\ \uparrow & & \uparrow \tilde{k} \\ X_\alpha & \longleftarrow & X \end{array} \tag{3.2}$$

In the same way, for $E_\beta \subset E_\alpha$, both invariant by b, we have commuting diagrams

$$\begin{array}{ccc} E_\alpha & \xrightarrow{i_\alpha} & E \\ {\scriptstyle i_{\beta\alpha}}\uparrow & \nearrow {\scriptstyle i_\beta} & \\ E_\beta & & \end{array} \qquad \begin{array}{ccc} X_\alpha & \xrightarrow{k_\alpha} & X \\ {\scriptstyle k_{\beta\alpha}}\uparrow & \nearrow {\scriptstyle k_\beta} & \\ X_\beta & & \end{array} \tag{3.3}$$

$\sigma_{\alpha\beta} : E'_\alpha \to E'_\beta$ denotes the transpose of $i_{\beta\alpha}$. By the Fréchet-Riesz theorem, the completion X of the scalar product space $\underset{\to}{\lim}\,(E_\alpha, s_\alpha)$ is isometric with the dual of this inductive limit. Hence X is the projective limit of the spaces $'(E_\alpha, s_\alpha) \simeq X_\alpha$. This proves the following.

3.3 The CUB lemma

Let $A = (E \xrightarrow{j} E', b)$ be a complex triplet. Let (E_α) be an increasingly directed family of vector subspaces of E, invariant with respect to b, such that $\bigcup E_\alpha$ is dense in (E,s). Then the map $f \to (\sigma_\alpha f)_\alpha : E' \to \Pi E'_\alpha$ induces an isometry of X on the subspace CUB $(X_\bullet)$ of $\Pi E'_\alpha$, consisting of all coherent and uniformly bounded families $(f_\bullet = f_\alpha) \in \Pi X$, i.e. such that

i) $E_\alpha \supset E_\beta \Rightarrow f_\beta = j^{\star}_{\beta\alpha}(f_\alpha)$

ii) $\| f_\bullet \| = \sup_\alpha \| f_\alpha \| < \infty$

These results are applied in the following way.

3.4 The semi-linear map J

Let $Q = (\varepsilon, X - X', \ell, b)$ be a basic complex quartet, such that there exists a semi-linear bijection J of $T^\varepsilon(X')$ s.t.

i) the sesquilinear form :

$$(t_1, t) = \langle J^{-1} L'^{-1} t_1, t \rangle \tag{3.4}$$

is a scalar product on $T^\varepsilon(X)$, and the corresponding scalar product space is separable.

ii) For any $X'_\alpha \subset\subset X$ satisfying (2.3), $T^\varepsilon(X'_\alpha)$ is invariant with respect to J.

3.5 The triplet $B = (T^\varepsilon(X) \subset F^\varepsilon(X') ; K^{-1})$

a) By § 1.4 , $T^\varepsilon(X)$ is canonically imbedded in the space of ε-symmetrical forms on X'. A bilinear form of duality is defined on $T^\varepsilon(X) \times F^\varepsilon(X')$ by :

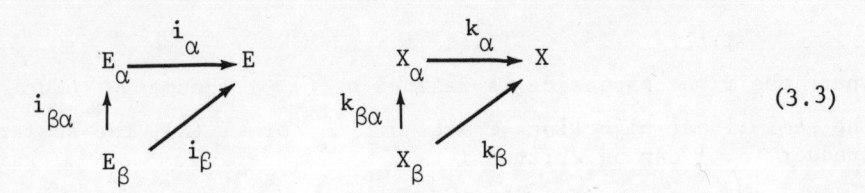

$$< t,f > \quad = \quad < L'^{-1}(t),f > \tag{3.5}$$

where the right-hand side is defined by (1.3). Hence introducing the semi-linear bijection $K = L'\,J\,L'^{-1}$ of $T^{\varepsilon}(X)$, the scalar product (3.4) can be written :

$$(t_1,t) = < L'^{-1}(L'\,J^{-1}\,L'^{-1})\,t_1,t > \quad = < K^{-1}(t_1),t > \tag{3.6}$$

i.e., this scalar product is of the type (3.1.i). Now $F^{\varepsilon}(X)$, isomorphic with the algebraic dual of $T^{\varepsilon}(X)$, is complete. More generally, the hypothesis (3.1. (i), (ii), (iii)) are fulfilled hence $(T^{\varepsilon}(X) \subset F^{\varepsilon}(X') \; ; K^{-1})$ is a complex triplet of vector spaces.

b) For any $X'_{\alpha} \subset\subset X'$, the operators induced by J and L in $T^{\varepsilon}(X'_{\alpha})$ are denoted by J_{α} and L_{α}, respectively. For arbitrary

$$t \in T^{\varepsilon}(X_{\alpha}), \quad t' \in T^{\varepsilon}(X'_{\alpha})$$
$$< t',t > \quad = \quad (L'\,J\,t',t) = (L'_{\alpha}\,J_{\alpha}\,t',t). \tag{3.7}$$

Hence for arbitrary $t,\ t_1 \in T^{\varepsilon}(X_{\alpha})$

$$(t_1,t) \quad = \quad < J_{\alpha}^{-1}\,L_{\alpha}^{-1}\,t_1\,,\,t > . \tag{3.8}$$

3.6 Examples of triplets B

a) Let $Q = Q_R$. By § 1.4, we have a canonical injection $j : T^{-}(E) \to F^{-}(E)$. The bilinear form $< t, j t' >$ on $T^{-}(E) \times T^{-}(E)$ is a scalar product : the completion is denoted by $F\,H^{-}(X)$. By application of the real version of Prop.3.2 we have a real triplet

$$B_R = (T^{-}(E) \subset F\,H^{-}(X) \subset F^{-}(E)) \tag{3.9}$$

The norm in the central space is

$$\| t \| = < t\,,\,j\,t >^{1/2} = \Big(\sum_k k! < t_k,t_k > \Big)^{1/2}$$

Hence the map $(t_k)_k \mapsto (k!^{1/2}\,t_k)$ is an isometry

$$F\,H^{-}(X) \longrightarrow \text{Fock}^{-}(X). \tag{3.10}$$

b) Let $Q = Q_{\varepsilon}$, $\varepsilon = \pm$. The scalar product of the Hilbert space $\overline{Z} \times Z$ is $x = (\overline{z}\,;z)$, $x_1 = (\overline{z}_1,z'_1) \mapsto (x,x_1) = \overline{(z,z_1)} + (z',z'_1)$

Using the duality (2.18) on $X \times X'$ an application of § 1.4 gives a canonical injection $T^{\varepsilon}(X) \subset F(X')$, with $X = \overline{G} \times G$. We introduce on $T^{\varepsilon}(X)$ the scalar product defining (modulo terms in k!) the scalar product of $\mathrm{Fock}^{\varepsilon}(\overline{Z} \times Z)$:

$$(t,u) = \sum_{o}^{\infty} k!\ (t_k, u_k)_{k,nat} \tag{3.11}$$

with

$$k!(x_i \ldots x_k, y_1 \ldots y_k)_{k,nat} = \sum_{\alpha \in Q(k)} sg_{\varepsilon}\alpha\ (x_{\alpha(1)}, y_1) \ldots (x_{\alpha(k)}, y_k)$$

We have to find a semi-linear bijection J of $T^{\varepsilon}(X')$ satisfying (3.4). Hence for arbitrary $G_{\alpha} \Subset G$, setting $X_{\alpha} = \overline{G}_{\alpha} \times G_{\alpha}$, the restriction J_{α} of J to $T^{\varepsilon}(X'_{\alpha})$ is characterized by (3.7). Denoting by $F H^{\varepsilon}(\overline{Z} \times Z)$ the completion of $T^{\varepsilon}(X)$, we obtain by Prop. 3.2 the following triplet of spaces of forms

$$B_{\varepsilon} = (T^{\varepsilon}(\overline{G} \times G) \subset F H^{\varepsilon}(\overline{Z} \times Z) \subset F^{\varepsilon}(\overline{G} \times G)) \tag{3.12}$$

§ 4 - L^2 PICTURES OF FOCK SPACES

4.1 Definition of normalized Laplace transform

By definition, the NL-transform associated to a basic quartet $(\varepsilon, X, X', \ell, b)$ maps any coform M on X onto the following ε-symmetric form on X'

$$(NL\ M)(\xi) = (\mathcal{L}\ M)(\xi)(\exp - b(\xi)) . \tag{4.1}$$

We note that $NL(\mu) = (\exp b)(\exp - b) = 1$. For this reason, NL is called a normalized Laplace transform.

The NL-transform associated to the quartet $(\varepsilon, X_{\alpha}, X'_{\alpha}\ \ell_{\alpha}, b_{\alpha})$ with X'_{α} satisfying (2.3) is denoted by NL_{α}. But any cylindrical coform M on X is characterized by a coherent family of coforms M_{α} on the dual spaces X_{α} ; see (§ 2.8, b). Hence by (2.13)

$$((NL)\ M)(i_{\alpha}\ \xi) = ((NL_{\alpha})\ M_{\alpha})(\xi) . \tag{4.2}$$

This permits the computation of a normalized Laplace transform by reduction to the finite dimensional case.

We consider now any complex quartet $Q = (\varepsilon, \ldots)$ with a semi-linear map J of $T^{\varepsilon}(X')$ as in § 3.4 . A semi-linear bijection

$$u \longmapsto u^{+} = W^{-1} J^{-1} W u \tag{4.3}$$

is defined in $T^{\varepsilon}(X')$. By § 3.4,ii),the subspaces $T^{\varepsilon}(X'_{\alpha})$ are invariant with respect to this bijection.

4.2 The complex version of the isomorphism theorem

a) The sesquilinear form

$$(\mu u,\mu u') = \int \mu u' u^{+} \tag{4.4}$$

is a scalar product on $\mu T^{\varepsilon}(X')$. Hence

$$A = (\mu T^{\varepsilon}(X') \subset F^{\varepsilon'}_{cyl}(X) ; Id) \tag{4.5}$$

is a complex triplet of spaces of coforms.

b) The map NL defines an isomorphism of triplets $A \to B$, i.e., NL defines a bijection between the external spaces of A and B, induces a bijection between the internal spaces, and preserves the scalar products :

$$\forall u \quad \text{and} \quad u' \in T^{\varepsilon}(X') \qquad \int \mu u' u^{+} = (\theta(\mu u), \theta(\mu u')) \tag{4.6}$$

Proof

The map $NL : F^{\varepsilon'}_{cyl}(X) \to F^{\varepsilon}(X')$ is the product of two bijections : $\mathcal{L}$ and the multiplication by the invertible form exp-b in $F^{\varepsilon}(X')$. Hence NL is bijective. Combining (2.6) and (2.15)

$$\forall u \in T^{\varepsilon}(X') \qquad NL(\mu u) = (L'W)(u) \tag{4.7}$$

Hence the map $NL_1 : \mu T^{\varepsilon}(X') \to T^{\varepsilon}(X)$ induced by NL is the product of the two isomorphisms $W \in End\, T^{\varepsilon}(X')$ and $L' : T^{\varepsilon}(X') \to T^{\varepsilon}(X)$. Hence NL_1 is a bijection. According to (4.7), formula (2.7) can be written

$$\int \mu u'u = \langle Wu, L'Wu' \rangle = (L'JWu, L'Wu') \tag{4.8}$$

Introducing u^{+} defined by (4.3), we have $L'JWu^{+} = L'Wu$; hence

$$\int \mu u'u^{+} = (L'Wu, L'Wu') = (NL(\mu u), NL(\mu u')). \tag{4.9}$$

In view of the bijectivity of NL_1, this shows that the sesquilinear form $\int \mu u'u^{+}$ on $T^{\varepsilon}(X')$ is a scalar product. By (4.9) this scalar product, and the scalar product of the triplet B are in correspondence by NL. Hence NL defines an isomorphism $A \to B$ of complex triplets.

4.3 The Hilbert space $\mu L^2(X)$

By the CUB lemma, the completion $\mu L^2(X)$ of $\mu T^{\varepsilon}(X')$ for the scalar product (4.4) is the space of coforms $M = (M_\alpha)$ on X' such that

a) for arbitrary $X'_\alpha \Subset X'$ satisfying (2.3), M_α belongs to the completion $\mu_\alpha L^2(X_\alpha)$ of $\mu_\alpha T^{\varepsilon}(X'_\alpha)$ for the scalar product induced by (4.4).

b) $\| M \| = \sup_\alpha \| M_\alpha \| < \infty$

An element of $\mu L^2(X)$ is conventionally denoted by μf or $(\mu_\alpha f_\alpha)_\alpha$. If $\mu u \to \mu u^+$ is continuous in $\mu T^{\varepsilon}(X')$, the continuous extension of this map in $\mu L^2(X)$ is denoted by $\mu f \to \mu f^+$. Hence we write for μf and $\mu g \in \mu L^2(X)$

$$(\mu f, \mu g) = \int \mu g f^+ . \tag{4.10}$$

In particular if $\mu g \in \mu_\alpha L^2(X_\alpha)$ for somme X'_α satisfying (2.3), then

$$\int_X \mu g f^+ = \int_{X_\alpha} \mu_\alpha g f_\alpha^+ . \tag{4.11}$$

This means that an infinite-dimensional ε-commutative integral can be computed by a finite dimensional ε-commutative integral.

4.4 Corollary (complex version)

With the hypothesis of the isomorphism theorem, the normalized Laplace transforms induces a bijective isometry of $\mu L^2(X)$ on the central Hilbert space of the complex triplet B.

We note that the real version of this corollary, applied to the quartet Q_R gives the explicit form

$$M \to \int e^{<x,\xi> - \|\xi\|^{2/2}} d M(x)$$

of one isometry $\theta : \nu L^2(X) \to F H(X)$. With the notations of the introduction we have $W^{-1}(q^k) = \dot{\Pi}_{i=1}^n W_i^{-1}(q_i^{k_i})$, where W_i denotes the convolution operator on the line with symbol $\exp \xi_i^{2/2}$. Hence $W_i^{-1}(q_i^{k_i})$ is the Hermite polynomial $H_{k_i}(q_i)$. By (4.7), θ maps νH_k on q^k. This proves that the product of θ with (3.10) is the Wiener isometry. A direct application of the theorem

to the quartets Q_ε, $\varepsilon = \pm$ gives us :

4.5 Proposition

Let G be a dense subspace of a complex and separable Hilbert space Z, $\varepsilon = \pm$. Then the normalized Laplace transform :

$$M \longrightarrow (\Theta M)(\bar{\zeta},\zeta) = \int M(\bar{z},z)\, e^{\bar{z}.\zeta + \bar{\zeta}.z - \bar{z}.z} \tag{4.12}$$

defines an isomorphism of the triplet of coforms

$$A_\varepsilon = \nu'\, T^\varepsilon(\bar{G} \times G) \subset \nu'\, L^2(\bar{Z} \times Z) \subset F^\varepsilon_{cyl}(\bar{G} \times G) \tag{4.13}$$

on the complex triplet B_ε of ε-symmetric forms.

§ 5 - CHARACTERISTIC FORMS OF A BASIC QUARTET

In view of Lemma 2.5, we consider only basic quartets $(\varepsilon, X, X' ..)$ with dim X finite.

5.1 Characteristic Forms of a basic Quartet

Let $(\varepsilon, X.X', \ell, b)$ be a basic quartet with dim X finite. Let $\{ f_i ,\ i \in I \}$ and $\{\varphi_i ;\ i \in I\}$ be dual basis in X and X'; the corresponding coordinates are denoted x_i and ξ_i. The left convolution operator W in $T^\varepsilon(X')$, with symbol exp b , is characterized by the set of cylindrical forms

$$u_\gamma(x) = W^{-1}(\varphi^\gamma) \quad ; \quad \gamma \in J(\varepsilon, I) \tag{5.1}$$

5.2 Properties of the Characteristic Forms u_γ

a) The following ε-symmetric forms on $X \times X'$ are identical

$$\sum_{\gamma \in J(\varepsilon,I)} \gamma!^{-1}\, u_\gamma(x)\, \xi'^{\gamma\vee} = \exp(-b(\xi') + x.\xi') \tag{5.2}$$

$$\sum_{\gamma \in J(\varepsilon,I)} \gamma!^{-1}\, \xi'^{\gamma\vee}\, u_\gamma(x) = \exp(\xi'.x - b(\xi')) \tag{5.3}$$

b) Setting $b'(x) = b(\ell^{-1}x)$

$$u_\gamma = \varepsilon^{|\gamma|}(\partial_{L(\varphi^\gamma)} e^{-b'})\, e^{b'} = (-1)^{|\gamma|}(e^{-b'} \partial_{L(\varphi^\gamma)})\, e^{b'} \tag{5.4}$$

c) For $b \in J(\varepsilon, I)$, $b \not\subseteq \gamma$, $\partial^b u_\gamma = 0$ and for $b \subseteq \gamma$:

$$\partial^b u_\gamma = \gamma!(\gamma - b)!^{-1}\, (b, \gamma \smallsetminus b)_\varepsilon\, (b)_\varepsilon\, u_{\gamma - b} \tag{5.5}$$

where the signs $(b,\gamma\grave{}b)_\varepsilon$ and $(b)_\varepsilon$ are identically + for $\varepsilon =-$; and such that

$$\varphi^{b}\ \varphi^{\gamma\grave{}b} = (b,\gamma\grave{}b)_{+}\,\varphi^{\gamma} \quad ; \quad \varphi^{b\wedge} = (b)_{+}\,\varphi^{b} \qquad (5.6)$$

Proof

a) Combining (5.1) and (2.1)

$$u_\gamma(x) = < (\exp - b)(\xi'') \ , \ (x + x'')^\gamma >$$

Using (1.19), the LHS I of (5.2) can be written

$$I = \sum \gamma!^{-1} < (\exp - b)(\xi'') \ , \ (x + x'')^\gamma\ \xi''^{\gamma\vee} >$$

$$= < (\exp - b)(\xi'') \ , \ \exp x''.\xi' > \exp x.\xi' = \exp(- b(\xi') + x.\xi') \ .$$

This proves (5.2). The proof of (5.3) is similar, but use for $\varepsilon = +$, the formula :

$$\bigstar \quad \sum \gamma!^{-1}\ \xi'^{\gamma\vee} < e^{-b(\xi'')}, (x + x'') > =$$

$$\sum \gamma!^{-1} < e^{-b(\xi'')}, \xi'^{\gamma\vee}(x + x'')^\gamma > \ .$$

In fact $(x + x'')^\gamma$ is a linear combination of terms $x''^\alpha\ x^\beta$ with $|\alpha| + |\beta| = |\gamma|$. Because $(\exp - b)(\xi'')$ has only even terms :

$$< \exp - b(\xi'') \ , \ \xi'^{\gamma\vee}\ x''^\alpha\ x^\beta > = < \exp - b(\xi''), \ x''^\alpha\ \xi'^{\gamma\vee} x^\beta >$$

This proves ★, hence (5.3).

b) We set $II = \sum \gamma!^{-1}\ \xi'^{\gamma\vee}\ u_\gamma(x)\ (\exp - b')(x)$. Combining (2.4) and (5.3) :

$$II = \exp \xi'.x - b(\xi') - b(\ell^{-1}x) = \exp - b'(x) - b(\xi') - \varepsilon x.\xi'$$

$$= \exp - b\,(\ell^{-1}x + \varepsilon\xi') \ .$$

By the generalized Taylor formula

$$(\exp - b)(\xi + \varepsilon\xi') = \sum \varepsilon^{|\gamma|}\ \gamma!^{-1}\ \xi'^{\gamma\vee}\ (\partial_{\varphi\gamma} \exp - b)(\xi)$$

Hence using Corollary 2.2.b),

$$II = (\exp - b)(\ell^{-1}x + \varepsilon\xi') = \sum \varepsilon^{|\gamma|}\ \gamma!^{-1}\ \xi'^{\gamma\vee}(\partial_{L(\varphi\gamma)} \exp - b'$$

Comparison of this formula with (5.3) gives the first formula (5.4). In the same way, starting from (5.2).

$$III = \sum \gamma!^{-1}\ u_\gamma(x)\ \xi'^{\gamma\vee}\ (\exp - b')(x)$$

$$= \exp\,(-b\,(\ell^{-1}x) - b(\xi') + x\,\xi') = \exp - b(\ell^{-1}x - \xi')\ .$$

But $\exp b(\xi - \xi') = \sum (-1)^{|\gamma|}\, \gamma!^{-1}((\exp - b)(\xi)\,\partial_{\varphi^\gamma})\,\xi'^{\gamma\vee}$

Hence using Corollary 2.2.b),

$$III = \sum (-1)^{|\gamma|} \quad \gamma!\ (e^{-b'}\partial_{L(\varphi^\gamma)})\,\xi'^{b\vee}\ .$$

A comparison with (5.2) gives the second formula (5.4).

c) In view of Corollary 2.2.a),

$$\partial^b u_\gamma = \partial_{\xi b}\ \partial_{W^{-1}}(\varphi^\gamma) = \partial_{W^{-1}}(\partial_{\xi b}\,\varphi^\gamma)$$

Hence (5.5) follows from the following expression of the left derivative of a monoform $\varphi^\gamma = x^\gamma$

$$\partial^b x^\gamma = \begin{cases} 0 & \text{if} \quad b \not\leqslant \gamma \\ \gamma!\ (\gamma\grave{}b)!^{-1}(b, \gamma\grave{}b)(b)x^{\gamma\grave{}b} & \text{if} \quad b \leqslant \gamma. \end{cases}$$

5.3 <u>Examples</u>

a) For the basis quartet Q_R with X of finite dimension d, we obtain the real Hermite polynomials

$$H_\gamma = W^{-1}(x^\gamma) = \Pi_{i=1}^{d} \quad H_{\gamma_i}(x_i) \tag{5.7}$$

b) We consider the quartet Q_ε, with the hermitian space G of finite dimension d. If $< e_i, i \in K = \{1,\dots d\} >$ is an orthonormal basis of G, the generic point of $X = \overline{G} \times G$ is $x = \sum e_i^\star\,\overline{z}_i + \sum e_j\,z_j$; hence $I = K \times K$. Setting $\varphi_i = \ell^{-1}(e_i)$, the generic point of X' is $\xi = \sum \varphi_i^\star\,\overline{\zeta}_i + \sum \varphi_j\,\zeta_j$. The duality (2.18) on $X \times X'$ identifies points of X(resp X') with linear forms on X' (resp X) ; for example

$$e_i^\star = \zeta_i\ ;\quad e_i = -\varepsilon\,\overline{\zeta}_i\ ;\quad \varphi_i^\star = -\varepsilon z_i\ ;\quad \varphi_i = \overline{z}_i \tag{5.8}$$

Hence any element $\gamma \in J(\varepsilon, K \times K)$ is identified with a pair $(\alpha ; \beta) \in J(\varepsilon, K)^2$.

Hence $\varphi^\gamma = \overline{z}^\alpha\, z^\beta = (-\varepsilon)^{|\beta|}\,\varphi^\alpha\,\varphi^{\star\beta}$

The corresponding characteristic form is denoted

$$H_{\alpha,\beta}(\overline{z}\ ;\ z) = W^{-1}(\varphi^\gamma) \tag{5.9}$$

Using (2.1)

$$H_{\alpha,\beta} = \langle \exp \bar{\zeta}'.\zeta' \ , \ (\varphi+\varphi')^{\alpha} \ (-\varepsilon\varphi^{\star} \ \varepsilon\varphi^{\star}{}')^{\beta} \rangle \quad (5.10)$$

Hence by (5.4)

$$H_{\alpha,\beta} = (-1)^{|\alpha|} \varepsilon^{|\beta|} (e^{-\bar{z}.z} \ \partial_{e^{\alpha} e^{\star\beta}}) \ e^{\bar{z}.z} \quad (5.11)$$

$$= (-1)^{|\alpha|} \varepsilon^{|\beta|} (e^{-\bar{z}.z} \ \partial^{\alpha}_{z} \partial^{\beta}_{\bar{z}}) \ e^{\bar{z}.z}$$

$$= \varepsilon^{|\alpha|} (-1)^{|\beta|} (\partial^{\alpha}_{z} \ \partial^{\beta}_{\bar{z}} \ e^{-\bar{z}.z}) \ e^{\bar{z}.z}$$

We indicate the following symmetrical expression

$$H_{\alpha,\beta} = (-1)^{(\alpha)+|\beta|} [\partial^{\beta}_{\bar{z}} (e^{-\bar{z}z}) \ \partial^{\alpha}_{z}] \ e^{\bar{z}.z} \quad (5.12)$$

For example $d = 1$, $\varepsilon = +$: (5.13)

$$H_{oo} = 1 \ ; \ H_{1o} = \bar{z} \ ; \ H_{o,1} = z \ ; \ H_{11} = 1 + \bar{z} \wedge z$$

The semi-linear map J^{-1} of $T^{\varepsilon}(X')$ can be computed explicitly using (3.8)

$$J^{-1} (\varphi^{\star\alpha} \varphi^{\beta}) = (-\varepsilon)^{|\alpha'|} \ \varphi^{\star\beta\vee} \varphi^{\alpha\vee} \quad (5.14)$$

Combining (5.9) and (4.3)

$$H^{+}_{\alpha,\beta} = W^{-1} J^{-1} W W^{-1} [(-\varepsilon)^{|\beta|} \varphi^{\alpha} \varphi^{\star\beta}]$$

$$= W^{-1} J^{-1} [(-\varepsilon)^{|\beta|} \varphi^{\alpha} \varphi^{\star\beta}] = W^{-1} [(-\varepsilon)^{|\beta|} . \varphi^{\beta\vee} \varphi^{\star\alpha\vee}]$$

Finally

$$H^{+}_{\alpha,\beta} = (-\varepsilon)^{|\alpha|} (\alpha) (\beta) H_{\beta,\alpha} \quad (5.15)$$

hence $H^{++}_{\alpha,\beta} = (-\varepsilon)^{|\alpha|} (\alpha)(\beta) H^{+}_{\beta,\alpha} = (-\varepsilon)^{|\alpha|+|\beta|} H_{\alpha,\beta}$

For $\varepsilon = -$, the map $f \to f^{+}$ is the familiar conjugation $f \to \bar{f}$.
For $\varepsilon = +$, the map $f \to f^{+}$ is not a conjugation.

For example, in the simple case (5.13) :

$$\bar{z}^{+} = -z \ ; \ z^{+} = \bar{z} \ , \ 1^{+} = 1 \ , \ (\bar{z}^{1} \wedge z)^{+} = (\bar{z} \wedge z) - 2 \neq z^{+} \wedge \bar{z}^{+}$$

REFERENCES

1 P. KRÉE Anticommutative integration and Dirac Fields. In Proceedings of "Bielefeld Encounters in Physics and Mathematics II, Quantum Fields, Algebras, Processes" (December 1978), (to be published).

2 P. KRÉE Equations aux dérivées partielles en dimension infinie. Séminaire 3ème année 1976 - 1977. Institut H.Poincaré (Paris). Secrétariat mathématique.

STATIONARY PHASE FOR THE FEYNMAN INTEGRAL AND TRACE FORMULA

S. Albeverio, Ph. Blanchard and R. Høegh-Krohn

Fakultät für Mathematik, Ruhr-Universität Bochum
Fakultät für Physik, Universität Bielefeld
Matematisk Institutt, Universitetet i Oslo

1. INTRODUCTION

In the Feynman formulation of quantum mechanics the formal expression for the solution of Schrödinger's equation in $L^2(\mathbb{R}^d)$

$$ih \frac{\partial\psi}{\partial t} = H\,\psi$$

$$\psi(o,x) = \varphi(x)$$

is given by

$$\psi(t,x) = (e^{-\frac{i}{h} tH}\varphi)(x) = N \int_{\gamma(t)=x} e^{\frac{i}{h} S_t(\gamma)} \varphi(\gamma(o))d\gamma \quad (1.1)$$

where $H = H_o + V$, H_o being the free energy operator $H_o = -\frac{h^2}{2m}\Delta$, and Δ being the Laplacian in $\mathbb{R}^d$. The classical action $S_t(\gamma)$ is equal to

$$S_t(\gamma) = \int_o^t \frac{m}{2}\dot{\gamma}^2(\tau)\,d\tau - \int_o^t V(\gamma(\tau))\,d\tau \quad (1.2)$$

In the heuristic expression (1.1) the "integral" should be over all paths which start anywhere at time $\tau = o$ and end at time $\tau = t$ in $x \in \mathbb{R}^d$ and N should be a suitable normalization. According to a beautiful idea of Dirac and Feynman the detailed approach to the classical limit (when Planck's constant h goes to zero) should

come out by a "stationary phase method in infinitely many dimensions". This should be intuitively so since the quantum mechanical quantities are represented by oscillatory path integrals

$$\int e^{\frac{i}{h} S_t(\gamma)} g(\gamma)\, d\gamma \qquad (1.3)$$

and as $h \to o$ only the behaviour in a neighborhood of the stationary points of the phase function $S_t(\gamma)$ should give a non vanishing contribution. However by Hamilton's principle these stationary points are precisely the "classical paths", i.e. the solutions of the classical Newton equations of motion. In order to transform these heuristic suggestions into mathematical results we should

1) give a mathematical meaning to the heuristic expression (1.1) as a linear continuous functional on a space of paths

2) study oscillatory integrals of the type

$$I(h) = \int_{\mathcal{H}} e^{\frac{i}{h}\Phi(\gamma)} g(\gamma)\, d\gamma \qquad (1.4)$$

where $\mathcal{H}$ is some infinite dimensional space, Φ is a real valued "phase function" on $\mathcal{H}$ and g is a complex-valued amplitude function on $\mathcal{H}$. For applications to quantum mechanics we are mainly interested in phase functions of the form

$$\Phi(\gamma) = (\gamma, B\gamma) - W(\gamma) \qquad (1.5)$$

where $(\gamma, B\gamma)$ is a quadratic form corresponding to the kinetic energy or, in the case of an anharmonic oscillator, the kinetic energy minus the potential energy of an harmonic oscillator i.e.

$$(\gamma, B\gamma) = \int_o^t \frac{1}{2}\dot{\gamma}^2(\tau)\, d\tau - \frac{1}{2}\int_o^t \gamma(\tau)\, A^2\gamma(\tau)\, d\tau \qquad (1.6)$$

and $W(\gamma)$ is a term coming from the potential.

In the special case where B^{-1} is a bounded operator we can prove that the asymptotic expansion of $I(h)$ defined in (1.4) is of the form

$$I(h) = \sum_{\gamma_c} F_h(\gamma_c) \tag{1.7}$$

where the sum is over all classical paths γ_c i.e.

$$d^{\Phi}(\gamma_c) = B\gamma_c - dW(\gamma_c) = o$$

$$\text{i.e.} \quad \gamma_c = B^{-1}\, dW(\gamma_c) \tag{1.8}$$

Moreover we will give an explicit expression for $F_h(\gamma_c)$. As an application we get asymptotic expansions in powers of h for the theta function

$$\theta(t) = \mathrm{Tr}\, e^{-\frac{i}{h} t H} = \sum_n e^{-\frac{i}{h} t\lambda n} \tag{1.9}$$

associated with the Schrödinger operator $H = -\frac{h^2}{2}\Delta + \frac{1}{2}(x, A^2 x)_d + V(x)$, A^2 being a symmetric positive matrix in $\mathbb{R}^d$, $x \in \mathbb{R}^d$, $V(x)$ a bounded continuous potential on $\mathbb{R}^d$, λ_n being the eigenvalues of H. The expansion is obtained by expressing $\theta(t)$ in terms of oscillatory integrals over a Hilbert space of paths and using then our method of stationary phase for such integrals (see [1]). We obtain in this way an asymptotic expansion in powers of h in terms of the periodic orbits of the corresponding classical mechanical anharmonic oscillator. This representation is a natural extension of the classical Poisson formula for the theta function. From it we deduce a trace formula for other associated functions like e.g. the ζ-function $\zeta(s) = \Sigma \frac{1}{\lambda_n{}^s}$. We give also asymptotic formulae as $h \to o$ for $\hat{g}(\lambda_n{}^h)$ where $\hat{g}$ has support around $\lambda_n{}^h$, $\lambda_n{}^h$ being the n-th eigenvalue of H and we obtain the proof of the Bohr-Sommerfeld quantization formula. These results give in particular a natural extension of those obtained in the mathematical literature for compact manifolds to the case of Schrödinger operators in $\mathbb{R}^d$. We can get indeed from the trace formula for $\theta(t) = \mathrm{tr}\, e^{-\frac{i}{h}tH}$ an asymptotic expression in powers of h for $h \to o$ which involves the classical closed orbits (thus the corresponding quantities to the closed

geodesics in our case). The reason why in the case of the Laplacian on a compact manifold the expression are obtained for all h is the homogeneity of the action in this case.

Our aim in this paper is simply to give a general idea of the methods and results obtained in our papers [1][2][3]. As for references to related work by other methods we have to ask the reader to look at the rather extensive list in [1][2][3].

2. FRESNEL INTEGRALS RELATIVE TO A NON SINGULAR QUADRATIC FORM

Let us recall the definition of a normalized integral with respect to a given bounded quadratic form, a particular case of the ones defined in [1] and [2].

Let $\mathcal{H}$ be a real separable Hilbert space and let B be an everywhere defined bounded symmetric operator on $\mathcal{H}$. Assume B^{-1} is also a bounded symmetric operator on $\mathcal{H}$. Let $\mathcal{F}(\mathcal{H})$ be the space of functions f on $\mathcal{H}$ which are Fourier transforms of complex measures on $\mathcal{H}$ i.e.

$$f(\gamma) = \int_{\mathcal{H}} e^{i(\gamma,\alpha)}\, d\mu_f(\alpha) \tag{2.1}$$

with $(\ ,\ )$ the scalar product in $\mathcal{H}$ and μ_f a bounded complex measure on $\mathcal{H}$, with finite total variation $\|\mu_f\| = \int_{\mathcal{H}} d|\mu_f|(\alpha)$. The mapping $f \to \mu_f$ is one to one and continuous. With the norm $\|f\|_o = \|\mu_f\|$, $\mathcal{F}(\mathcal{H})$ is a Banach function algebra, whose elements are going to be the integrable functions with respect to the following integral. For $f \in \mathcal{F}(\mathcal{H})$ define

$$\tilde{\int_{\mathcal{H}}} e^{\frac{i}{2}(\gamma,B\gamma)} f(\gamma)\, d\gamma = \int_{\mathcal{H}} e^{\frac{i}{2}(\alpha,B^{-1}\alpha)}\, d\mu_f(\alpha) \tag{2.2}$$

The symbol on the left hand side is defined by the right hand side, which exists as an integral on $\mathcal{H}$ since the function $e^{\frac{i}{2}(\alpha,B^{-1}\alpha)}$ is

continuous and bounded. The complex-valued functional

$$f \to I(f) \equiv \widetilde{\int_{\mathcal{H}}} e^{\frac{i}{2}(\gamma, B\gamma)} f(\gamma)\, d\gamma \tag{2.3}$$

is shown to be linear, continuous and normalized $(I(1) = 1)$ on the Banach algebra $\mathcal{F}(\mathcal{H})$, in fact $|\, I(\prod_{j=1}^{n} f_j)\, | \leq \prod_{j=1}^{n} \| f_j \|_o$, and is an extension to the infinite dimensional case of

$$\widetilde{\int_{\mathbb{R}^d}} e^{\frac{i}{2}(\gamma, B\gamma)} f(\gamma)\, d\gamma = (2\pi)^{-\frac{d}{2}} |\mathrm{Det}\, B|^{1/2} e^{\frac{i\pi}{4}\sigma(B)} \int_{\mathbb{R}^d} e^{\frac{i}{2}(\gamma, B\gamma)} f(\gamma) d\gamma \tag{2.4}$$

where $|\mathrm{Det}\, B|$ is the absolute value of the determinant of the matrix B in $\mathbb{R}^d$ and $\sigma(B)$ is the signature of the matrix B. We also recall the behaviour under translations of the normalized integral expressed by

$$\widetilde{\int} e^{\frac{i}{2}(\gamma+\alpha,\, B(\gamma+\alpha))} f(\gamma+\alpha)\, d\gamma = \widetilde{\int} e^{\frac{i}{2}(\gamma, B\gamma)} f(\gamma)\, d\gamma \tag{2.5}$$

For other properties of the normalized integrals $I(f)$, in particular a Fubini theorem about iterated integration, see [1] and [2].

<u>Remark</u>: An intrinsic characterization of $\mathcal{F}(\mathcal{H})$ is e.g. as the complex linear hull of those positive definite functions which are continuous in the so-called Minlos-Sazonov-Gross topology i.e. those continuous positive definite functions f on $\mathcal{H}$ for which for any $\varepsilon > o$ there exists a nuclear operator (positive, symmetric, trace class) N_ε such that $R_e(f(o)-f(\gamma|) < \varepsilon$ whenever $(\gamma, N_\varepsilon \gamma) \leq 1$.

We shall now use this normalized integral to express quantities associated with anharmonic oscillators on $\mathbb{R}^d$. Consider the system given by the classical action

$$S_t(\gamma) = \frac{1}{2}\int_o^t \dot{\gamma}^2(\tau)\, d\tau - \frac{1}{2}\int_o^t \gamma(\tau).A^2\gamma(\tau) - \int_o^t V(\gamma(\tau))\, d\tau \tag{2.6}$$

where A^2 is a strictly positive symmetric operator on $\mathbb{R}^d$ and assume that $V \in \mathcal{F}(\mathbb{R}^d)$ and is real. Consider the Schrödinger's

operator

$$H = \frac{h^2\Delta}{2} + \frac{1}{2}\, x\, A^2 x + V(x) \tag{2.7}$$

in $L^2(\mathbb{R}^d)$. H is essentially self-adjoint on the domain $C_o^\infty(\mathbb{R}^d)$ and its spectrum $\sigma(H)$ is contained in $[\inf V, +\infty)$ and by a theorem of Friedrichs, it is discrete. Let $\varphi \in D(H)$ we have that $\psi(t,x) = e^{-\frac{i}{h} tH}\varphi(x)$ solves the Schrödinger equation

$$i\, h \frac{\partial\psi}{\partial t}(t,x) = H\, \psi(t,x) \tag{2.8}$$

with initial condition $\psi(o,x) = \varphi(x)$. It is proved in [1] that for all values of t such that cos At is non singular one has

$$(e^{-\frac{i}{h} tH}\varphi)(x) = \psi(t,x) = |\cos At|^{1/2} \sim \int_{\mathcal{H}_o} e^{\frac{i}{2}(\gamma,B\gamma)} f(\gamma)\, d\gamma \tag{2.9}$$

with

$$f(\gamma) = e^{\frac{i}{2}(\beta,B\beta)}\, e^{\frac{i}{h}\int_o^t V(\gamma(\tau)+\beta(\tau))d\tau}\, \varphi(\gamma(o)+\beta(o)) \tag{2.10}$$

and $$|\cos At|^{1/2} = |\mathrm{Det}\, \cos At|^{1/2}\, e^{\frac{i\pi}{4}\sigma(\cos At)} \tag{2.11}$$

Here $\mathcal{H}_o$ is the real separable Hilbert space of absolutely continuous functions γ from $[o,t]$ into $\mathbb{R}^d$ such that $\gamma(t) = o$, with finite kinetic enery $\frac{1}{2}\int_o^t \dot\gamma^2(\tau)\, d\tau$ and norm given by

$$|\gamma|^2 = \int_o^t \dot\gamma^2(\tau)\, d\tau \tag{2.12}$$

B is the bounded symmetric operator on $\mathcal{H}_o$ given by

$$(\gamma,B\gamma) = \frac{1}{h}\int_o^t [\dot\gamma^2(\tau) - \gamma(\tau)\, A^2\, \gamma(\tau)]\, d\tau \tag{2.13}$$

In this case it is easy to see that B^{-1} is also bounded symmetric on $\mathcal{H}_o$. $\beta(\tau)$ is the path such that

$$\beta + A^2\beta = o \quad \beta(t) = x \quad \dot\beta(o) = o \quad \text{i.e. } \beta(\tau) \equiv \frac{\cos A\tau}{\cos At}\, x \tag{2.14}$$

We see also that $(e^{-\frac{i}{h}tH}\varphi)(x)$ is expressed through an oscillatory integral of the type considered in [1] and can be used for deriving asymptotic expansions in powers of h by the method developed in section 4 of [1] and which we will sketch in the next section. It is convenient to consider the Green function $K(t,x,y)$ for the Cauchy problem. We have

$$(e^{-\frac{i}{h}tH}\varphi)(x) = \int_{\mathbb{R}^d} K(t,x,y)\,\varphi(y)dy \tag{2.15}$$

The representation of $K(t,x,y)$ through an oscillatory integral is given by the following

Theorem 2.1

The Green's function $K(t,x,y)$ for the Schrödinger equation

$$i\,h\,\frac{\partial\psi}{\partial t}(t,x) = [-\frac{h^2}{2} + \frac{1}{2}\,x\,A^2\,x + V(x)]\,\psi(t,x)$$

with $V \in \mathcal{F}(\mathbb{R}^d)$ real and A^2 a symmetric strictly positive matrix in $\mathbb{R}^d$ is given by

$$K(t,x,y) = K_o(t,x,y)\,\tilde{\int}_{\mathcal{H}_{o,o}} e^{\frac{i}{2}(\gamma,B\gamma)}\,g_x(\gamma)\,d\gamma$$

$$g_x(\gamma) = e^{-\frac{i}{h}\int_o^t V(\gamma(\tau) + \alpha(x,y)(\tau) + \beta(\tau))\,d\tau}$$

where $K_o(t,x,y) = \left|\mathrm{Det}\,\frac{A}{\sin At}\right|^{1/2}(2\pi i)^{-\frac{d}{2}}\,e^{\frac{i}{2h}(x,A\,\mathrm{cotg}.\,At\,x)_d}$

$$e^{-\frac{i}{h}(x,\frac{A}{\sin At}y)_d}\,e^{\frac{i}{2h}(y,A\,\mathrm{cotg}\,At\,y)_d}$$

is the corresponding Green's function for the harmonic oscillator and $\alpha(x,y) \equiv \eta_{y-\frac{x}{\cos At}}$ with $\eta_z(\tau) = \cos A\tau\,z - (\cos At\,\sin A\tau)z$ and $\beta(\tau) \equiv \frac{\cos A\tau}{\cos At}x$. $\mathcal{H}_{o,o}$ is the closed subspace of $\mathcal{H}_o$ consisting of paths γ such that $\gamma(o) = o$.

Remark about the proof of Theorem 2.1

We can write symbolically the Green's function in the form

$$K(t,x,y) = \tilde{\int}_{\substack{\gamma(t)=x \\ \gamma(o)=y}} e^{\frac{i}{h} S_t(\gamma)} d\gamma \qquad (2.16)$$

The symbolic notation is of course to be interpreted by formulating the integral over the space of paths as an integral over a linear space of paths i.e. by translating suitably the integration variables in such a way that the new integration variable $\tilde{\gamma}$ satisfies $\tilde{\gamma}(o) = \tilde{\gamma}(t) = o$. The result can be formally written

$$(e^{\frac{-itH}{h}}\varphi)(x) = |\cos At|^{-1/2} \tilde{\int}_{\gamma(t)=x} e^{\frac{i}{h} S_t(\gamma)} \varphi(\gamma(o))\, d\gamma \qquad (2.17)$$

and can be obtained by going from γ to $\tilde{\gamma} + \alpha(x,y) + \beta$, and splitting the integral into an integral over $d\tilde{\gamma}$ and one over R^d. For a proof of Theorem 2.1 see [3].

3. ASYMPTOTIC EXPANSION FOR THE CASE OF NORMALIZED INTEGRALS WITH RESPECT TO A QUADRATIC FORM

We shall now shortly indicate the type of results obtained in [1] for the asymptotic expansion of the normalized integrals with respect to a non degenerate not necessarily positive - or negative - definite quadratic form in the special case where B and B^{-1} are bounded symmetric operators. These are thus oscillatory integrals of the form

$$I(h) = \tilde{\int}_{\mathcal{H}} e^{\frac{i}{2h}(\gamma, B\gamma)} e^{-\frac{i}{h} W(\gamma)} g(\gamma)\, d\gamma \qquad (3.1)$$

where $W, g \in \mathcal{F}(\mathcal{H})$. By an expansion of $e^{-\frac{i}{h} W(\gamma)}$ under the normalized

integral in $I(h)$ and an interchange of the operations of summation and taking the normalized integrals (possible because of the continuity of the normalized integral and the fact that the space $\mathcal{F}(\mathcal{H})$ of integrable functions is a Banach algebra) we get that $I(h)$ is equal to

$$I(h) = \sum_{n=0}^{\infty} \left(\frac{-i}{h}\right)^n \frac{1}{n!} \widetilde{\int_{\mathcal{H}}} e^{\frac{i}{2h}(\gamma, B\gamma)} W(\gamma)^n g(\gamma)\, d\gamma \tag{3.2}$$

$$= \sum_{n=0}^{\infty} \frac{1}{n!}\left(-\frac{i}{h}\right)^n \int_{\mathcal{H}} \cdots \int_{\mathcal{H}} e^{-i\frac{h}{2}\left(\sum_{j=1}^{n} \alpha_j + \beta,\, B^{-1}\left(\sum_{k=1}^{n} \alpha_k + \beta\right)\right)} \prod_{j=1}^{n} d\mu(\alpha_j)\, d\nu(\beta) \tag{3.3}$$

where $W(\gamma) = \int_{\mathcal{H}} e^{i(\gamma,\alpha)}\, d\mu(\alpha)$ and $g(\gamma) = \int_{\mathcal{H}} e^{i(\gamma,\beta)}\, d\nu(\beta)$

We shall now describe the results when there is one and only one stationary point.

<u>Theorem 3.1</u>

Let $W(\gamma) = \int_{\mathcal{H}} e^{i(\alpha,\gamma)}\, d\mu(\alpha)$ where μ is a finite complex measure such that $\int_{\mathcal{H}} e^{\sqrt{2\|B^{-1}\|^{\frac{1}{2}}}|\alpha|}\, d|\mu|(\alpha) < +1$ and $g(\gamma) = \int_{\mathcal{H}} e^{i(\gamma,\beta)}\, d\nu(\beta)$ with $\int_{\mathcal{H}} e^{\sqrt{2}\|B^{-1}\|^{\frac{1}{2}}|\beta|}\, d|\nu|(\beta) < +\infty$. Then there is a unique point $\gamma_c \in \mathcal{H}$ such that $B\gamma_c = dW(\gamma_c)$. Let

$$I(h) = \widetilde{\int_{\mathcal{H}}} e^{\frac{i}{h}(\gamma,B\gamma)} e^{-\frac{i}{h}W(\gamma)} g(\gamma)\, d\gamma$$

Then $I^*(h) = e^{-\frac{i}{h}\left[\frac{1}{2}(\gamma_c, B\gamma_c) - W(\gamma_c)\right]} I(h)$ is a C^∞ function of h on the real line. Moreover its value at zero is given by

$$I^*(o) = |\mathbb{1} - B^{-1} d^2W(\gamma_c)|^{1/2} g(\gamma_c)$$

where $|\mathbb{1} - B^{-1}d^2W(\gamma_c)|$ is the Fredholm determinant of the operator $\mathbb{1} - B^{-1} d^2W(\gamma_c)$.

For the proof the formal idea is to consider the translated integral

$$\tilde{\int_{\mathcal{H}}} e^{\frac{i}{h}\Phi(\gamma+\gamma_c)} g(\gamma+\gamma_c)d\gamma \quad \text{where} \quad \Phi(\gamma) = \frac{1}{2}(\gamma,B\gamma) - W(\gamma)$$

and to expand $W(\gamma+\gamma_c)$ around $\gamma = o$, whereby then one is reduced to the case where the stationary point is at the origin.

In the case where $\mathcal{H}$ **is finite** dimensional the treatment of phase functions with more than one stationary point, with no accumulation points, is done by a decomposition of the unit χ_n for g, the decomposition of the unit being such that $g\,\chi_n$ has support containing only one stationary point, and then summing over the contributions coming from the individual stationary points according to Theorem 3.1. This method is not immediately applicable to the case where $\mathcal{H}$ is infinite dimensional, because one needs $\int e^{\sqrt{2}\|B^{-1}\|^{1/2}|\beta|}\, d|\nu|(\beta) < +\infty$, which makes g entire hence not with compact support. This problem has been overcome in [1] under the assumptions

$$\int e^{\sqrt{2}\|B^{-1}\|^{1/2}\lambda|\alpha|}\, d|\mu|(\alpha) < \infty \quad \int d|\mu|(\alpha) < \lambda^2 \qquad (3.4)$$

for some λ. The condition for having just one stationary point is no more satisfied, and in general one will have several stationary points. Suppose there exists a splitting of $\mathcal{H}$ of the form $\mathcal{H} = \mathcal{H}_1 + \mathcal{H}_2$ where $\mathcal{H}_2 = B^{-1}\mathcal{H}_1^{\perp}$ and $\dim \mathcal{H}_2$ is finite and the restriction of the quadratic form $(\gamma,B\gamma)$ to $\mathcal{H}_1 \times \mathcal{H}_1$ is non degenerate. Note that the sum $\mathcal{H} = \mathcal{H}_1 + \mathcal{H}_2$ is then a direct one with respect to the quadratic form $(\gamma,B\gamma)$ in the sense that γ $\gamma \in \mathcal{H}$ can be represented as $\gamma = \gamma_1 + \gamma_2$ $\gamma_1 \in \mathcal{H}_1$ $\gamma_2 \in \mathcal{H}_2$ and $(\gamma_1,B\gamma_2) = o$. Using the Fubini Theorem for infinite dimensional oscillatory integrals over the infinite dimensional subspace $\mathcal{H}_1$ with a partial phase function $\Phi_1(\gamma) = \Phi(P_1\gamma), \mathcal{H}_1 = P_1\mathcal{H}, P_1 = P_1 = P_1^2$ having one and only one stationary point and a oscillatory integral over the finite dimensional subspace $\mathcal{H}_2$, possibly with infinitely

many stationary points. The first normalized integral over $\mathcal{H}_1$ is then treated by Theorem 3.1 and the oscillatory finite dimensional integral is then treated by the finite dimensional theory.

If the equation $B^{-1}\, dW(\gamma) = \gamma$ has only solutions γ_c such that none of the operators $\mathbb{1} - B^{-1}d^2W(\gamma_c)$ has zero as an eigenvalue then the oscillatory integral

$$I(h) = \int_{\mathcal{H}} e^{\frac{i}{2h}(\gamma, B\gamma)}\, e^{-\frac{i}{h} W(\gamma)}\, g(\gamma)\, d\gamma$$

is of the following form for $h \to o$

$$I(h) = \sum_k e^{\frac{i}{h}[\frac{1}{2}(\gamma_c^{\ k}, B\gamma_c^{\ k}) - W(\gamma_c^{\ k})]}\, I^{*k}(h) \qquad (3.5)$$

where $I^{*k}(h)$ is a C^∞ function of h such that

$$I^{*k}(o) = e^{\frac{i\pi}{2} n_k}\, |\, \mathrm{Det}\, (\mathbb{1} - B^{-1}d^2W(\gamma_c^{\ k}))\, |^{-1/2}\, g(\gamma_c^{\ k}) \qquad (3.6)$$

where n_k is the number of eigenvalues of $B^{-1}d^2W(\gamma_c^{\ k})$ which are larger than 1. We can write (3.5) in the form

$$I(h) = \sum_k e^{\frac{i}{h} S(\gamma_c^{\ k})}\, I^{*k}(h) \qquad (3.7)$$

Remark: In the case where there is a degeneracy we have an asymptotic expansion for I(h) in which the contribution from degenerate stationary point $\hat{\gamma}_c$ is of the form

$$e^{\frac{i}{h} S(\hat{\gamma}_c)}\, G(h, \hat{\gamma}_c)$$

where the function $G(h,\hat{\gamma}_c)$ depends only on h, $\hat{\gamma}_c$ and the type of degeneracy of the phase $S(\gamma)$ at $\hat{\gamma}_c$. See section 5 of [1] See also [4] for analogous results in the case where $B = \mathbb{1}$.

4: THE TRACE FORMULA

As remarked in section 2 the spectrum of H given by (2.7) is discrete. Let us call λ_n $n=0,1,2,\ldots$ the eigenvalues of H. We have $\lambda_0 = \inf \sigma(H) \geq \frac{1}{2} \operatorname{tr} A + \inf V(x)$ and $\lambda_0 \leq \lambda_1 \leq \lambda_2 \leq \ldots$ $\lambda_n \to +\infty$. We will now give a meaning to the formal expression

$$\theta(t) \equiv \operatorname{Tr} e^{-itH} \equiv \sum_{n=0}^{\infty} e^{-it\lambda_n} \qquad (4.1)$$

Although e^{-itH} is not of trace class we shall see that (4.1) is well defined in the sense of distributions and is expressed by oscillatory integrals. The distributional kernel of e^{-itH} is given by

$$e^{-itH}(x,y) = K(t,x,y) = \sum_{k=0}^{\infty} e^{-it\lambda_k} \overline{f_k(x)}\, f_k(y) \qquad (4.2)$$

where $\{ f_k \}_{k\in\mathbb{N}}$ is a basis of normalized eigenfunctions in $L^2(\mathbb{R}^d)$, f_k being the eigenfunction of H corresponding to the eigenvalue λ_k. On the other hand we have seen in Theorem 2.1 that $K(t,x,y)$ is expressible by normalized integrals. We have also

$$(f_k, e^{-itH} f_k) = e^{-it\lambda_k} \qquad (4.3)$$

But by the definition of $e^{-itH}(x,y)$ the left hand side of (4.3) is equal to

$$\int_{\mathbb{R}^d} \overline{f_k(x)} \left(\int_{\mathbb{R}^d} e^{-itH}(x,y)\, f_k(y)\, dy \right) dx = \langle e^{-itH}, \bar{f}_k \otimes f_k \rangle \qquad (4.4)$$

Integrating the bounded continuous function (4.3) against an integrable φ with Fourier transform $\hat{\varphi}$ continuous with compact support we have

$$\hat{\varphi}(\lambda_k) = \int_{\mathbb{R}} \varphi(t)\, e^{-it\lambda_k}\, dt = \int_{\mathbb{R}} \varphi(t) \langle e^{-itH}, \bar{f}_k \otimes f_k \rangle\, dt \qquad (4.5)$$

Summing over k we get

$$\sum_k \hat{\varphi}(\lambda_k) = \int_{\mathbb{R}} \varphi(t) < e^{-itH}, \sum_k \bar{f}_k \otimes f_k > dt \tag{4.6}$$

But by the completeness of the $\{f_k\}_{k\in\mathbb{N}}$ we have

$$\sum_k \bar{f}_k(x) \otimes f_k(y) = \delta(x-y) \tag{4.7}$$

Hence from (4.6) and (4.7) we get

$$\sum_k \hat{\varphi}(\lambda_k) = \int_{\mathbb{R}} \varphi(t) \left(\int_{\mathbb{R}^d} e^{-itH}(x,x)\, dx \right) dt \tag{4.8}$$

Note that the left hand side of (4.8) is finite by the assumptions on φ hence $\int_{\mathbb{R}^d} e^{-itH}(x,x)\, dx$ is a well defined distribution in t. On the other hand this distribution can also be written in the form

$$\tilde{\int}_{\substack{\gamma(t)=x \\ \gamma(o)=x}} e^{iS_t(\gamma)}\, d\gamma \tag{4.9}$$

Let us formulate the above result as

<u>Theorem 4.1</u>

Let $H = -\frac{1}{2}\Delta + \frac{1}{2} x A^2 x + V(x)$ with A^2 a symmetric strictly positive $d \times d$ matrix and $V \in \mathcal{F}(\mathbb{R}^d)$ real. Let λ_k be the eigenvalues of H. Then in the sense of distributions in t we have

$$\theta(t) = \mathrm{Tr}\, e^{-itH} = \sum_K e^{-it\lambda_K} = \int_{\mathbb{R}^d} \left(\tilde{\int}_{\substack{\gamma(t)=x \\ \gamma(o)=x}} e^{iS_t(\gamma)}\, d\gamma \right) dx$$

where the path integral is defined by

$$\tilde{\int}_{\substack{\gamma(t)=x \\ \gamma(o)=x}} e^{iS_t(\gamma)}\, d\gamma = K_o(t,x,x) \tilde{\int}_{\mathcal{H}_{o,o}} e^{\frac{i}{2}(\gamma, B\gamma)} g_x(\gamma)\, d\gamma$$

where $S_t(\gamma)$ is the classical action along γ, $\mathcal{H}_{o,o}$ is the Hilbert space of paths of finite kinetic energy beginning and ending

at the origin,

$$K_o(t,x,x) = \left| \det \frac{A}{\sin At} \right|^{1/2} e^{-i(x, \frac{A}{\sin At}(\cos At - 1)x)_d}$$

$$g_x(\gamma) = \exp \left[-i \int_o^t V(\gamma(\tau) + \alpha(x,x)(\tau) + \beta(\tau))\, d\tau \right. .$$

We now derive an asymptotic expression as $h \to o$ of the quantities entering the trace formula. The results are as follows. Assume the Schrödinger potential V is in $\mathfrak{F}(\mathbb{R}^d)$ and the measure μ_V of which it is the Fourier transform satisfies

$$\int_{\mathbb{R}^d} e^{\varepsilon|\beta|}\, d|\mu_V|(\beta) < +\infty \tag{4.1o}$$

for some $\varepsilon > o$. It can be shown (see [3] Section 4) that this assumption (implying of course analyticity of V) is actually enough to permit that the result of the preceding section can be applied. These results give then the general asymptotic representation of the oscillatory integral over $\mathcal{H}_{o,o}$ as a sum of terms which represent contributions from each stationary point of the phase

$$\Phi(\gamma) \equiv \int_o^t \frac{1}{2} [\dot\gamma^2(\tau) - \gamma(t)\, A^2\gamma(\tau)]\, dt - \int_o^t V(\gamma(\tau)+\alpha_x(\tau)+\beta(\tau))d\tau \tag{4.11}$$

with $\alpha_x(\cdot) = \alpha_{xx}(\cdot)$.

Now the stationary points of the phase $\Phi(\gamma)$ are the solutions of $d\Phi(\gamma) = o$. This is equivalent with Newton's equation of motion

$$\ddot\gamma_x{}^t(\tau) + A^2\, \gamma_x^t(\tau) = -\text{grad}\ V(\gamma_x{}^t(\tau)) \tag{4.12}$$

for a particle in the total potential $\frac{1}{2}(z, A^2z)_d + V(z)$ and with boundary conditions $\gamma_x^t(o) = \gamma_x{}^t(t) = x$. Assuming that the orbits are non degenerate we obtain for the diagonal part $K(t,x,x)$ of the Green's function the following asymptotic behaviour as $h \to o$

$$K(t,x,x) = \widetilde{\int}_{\substack{\gamma(t)=x \\ \gamma(o)=x}} e^{\frac{i}{h} S_t(\gamma)} \, d\gamma$$

$$= \sum_{\gamma_x^t} \frac{e^{\frac{i}{h} S_t(\gamma_x^t)} \, e^{i\frac{\pi}{2} n(\gamma_x^t)}}{D(\gamma_x^t)^{1/2}} + h\, O(1) \qquad (4.13)$$

where the sum is over all orbits which solve the equation of motion, $-n(\gamma_K^t)$ is the number of negative eigenvalues of $\mathbb{1} - B^{-1} d^2 W(\gamma_x^t)$ and $D(\gamma_x^t) = \mathrm{Det}\,(\mathbb{1} - B^{-1} d^2 W(\gamma_x^t))$. Note that under our assumptions the potential is analytic and one can show that the set of degenerate critical points is discrete. We can also compute the determinant $D(\gamma_x^t)$ appearing in (4.13)

$$D(\gamma_x^t) = \left| \mathrm{Det} \; \frac{\partial \gamma_{x,j}^t}{\partial p_{o,k}} \right|^{-1} \qquad (4.14)$$

where $\gamma_{x,j}^t$ $j = 1\ldots d$ is the j-th component of the closed orbit γ_x^t and $p_{o,k} = \left.\frac{\partial \gamma_{x,k}^t}{\partial \tau}\right|_{\tau=o}$ is the k-th component of the initial momentum on the orbit γ_x^t $k = 1\ldots d$. Consider now the theta function θ_h defined by $\theta_h(t) = \mathrm{tr}\, e^{-\frac{i}{h}tH}$ as written as an oscillatory integral. Using our preceding result we have

$$\theta_h(t) = \int_{\mathbb{R}^d} \Big(\sum_{\gamma_x^t} \frac{e^{\frac{i}{h} S(\gamma_x^t)}}{D(\gamma_x^t)} \, e^{-i\frac{\pi}{2} m(\gamma_x^t)} + h\, O(1)\Big)\, dx \qquad (4.15)$$

We now remark that under our assumptions on the potential all closed orbits are bounded in the sense that the set of x such that x is the starting point of some closed orbit is bounded. Since the integrands in (4.15) are bounded and continuous we can interchange the sum over the closed orbits with the integral. We shall now study the remaining integrals over x by the finite dimensional method of stationary phase. The asymptotic expansions of these integrals are

given by the stationary points of the total phase. The stationary points are those where

$$p_x(t) = p_x(o) \tag{4.16}$$

hence the orbits γ_x^t are not only closed but also periodic. Thus we see that we get only contributions to the leading term of (4.15) from classical periodic orbits. To determine the leading term we look at the second variation of the phase at the stationary points. We have the following

Theorem 4.2

Let V be a real potential which is the Fourier transform of a complex measure μ_V such that $\int_{\mathbb{R}^d} e^{\varepsilon|\alpha|} d|\mu_V|(\alpha) < \infty$ for some $\varepsilon > o$. Then the theta function $\theta_h(t)$ for the Schrödinger operator $-\frac{h^2}{2}\Delta + \frac{1}{2} x A^2 x + V(x)$ where A^2 is a symmetric positive d x d-matrix has under the assumption that all classical periodic orbits are non degenerate the following asymptotic expansion as $h \to o$

$$\theta_h(t) = \sum_{n=1}^{\infty} \sum_{\gamma^{t/n}} e^{\frac{i}{h} n S_{t/n}(\gamma^{t/n})} e^{-i\frac{\pi}{2} n m(\gamma^{t/n})} A(\gamma^{t/n}) + h\,\mathcal{O}(1)$$

where the sum is over all existing classical periodic orbits $\gamma^{t/n}$ of minimal period t/n, $S_{t/n}(\gamma^{t/n})$ is the classical action along the orbit $\gamma^{t/n}$, $m(\gamma^{t/n})$ is the Maslov index of the orbit and $A(\gamma^{t/n})$ is given by

$$A(\gamma^{t/n}) = \int \frac{1}{\left| \operatorname{Det} \dfrac{\partial \gamma_i^{t/n}}{\partial p_{x,j}(o)} \right|^{1/2}} \; \frac{1}{|\operatorname{Det}(d_{x_T}(p_x(t)-p_x(o))|^{1/2}} \, dx_L$$

where $p_x(\tau) \equiv \frac{\partial \gamma^{t/n}(\tau)}{\partial \tau}$ $x \in \gamma^{t/n}$ and x_L, x_T are longitudinal resp. transversal.

Remark 1:

In the one dimensional case (d=1) there is no need for introducing the transversal coordinates, in other words we get the same expression for $\theta_h(t)$ as in Theorem 4.2. but with $|\mathrm{Det}\, dx_T(p_x(t)-p_x(o))|^{1/2}$ replaced by 1. Moreover we can in this case express the quantities $A(\gamma^{t}/n)$ in the following way

$$A(\gamma^{t}/n) = t \left| \frac{dE(\gamma^{t}/n)}{dt} \right|^{1/2}$$

where E is the energy associated with the orbit γ^{t}/n of primitive period $^{t}/n$.

Remark 2:

Our theorem give the expansion of the theta function in terms of classical periodic orbits. Therefore it is interesting to have information about the number and structure of such orbits. Some results can be extracted for the existing literature, however a systematic discussion for the case at hand is still lacking.

It is now interesting to study the singularities of the theta function $\theta_h(t)$. Let us take a test function g such that the Fourier transform $\hat{g}$ of g has support such that $\mathrm{supp}\, \hat{g} \cap \sigma(H) = \frac{1}{h} \lambda_n^{h}$, where $\lambda_n(h)$ is an eigenvalue of H . We have

$$\hat{g}\left(\frac{1}{h} \lambda_n(h)\right) = \int_{\mathbb{R}} \theta_h(t)\, f(t)\, dt \tag{4.17}$$

Consider

$$< e^{\frac{i}{h}\lambda t} f\, ,\ \theta_h > = \int_{\mathbb{R}} e^{\frac{i}{h}\lambda t} f(t)\, \theta_h(t)\, dt \tag{4.18}$$

with $f \in \mathcal{S}(\mathbb{R}+)$. Our method gives an asymptotic expansion of $\theta_h(t)$ as $h \to o$. In particular we have

$$\theta_h(t) = \theta_h^{o}(t) + h\, O_t(1) \tag{4.19}$$

Observing that $O_t(1)$ is slowly increasing in t we have that

$$< e^{+\frac{i}{h}\lambda t} f\,,\,\theta_h > = < e^{\frac{i}{h}\lambda t} f,\, \theta_h{}^o > + h\, O(1) \tag{4.20}$$

Now we can insert the expression for the leading term $\theta_h{}^o$ and apply the method of the stationary phase with respect to the t-integration. We obtain a sum over all existing periodic orbits with period $t(\lambda)$, where $t(\lambda)$ are the solutions of the equation

$$\frac{\partial S_{t/n}(\gamma^t/n)}{\partial t} + \lambda = o \tag{4.21}$$

It is well known that if γ^t is a solution of Newton's equation of motion one has

$$\frac{\partial S_t(\gamma^t)}{\partial t} + E = o \tag{4.22}$$

where E is the energy associated with the orbit γ^t, in other words we have $E = \lambda$. Introduce now the Legendre transform W_E of the action function S_t by

$$W_E = S_{t(E)} + Et(E) \tag{4.23}$$

We get

$$< e^{\frac{iEt}{h}} f(t),\, \theta_h{}^o(t) > \;=\; \sum_{n=1}^{\infty} \sum_{\Gamma(E)} f(t(E))\, e^{-\frac{i\pi}{2} n\, \tilde{m}\, (\gamma^{nt(E)})} \cdot \frac{e^{i\frac{n}{h}W_E}}{\left|\frac{dE}{dt}\right|^{1/2}} A(\gamma^{nt(E)}) \tag{4.24}$$

where the sum is over the class $\Gamma(E)$ consisting of all pairs $(t(E), \gamma^{t(E)})$ such that $\gamma^{t(E)}$ is a periodic orbit of primitive period $t(E)$ and energy E. If we now suppose that $\Gamma(E)$ consists of one primitive orbit then we can effectuate the sums in (4.24)

$$\langle e^{\frac{i}{h}Et} f, \theta_h \rangle = \mathrm{Tr}(\hat{f}(H-E))$$

$$= f\,(t(E))\,t(E)\,\frac{e^{\frac{i}{h}[W_E - \frac{\pi}{2} hm']}}{1 - e^{\frac{i}{h}[W_E - \frac{\pi}{2} hm']}} + h\,O(1) \tag{4.25}$$

In (4.24) and (4.25) $\tilde{m}$ and m' are Maslov-Arnold indices. It follows from (4.25) that the singularities of $\mathrm{Tr}(\hat{f}\,(H-E))$ are given by the values of E satisfying the extended Bohr-Sommerfeld quantization conditions

$$W_E = \oint p\,dq + E\,t\,(E) = 2\pi\,(\,n + \frac{1}{4}\,m')\,h \tag{4.26}$$

In particular if $\hat{f}$ has support only containing the eigenvalue λ_n of H and is identically one around λ_n then we obtain relations between eigenvalues of the quantum mechanical problem and the periods of the corresponding classical orbits.

References

[1] S. Albeverio, Ph. Blanchard, R. Høegh-Krohn "Oscillatory integrals and the method of stationary phase in infinitely many dimensions II", Preprint Bielefeld 198o.

[2] S. Albeverio, R. Høegh-Krohn "Mathematical theory of Feynman Paths Integral", Lecture Note in Math. 523 Berlin Heidelberg New York Springer Verlag (1976)

[3] S. Albeverio, Ph. Blanchard, R. Hoegh-Krohn "The trace formula for the Schrödinger Operators," Preprint Bielefeld 1980.

[4] S. Albeverio, R. Høegh-Krohn "Oscillatory integrals and the Method of stationary phase in infinitely many dimensions, with applications to the classical limit of quantum mechanics" I., Inventiones math. 4o-1o6 (1977).

WHITE NOISE ANALYSIS AND THE FEYNMAN INTEGRAL

L. Streit

Fakultät für Physik
Universität Bielefeld
D-48oo Bielefeld 1

I. INTRODUCTION

As one can see at this conference, and similarly as with some other concepts of theoretical physics, the Feynman integral is being used as an important tool of quantum dynamics at a time when its mathematical formalization is still being developed , - a novel and remarkable example of such development was presented by Mme Sirugue [1].

Here, on the basis of joint work with T. Hida [2], I shall present another passage from intuition to definition.

We start from the intuition that

$$\left\langle e^{\frac{im}{2\hbar}\int \dot{x}^2\, dt}\; e^{-\frac{i}{\hbar}\int V[x]dt}\; \Phi[x] \right\rangle \tag{1}$$

should imply some kind of averaging over fluctuating trajectories, such as

$$x(t) = x_0 + vt + \alpha\, B_T(t) \tag{2}$$

where v is the velocity of the "straight line" free path

$$v = T^{-1}(x(T) - x_0)$$

and B_T is the Brownian bridge

$$B_T(t) = B(t) - \frac{t}{T} B(T)$$

In our formal expression (1), the kinetic energy term turns out to be the hardest to cope with, since

$$\dot{x}(t) = \alpha \dot{B}(t) + \ldots..$$

which would lead to nonlinear functionals of "white noise" $\dot{B}(t)$ which, we recall, is a distribution valued "generalized process".

$$e^{i\int \dot{B}^2(t)\, dt} = ?$$

How to square white noise? An answer can be found in the framework of "White Noise Analysis" developped by T. Hida [3].

II. WHITE NOISE ANALYSIS

The theory of nonlinear functionals of white noise can be found in [3]. Here we shall introduce only the bare minimum necessary for the discussion of Feynman integration.

To fix concepts and notation we introduce **white noise $\dot{B}(t)$** through its characteristic functional

$$C(f) \equiv \langle e^{i(f,\dot{B})} \rangle = e^{-\frac{1}{2}(f,f)} = \int_{\mathcal{S}^*} e^{i(f,\dot{B})}\, d\mu(\dot{B}) \qquad (3)$$

for f in the Schwartz space $\mathcal{S}(\mathbb{R})$.

Abstractly, a large class of nonlinear functionals of $\dot{B}$ is furnished by

$$(L^2) \equiv L^2(\mathcal{S}^*, d\mu).$$

The problem is to find a handy realization of (L^2), - in particular it should not obscure the causal structure of (L^2) (note that functionals

$$\Phi(\dot{B}(t)\ ;\ t \in I_V)$$

are statistically independent if their "supports" I_v are disjoint).

We consider for this purpose the following linear map τ

$$\tau : (L^2) \ni \Phi(\dot{B}) \to (\tau\Phi)(f) \equiv \int e^{i(f,\dot{B})} \Phi(\dot{B})\, d\mu(\dot{B}) \in \mathfrak{F}.$$

In particular one sees immediately that

$$\tau \ : \ e^{-i(\dot{B},g)} \to C(f-g)$$

so that

$$(\tau\Phi)(g) = \int e^{i(\dot{B},g)} \Phi(B)\, d\mu\,(\dot{B}) = (e^{i(\dot{B},g)}\, , \Phi(\dot{B}))_{(L^2)}$$

$$= (C(\cdot\, -g)\ ,\ \tau\Phi(\cdot))_{\mathfrak{F}}$$

and one can prove that under τ, (L^2) is isomorphic to the reproducing kernel Hilbert space $\mathfrak{F}$ with kernel $C(f-g)$.

Further insight is gained by introducing the following projection operators P_n in $\mathfrak{F}$:

$$(P_n F)\ (f) \equiv \frac{1}{n!}\, C(f)\left(\frac{d}{d\lambda}\right)^n \frac{F(\lambda f)}{C(\lambda f)}\Bigg|_{\lambda=o}$$

They project onto those elements of $\mathfrak{F}$ which are, up to a factor $C(f)$, n-linear in f:

$$P_n\mathfrak{F} = \{\ C(f) \int F(t_1,\dots,t_n)\ f(t_1)\dots f(t_n) d^n t \,|\, F \in \mathrm{Sy}\ L^2(\mathbb{R}^n)\}$$

Hence there is a further isomorphism, with the space $\mathcal{K}$ of symmetric kernel functions

$$\begin{array}{l} (L^2) = \bigoplus_{n=o}^{\infty} \mathcal{H}_n \\ \quad \updownarrow \tau \\ \mathfrak{F} = \bigoplus_{n=o}^{\infty} P_n \mathfrak{F} \\ \quad \updownarrow \\ \mathcal{K} = \bigoplus_{n=1}^{\infty} \mathrm{Sy}\ L^2(\mathbb{R}^n) \end{array} \qquad (4)$$

which induces the Wiener-Ito decomposition of (L^2) into subspaces of n-ple Wiener integrals.

Example: For $e \in L^2(\mathbb{R})$ with $\|e\| = 1$ the function $\prod_{i=1}^{n} e(t_i) \in Sy\, L^2(\mathbb{R}^n)$ is transformed as follows by the above isomorphisms

$$\left(\frac{i}{\sqrt{2}}\right)^n H_n\left(\frac{(e,\dot{B})}{\sqrt{2}}\right) \in \mathcal{H}_n$$

$$\updownarrow \tau$$

$$C(f)(e,f)^n \in P_n \mathcal{F}$$

$$\updownarrow$$

$$e(t_1) \ldots e(t_n) \in Sy\, L^2(\mathbb{R}^n)$$

For $n=2$ in particular, this yields

$$\tau\,((e,\dot{B})^2 - (e,e))\,(f) = -\,C(f)\,(e,f)^2$$

and extends by linearity to

$$\tau\,((\dot{B},A\,\dot{B}) - \mathrm{Tr}\,A) = \tau(:(\dot{B},\,A\,\dot{B}):) = -\,C(f)\,(f,\,A\,f) \qquad (5)$$

for $(\dot{B},\,A\,\dot{B}) \equiv \sum_n a_n\,(\dot{B},\,e_n)^2$

and A a trace class operator with kernel

$$A(t_1,t_2) = \sum a_n\, e_n(t_1) e_n(t_2),$$

(e_n) an orthonormal basis.

Of course the r.h.s. of equation (5) makes sense beyond trace class, so that e.g. for

$$A = \mathbb{1}$$

one would want to set

$$\int :\dot{B}^2(t): dt \equiv \tau^{-1}(-C(f)\int f^2(t)\,dt)$$

Note however that the corresponding kernel "function"

$$F(t_1,t_2) = -\delta(t_1-t_2)$$

in <u>not</u> an element of $\text{Sy } L^2(\mathbb{R}^2) \subset \mathcal{K}$.

As a consequence, expressions such as

$$\int : \dot{B}^2(t) : dt$$

can be considered as "generalized Brownian functionals" in the following way.

First one embeds each kernel space $\text{Sy } L^2(\mathbb{R}^2)$ in a triplet with a space of smooth functions $\mathcal{K}_{(n)}$ and the dual space $\mathcal{K}^{(n)}$ of generalized functions, then extends this structure to the space (L^2) by the isomorphism (4), obtaining spaces of smooth resp. "generalized Brownian functionals":

$$\begin{array}{ccccc} \mathcal{K}_{(n)} & \subset & \text{Sy } L^2(\mathbb{R}^n) & \subset & \mathcal{K}^{(n)} \\ \updownarrow & & \updownarrow & & \updownarrow \\ \mathcal{H}_{(n)} & \subset & \mathcal{H}_n & \subset & \mathcal{H}^{(n)} \end{array} \qquad (6)$$

In the next section we shall see how these concepts relate to the Feynman integral.

III. THE FEYNMAN INTEGRAL

For simplicity we shall consider the following straight line path plus Brownian fluctuations

$$x(t) = \frac{X}{T}\, t \quad + \left(\frac{\hbar}{m}\right)^{1/2} B_T(t) \qquad (7)$$

i.e. one that leads from $x(o) = o$ to $x(T) = X$.

For the free action

$$S_o[x] = \frac{1}{2m} \int_o^T \dot{x}^2(t)\, dt$$

the following ansatz then suggests itself

$$\frac{1}{\hbar} S_o[x] = \frac{1}{2} \int_o^T :B^2(t) : dt + \text{reg. terms},$$

but fails attempts to exponentiate it. This becomes clear if one looks at exponentials of smoother quadratic expressions.

For small K in <u>trace class</u>

$$\tau(e^{(\dot{B},K\dot{B})}) = e^{-\frac{1}{2} \mathrm{Tr}\ \ln(1-2K)} \ e^{-\frac{1}{2}(f,\frac{1}{1-2K} f)}$$

is well defined. The use of $:(\dot{B},K\dot{B}):$ in the exponent leads to

$$\tau (e^{:(\dot{B},K\dot{B}):}) = e^{- \frac{1}{2} \mathrm{Tr}(\ln(1-2K) +2K)} \ e^{-\frac{1}{2}(f, \frac{1}{1-2K} f)}$$

which extends to K in the <u>Hilbert Schmidt</u> class.

By this we are led to consider further a "normalized exponential", which we define by

$$\mathbb{N}\exp ((\dot{B},K\dot{B})) \equiv \tau^{-1} (e^{-\frac{1}{2}(f,\frac{1}{1-2K} f)}) \tag{8}$$

for $(1-2K)^{-1}$ bounded.

In particular we may set

$$\Phi_{X,T} (\dot{B}) \equiv G_o(X,T) \quad \exp \{ (\tfrac{i}{2} + \tfrac{1}{2}) \int_o^T B^2(t)\, dt \} , \tag{9a}$$

defined in the above sense by

$$(\tau\Phi_{X,T})(f) = G_o(X,T) \ e^{\frac{i}{2} \int_o^T f^2(t)dt - \frac{1}{2} \int_{\mathbb{R}-[o,T]} f^2(t)\, dt}$$

$$= \left\langle e^{i(\dot{B},F)} \ \Phi_{X,T} (\dot{B}) \right\rangle \tag{9b}$$

In the above expressions G_o stands for the free particle Green's function, and apart from the "infinite renormalization" inherent in the definition of the normalized exponential $\mathbb{N}\exp$, it is formally obtained by inserting the fluctuating trajectories (7) into

$$\exp\{\frac{i}{\hbar} S_o[x]\} ,$$

except, of course, for the real parts of the exponent in equs.(9) (the term with $^1/2$ in front). Why do we need it to generate solutions of the Schroedinger equation? Formally, again, this term cancels the Gaussian damping of white noise which is alien to the Feynman integral.(If instead we use just the normalized exponential for the free action, without setting

$$\alpha = (\frac{\hbar}{m})^{\frac{1}{2}}$$

for the amount of fluctuation in (7), we find accordingly that a solution of the Schroedinger equation is obtained for $\alpha \to \infty$).

The action of $\Phi_{X,T}$ on Gaussian test functionals can be evaluated in closed form:

$$\left\langle \Phi_{X,T} \; e^{(\dot{B},K\dot{B}) + i(\dot{B},f)} \right\rangle \tag{1o}$$

$$= G_o(X,T) \; e^{-\frac{1}{2}\,\mathrm{Tr}\,\ln\,(1-2iK)} \; e^{-\frac{i}{2}(f,(1-2iK)^{-1}f)}$$

if $f \in L^2([o,T])$ and e.g. K with trace class norm less than $^1/2$.

Equation (1o) suffices to verify that one obtains the Green's function of the harmonic oscillator, for which $V(x) = \frac{1}{2} m\,\omega^2 x^2$, by

$$G(X,T) = \langle \Phi_{X,T} \; e^{-\frac{i}{\hbar} S_I[x]} \rangle \tag{11}$$

with the potential term of the action functional given by

$$-\frac{i}{\hbar} S_T[x] = -\frac{i}{2\hbar} m\omega^2 \int_0^T x^2(t)\,dt$$

$$= (\dot{B}, K\dot{B}) + i(\dot{B}, f) - \frac{i}{\hbar}\int_0^T V(\frac{X}{T}t)\,dt \tag{12}$$

so that

$$K(t_1,t_2) = \frac{i}{2}\,\omega^2 (t_1 \vee t_2 - \frac{1}{2T}(t_1{}^2 + t_2{}^2) - \frac{T}{3}) \tag{13}$$

$$f(t) = -\frac{1}{2}\,(\frac{m}{\hbar})^{1/2}\,\omega^2\,\frac{X}{T}\{t^2 - \frac{T^2}{3}\} \tag{14}$$

The harmonic oscillator Green's function is thus obtained by evaluating (11) with the help of (1o):

$$G(X,T) = G_o(X,T)\cdot e^{-\frac{1}{2}\,\mathrm{Tr}\,\ln\,(1-2iK)} \cdot e^{-\frac{i}{2}(f,(1-2iK)^{-1}f)} \cdot e^{-\frac{i}{\hbar}\int_o^T V(\frac{X}{T}t)\,dt} \tag{15}$$

The operator K with kernel given by (13) is easy to diagonalize. Hence we can calculate (15) explicitly. To show how the various factors conspire we give them separated by dots in the same sequence as in (15). The result is

$$G(X,T) = -i\sqrt{\frac{m}{2\pi i\hbar T}}\; e^{\frac{imx^2}{2\hbar T}} \cdot \sqrt{\frac{\omega T}{\sin\omega T}} \cdot e^{\frac{-imx^2}{2\hbar T} + \frac{im\omega x^2}{2\hbar}\,\mathrm{ctg}\,\omega T + \frac{im\omega^2 x^2 T}{6\hbar}} \cdot e^{\frac{-im\omega^2 x^2 T}{6\hbar}}$$

$$= -i\sqrt{\frac{m\omega}{2\pi i\hbar\sin\omega T}}\; e^{\frac{im\omega x^2}{2\hbar}\,\mathrm{ctg}\,\omega T}$$

So much for the harmonic oscillator. A large class of further examples is obtained by considering potentials which are Fourier transforms of bounded complex measures

$$V(x) = \int d\mu(\alpha)\, e^{i\alpha x}.$$

Expanding the functionals

$$e^{-\frac{i}{\hbar} S_i[x]} = \sum_{n=o}^{\infty} \frac{\left(-\frac{i}{\hbar}\right)^n}{n!} \prod_{k=1}^{n} \left(\int d\mu(\alpha_k) \int_o^T dt_k\right) \underline{e^{i \sum_{n=1}^{n} \alpha_k x(t_k)}} \tag{16}$$

has the effect of reducing it to a linear combination of exponential functionals, underlined above. These can be seen by $\Phi_{X,T}$: using (9b) one obtains the Dyson series, which, as shown by Albeverio and Hoegh-Krohn [4], solves the Schroedinger equation for the class of potentials at hand.

IV. AN APPROXIMATION

Writing once more

$$G(X,T) = G_o < (N\exp \frac{1+i}{2} \int_o^T \dot{B}^2 dt)\, e^{-\frac{i}{\hbar} S_I[vt + (\frac{h}{m})^{1/2} B_T]} > \tag{17}$$

$$\uparrow \qquad\qquad\qquad \uparrow \qquad \uparrow$$

we have marked the occurrences of $\hbar$ by arrows. An expansion of S_I in powers of $\hbar^{1/2}$ suggests itself. It is obtained by taking functionals derivatives S_I', S_I'', etc. of S_I with respect to white noise along the free path $x(t) = vt$:

$$S_I[x] = S_I[vt] + \frac{\hbar^{1/2}}{1!}(S_I', \dot{B}) + \frac{\hbar}{2!}(\dot{B}, S_I'' \dot{B}) + \ldots$$

As long as we approximate S_I by these first three terms only, we can evaluate the expression (17) for the Green's function explicitly with the aid of (1o) and obtain

$$G(X,T) \approx -i \sqrt{\frac{m}{2\pi i h T}}\; e^{\frac{i}{\hbar}\{\frac{mx^2}{2T} - \frac{1}{2}(S_I', (1-S_I'')^{1} S_I') - S_I\}} \cdot e^{-\frac{1}{2} \mathrm{Tr} \ln(1-S_I'')}$$

and, of course, similar expressions would result for the time development of wave functions.

Contrary to the usual semiclassical approximation this does not presuppose the knowledge of the classical solution since the functional derivatives are taken for free trajectories. One would expect it to be close to the former as long as classically a quadratic expansion of the interaction Lagrangian around the free path is good, but details remain to be explored.

* * *

Heartfelt thanks are due to S. Albeverio for helpful, even crucial discussions, to J.P. Antoine and his collaborators for bringing about the very stimulating exchange of ideas represented in this volume, to Ch. Berger for important words of encouragement, and to T. Hida whose ideas were central to our joint work.

References

[1] Ph. Combe, R. Høegh-Krohn, R. Rodriguez, M. Sirugue, M. Sirugue-Collin: Poisson Processes on Groups and Feynman Path Integrals. Marseille preprint, Sept. 1979, and these Proceedings.

[2] T. Hida, L. Streit: Generalized Brownian Functionals and Feynman Integrals. To appear.

[3] T. Hida: Analysis of Brownian Functionals. Carleton Mathematical Lecture Notes, No. 13. 2nd ed., 1978.
T. Hida: Causal Analysis in Terms of White Noise. In "Quantum Fields-Algebras, Processes", ed. by L. Streit, Springer, Vienna, 198o.

[4] S. Albeverio, R. Hoegh-Krohn: Mathematical Theory of Feynman Path Integrals. Lecture Notes in Mathematics 523, Springer, Berlin, 1976.

FEYNMAN FORMULA AND POISSON PROCESSES FOR GENTLE PERTURBATIONS

Ph. Combe *, R. Høegh-Krohn **, R. Rodriguez *,
M. Sirugue ***, M. Sirugue-Collin ****

Centre de Physique Théorique
C.N.R.S. - LUMINY - CASE 907
F-13288 MARSEILLE CEDEX 2 (FRANCE)

I. INTRODUCTION

Let $H = H_0 + V$ be a Hamiltonian, the solution of the corresponding Schrödinger equation is expected to be given by the Feynman path integral [1]

$$\psi(x,T) = \int_\Gamma e^{-iS_0(x,\gamma)-i\int_0^T V(x-\gamma(t))dt}\ \psi(x-\gamma(o))d\gamma$$

where S_0 is the free classical action associated with a path $\gamma \in \Gamma$, V is the potential and $d\gamma$ is expected to be a measure.

Unfortunatly, as it stands, the previous formula is not well defined. In particular $d\gamma$ is not a measure [2]. In the euclidean case one can incorporate $\exp(-S_0(\gamma))$ to $d\gamma$, then $d\omega(\gamma) = \exp(-S_0(\gamma))d\gamma$ is a bona fide measure (a Gaussian measure) on a space Γ which is a Hilbert space.

We take an alternative point of view. Namely for a large class of potentials there exists a measure space Ω and a measure on Ω which is roughly speaking :

* Faculté des Sciences de Luminy and Centre de Physique Théorique, CNRS, Marseille.
** Matematisk Institutt, Universitet i Oslo.
*** Centre de Physique Théorique, CNRS, Marseille.
**** Université de Provence and Centre de Physique Théorique, CNRS, Marseille.

$$e^{-i \int_0^T V(x-\gamma(t))dt} \, d\gamma = P(d\gamma)$$

such that, in the p representation,

$$\psi(p,T) = \int_\Omega \{e^{-i S_0(X)} \psi(p-X(o))\} (\omega) \, P(d\omega) .$$

X is a generalized Poisson process and P is a Poisson measure.

Results in this direction were obtained by Chebotarev and Maslov [3], [4] for velocity independant smooth potential. Our results may be considered as an extention of their ideas to interactions with velocity dependant potentials. However with our methods we are also able to treat more general systems like Fermi-spins systems, etc...

In order to describe the basic ideas we restrict ourselves in the next two sections to ordinary quantum mechanics, but treat velocity dependant potentials.

More precisely section 2 describes the measure space Ω, the Poisson measure P and the process X_t.

In section 3, we give explicitly the derivation of the Feynman formula.

In section 4, we show that the right context is to consider some unitary projective representation of groups and we derive in that case the corresponding Feynman formula.

Finally we list a series of examples where these general results apply. In particular we want to mention that we have treated along these lines an a priori quite different system like the Fermi system.

II. POISSON PROCESS ON Ω .

1) Probability space

The underlying probability space Ω is defined as follows :

Let $[0,T]$ be a closed interval of the real line

$$\Omega = \{\omega = (n \, ; t_1 \ldots t_n \, ; g_1 \ldots g_n) \, ; n \in \mathbb{N}, \quad 0<t_1<t_2 \ldots <t_n<T , \quad g_i = (p_i,q_i) \in \mathbb{R}^2\} \cup \{\omega_0\} \tag{2.1}$$

Notice that $\Omega = \bigcup_{n=o}^{\infty} \Omega^{(n)}$ with an obvious definition of $\Omega^{(n)}$.

Let $\mathcal{E}$ be the topology on Ω which is generated by the subsets $v^{(n)}_{\{a_i\}\ \{\mathcal{B}_i\}_{i=1\ldots n}}$ of Ω. The $v^{(n)}$ (n>0) are defined for any sequence $\{\mathcal{B}_i\}$ $i=1,\ldots,n$ of Borel subsets of $\mathbb{R}^2$ and for any sequence $\{a_i\}_{\ i=1\ldots n}$ of ordered, non intersecting, Borel subsets of $[0,T]$ i.e. satisfying the condition

$$\forall\, t_i \in a_i\ ,\ \forall\, t_j \in a_j \quad i < j \Longrightarrow t_i < t_j\ , \tag{2.2}$$

by

$$v^{(n)}_{\{a_i\}\ \{\mathcal{B}_i\}} = \{\omega = (n,\ t_1 \ldots t_n\ ;\ g_1 \ldots g_n)\ ;\ t_i \in a_i \quad g_i \in \mathcal{B}_i\} \tag{2.3}$$

Morever

$$v^{(o)} = \{\omega_0\} \tag{2.4}$$

Let $\mathcal{F}$ be corresponding Borel σ-algebra i.e. the smallest σ-algebra containing $\mathcal{E}$.

Given a positive bounded measure m on $\mathbb{R}^2$ one can define a probability measure P_m on Ω as the unique σ-additive measure on Ω which extends the additive function on the $v^{(n)}$'s défined by

$$P_m(v^{(o)}) = e^{-T\, m(\mathbb{R}^2)} \tag{2.5}$$

$$P_m(v^{(n)}_{\{a_i\}\{\mathcal{B}_i\}}) = e^{-T\, m(\mathbb{R}^2)} \prod_{i=1}^{n} |a_i|\ m(\mathcal{B}_i) \tag{2.6}$$

$|a_i|$ being the Lebesque measure of a_i.

Notice that the previous formulas define for a complex measure m a complex measure on Ω.

Then $(\Omega, \mathcal{F}, P_m)$ is a probability space.

Given a measurable function F on Ω its expectation value is given by

$$E(F) = \int F(\omega)\, P(d\omega) = e^{-Tm(\mathbb{R}^2)} \sum_{k\geqslant 0} \int_0^T dt_k \int_0^{t_k} \cdots \int_0^{t_2} dt_1 \tag{2.7}$$

$$\int_{\mathbb{R}^2} dm(g_k) \cdots \int_{\mathbb{R}^2} dm(g_1)\, F(n\, ;\, t_1 \ldots t_k\, ;\, g_1 \ldots g_k)$$

2) Sub σ-algebras $\mathfrak{F}_t$ of $\mathfrak{F}$

We shall consider in the following a family of sub σ-algebras $\mathfrak{F}_t$ $(t \in]0,T[)$ of $\mathfrak{F}$ which are defined as follows :

$\mathcal{C}_t$ is the topology generated by the subsets $v^{(n)}_{t,\{a_i\},\{\mathcal{B}_i\}}$ of Ω. The $v^n_{t,\{a_i\},\{\mathcal{B}_i\}}$ are defined for $n>0$, for any sequence of Borel subsets $\{\mathcal{B}_i\}_{i=1\ldots n}$ of $\mathbb{R}^2$ and for any sequence $\{a_i\}_{1\ldots n}$ of ordered, non intersecting Borel subsets of $]t,T]$, by

$$v^{(n)}_{t,\{a_i\}\{\mathcal{B}_i\}} = \{\{k+n;\, u_1 .. u_k, t_1 .. t_n\, ;\, h_1 .. h_k, g_1 .. g_n\} \tag{2.8}$$

$$k \in \mathbb{N} \quad 0 \leqslant u_1 < \ldots < u_k \leqslant t < t_1 \quad t_i \in a_i \quad h_j \in \mathbb{R}^2 \quad g_i \in \mathcal{B}_i\}$$

$$v^0_t = \{\{k,\, u_1 .. u_k\, ;\, h_1 .. h_k\} \quad 0<u_1 .. <u_k \leqslant t \quad h_j \in \mathbb{R}^2\} \tag{2.9}$$

Obviously

$$v^{(n)}_{t,\{a_i\},\{\mathcal{B}_i\}} = \bigcup_{k\geqslant 0} \bigcup_{b_i \subset [0,T]} V^{(k+n)}_{b_1 .. b_k, a_1 .. a_n; \mathbb{R}^2 .. \mathbb{R}^2, \mathcal{B}_1 .. \mathcal{B}_n} \tag{2.10}$$

Hence $\mathfrak{F}_t$, the corresponding Borel σ-algebra, is a decreasing family of σ-algebras

$$\mathfrak{F}_t \subset \mathfrak{F}_s \subset \mathfrak{F} (\equiv \mathfrak{F}_0) \text{ if } 0 < s < t < T \tag{2.11}$$

Corresponding to these sub σ-algebras one can compute explicitly the conditional expectation value $E(\cdot|\mathfrak{F}_t)$ $t \in]0,T[$. More precisely let F be a measurable function on Ω, $E(F|\mathfrak{F}_t)$ is a random variable defined by $(u_k \leqslant t < t_2)$:

$$E(F|\mathcal{F}_t)(k+n;u_1..u_k,t_1..t_n;h_1..h_k,g_1..g_n) = \qquad (2.12)$$

$$e^{-tm(\mathbb{R}^2)} \sum_{\ell\geq 0} \int_0^t dv_\ell \int^{v_\ell} dv_{\ell-1} \ldots \int_0^{v_2} dv_1 \int_{\mathbb{R}^2} dm(h'_\ell) .. \int_{\mathbb{R}^2} dm(h'_1)$$

$$F(\ell+n,\ v_1..v_\ell,\ t_1..t_n;\ h'_1..h'_\ell,\ g_1..g_n)$$

Roughly speaking $E(F|\mathcal{F}_t)$ is independant of what happens before t.

3) Jump processes X_t^K on Ω

Given a continuous fonction K on $\mathbb{R}^2$ with values in $\mathbb{R}$ we shall define a jump process X_t^K, $t \in [0,T]$, on Ω by

$$X_t^K(n,t_1\ldots t_n,\ g_1\ldots g_n) \begin{cases} = \sum\limits_{i,t_i\geq t} K(g_i) \\ = 0 \quad \text{if } t_n < t \end{cases} \qquad (2.13)$$

Figure

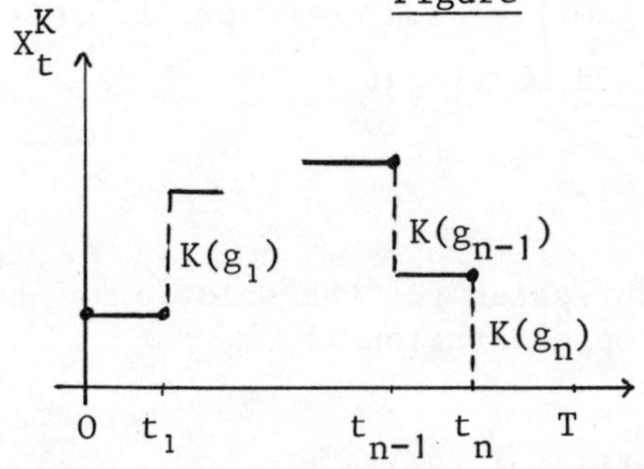

Proposition (2.14)

X_t^K is a measurable process whose trajectories are piecewise constant, left continuous, with a finite number of jumps (see figure).

Moreover assume that

$$e(|K|) = \int_{\mathbb{R}^2} |K(g)|\,dm(g) < \infty$$

$$e(K^2) = \int_{\mathbb{R}^2} [K(g)]^2\,dm(g) < \infty$$

then one can compute explicitly

$$E(X_t^K) = e(K)(T-t)$$

$$E\left[(X_t^K - E(X_t^K))^2\right] = e(K^2)(T-t)$$

$$E\left[(X_t^K - X_s^K - E(X_t^K - X_s^K))^2\right] = e(K^2)\ |s-t|$$

Let us notice that the function $N(x,y) = 1$ corresponds the usual Poisson process in the sense that

$$P_m(\omega;\ X_t^N(\omega) = n) = e^{-(T-t)m(\mathbb{R}^2)} \frac{(T-t)^n}{n!} \left[m(\mathbb{R}^2)\right]^n \qquad (2.15)$$

Nevertheless in the general case one can state the

Proposition (2.16)

If K is a continuous fonction on $\mathbb{R}^2$, X_t^K is $\mathfrak{F}_t$ measurable (in fact $\mathfrak{F}_t$ is an adapted familly) and moreover, if e(K) is finite, $\overline{X}_t^K = X_t^K - (T-t)\ e(K)$ is a martingale.

III. FEYNMAN FORMULA

We want to give an expression for the solution of the Schrödinger equation in the p-representation :

$$i \frac{\partial}{\partial t} \psi(p,t) = h_0(p)\ \psi(p,t) + (V\psi)(p,t) \qquad (3.1)$$

h_0 is the free hamiltonian and V a bounded operator of the form

$$V = \int_{\mathbb{R}^2} dm(x,p)\ W_{xp} \qquad (3.2)$$

where W_{xp} is a Weyl system

$$W_{xp}\ W_{x'p'} = e^{-(i/2)(xp'-x'p)}\ W(x+x',p+p') \qquad (3.3)$$

acting on the functions of $L_2(\mathbb{R})$.

In other terms

$$(V\psi)(\pi) = \int_{\mathbb{R}^2} dm(x,p)\, e^{(i/2)\,xp}\, e^{i\pi x}\, \psi(\pi+p) \tag{3.4}$$

Theorem (3.5)

The solution of the equation (3.1) which takes at t = 0 the value ψ, where ψ is a continuous, L_2 function, is given by

$$\psi(p,T) = \int_{\Omega} \{e^{-i\int_0^T dt\, h_0(p-P_t) - i\int_0^T P_t\, dX_t - i\, p\, X_0}\}(\omega) \cdot$$

$$\cdot\ \{\psi(p - P_0)\}(\omega)\, P_{m'}(d\omega) \tag{3.6}$$

where P_t and X_t, $t \in [0,T]$, are the jump processes defined respectively by the functions K_1 and K_2 on $\mathbb{R}^2$

$$K_1(x,p) = -p$$

$$K_2(x,p) = -x$$

and $P_{m'}$ is the measure on Ω corresponding to the bounded measure on $\mathbb{R}^2$: $dm'(x,p) = -i\, e^{+i\, xp/2}\, dm(x,p)$

Proof

Let $\omega = (n, t_1, \ldots, t_n, g_1 \ldots g_n)$ where $g_i = (x_i, p_i)$.

If h_0 is a continuous function then

$$\{\exp -i\int_0^T h_0(p-P_t)dt\}(\omega) = \exp\{-i\{(T-t_n)\, h_0(p) +$$

$$+(t_n - t_{n-1})\, h_0(p+p_n) + \ldots + t_1\, h_0(p+p_n+p_{n-1}\ldots+p_1)\}\ \}$$

is a measurable function on Ω , as well as the functions :

$$\{\exp -i\int_0^T P_t\, dX_t\}(\omega) = \exp\{-i \sum_{k=1}^{n} x_k(p_n+\ldots+p_k)\}$$

$$\{\exp(-i\, p\, X_0)\}(\omega) = \exp\{-\, i\, p \sum_{j=1}^{n} x_j\}$$

and $\psi(p-P_0)(\omega) = \psi(p - \sum_{j=1}^{n} p_j)$ (if ψ is continuous).

Moreover if ψ is L_2 the integral is finite.

Furthermore we can compute explicitly the left hand side of the equation (3.6)

$$\psi(p,T) = e^{-ih_0(p)T}\,\psi(p) + \sum_{n=1}^{\infty} (-i)^n \int_0^T dt_n \dots \int_0^{t_2} dt_1$$

$$\int_{\mathbb{R}^2} \dots \int_{\mathbb{R}^2} dm(x_1,p_1)\dots dm(x_n,p_n) \quad \exp\left(\frac{i}{2} \sum x_k\, p_k\right)$$

$$\exp -i\{(T-t_n)h_0(p)+(t_n-t_{n-1})h_0(p+p_n) + \dots$$

$$+t_1 h_0(p+p_n \dots +p_1)\}$$

$$\exp -i\{\sum_{k=1}^{n} x_k(p_n+p_{n-1}+\dots+p_k)+p(x_n+\dots+x_1)\}$$

$$\psi(p+p_n+p_{n-1}\dots+p_1)\ .$$

If we define H_0 through

$$(H_0\ \psi)(p) = h_0(p)\ \psi(p)$$

then after some algebra we have

$$\psi(p,T) = (e^{-i\,H_0 T}\psi)(p) + \sum_{n\geq 1} (-i)^n \int_0^T dt_n \int_0^{t_2} dt_1\ .$$

$$.\ \{e^{-i(T-t_n)H_0}\ V\ e^{-i(t_n-t_{n-1})H_0}\ V\dots V e^{-i\,t_1 H_0}\psi\}(p)$$

which is nothing but the Dyson's convergent expansion of the solution of

$$i\,\frac{\partial}{\partial t}\,\psi = (H_0+V)\psi$$

As a special case we can consider potentials corresponding to a measure of the type $m = \delta \otimes m_1$, where δ is the Dirac measure on $\mathbb{R}$ and m_1 a bounded measure on $\mathbb{R}$. In the x representation V is a multiplicative potential whose Fourier transform is $m_1(p)$.

In that case formula (3.6) simplifies and we recover the results of Maslov-Chebotarev

$$\psi(p,T) = \int_{\Omega'} \{e^{-i\int_0^T h_0(p-P_t)dt}\ \psi(p-P_0)\}(\omega)\ P_{m'_1}(d\omega)$$

where $\Omega' = \{(n;\ t_1 \ldots t_n;\ p_1 \ldots p_n)\ ,\ 0 < t_1 \ldots < t_n < T,\ p_i \in \mathbb{R}\}$

$$m'_1 = -i\ m_1$$

IV. GENERAL CASE

Theorem (3.5) is a special case of a much more general result that we want to describe now.

The natural context of such an extension is some projective unitary representation of a topological group G induced by an action of G on a topological space $\mathcal{H}$ [5].

Let G be a topological group, $\mathcal{H}$ a topological space and consider a continuous action of G on $\mathcal{H}$ which we denote by

$$(x,g) \in \mathcal{H} \times G \to xg \in \mathcal{H} \tag{4.1}$$

Let ξ be a continuous multiplier on G, i.e. a continuous function from G × G to the torus T such that

$$\xi(g_1,g_2)\ \xi(g_1g_2,g_3) = \xi(g_1,g_2g_3)\ \xi(g_2,g_3) \tag{4.2}$$

Let μ be a positive measure on $\mathcal{H}$, quasi-invariant with respect to the action of G. Let Z be a continuous function of $\mathcal{H} \times G \to T$ satisfying

$$Z(x,g)\ Z(xg_1,g_2) = \xi(g_1,g_2)\ Z(x,g_1g_2) \tag{4.3}$$

then

$$\left[U^Z(g)f\right](x) = Z(x,g)\ \sqrt{\frac{d\mu(xg)}{d\mu(x)}}\ f(xg) \qquad f \in L_2(\mathcal{H},\mu) \tag{4.4}$$

defines a continuous unitary projective representation of G on $L_2(\mathcal{H},\mu)$.

For special action of G on $\mathcal{H}$ one has the more precise result :

Proposition (4.5)

Let G be an abelian topological group and H a closed, invariant, subgroup of G. Let $g \in G \to [g] \in G/H$ be the canonical surjective homomorphism of G onto G/H. Let ξ be a continuous multiplier on G such that there exists a continuous function $\lambda : G \to T$ with the property

$$\xi(h,g) = \lambda(h)\,\lambda(g)\,\overline{\lambda(hg)} \qquad \text{for } h \in H\ ,\ g \in G$$

Let us consider the natural action of G onto G/H

$$[g]g' = [gg'] \qquad [g] \in G/H \qquad g' \in G$$

and let μ be a quasi-invariant positive measure on G/H for this action. Then any unitary projective representation U of G onto $L_2(G/H,\mu)$ is given by :

$$[U(g)f][g'] = \overline{\lambda(g'')}\,\lambda(g''g)\,\xi(g'',g)\,\chi_0(g)$$

$$u([g'])\,\overline{u([g'g])}\left[\frac{d\mu([g'g])}{d\mu([g'])}\right]^{1/2} f([g'g])$$

for some character χ_0 of G, some function $u : G/H \to T$ and for g'' an arbitrary element of G such that $[g''] = [g']$.

Conversely for any u and χ_0 the previous formula defines an unitary projective representation of G.

This is the general framework where we can state a theorem whose special case has been given in theorem (3.5).

Theorem (4.6)

With the same definitions and notations as above the solution of the equation

$$\frac{i\partial}{\partial t}\psi_t = (H_0 + V)\psi_t$$

where ψ_0 is a continuous function in $L_2(\mathcal{X},\mu)$, H_0 a self adjoint operator such that

$$(H_0\,\psi)(x) = h_0(x)\,\psi(x) \quad ,$$

h_0 being a continuous function on $\mathcal{X}$, and V a bounded operator on $L_2(\mathcal{X},\mu)$ such that

$$(V\psi)(x) = \int_G dm(g) \; (U^Z(g)\psi)(x) \; ,$$

where m is a bounded measure on G, is given by :

$$\psi_T(x) = \int_\Omega \{e^{-i \int_0^T h_0(x X_t^{-1}) dt} \; \Xi_\xi(X) \; Z(x, X_0^{-1}) \sqrt{\frac{d\mu(x X_0^{-1})}{d\mu(x)}} \; \psi(x X_0^{-1})\}(\omega) \; P_{m'}(d\omega)$$

where

$$\Omega = \{(n, t_1 \ldots t_n \; ; \; g_1 \ldots g_n) \; , \; 0 < t_1 \ldots < t_n < T \; , \; g_i \in G\} \; ,$$

X is a jump process in the sense that $X : [0,T] \times \Omega \to G$.

$$X_t(n \; ; \; t_1 \ldots t_n \; ; \; g_1 \ldots g_n) = (g_n \ldots g_k)^{-1} \quad \text{if } t_{k-1} < t \leq t_k$$

$$X_t(n \; ; \; t_1 \ldots t_n \; ; \; g_1 \ldots g_n) = e \quad \text{if } t_n < t$$

and

$$\Xi_\xi(n \; ; \; t_i \; ; \; g_i) = \xi(g_n, g_n^{-1} g_{n-1}) \ldots \xi(g_n \ldots g_k \; , \; g_k^{-1} g_{k-1}) \ldots \xi(g_n \ldots g_2, \; g_2^{-1} g_1)$$

is a measurable function.

$P_{m'}$ is the Poisson measure on Ω associated with the measure (-im) on G.

As an illustration of the generality of the previous results we list some examples where this formalism applies :

1) As we have seen the ordinary quantum mechanics in the p representation

2) Zak's kq representation

3) In general problems ([5] and references therein), where $G = \mathcal{G} \times \hat{\mathcal{G}}$

- quantum spins on a lattice in the Fock representation

- trace-class perturbation of hamiltonian with purely discrete spectrum

4) and also problems where $G = \mathcal{G}_1 \times \mathcal{G}_2 \qquad \mathcal{G}_2 \not\subset \hat{\mathcal{G}}_1$

This case covers both Fermi systems and Bose systems [6] with infinite numbers of degrees of freedom.

REFERENCES

1. R.P. Feynman, Review of Modern Physics, 20, 367 (1948).
2. R.H. Cameron, Journal of Math. and Phys., 39-126 (1960).
3. V.P. Maslov, A.M. Chebotarev, Sov. Math. Dok 17, 4-975 (1976).
4. V.P. Maslov, A.M. Chebotarev, Proceeding of the Conference on Feynman Path Integrals, Marseille (1978). Lecture Notes in Physics, 106, Springer-Verlag (1979).
5. P. Combe, R. Høegh-Krohn, R. Rodriguez, M. Sirugue, M. Sirugue-Collin, Poisson Processes on Groups and Feynman Path Integrals, Preprint CPT 79/P1139 Marseille.
6. P. Combe, R. Høegh-Krohn, R. Rodriguez, M. Sirugue, M. Sirugue-Collin , Poisson Processes Associated to Perturbation of Free Evolutions (in preparation).

THE CLASSICAL LIMIT OF QUANTUM MECHANICS IN A CURVED SPACE BACKGROUND

David Elworthy and Aubrey Truman

Mathematics Institute, University of Warwick
Coventry, England
Mathematics Department, Heriot-Watt University
Edinburgh, Scotland

ABSTRACT

Quasiclassical representations are given for the diffusion (heat) equation and the Schrödinger equation on a Riemannian manifold. These give an unambiguous functional integral expression for the solution of the diffusion (heat) equation and a (formal) unambiguous functional integral expression for the wave function solution of the Schrödinger equation intimately related to a corresponding classical mechanical problem on the manifold. Guided by these expressions we prove that in the curved space background of a Riemannian manifold quantum mechanics tends to classical mechanics as $\hbar$ tends to zero.

1. INTRODUCTION

In this paper we give a summary of some of the results which we have obtained on the classical limit of quantum mechanics in a curved space background[1]. In particular we discuss the limiting case $\mu^2 \to 0$ of the Cauchy problem

$$\frac{\partial g^\mu}{\partial t}(x,t) = \frac{\mu^2}{2}\,\Delta_x g^\mu(x,t) + \frac{V(x)}{\mu^2}\,g^\mu(x,t)\ , \qquad (1)$$

where Δ_x is the Laplace-Beltrami operator for a finite dimensional Riemannian manifold N, V is a real-valued potential and g^μ has initial data

$$g^{\mu}(x,0) = g_o^{\mu}(x) = \exp\{-S_o(x)/\mu^2\}\,\phi_o(x) \;, \tag{2}$$

S_o being real-valued, S_o and ϕ_o being independent of μ. We consider this Cauchy problem for both real and pure imaginary values of μ^2.

When $\mu^2 = i\hbar$ is pure imaginary, the above equation is a Schrödinger equation on the Riemannian manifold N. The above initial data in this case corresponds to an initial particle density ρ and a limiting value of the probability current $j_{\hbar=o}$, where

$$\rho(x) = |\phi_o(x)|^2, \qquad j_{\hbar=o}(x) = \rho(x)\,\nabla S_o(x) \;, \tag{3}$$

i.e., the initial particle flux is associated with the velocity field ∇S_o. Thus, the above initial conditions lead us to the corresponding classical mechanical problem

$$\frac{D^2X(s)}{\partial s^2} = -\nabla V[X(s)] \;, \qquad 0 \leq s \leq t \;, \tag{4}$$

with boundary conditions

$$X(t) = x, \qquad \dot{X}(0) = \nabla S_o(X(0)) \;. \tag{5}$$

Our results below give some simple relationships between the Cauchy problem for the Schrödinger equation above and the corresponding classical mechanical problem. Similar formal relationships exist for the Cauchy problem for the Green's function of the Schrödinger equation and the corresponding classical mechanical problem.

When $\mu^2 = \lambda$ is real, the above equation is a diffusion (heat) equation on the Riemannian manifold N. Given certain technical assumptions, which we outline below, using some ideas of Eells and Elworthy,[2] we obtain a quasiclassical representation (qcr) for g^{μ}, the solution to this diffusion (heat) equation. This qcr expresses g^{μ} as a formal power series in $\mu^2 = \lambda$, the coefficients of which are Wiener integrals related to the corresponding classical mechanical problem (Theorem 2.1). When $\mu^2 = i\hbar$ and the above equation reduces to a Schrödinger equation, this formal power series becomes a formal power series in $\mu^2 = i\hbar$ with coefficients which are Feynman integrals again determined by the corresponding classical problem (Eq 44). Unlike previous formal Feynman integral expressions for g^{μ} the qcr does not seem to be afflicted with infinities or ambiguities.

The first term of the qcr is exactly computable and gives the Pauli Van-Vleck De Witt WKB term[3]. That this is the correct limiting value of g^{μ} as μ tends to zero is proven in Theorem 3.1. This theorem uses simple Hilbert space methods, but we were led to

the result by the functional integral expressions which we encountered in the qcr. Our Hilbert space result proves that for small times quantum mechanics tends to classical mechanics in the curved space background of the Riemannian manifold N as $\hbar$ tends to zero.

Because of lack of space we have given only outline proofs in this paper. Nevertheless we have striven to make the methods of proof as transparent as possible. For further details and other results the interested reader should consult Reference 1.

2. THE DIFFUSION (HEAT) EQUATION ON A RIEMANNIAN MANIFOLD

In this section we derive the qcr for the diffusion (heat) equation on the Riemannian manifold N - Eqs (1) and (2). To simplify our working we make the following assumptions:-

1. The real-valued functions V and S_o and the complex-valued function ϕ_o are smooth, as is the complete, paracompact, n-dimensional Riemannian manifold N, V being bounded, S_o bounded below.

2. The Riemannian manifold N is stochastically complete so that the Brownian motion on N is defined for all time. This will be the case for instance if N is compact.

Let $\pi : O(N) \to N$ denote the orthonormal frame bundle of N. Here we consider an orthonormal frame $u_o \in \pi^{-1}(x_o)$, for $x_o \in N$, as an isometry $u_o : \mathbb{R}^n \to T_{x_o}N$, where for $e = (e^1, e^2, \ldots, e^n) \in \mathbb{R}^n$, $u_o(e) \in T_{x_o}N$ is the vector with components $(e^1, \ldots, e^n)$ relative to the orthonormal frame u_o.

The Levi-Civita connection on N determines a map $X : O(N) \times \mathbb{R}^n \to TO(N)$, trivialising the horizontal tangent bundle to O(N), so that if $(u,e) \in O(N) \times \mathbb{R}^n$, then $X(u,e)$ is the unique horizontal vector in $T_uO(N)$ with

$$\pi' X(u,e) = u(e) \ . \tag{6}$$

Take a fixed value of the time $t > 0$ and consider Brownian motion ω on $\mathbb{R}^n$ defined upto time t. We take this to be defined by the Wiener measure Γ on the space $\Omega = C_o(\mathbb{R}^n)$ of continuous paths $\omega : [0,t] \to \mathbb{R}^n$ with $\omega(0) = x_o$.

For fixed $x_o \in N$ and $u_o \in \pi^{-1}(x_o)$, let $u^\mu : [0,t] \times \Omega \to O(N)$, $\mu > 0$ be the solution of the Stratanovich stochastic differential equation

$$du^\mu = X(u^\mu, \mu d\omega) \ , \tag{7}$$

with $u^{\mu}(0,\omega) = u_o$, for all $\omega \in \Omega$. Define $x^{\mu} : [0,t] \times \Omega \to N, \mu > 0$, by $x^{\mu} = \pi u^{\mu}$. Then $x^{\mu=1}$ represents 'Brownian motion on N' and $u^{\mu=1}$ is its horizontal lift. By Eqs (6) and (7), $x^{\mu}(\cdot,\omega)$ satisfies in some sense

$$dx^{\mu}(s,\omega) = \mu u^{\mu}(s,\omega)d\omega(s) , \tag{8}$$

with $x^{\mu}(o,\omega) = x_o$, for all $\omega \in \Omega$, fixed $\mu > 0$.

The mapping $C_o(\mathbb{R}^n) \to C_{x_o}(N)$ defined almost everywhere by $\omega \to x^{\mu=1}(\cdot,\omega)$ with values in the space of continuous paths $\alpha : [0,t] \to N$ with $\alpha(0) = x_o$ is the 'stochastic development'. For a smooth path ω, $x^{\mu=1}(\cdot,\omega)$ is exactly the Cartan development obtained by rolling the curve $(u_o \circ \omega) : [0,t] \to T_{x_o}N$ on the manifold N.

The crucial fact is that the solution g^{μ} to Eqs (1) and (2) is given by the Feynman-Kac formula

$$g^{\mu}(x_o,t) = \int_{\Omega} \exp\left\{\mu^{-2} \int_0^t V[x^{\mu}(s,\omega)]\, ds\right\} g_o^{\mu}[x^{\mu}(t,\omega)]\, d\Gamma(\omega) . \tag{9}$$

This is basic in what follows. (For a proof of this result see Reference 2.)

Suppose now that $Z : [0,t] \to N$ satisfies the classical equation

$$\frac{D^2 Z(s)}{\partial s^2} = - \nabla V[Z(s)] , \tag{10}$$

with $Z(0) = x_0$ and $\dot{Z}(t) = - \nabla S_0[Z(t)]$. Then there is a unique smooth path $\sigma(\cdot)$ in $\mathbb{R}^n$ which has Z as the development of $(u_o \circ \sigma)$.

Let $v^{\mu} : [0,t] \times \Omega \to O(N)$ satisfy the Stratanovich stochastic differential equation

$$dv^{\mu} = X(v^{\mu}, \mu d\omega + \dot{\sigma} ds) , \tag{11}$$

with $v^{\mu}(0,\omega) = u_0$, for all $\omega \in \Omega$. As above define $y^{\mu} = \pi v^{\mu}$. Then $y^{\mu=0}(\cdot,\omega)$ is independent of ω and coincides with $Z(\cdot)$. From Eqs (6) and (11) in some sense

$$dy^{\mu}(s,\omega) = \mu v^{\mu}(s,\omega)d\omega(s) + v^{\mu}(s,\omega)\, \dot{\sigma}(s)ds , \tag{12}$$

with $y(0,\omega) = x_o$, for all $\omega \in \Omega$, fixed $\mu > 0$.

By the Girsanov-Cameron-Martin formula the measures $y^\mu(\Gamma)$ and $x^\mu(\Gamma)$ are equivalent and so for $\mu > 0$

$$g^\mu(x_0,t) = \int_\Omega \exp\left\{\mu^{-2}\int_0^t V[y^\mu(s,\omega)]\,ds - \mu^{-1}\int_0^t <\dot\sigma(s),d\omega(s)> - 2^{-1}\mu^{-2}\int_0^t |\dot\sigma(s)|^2 ds\right\} g_0^\mu[y^\mu(t,\omega)]\,d\Gamma(\omega) . \tag{13}$$

Setting $S = S_0[Z(t)] + 2^{-1}\int_0^t |\dot Z(s)|^2 ds - \int_0^t V[Z(s)]\,ds$, substituting for g_0^μ from Eq (2) and using $|\dot Z(s)| = |\dot\sigma(s)|$, gives

$$\exp\{\mu^{-2}S\}g^\mu(x_0,t) = \int \phi_0[y^\mu(t,\omega)]\exp\{A(\mu,\omega)\}d\Gamma(\omega) , \tag{14}$$

where

$$A(\mu,\omega) = \mu^{-2}\int_0^t \{V[y^\mu(s,\omega)] - V[Z(s)]\}ds - \mu^{-2}\{S_0[y^\mu(t,\omega)] - S_0[Z(t)]\} - \mu^{-1}\int_0^t <\dot\sigma(s),d\omega(s)> . \tag{15}$$

Apparently $A(\mu,\omega)$ is singular in μ at $\mu = 0$. The interesting fact about the qcr is that $A(\mu,\omega)$ is <u>not</u> singular at $\mu = 0$ at all. This is explained below. (See Reference 4.)

By results of Baxendale and Malliavin for a class of manifolds N (including compact N) there exists a version of y^μ which is almost surely C^∞ in μ.[5,6] Denote by $\delta y^\mu : [0,t]\times\Omega \to TN$ the first derivative with respect to μ of y^μ and set, for integer r,

$$\delta^r y^\mu = \frac{D}{\partial\mu}\delta^{r-1}y^\mu , \quad r \geq 2 , \tag{16}$$

$\delta^2 y^\mu : [0,t]\times\Omega \to TN$.

Expanding in powers of μ and integrating by parts in the last term of $A(\mu,\omega)$ gives

$$A(\mu,\omega)=\mu^{-1}\int_0^t dV[Z(s)]\{\delta y(s)-v^o(s)\omega(s)\}ds-\mu^{-1}dS_o[Z(t)]\{\delta y(t)-v^o(t)\omega(t)\}$$

$$+2^{-1}\int_0^t \nabla dV[Z(s)](\delta y(s),\delta y(s))ds - 2^{-1}\nabla dS_o[Z(t)](\delta y(t),\delta y(t))$$

$$+2^{-1}\int_0^t dV[Z(s)]\delta^2 y(s)ds - 2^{-1}dS_o[Z(t)]\delta^2 y(t) + R_1(\mu,\omega) + R_2(\mu,\omega)\ , \tag{17}$$

where $\delta^r y = \delta^r y^{\mu=o}$, $r = 1,2$ and $v^o(\cdot)$ is the orthonormal frame u_o parallel-translated along $Z(\cdot)$. Here $R_1(\mu,\omega)$ and $R_2(\mu,\omega)$ are remainder terms each of which is $O(\mu)$. Explicit equations for R_1 and R_2 are given in Reference 1 but the detailed nature of these terms will not concern us here.

We must now show that the coefficient of μ^{-1} in above expression for $A(\mu,\omega)$ is zero. The key result is the lemma below.

Lemma 2.1

The process $[\omega(s) - v^o(s)^{-1}\delta y(s)]$ has almost surely C^2 sample paths with

$$\frac{d}{ds}\left[v^o(s)^{-1}\delta y(s) - \omega(s)\right] = \int_0^s v^o(r)^{-1} R[\dot Z(r), \delta y(r)] v^o(r)\dot\sigma(s)dr\ , \tag{18}$$

R being the curvature tensor of N, with sign conventions of Reference 7.

Proof

Assume first that we solve Eq (12) as an ordinary differential equation with $\omega = \alpha$ a piecewise smooth path giving a piecewise smooth path $v^\mu(\cdot,\alpha)$ in $O(N)$ projecting to a piecewise smooth path $y^\mu(\cdot,\alpha)$ in N. With this assumption taking the covariant derivative $\frac{D}{\partial\mu}$ of Eq (12) and setting $\mu = 0$, we obtain, with $v^o(s,\alpha) = v^o(s)$,

$$\frac{D}{\partial s}\delta y(s,\alpha) = v^o(s)\,\dot\alpha(s) + \frac{D}{\partial\mu}[v^\mu(s,\alpha)\,\dot\sigma(s)]\Big|_{\mu=o}\ . \tag{19}$$

Also , using the fact that $v^{\mu}(\cdot,\alpha)\,\dot{\sigma}(s_0)$ is just the parallel translate of $(u_0 \circ \dot{\sigma})(s_0)$ along $y^{\mu}(\cdot,\overset{o}{\alpha})$,

$$\frac{D}{\partial s}\frac{D}{\partial \mu}[v^{\mu}(s,\alpha)\,\dot{\sigma}(s_0)]\Big|_{\mu=0} = \frac{D}{\partial \mu}\frac{D}{\partial s}[v^{\mu}(s,\alpha)\,\dot{\sigma}(s_0)]\Big|_{\mu=0} + R[\dot{Z}(s),\delta y(s,\alpha)]v^{0}(s)\,\dot{\sigma}(s_o)$$

$$= R[\dot{Z}(s),\delta y(s,\alpha)]v^{0}(s)\,\dot{\sigma}(s_o)\ . \tag{20}$$

Working in the parallel translated orthonormal frame $v^{0}(s)$, we therefore obtain

$$\frac{d}{ds}\left\{v^{0}(s)^{-1}\frac{D}{\partial\mu}[v^{\mu}(s,\alpha)\dot{\sigma}(s_o)]\right\}\Big|_{\mu=o} = v^{0}(s)^{-1}R[\dot{Z}(s),\,\delta y(s,\alpha)]v^{0}(s)\,\dot{\sigma}(s_o)\ . \tag{21}$$

Equivalently

$$\left\{v^{0}(s)^{-1}\frac{D}{\partial\mu}[v^{\mu}(s,\alpha)\,\dot{\sigma}(s)]\right\}\Big|_{\mu=o} = \int_0^s v^{0}(r)^{-1}R[\dot{Z}(r),\,\delta y(r,\alpha)]v^{0}(r)\,\dot{\sigma}(s)dr\ . \tag{22}$$

The last equation taken in conjunction with Eq (19) establishes Eq (18) for $\omega = \alpha$ a piecewise smooth path. The result in the lemma can now be obtained by taking a suitable limit over piecewise smooth paths α . (See Reference 1.) □

<u>Corollary</u>

$$A(\mu,\omega) = 2^{-1}\int_0^t \nabla dV[Z(s)](\delta y(s),\,\delta y(s))ds - 2^{-1}\nabla dS_0[Z(t)](\delta y(t),\,\delta y(t))$$
$$+ 2^{-1}\int_0^t dV[Z(s)]\,\delta^2 y(s)ds - 2^{-1}dS_0[Z(t)]\,\delta^2 y(t) + R_1(\mu,\omega) + R_2(\mu,\omega)\ . \tag{23}$$

Proof

The coefficient of μ^{-1} in $A(\mu,\omega)$ is just

$$<\dot{Z}(t),\ \delta y(t) - v^{o}(t)\omega(t)> - \int_0^t <\ddot{Z}(s),\ \delta y(s) - v^{o}(s)\omega(s)> ds$$

$$= \int_0^t <\dot{Z}(s),\ \frac{D}{\partial s}[\delta y(s) - v^{o}(s)\omega(s)] > ds \ , \tag{24}$$

by partial integration. However, $v^{o}(r)^{-1} R[\dot{Z}(r), \delta y(r)] v^{o}(r) : T_{y^{o}(r)}N \to T_{y^{o}(r)}N$ is skew-symmetric for each r and therefore so is its integral with respect to r, giving from last lemma

$$<\dot{Z}(s),\ \frac{D}{\partial s}[\delta y(s) - v^{o}(s)\omega(s)]> = 0\ , \qquad 0 \le s \le t\ . \tag{25}$$

This proves the corollary. □

We now rewrite the terms in $\delta^2 y$ in a more convenient form.

Lemma 2.2

$$A(\mu,\omega) = \int_0^t <\frac{d}{ds}[\omega(s) - v^{o}(s)^{-1}\delta y(s)], d\omega(s)> - \frac{1}{2}\int_0^t \left|\frac{d}{ds}[\omega(s) - v^{o}(s)^{-1}\delta y(s)]\right|^2 ds$$

$$+ \frac{1}{2}\int_0^t \nabla dV[Z(s)](\delta y(s), \delta y(s)) ds - \frac{1}{2}\int_0^t <R[\delta y(s), \dot{Z}(s)]\delta y(s), \dot{Z}(s)> ds$$

$$- \frac{1}{2}\nabla dS_o[Z(t)](\delta y(t), \delta y(t)) + R_1(\mu,\omega) + R_2(\mu,\omega)\ . \tag{26}$$

Proof

The proof depends upon the identity:

$$<\delta^2 y(t), \dot{Z}(t)> + \int_0^t <\delta^2 y(s), \nabla V[Z(s)]> ds = 2\int_0^t <\frac{d}{ds}[\omega(s) - v^{o}(s)^{-1}\delta y(s)], d\omega(s)>$$

$$- \int_0^t \left|\frac{d}{ds}[\omega(s) - v^{o}(s)^{-1}\delta y(s)]\right|^2 ds - \int_0^t < R[\delta y(s), \dot{Z}(s)]\delta y(s), \dot{Z}(s)> ds\ , \tag{27}$$

almost surely.

The last equation can be deduced by integrating with respect to s the identity, valid for piecewise smooth α,

$$\frac{d}{ds} < \delta^2 y(s,\alpha), \dot{Z}(s) > - < \delta^2 y(s,\alpha), \ddot{Z}(s) > = - \left| \frac{d}{ds} [\alpha(s) - v^o(s,\alpha)^{-1} \delta y(s,\alpha)] \right|^2$$

$$+ 2 < \frac{d}{ds} [\alpha(s) - v^o(s,\alpha)^{-1} \delta y(s,\alpha)], \dot{\alpha}(s) > \tag{28}$$

$$- < R[\delta y(s,\alpha), \dot{Z}(s)] \delta y(s,\alpha), \dot{Z}(s) > .$$

We leave the proof of this equation as an exercise. (See Reference 1.) □

The first two terms in our final expression for $A(\mu,\omega)$ suggest that we now make the change of integration variables $\theta : C_o(\mathbb{R}^n) \to C_o(\mathbb{R}^n)$ defined by

$$\theta(\omega)(s) = v^o(s)^{-1} \delta y(s,\omega) . \tag{29}$$

Setting $\theta_0 = \theta - I$, where I is the identity map, Lemma 1 gives an explicit expression for θ_0 as an iterated Volterra operator. Restricted to the reproducing kernel Hilbert space $L_o^{2,1}(\mathbb{R}^n)$ of Γ, it follows that θ_0 determines a trace-class operator with no non-zero eigenvalues. Consequently the Fredholm determinant $\det \theta$ must be unity. By the Cameron-Martin formula $\theta^{-1}(\Gamma) \approx \Gamma$ with Radon-Nikodym derivative

$$\frac{d\theta^{-1}(\Gamma)(\omega)}{d\Gamma} = \exp \left\{ - \int_0^t < \frac{d}{ds} [\theta(\omega)(s) - \omega(s)], d\omega(s) > \right. \tag{30}$$

$$\left. - 2^{-1} \int_0^t \left| \frac{d}{ds} [\theta(\omega)(s) - \omega(s)] \right|^2 ds \right\} .$$

Hence we have proven Theorem 2.1.

Theorem 2.1

Let Z satisfy the classical equations of motion

$$\frac{D^2 Z(s)}{\partial s^2} = - \nabla V[Z(s)] , \qquad 0 \le s \le t , \tag{31}$$

with $Z(0) = x_o$ and $\dot{Z}(t) = -\nabla S_o[Z(t)]$. Let $g^\mu(x_o,t)$ be the solution of the equation

$$\frac{\partial g^\mu}{\partial t} = \frac{\mu^2}{2}\Delta_{x_o} g^\mu + \frac{V(x_o)}{\mu^2} g^\mu , \tag{32}$$

with $g^\mu(\cdot,0) = \exp\left\{-S_o(\cdot)\right\}\phi_o(\cdot)$, for smooth ϕ_o, S_o, V, real V and S_o; V being bounded above. Then, if $S = S_o[Z(t)] + 2^{-1}\int_0^t |\dot{Z}(s)|^2\, ds - \int_0^t V[Z(s)]ds$, we obtain

$$\exp\{\mu^{-2}S\}g^\mu(x_o,t) = \int_\Omega \phi_o[z^\mu(t,\omega)]\exp\{B(\mu,\omega)\}d\Gamma(\omega) , \tag{33}$$

where $z^\mu(s,\omega) = y^\mu(s,\theta^{-1}\omega)$, $0 \le s \le t$, $\mu \ge 0$ and

$$B(\mu,\omega) = 2^{-1}\int_0^t \nabla dV[Z(s)](v^o(s)\omega(s),v^o(s)\omega(s))ds$$

$$- 2^{-1}\int_0^t \langle R[v^o(s)\omega(s),\dot{Z}(s)]\, v^o(s)\omega(s),\dot{Z}(s)\rangle ds \tag{34}$$

$$- 2^{-1}\nabla dS_o[Z(t)](v^o(t)\omega(t),v^o(t)\omega(t)) + \rho(\mu,\omega) ,$$

with $\rho(\mu,\omega) = R_1(\mu,\theta^{-1}\omega) + R_2(\mu,\theta^{-1}\omega)$. In particular $\rho(\mu,\omega) \to 0$ and $z^\mu(t,\omega) \to Z(t)$ almost surely as $\mu \to 0$.

Theorem 1 gives the quasiclassical representation for the diffusion (heat) equation on a Riemannian manifold N. We shall give the analogous result for the Schrödinger equation on a Riemannian manifold N in the next section. Our principal result in the next section is equivalent to proving that in curved space quantum mechanics $\to$ classical mechanics as $\hbar \to 0$. (See Reference 8.)

3. THE SCHRÖDINGER EQUATION ON A RIEMANNIAN MANIFOLD

To facilitate comparison with earlier treatments we use time-reversed paths in this section. Thus, letting $O(N)$ denote the orthonormal frame bundle of the Riemannian manifold N, with $\pi : O(N) \to N$, we define ${}^\mu x = \pi({}^\mu u)$, where ${}^\mu u$ satisfies the

(Stratanovich) stochastic differential equation

$$d\,{}^{\mu}u = X({}^{\mu}u, \mu d\omega) \ , \tag{35}$$

for some fixed $\mu > 0$, with ${}^{\mu}u(t,\omega) = u_f$, for some fixed $u_f \in \pi^{-1}(x_f)$, fixed $x_f \in N$, for all $\omega \in \Omega$, ω being (time-reversed) Brownian motion in $\mathbb{R}^n$. Here as before $X : O(N) \times \mathbb{R}^n \to TO(N)$ is determined by the Levi-Civita connection so that

$$\pi' X(u,e) = u(e) \in T_{\pi(u)}N \ , \tag{36}$$

$(u,e) \in O(N) \times \mathbb{R}^n$. Hence ${}^{\mu}x$ satisfies in some sense the (Stratanovich) stochastic differential equation

$$d\,{}^{\mu}x(s,\omega) = \mu\,{}^{\mu}u(s,\omega)d\omega(s) \ , \tag{37}$$

with ${}^{\mu}x(t,\omega) = x_f$, for all $\omega \in \Omega$, fixed $\mu > 0$.

Suppose now that $Z : [0,t] \to N$ satisfies the classical equation of motion

$$\frac{D^2 Z(s)}{\partial s^2} = - \nabla V[Z(s)] \ , \tag{38}$$

with $Z(t) = x_f$ and $\dot{Z}(0) = \nabla S_o[Z(0)]$. Then there is a unique smooth path σ in $\mathbb{R}^n$ for which Z is the development of $(u_f \circ \sigma)$. For this path σ, let ${}^{\mu}v : [0,t] \times \Omega \to O(N)$ satisfy the time-dependent (Stratanovich) stochastic differential equation

$$d\,{}^{\mu}v = X({}^{\mu}v, \mu d\omega + \dot{\sigma}\, ds) \ , \tag{39}$$

with ${}^{\mu}v(t,\omega) = u_f$, for all $\omega \in \Omega$, $\mu > 0$. Define ${}^{\mu}y : [0,t] \times \Omega \to N, \mu > 0$, by ${}^{\mu}y = \pi({}^{\mu}v)$. Then, as before,

$$d\,{}^{\mu}y(s,\omega) = \mu\,{}^{\mu}v(s,\omega)d\omega(s) + {}^{\mu}v(s,\omega)\,\dot{\sigma}(s)ds \ , \tag{40}$$

with ${}^{\mu}y(t,\omega) = x_f$, for all $\omega \in \Omega$, fixed $\mu > 0$. Evidently $Z(\cdot) = {}^{\mu=0}y(\cdot,\omega)$ is independent of ω.

Arguing as in the last section with time reversed paths, making the substitutions $V \to \sigma^{-1}V$, $\Delta \to \sigma\,\Delta$, for some $\sigma > 0$, we see that, if $g^{\mu\sigma^{\frac{1}{2}}}(x_f,t)$ satisfies

$$\frac{\partial g^{\mu\sigma^{\frac{1}{2}}}}{\partial t} = \left[\frac{\mu^2\sigma}{2}\,\Delta_{x_f} + \frac{V(x_f)}{\mu^2\sigma}\right] g^{\mu\sigma^{\frac{1}{2}}} \ , \tag{41}$$

for fixed $\mu > 0$, with $g^{\mu\sigma^{\frac{1}{2}}}(\cdot,0) = \exp\{-\mu^{-2}\sigma^{-1}S_o(\cdot)\}\phi_o(\cdot)$, for smooth ϕ_o, S_o, V; real valued S_o, V, V bounded above,

$$\exp\{\mu^{-2}\sigma^{-1}S\}\, g^{\mu\sigma^{\frac{1}{2}}}(x_f,t) = \mathbb{E}^{\sigma}[\phi_o[{}^{\mu}z(0,\omega)]\exp\{\sigma^{-1}B(\mu,\omega)\}], \quad (42)$$

where ${}^{\mu}z(s,\omega) = {}^{\mu}y(s,\theta^{-1}\omega)$, $0 \le s \le t$,

$$S = S_o[Z(0)] + 2^{-1}\int_0^t |\dot{Z}(s)|^2\, ds - \int_0^t V[Z(s)]\, ds, \quad \text{and}$$

$$B(\mu,\omega) = 2^{-1}\int_0^t \nabla dV[Z(s)]({}^{o}v(s)\omega(s),\ {}^{o}v(s)\omega(s))\, ds$$

$$- 2^{-1}\int_0^t \langle R[{}^{o}v(s)\omega(s), \dot{Z}(s)]\,{}^{o}v(s)\omega(s), \dot{Z}(s)\rangle\, ds \quad (43)$$

$$- 2^{-1}\nabla dS_o[Z(0)]({}^{o}v(0)\omega(0),\ {}^{o}v(0)\omega(0)) + \rho(\mu,\omega),$$

with $\rho(\mu,\omega) = R_1(\mu\ \theta^{-1}\omega) + R_2(\mu,\theta^{-1}\omega)$; R_1, R_2 and θ being defined as in the last section (save for the replacement of t by 0 in S_o terms), $\mathbb{E}^{\sigma}$ being the integral with respect to $d\Gamma^{\sigma}(\omega)$ Wiener measure with parameter σ.

For $\sigma = 1$, the above equation expresses the solution of the diffusion (heat) equation as a formal power series in $\mu^2 = \hbar$, the coefficients of the ascending powers of $\hbar$ being Wiener integrals intimately related to a corresponding classical mechanical problem. By varying the parameter σ, we seek an analogous result for the Schrödinger equation, a formal power series in $\hbar$ for the solution with the coefficients of successive powers of $\hbar$ being Feynman integrals.

Now using the results of McShane[9] (See also Reference 10.) for a large class of manifolds N (including compact N) and a restricted class of potentials V and initial data S_o, ϕ_o, the Wiener integral on r.h.s. above can be defined by replacing ω by its piecewise linear polygonal approximation and taking a suitable limit. This amounts to defining the Wiener integral by the (analytically continued) Feynman map definition of the Feynman integral. (In this case $x^{\mu}(\cdot,\omega)$ (and ${}^{\mu}x(\cdot,\omega)$) become piecewise geodesic and a formal limit can be evaluated determining anomalous curvature terms in Eq (9). (See Reference 1.))

In addition for complete manifolds N, according to Gaffney,[11] $\bar{\Delta}$, the closure of the Laplace-Beltrami operator for N, is self-adjoint on some suitable domain in $L^2(N,d\nu)$, ν being the Riemannian volume element on N. For Kato potentials relative to $(-\hbar^2\bar{\Delta}/2)$, imitating Nelson,[12] $g^{\mu\sigma^{\frac{1}{2}}}$ can be analytically continued through $\mathrm{re}(\sigma) \geq 0$ to give $g^{\hbar^{\frac{1}{2}} e^{i\pi/4}} = \psi_\hbar$, where $\psi_\hbar$ is a solution of the Schrödinger equation on the Riemannian manifold N, satisfying Eqs (1) and (2), with $\mu^2 = i\hbar$.

Analytically continuing in σ on r.h.s. of above equation, we therefore obtain the formal result

$$\exp\{-iS/\hbar\}\,\psi_\hbar(x_f,t) = \mathscr{F}\left[\phi_o[{}^{\mu}z(0,\gamma)]\exp\{-iB(\mu,\gamma)\}\right], \qquad (44)$$

with $\mu = \hbar^{\frac{1}{2}}$, $B(\mu,\gamma)$ and ${}^{\mu}z(\cdot,\gamma)$ being defined as above, $\mathscr{F}$ being the Feynman integral with integration variables γ. This is the quasiclassical representation for the Schrödinger equation on the Riemannian manifold N. (A similar, but more complicated, formal result can be obtained for the Green's function of the Schrödinger equation or propagator.)

Working in the parallel-translated orthonormal frame ${}^{o}v(\cdot)$, letting , denote covariant derivative and setting

$$p_{\alpha\beta}(s) = V_{,\alpha,\beta}(Z(s)) - R_{\alpha\gamma\beta\delta}(Z(s))\dot{Z}^{\gamma}(s)\dot{Z}^{\delta}(s), \qquad (45)$$

$$q_{\alpha\beta} = S_{o,\alpha,\beta}(Z(0)),\quad \alpha,\beta = 1,2,\ldots,n,$$

where $R^{\alpha}{}_{,\beta\gamma\delta}$ is the mixed curvature tensor of N, we obtain from above the formal result

$$\exp\left\{-iS(x_f,t)/\hbar\right\}\psi_\hbar(x_f,t)$$

$$= \mathscr{F}\left[\exp\left\{-\frac{i}{2}\int_0^t \gamma^{\alpha}(s')p_{\alpha\beta}(s')\gamma^{\beta}(s')ds'\right\}\exp\left\{\frac{i\gamma^{\alpha}(0)q_{\alpha\beta}\gamma^{\beta}(0)}{2}\right\}\right]\phi_o(Z(0)) + O(\hbar), \qquad (46)$$

$S(x_f,t)$ being $S = S_o(Z(0)) + 2^{-1}\int_0^t |\dot{Z}(s)|^2 ds - \int_0^t V[Z(s)]\,ds$.

Denote by $x[x_o, p_o, \cdot]$ the solution (assumed unique) of the Newton equation

$$\frac{D^2 x[x_o, p_o, s]}{\partial s^2} = -\nabla V[x[x_o, p_o, s]] , \tag{47}$$

with $x[x_o, p_o, 0] = x_o \varepsilon N$ and $\dot{x}[x_o, p_o, 0] = p_o \varepsilon T_{x_o}N$. Then, setting $p_o = \nabla S_o(x_o)$, $Z(\cdot) = x[x_o, \nabla S_o(x_o), \cdot]$, if $x_o = x_o(x_f, t)$ is chosen so that $x[x_0, \nabla S_0(x_0), t] = x_f \varepsilon N$. An exact evaluation of the above Feynman integral then gives

$$\psi_\hbar(x_f,t) = \phi_o[x_o(x_f,t)]\exp\{iS(x_f,t)/\hbar\}\, g^{-\frac{1}{4}}(x_f)\left|\det \frac{\partial x_o^\alpha(x_f,t)}{\partial x_f^\beta}\right|^{\frac{1}{2}} \tag{48}$$

$$g^{\frac{1}{4}}(x_o(x_f,t))\exp\left\{\frac{-i\pi M(Z)}{2}\right\} + O(\hbar) ,$$

g being $|\det g_{\alpha\beta}|$, $M(Z)$ being the Maslov index of Z. (See Reference 13.)

We now go on to prove the above relationship in the simplest possible case when Z is unique and $M(Z)$ is zero. Our proof is a simple Hilbert space result, which we were led to by the functional integrands above. We detail the assumptions for our Hilbert space result below:-

1. To avoid counting derivatives we assume that the real-valued V, S_o are smooth and N is smooth. We assume that V is a Kato potential relative to $(-\hbar^2\bar{\Delta}/2)$, $\bar{\Delta}$ being the self-adjoint closure of Laplace-Beltrami operator Δ, so that $H = (-\hbar^2\bar{\Delta}/2 + V)$ generates a unitary one parameter group $\exp\{-iHt/\hbar\} : L^2(N,d\nu) \to L^2(N,d\nu)$, which according to Stone's theorem solves the Schrödinger equation for initial data in $\mathfrak{D}(\bar{\Delta})$. (See Reference 14.)

2. Define $\Phi_s : N \to N$ by

$$\Phi_s(x_o) = x[x_o, \nabla S_o(x_o), s] , \tag{49}$$

where $x[x_o, \nabla S_o(x_o), s]$ is defined as above, $x[x_o, \nabla S_o(x_o), s]$ being assumed to exist and be unique for $s \varepsilon [0,T']$, for some $T' > 0$. We assume, as can be shown from the standard theory of o.d.e. on manifolds, that $\Phi_s(x_o)$ is jointly continuous in (s, x_o) and, for each fixed s, $\Phi_s(x_o)$ is smooth in x_o with derivative denoted $T_{x_o}\Phi_s$.

3. Let the matrices p and q be defined as above. Let $\| \ \|$ denote matrix norm and assume $\lambda^2 = \sup_{\substack{x_f \in N \\ s\in[0,T']}} \|p_{\alpha\beta}(s)\| < \infty$. (This will follow from energy conservation if R is uniformly bounded and V has second order covariant derivatives uniformly bounded.) Also set $\mu_{min} = \inf_{x_f \in N} \mu_{min} - q(Z(0))$, $\mu_{max} = \sup_{x_f\in N} \mu_{max} - q(Z(0))$, μ_{min} and μ_{max} being assumed finite where $\mu^{min}_{max} - q(Z(0))$ are respectively the minimum and maximum eigenvalues of the matrix $-q(Z(0))$.

We prove first that necessarily $\Phi_s : N \to N$ is a diffeomorphism for some finite range of values $s \in [0,T]$. This result depends upon the global inverse function theorem for Riemannian manifolds contained in the proposition below.

Proposition 3.1

Let M and N be connected Riemannian manifolds with $\dim M = \dim N < \infty$. Suppose $\Phi : M \to N$ is smooth, with some $K > 0$, such that for all $v \in T_m M$, for all $m \in M$,

$$|T_m \Phi(v)| \geq K|v| , \tag{50}$$

$T_m \Phi : T_m M \to T_{\Phi(m)} N$ being the linear derivative mapping of Φ at m. Then if M is complete Φ is a covering map and N is complete. If also Φ is homotopic to a homeomorphism then Φ is a diffeomorphism.

Proof

We change the Riemannian metric on M so that Φ is a local isometry i.e. $T_m \Phi : T_m M \to T_{\Phi(m)} N$ is an isometry. This proves that, for complete M, N is complete and Φ is surjective. The injectivity of Φ follows from a simple homotopy argument.

Define the new metric $\tilde{d}$ on M by $\langle u,v\rangle_{\tilde{M}} = \langle T_m\Phi(u), T_m\Phi(v)\rangle_N$. Then, by the hypothesis $|T_m\Phi(v)| \geq K|v|$, $(M,\tilde{d})$ is complete and Φ is clearly a local isometry. It follows that, for $m \in M$, $\tilde{v} \in T_m M$, $v = T_m\Phi(\tilde{v})$,

$$\Phi[\tilde{\gamma}(t)] = \exp_{\Phi(m)}(tv) , \tag{51}$$

where $\tilde{\gamma}(t) = \exp_m(t\tilde{v})$. Hence $U = \Phi(M)$ is geodesically complete hence metrically complete and so is closed in N. The local inverse function theorem shows that U is open. By connectivity $U = N$ and Φ is

surjective. A standard result in Riemannian geometry[15] gives that, for complete M and surjective Φ, Φ must be a covering map. The injectivity of Φ follows because Φ is homotopic to a homeomorphism and $\Phi(m) = n$ gives $\Phi_* : \pi_1(M,m) \approx \pi_1(N,n)$. Letting $m, m^1 \in \Phi^{-1}(n)$ with m, m^1 distinct, taking σ in M with $\sigma(0) = m$ and $\sigma(1) = m^1$, implies $\Phi(\sigma)$ does not lie in $\Phi_*(\sigma)$, which is a contradiction. Hence $m = m^1$ and Φ is injective. □

We can now prove:

Proposition 3.2

$\Phi_s : N \to N$ is a diffeomorphism for $s \in [0,T)$, T being the least positive solution of the equation

$$\left(1 - \mu_{max} t\right)\left\{2 - \mu_{max} t - \mu_{min}[t - \lambda^{-1} \sinh \lambda t] - \cosh \lambda t\right\} = 0. \quad (52)$$

Proof

Let $K(s)$ be the matrix representation of $T_{x_0}\Phi_s : T_{x_0}N \to T_{\Phi_s(x_0)}N$, in parallel translated orthonormal co-ordinates. Then a simple but tedious calculation shows that $K(s)$ satisfies the second order linear matrix differential equation

$$\ddot{K}(s) + p(s)K(s) = 0 , \qquad s \in [0,t] , \quad (53)$$

with $K(0) = 1$ and $\dot{K}(0) = q(x_0)$, p and q being the matrices detailed above. Hence, we obtain

$$K(s) = I + sq(x_0) - \int_0^s ds' \int_0^{s'} p(s'')\, K(s'')\, ds'' . \quad (54)$$

Set $A(s) = I + sq(x_0)$ and $B(s) = -\int_0^s ds' \int_0^{s'} ds'' p(s'') K(s'')$. Then, if $\| \ \|$ denotes matrix norm,

$$\|B(s)\| \leq \lambda^2 f(s) , \qquad f(s) \overset{def}{=} \int_0^s ds' \int_0^{s'} \|K(s'')\|\, ds'' \geq 0 . \quad (55)$$

From above

$$\ddot{f}(s) = \|K(s)\| \leq \|A(s)\| + \lambda^2 f(s) , \quad f(0) = \dot{f}(0) = 0. \tag{56}$$

Define $g(s)$ by

$$\ddot{g}(s) = \|A(s)\| + \lambda^2 g(s) , \quad g(0) = \dot{g}(0) = 0 . \tag{57}$$

Then

$$\frac{d^2}{ds} (g - f) \geq \lambda^2 (g - f) , \tag{58}$$

and for $s \geq 0$ it follows that $g(s) \geq f(s)$. However, g can be evaluated explicitly giving

$$g(s) = \lambda^{-1} \int_0^s \sinh[\lambda (s - s')][1 - \mu_{min}(x_o)s'] ds' . \tag{59}$$

Now, using the fact that $f(s) \leq g(s)$, $s \geq 0$, and the result that when A is invertible and B satisfies $\|B\| < \|A^{-1}\|^{-1}$ $(A + B)$ is invertible with $\|(A+B)^{-1}\| < |\|A^{-1}\|^{-1} - \|B\||^{-1}$, we see that $K(s)$ is invertible and

$$\|K^{-1}(s)\| \leq [\|A^{-1}(s)\|^{-1} - \lambda^2 g(s)]^{-1} , \tag{60}$$

as long as $\lambda^2 g(s) \leq \|A^{-1}(s)\|^{-1} = 1 - \mu_{max}(x_o)s$, $s < \mu^{-1}_{max}(x_o)$.

Substitution of above explicit value for $g(s)$ leads to the result that $T_{x_o}\Phi_s = K(s)$ is invertible for all $x_o \varepsilon N$ and $\sup_{x_o} \|(T_{x_o}\Phi_s)^{-1}\| \leq M < \infty$, for $s \varepsilon [0,t]$, $t \varepsilon [0,T)$, T being the least positive solution of the equation

$$(1 - \mu_{max} t)\left\{2 - \mu_{max} t - \mu_{min}(t - \lambda^{-1}\sinh \lambda t) - \cosh \lambda t\right\} = 0. \tag{61}$$

This is equivalent to the existence of $K = M^{-1} > 0$ in last proposition. Result follows since Φ_s is homotopic to the identity. □

It is interesting to observe that the above result is a best possible result in the sense that when $N = \mathbb{R}$ and $V = 0$ the above equation reduces to $(1 - \mu \max t)^2 = 0$ i.e. $T = \mu_{max}{}^{-1}$. However, for $V \equiv 0$, a simple calculation gives $T_{x_o}\Phi_s = \left[1 + s\frac{\partial^2 S_o}{\partial x_o{}^2}(x_o)\right]$ and

to restrict Φ_s to be a bijection in one dimension Φ_s must be monotonic $s \varepsilon [0,t)$. Hence, we must insist $t < \mu_{max}^{-1}$.

We now require three lemmas before proving the main result of this section. For $s \varepsilon [0,t]$, $t \varepsilon [0,T)$, we shall set $\Phi_s^{-1}(x) = x_o(x,s)$.

Lemma 3.1

Let $S(x,s)$ be defined by $S(x,s) = S_o[x_o(x,s)] + \int_0^s \left\{2^{-1}|\dot{Z}(s')|^2 - V[Z(s')]\right\} ds'$. Then S satisfies the Hamilton-Jacobi equation

$$2^{-1}\partial^\alpha S(x,s)\partial_\alpha S(x,s) + \frac{\partial S(x,s)}{\partial s} + V(x) = 0, \quad x \varepsilon N, s \varepsilon [0,t], \tag{62}$$

with initial condition $S(x,0) = S_o(x)$.

Let $J(x,s)$ be defined by $J(x,s) = \det\left(\frac{\partial x_o^\alpha(x,s)}{\partial x^\beta}\right)$ and set $\rho(x,s) = g^{-\frac{1}{2}}(x)\, J(x,s) g^{\frac{1}{2}}(x_o(x,s))$, where $g(x) = \det(g_{\alpha\beta}(x))$. Then $\rho(x,s)$ satisfies the continuity equation

$$\frac{\partial\rho(x,s)}{\partial s} + \mathrm{div}_x[\nabla_x S(x,s)\rho(x,s)] = 0, \quad x \varepsilon N, \ s \varepsilon [0,t]. \tag{63}$$

Proof

Compute derivatives. (See Reference 1.) □

Lemma 3.2

For each fixed $t \varepsilon [0,T)$, T being least positive solution of Eq (52), define $\theta_t \varepsilon L^2(N,d\nu)$ by

$$\theta_t(x) = \exp\{iS(x,t)/\hbar\}\rho^{\frac{1}{2}}(x,t)\theta[x_o(x,t)], \qquad \theta \varepsilon C_o^\infty(N), \tag{64}$$

then $\|\theta_t\| = \|\theta\|$, $\| \ \|$ being $L^2(N,d\nu)$ norm.

Assuming V, S_o are as above and $t \in [0,T)$, then

$$\frac{(\theta_{t+k} - \theta_t)}{k} \xrightarrow{L^2(N,d\nu)} \frac{\partial\theta_t}{\partial t}, \tag{65}$$

as $k \to 0$, where

$$\frac{\partial\theta_t(x)}{\partial t} = \left[2^{-1}\rho^{-1}(x,t)\frac{\partial\rho}{\partial t}(x,t) + i\hbar^{-1}\frac{\partial S}{\partial t}(x,t)\right]\theta_t(x)$$
$$- e^{iS(x,t)/\hbar}\rho^{\frac{1}{2}}(x,t)\nabla_x S(x,t)\cdot\nabla_x\theta[x_o(x,t)]. \tag{66}$$

Moreover, $\theta_t \in \mathfrak{D}(\bar{\Delta}) = \mathfrak{D}(H)$, and θ_t is an <u>approximate</u> solution of the Schrödinger equation in the sense that

$$\frac{iH}{\hbar}\theta_t(\cdot) + \frac{\partial\theta_t(\cdot)}{\partial t} = -i2^{-1}\hbar\exp\{iS(\cdot,t)/\hbar\}\Delta.\left[\rho^{\frac{1}{2}}(\cdot,t)\theta[x_o(\cdot,t)]\right], \tag{67}$$

H being the quantum mechanical Hamiltonian $H = \left(\frac{-\hbar^2\bar{\Delta}}{2} + V\right)$.

<u>Proof</u>

First part of lemma follows by changing integration variables from x to $x_o(x,t)$ using Proposition 3.2. Also from Proposition 3.2 it follows that $\theta_t \in C_o^\infty(N)$, $t \in [0,T)$. Since for each fixed x, $\theta_t(x)$ is continuously differentiable w.r.t. t, $k^{-1}(\theta_{t+k} - \theta_t) \to \frac{\partial\theta_t}{\partial t}$, pointwise for each $x \in N$. The result that $k^{-1}(\theta_{t+k} - \theta_t) \xrightarrow{L^2} \frac{\partial\theta_t}{\partial t}$ follows from the joint continuity of $\Phi_s(x)$ and the dominated convergence theorem for the measure $d\nu$. The rest of the lemma is computation using Lemma 3.1 above.

<u>Lemma 3.3</u>

Let $\theta \in C_o^\infty(N)$ and define θ_t as above. Let $\psi_t \in L^2(N,d\nu)$ be defined by $\psi_t = \exp(-iHt/\hbar)\psi_o$ with $\psi_o \in \mathfrak{D}(H) = \mathfrak{D}(\bar{\Delta})$. Then assuming V satisfies above conditions, for $t \in [0,T)$,

$$\frac{d}{dt}(\theta_t,\psi_t)_{L^2(N,d\nu)} = i2^{-1}\hbar\left(\Delta.\rho^{\frac{1}{2}}(\cdot,t)\theta\,[\Phi_t^{-1}(\cdot)],\ e^{-iS(\cdot,t)/\hbar}\psi_t(\cdot)\right)_{L^2(N,d\nu)}. \tag{68}$$

Proof

Apply above lemma and Stone's theorem. □

We can now prove the main result of this section. (See also Reference 8 and for formal results Reference 16.)

Theorem 3.1

Let the real-valued smooth Kato potential V and the real-valued smooth function S_0 satisfy the conditions above (so that T the solution of Eq (52) is well defined). Set $\psi_\hbar(x,t) = \exp(-iHt/\hbar)\psi_0(x)$, where $H = [-2^{-1}\hbar^2\bar{\Delta}_x + V(\underline{x})]$ is the self-adjoint quantum mechanical Hamiltonian on $\mathfrak{D}(\bar{\Delta})$, $\bar{\Delta}$ being the self-adjoint Laplace-Beltrami operator for the smooth complete connected Riemannian manifold N, $d\nu$ being the Riemannian volume element on N, with $\psi_0(x) = \exp\{iS_0(x)/\hbar\}\phi_0(x)$, $\phi_0 \in C_0^\infty(N)$, S_0, ϕ_0 being independent of $\hbar$. Then, for each fixed $t \in [0,T)$,

$$\psi_\hbar(x,t) \xrightarrow{L^2(N,d\nu)} \exp\{iS(x,t)/\hbar\}\,\rho^{\frac{1}{2}}(x,t)\phi_0[x_0(x,t)]\ , \tag{69}$$

uniformly in t, as $\hbar \to 0$, where

$$S(x,t) = S_0[x_0(x,t)] + \int_0^t 2^{-1} g_{\alpha\beta}[Z(s)]\dot{Z}^\alpha(s)\dot{Z}^\beta(s) - V[Z(s)]\,ds\ ,$$

$$\rho(x,t) = g^{-\frac{1}{2}}(x)\det\left(\frac{\partial x_0^\alpha(x,t)}{\partial x^\beta}\right)g^{\frac{1}{2}}[x_0(x,t)]\ ,\ g(x) \text{ being } |\det g_{\alpha\beta}(x)|,$$

$x_0(x,t)$ being $\Phi_t^{-1}(x)$, $x \in N$.

Proof

Define the unitary $\exp(-iS_t/\hbar) : L^2(N,d\nu) \to L^2(N,d\nu)$ by $(\exp(-iS_t/\hbar)\theta)(x) = \exp(-iS(x,t)/\hbar)\,\theta(x)$, $\theta \in L^2(N,d\nu)$. From the above with $\|\ \|$ denoting $L^2(N,d\nu)$ norm, setting $\phi_{ot} = (\phi_0)_t$ and observing that $\|\phi_{ot}\|^2 = \|\psi_t\|^2 = \|\phi_0\|^2$, we see

$$\|\exp(-iS_t/\hbar)(\phi_{ot} - \psi_t)\|^2 = 2\|\phi_0\|^2 - 2\text{R.P.}(\phi_{ot},\psi_t) \leq 2|(\phi_0,\phi_0) - (\phi_{ot},\psi_t)|. \tag{70}$$

However, from previous lemma

$$(\phi_{ot},\psi_t) - (\phi_o,\phi_o) = (\phi_{ot},\psi_t) - (\phi_{oo},\psi_o)$$
$$= i\hbar 2^{-1}\int_0^t (\Delta.\rho^{\frac{1}{2}}(\cdot,s)\phi_o[\Phi_s^{-1}(\cdot)], e^{-iS(\cdot,s)/\hbar}\psi_s(\cdot))ds\,, \tag{71}$$

(,) being $L^2(N,d\nu)$ inner product. From the Cauchy-Schwarz inequality, using $\|\psi_s\| = \|\phi_o\|$, we obtain

$$\|\exp(-iS_t/\hbar)(\phi_{ot} - \psi_t)\|^2 < 2^{-1}\hbar\,\|\phi_o\| \int_0^t F(s)ds\,, \tag{72}$$

where $F(s) = \|\Delta.\rho^{\frac{1}{2}}(\cdot,s)\phi_o[\Phi_s^{-1}(\cdot)]\| \in L^1(0,t)$, Φ_s being a diffeomorphism $\Phi_s : N \to N$, $t \in [0,T)$. The result follows letting $\hbar \to 0$. □

4. CONCLUSION

Given the assumptions above, we have seen that $\psi_\hbar(x,t)$, the solution of Eqs (1) and (2), for $t \in [0,T)$, T being the solution of Eq (52), satisfies

$$\psi_\hbar(x,t) \xrightarrow{L^2(N,d\nu)} \exp\{iS(x,t)/\hbar\}|J(x,t)|^{\frac{1}{2}} g^{-\frac{1}{4}}(x) g^{\frac{1}{4}}(x_o(x,t))\phi_o[x_o(x,t)]\,, \tag{73}$$

as $\hbar \to 0$, $d\nu$ being the Riemannian volume element of N, $d\nu = g^{\frac{1}{2}}(x)d^n x$, $J(x,t)$ being $\left|\det \frac{\partial x_o^\alpha(x,t)}{\partial x^\beta}\right|_{\alpha,\beta=1,2,\ldots,n}$.

Now let Ω be any measurable subset of the configuration space Riemannian manifold N and denote by $P(t,\Omega)$ the limiting value as $\hbar \to 0$ of the quantum probability that the mechanical system is in Ω at time t. Then, changing integration variables using Proposition 3.2,

$$P(t,\Omega) = \lim_{\hbar\to 0}\int_\Omega |\psi_\hbar(x,t)|^2 d\nu(x) = \lim_{\hbar\to 0}\int_{\Phi_t^{-1}\Omega} |\psi_\hbar(x,0)|^2 d\nu(x) = P(0,\Phi_t^{-1}\Omega)\,. \tag{74}$$

Hence, in the limit as $\hbar \to 0$, the mechanical system in the configuration space N, as determined by Eqs (1) and (2), can quantum mechanically arrive at points of N only if it starts out at the corresponding classically correct initial points. Shrinking the support of the initial wave function $\psi_\hbar(x,0)$, we see that, for small $\hbar$, the support of $\psi_\hbar(x,t)$ is concentrated in a neighbourhood of the corresponding classical mechanical flow. In this sense quantum mechanics tends to classical mechanics on the Riemannian manifold N as $\hbar$ tends to zero.

Acknowledgements

Part of the work on this article was done while the first named author was a visiting professor at the Center for Relativity, Department of Physics, University of Texas at Austin, on Sabbatical leave from the University of Warwick; and while the second named held a Science Research Council Senior Visiting Fellowship at Princeton University, Mathematics and Physics Departments, arranged by B. Simon and A.S. Wightman. Discussions and correspondence with C. DeWitt-Morette, and B. Simon were very helpful.

REFERENCES

1. K.D. Elworthy, and A. Truman, Classical Mechanics, the Diffusion (heat) equation and the Schrödinger equation on Riemannian manifolds, Warwick University and Heriot-Watt University preprint (1979).
2. K.D. Elworthy, "Stochastic Differential Equations on Manifolds," notes of seminars by J. Eells and K.D. Elworthy, Department of Mathematics, University of Warwick, Coventry (1978).
3. C. DeWitt-Morette, A. Maheshwari, and B. Nelson, Path Integration in nonrelativistic quantum mechanics, Physics Reports, 50, 257 (1979).
4. A. Truman, Polygonal path formulation of the Feynman path integral in "Feynman Path Integrals," Albeverio et al., ed., Springer Lecture Notes in Physics, 106, (1979).
5. N. Ikeda, S. Nakao, and Y. Yamato, A class of approximations of Brownian motion, Publ. RIMS, Kyoto University 13 (1977).
6. P. Malliavin, Un principe de transfert et son application au Calcul des Variations, C.R. Acad. Sc., Paris, 284, Série A (1977).
7. S. Kobayashi, and K. Nomizu, "Foundations of Differential Geometry," Vol I, Interscience, New York (1963).

8. A. Truman, Classical Mechanics, the Diffusion (heat) equation and the Schrödinger equation, J. Math. Phys., 18, 2308 (1977).
9. E.J. McShane, "Stochastic Calculus and Stochastic Models," Academic Press, New York (1974).
10. K.D. Elworthy, Stochastic Dynamical Systems and their flows in "Stochastic Analysis," A. Friedman, and M. Pinsky, eds., Academic Press, New York (1978).
11. M. Gaffney, A Special Stoke's theorem for complete Riemannian manifolds, Ann. of Math. 60, 140 (1954).
12. E. Nelson, Feynman integrals and the Schrödinger equation, J. Math. Phys., 5, 332 (1964).
13. K.D. Elworthy, and A. Truman, Feynman maps, Cameron-Martin formulae, and the anharmonic oscillator, in preparation.
14. M. Reed, and B. Simon, "Methods of Modern Mathematical Physics, II, Fourier Analysis, Self-Adjointness," Academic Press, New York (1975).
15. M. Berger, "Lectures on Geodesics in Riemannian Geometry," Tata Institute Notes, Bombay (1965).
16. F. Langouche, D. Roekaerts, and E. Tirapegui in these proceedings.

INTEGRATION IN HILBERT SPACE AND QUANTUM THEORY

Alexander Bach

Institut für Theoretische Physik I
Universität Münster
D-4400 Münster, Germany

1. FUNCTIONAL INTEGRATION AND QUANTUM THEORY

The most familiar connection between quantum mechanics and functional integration is provided by Feynman's path integral formalism. Path integrals are special linear functionals defined on an appropriate space of paths. They are close to the concept of an ordinary integral but cannot be represented as an integral w.r. to some measure (cf. 1). On the other hand - in classical physics - we are acquainted with the theory of integration in function spaces by means of integrals which are defined by some measure. In non-equilibrium statistical mechanics, e.g., the Wiener integral is widely used (cf. 2).

Integration in infinite-dimensional spaces is discerned from the finite-dimensional case by the fact that there exists no translation invariant measure which can be used in analogy to the Lebesgue measure. Our concern is to demonstrate that integration theory applied to Hilbert space if regarded as a measurable space is useful in quantum theory from a structural point of view as well as from the conceptual foundations. Especially we show how the expectation value of quantum theory can be represented as an integral on Hilbert space.

The fundamental observation is constituted by the fact that the statistical operators of quantum theory and the covariance operators of probability measures on Hilbert space are structurally identical up to an isometry [3]. Due to this property it is possible to set up a measure on Hilbert space (which is determined by the statistical operator) and a measurable functional (which is determined by the ob-

servable) such that the combination permits a representation of quantum theory by means of integration in Hilbert space. We discuss this representation which constitutes a formal hidden variables theory with respect to the structural analogy between classical statistical mechanics and quantum mechanics.

2. PROBABILITY MEASURES ON A REAL SEPARABLE HILBERT SPACE (cf.[4,5]).

Let $(H_o, \langle\cdot|\cdot\rangle_o)$ be a real separable Hilbert space. The norm $|\overset{o}{\cdot}|_o = (\langle\overset{o}{\cdot}|\cdot\rangle_o)^{1/2}$ induces a metric by which H_o becomes a topological vector space. The σ-field generated by the open subsets of H_o is the Borel field $\mathcal{B}(H_o)$ of H_o. Together with $\mathcal{B}(H_o)$ the Hilbert space H_o is a measurable space $(H_o, \mathcal{B}(H_o))$ and in the following we consider probability measures μ on H_o.

In analogy to probability measures on finite dimensional spaces we define the mean vector $m_\mu \in H_o$ by

$$\langle x|m_\mu\rangle_o = \int_{H_o} d\mu(y)\ \langle x|y\rangle_o \quad , \quad x,y \in H_o \tag{1}$$

and the covariance operator C_μ by

$$\langle x|C_\mu\, y\rangle_o = \int_{H_o} d\mu(z)\ \langle x|z\rangle_o\ \langle z|y\rangle_o \tag{2}$$

where $x,y,z \in H_o$. The operator

$$K_\mu = C_\mu - |m_\mu\rangle\langle m_\mu| \tag{3}$$

is the correlation operator of the measure μ. From the defining properties it is obvious that C_μ - if it exists - is symmetric and positive definite

$$C_\mu = C_\mu^+ \quad , \quad C_\mu \geq 0 \tag{4}$$

and that the same holds for K_μ.

In order to classify the operators under consideration we define the following sets of operators on H_o:

$\mathcal{L}(H_o)$: Banach space of linear, bounded operators
$\mathcal{L}_1(H_o)$: Banach space of trace class operators
$\mathcal{R}(H_o)$: self-adjoint elements of $\mathcal{L}(H_o)$.

An operator $A \in \mathcal{L}(H_o)$ is called nuclear or a S-operator if (i) $A \in \mathcal{L}_1(H_o)$, (ii) $A = A^+$, (iii) $A \geq 0$.

The set of nuclear operators on H_o is denoted by $S(H_o)$. Especially we are concerned with the convex set

$$S_c(H_o) = \{ A \in S(H_o) \; ; \; \mathrm{tr}\, A = c \in \mathbb{R} \} . \tag{5}$$

By means of the monotone convergence theorem it can be shown that $C_\mu \in S(H_o)$ if

$$\int_{H_o} d\mu(x) \; |x|_o^2 < \infty . \tag{6}$$

Furthermore in this case

$$\mathrm{tr}(C_\mu) = \int_{H_o} d\mu(x) \; |x|_o^2 . \tag{7}$$

The moment functions (1),(2) can also be defined in terms of the characteristic functional Φ_μ of the probability measure μ which is given by

$$\Phi_\mu(x) = \int_{H_o} d\mu(y) \; \exp(i\langle x|y\rangle_o) . \tag{8}$$

As in the finite-dimensional version the measure is uniquely determined by the characteristic functional if it exists.

It is well known that a measure is not uniquely determined by the mean vector and the covariance operator (the correlation operator respectively). The most important exceptions are Gaussian measures. A Gaussian γ with mean vector m and correlation operator K, which we denote by $\gamma(m,K)$, is determined by the characteristic functional

$$\Phi_\gamma(x) = \exp \left(i\langle x|m\rangle_o - \frac{1}{2} \langle x|K|x\rangle_o \right) . \tag{9}$$

If γ is Gaussian then necessarily $C_\gamma \in S(H_o)$.
As $\mathbb{1}_{H_o} \notin S(H_o)$ if $\dim_{\mathbb{R}}(H_o)=\infty$ there is no rotation invariant Gaussian on $(H_o, \mathcal{B}(H_o))$ in the infinite-dimensional case.

As an example for a measure on H_o consider the Dirac measure δ_y which is defined by, $y \in H_o$

$$\delta_y(B) = \begin{cases} 1 & \text{if} \quad y \in B \\ 0 & \text{if} \quad y \notin B \end{cases} , \quad B \in \mathcal{B}(H_o) . \tag{10}$$

The mean vector of δ_y is just given by y and for the covariance operator we obtain

$$C_{\delta_y} = |y\rangle\langle y| . \tag{11}$$

3. THE CANONICAL ISOMETRY BETWEEN HILBERT SPACES.

In quantum theory we are used to deal with complex Hilbert spaces. To get a connection between the real Hilbert space which is used in measure theory and the complex one we define an isometry between these spaces over different fields.

Let $(H,\langle\cdot|\cdot\rangle)$ be a complex separable Hilbert space and $(H_o,\langle\cdot|\cdot\rangle_o)$ a real separable one such that $\dim_{\mathbb{C}}(H) = \frac{1}{2}\dim_{\mathbb{R}}(H_o)$. Let $\{\phi_n\}_{n=1}^{\infty}$ be a complete orthonormal system of H and assume that $\{e_n\}_{n=1}^{\infty}$ is a complete orthonormal system of H_o. For $|\psi\rangle \in H$, $z_n \in \mathbb{C}$, $a_n, b_n \in \mathbb{R}$

$$|\psi\rangle = \sum_n z_n |\phi_n\rangle = \sum_n (a_n + ib_n)|\phi_n\rangle \tag{12}$$

the mapping $U: H \to H_o$

$$U|\psi\rangle = \sum_n (a_n |e_{2n-1}\rangle + b_n |e_{2n}\rangle) \tag{13}$$

defines an isometry between H and H_o as

$$\langle U\psi|U\psi\rangle_o = \langle\psi|\psi\rangle \quad \text{for all } |\psi\rangle \in H \quad . \tag{14}$$

Note that U is R-linear but not linear. U is one-to-one such that the mapping U^{-1} exists and defines an isometry as well.

Operators $A \in \mathcal{L}(H)$ can be represented by their isometrically equivalent ones on H_o by means of the mapping $\mathfrak{U}$ which is defined by $\mathfrak{U}: \mathcal{L}(H) \to \mathcal{L}(H_o)$

$$\mathfrak{U} A = U A U^{-1} =: A_o \quad . \tag{15}$$

$\mathfrak{U}$ is an $\mathbb{R}$-linear mapping which defines an isometry between $\mathcal{L}(H)$ and $\mathcal{L}(H_o)$ w.r. to the uniform norm.

By means of this isometry each element of $\mathfrak{A}(H)$ or S(H) is represented by an isometrically equivalent one which is an element of $\mathfrak{A}(H_o)$ or $S(H_o)$ respectively. A matrix element $A_{nm} = \langle\phi_n|A\phi_m\rangle$ of an element $A \in \mathcal{L}(H)$ transforms as

$$A_{nm} \overset{\mathfrak{U}}{\to} \begin{pmatrix} \mathrm{Re}(A_{nm}) & -\mathrm{Im}(A_{nm}) \\ \mathrm{Im}(A_{nm}) & \mathrm{Re}(A_{nm}) \end{pmatrix} \tag{16}$$

This demonstrates that the operators belonging to $S_1(H)$ are represented by elements of $S_2(H_o)$. More explicitly :

$$\mathrm{tr}_H(A) = \frac{1}{2}\,\mathrm{tr}_{H_o}(A_o) \quad . \tag{17}$$

Finally we remark that for $A \in \mathfrak{A}(H)$ the isometry U acts like a unitary operator on the diagonal elements

$$\langle x|UAU^{-1}|x\rangle_o = \langle U^{-1}x|A|U^{-1}x\rangle \quad , \quad x \in H_o \tag{18}$$

4. QUANTUM THEORY AND INTEGRATION IN HILBERT SPACE

The quantum mechanical expectation value $E_W(A)$ of an observable $A \in \mathfrak{A}(H)$, in the state given by the statistical operator $W \in S_1(H)$, reads

$$E_W(A) = \frac{1}{2}\, tr_{H_o}(W_o\, A_o) \quad . \tag{19}$$

Using the isometries defined in the last section this trace can equally well be represented on the real Hilbert space H_o as

$$tr_H(WA) = tr_{H_o}(W_o\, A_o) \quad . \tag{20}$$

The operator $W_o \in S_2(H_o)$ which is isometrically equivalent to the statistical operator W is nuclear and can be considered therefore as the covariance operator of some probability measure on H_o.

We use this fact to define a probability measure μ_{W_o} on H_o which is characterized by the fact that its covariance operator is just given by W_o. Note that by this procedure μ_{W_o} is by no means uniquely determined. This definition allows to demonstrate the following identity

$$tr_{H_o}(W_o\, A_o) = \int_{H_o} d\mu_{W_o}(x)\; \langle x|A_o|x\rangle_o \quad . \tag{21}$$

For the proof of (21) we assume that (19) exists and apply Lebesgue's dominated convergence theorem as well as the definition of the covariance operator (2)

$$\begin{aligned}
&\int_{H_o} d\mu_{W_o}(x)\; \langle x|A_o|x\rangle_o \\
&= \sum_{n,m} \int_{H_o} d\mu_{W_o}(x)\; \langle x|e_n\rangle_o \langle e_n|A_o|e_m\rangle_o \langle e_m|x\rangle_o \\
&= \sum_{n,m} \langle e_n|A_o|e_m\rangle_o \int_{H_o} d\mu_{W_o}(x)\; \langle e_m|x\rangle_o \langle x|e_n\rangle_o \\
&= \sum_{n,m} \langle e_n|A_o|e_m\rangle_o \langle e_m|W_o|e_n\rangle_o = tr_{H_o}(A_o\, W_o)
\end{aligned} \tag{22}$$

For convenience we express the integral in (21) as an integral on

H. This is obtained by means of the image measure of μ_{W_0} w.r. to the continuous - hence measurable - mapping U^{-1}. In terms of this measure, which we denote by μ_W,

$$\mu_W(B) = \mu_{W_0}(U(B)) \quad , \quad B \in \mathcal{B}(H) \tag{23}$$

the quantum mechanical expectation value reads

$$tr_H(WA) = \int_H d\mu_W(\phi) \, \frac{1}{2} \langle U\phi | UAU^{-1} | U\phi \rangle_o \quad . \tag{24}$$

Using equ. (18) we obtain

$$tr(WA) = \int_H d\mu_W(\phi) \, \frac{1}{2} \langle \phi | A | \phi \rangle \quad . \tag{25}$$

This formula contains the central result. It states that the expectation value of quantum theory can be represented as an integral on that the Hilbert space H which is associated with the system as

$$E_W(A) = \int_H d\mu_W(\phi) \quad f_A(\phi) \tag{26}$$

where the expectation functional f_A is given by

$$f_A(\phi) = \frac{1}{2} \langle \phi | A | \phi \rangle \quad . \tag{27}$$

Let us briefly discuss a plausibility argument for the existence of such a representation. The expectation functional $f_A(\phi)$ can be regarded as the expectation value of the operator A in the unnormalized state $\frac{1}{2}|\phi\rangle\langle\phi|$ such that it already contains all the essential quantum mechanical properties. In contrast to the formula tr(WA) where the matrix elements w.r. to a complete orthonormal system are required the present representation exists of an appropriate "continuous summation" of all diagonal elements of A. That this is sufficient is explained by the fact that for $A \in \mathfrak{A}(H)$ or $A_0 \in \mathfrak{A}(H_0)$ every matrix element can be constructed from the diagonal ones by means of the polarization identity. Denoting the unit vector in the direction of $|\phi\rangle$ by $|e_\phi\rangle$, the neccessary contributions to the expectation value of an observable A consist of the contributions of the expectation values of all pure states, $tr(|e_\phi\rangle\langle e_\phi|A)$, which are appropriately summed up if we define a measure which incorporates the factor 1/2 and the effect of the normalization.

5. CONNECTION WITH HIDDEN VARIABLES THEORIES.

The relations (the second one is multivalued)

$$A \to f_A \quad \text{and} \quad W \to \mu_W$$

in combination with formula (26) just fulfil the requirements of a hidden variables theory as it is defined, e.g., in ref.[6] p. 262. We stress that this only referes to the structural aspects of such a theory as it is evident that the hidden variables which are the wave-functions (vectors of H) have no immediate empirical meaning. Nontheless it is interesting to analyze the conditions which permit such a representation of quantum theory as most of the impossibility proofs concerning hidden variables do not depend on the physical nature of the assumed hidden variables.

It has been shown by v.Neumann[7] that quantum theory does not admit dispersion-free states. Here a state W is called dispersion-free if

$$E_W(A^2) - (E_W(A))^2 = 0 \tag{28}$$

for all $A \in \mathfrak{A}(H)$. From this viewpoint it seems that a representation of the expectation value in terms of classical probability theory on $(H, \mathfrak{B}(H))$ seems impossible as (i) pure states can be represented by Dirac measures on H and (ii) Dirac measures are dispersion-free on every measure space. On the other hand equ. (25) is a strict mathematical identity which provides us with a representation of the expectation value which is alternative to the one of Gleason[8].

This situation arises from the different use of the term "dispersion free". The integral representation of (28) reads

$$\int_H d\mu_W(\phi)\, f_{(A^2)}(\phi) - \{ \int_H d\mu_W(\phi)\, f_A(\phi) \}^2 = 0 \tag{29}$$

which is different from the usual definition of a dispersion-free random variable f_A on H for which

$$\int_H d\mu_W(\phi) \{ f_A(\phi) \}^2 - \{ \int_H d\mu_W(\phi)\, f_A(\phi) \}^2 = 0 \tag{30}$$

holds. As in general $f_{(A^2)} \neq f_A^2$ it is obvious that w.r. to the quantum mechanical meaning of dispersion-free f_A cannot be regarded as an ordinary random variable on H. These formulae demonstrate explicitely that the non-existence of quantum mechanical dispersion-free states depends on the expectation functional f_A and not on the measure μ_W.

This is connected with the fact that w.r. to operator valued functions k(A) the mapping f_A does not transform as an ordinary random value on H as

$$f_{k(A)} = k(f_A) \tag{31}$$

cannot be effected by a substitution of the variable $\phi \in H$. The failure of (31) for an arbitrary formulation of quantum mechanics in terms of classical probability theory has already been remarked by Kochen and Specker[9]. Whereas they used this as an argument against hidden variables theories we conclude that the failure of (31) demonstrates that the concepts of classical probability theory are not appropriate for quantum theory although a classical probabilistic representation of the expectation value is possible.

Due to the non-existence of dispersion-free states there is no deterministic subdynamics. Moreover, the formal hidden variables representation is non-local as we have

$$f_{AB} \neq f_A \, f_B \quad . \tag{32}$$

This agrees with the statement of Bell's theorem[10]. We note, however, that the non-locality refers to the Hilbert space and not to the empirical space. It may imply an action-at-a distance in H. From this viewpoint it seems worth-while to consider anew the EPR paradox and the measurement problem of quantum mechanics (cf.[6]).

6. ON THE DIFFERENCE BETWEEN CLASSICAL MECHANICS AND QUANTUM MECHANICS

Although the representation we have set up does not define a hidden variables theory with empirical implications, it is valuable in its own from a formal viewpoint as it provides us with a formulation of quantum theory which structurally is quite analogous to the representation of classical statistical mechanics: the state space of the system is the Hilbert space, states and observables are represented by measures and measurable functions respectively. Therefore this representation is useful to elucidate the difference between classical mechanics and quantum mechanics.

The fundamental property from which all the substantial difference emerges is established by the fact that for a given statistical operator W the measure μ_W (or μ_{W_o}) is not uniquely defined: only the covariance operator is prescribed by our procedure. Thus we conclude that the quantity which should be considered as hidden in quantum theory is the measure in state space which describes the state of the system.

The far reaching arbitrariness of the measures is related to the structure of the expectation functional f_A. Preparation and measurement of observables are expressed by this special quadratic form which, by its structure, only allows to determine the covariance operator of the measure. This implies that most of the

information which could be deduced from a measure in H is empirically meaningless.

As an example for this statement let us consider the quantity

$$\mu_W(B) = \int_H d\mu_W(\phi)\ \chi_B(\phi) \quad , \quad B \in \mathcal{B}(H) \tag{32}$$

where χ_B is the characteristic function of the set B. The analogous formula in classical statistical mechanics determines uniquely the probability to localize the system in a certain region of phase space. As the measure is not uniquely determined (32) cannot define any empirical probability. This is due to the fact that the characteristic function cannot be expressed as a quadratic form.

The indeterminateness of the measures has natural consequences w.r. to quantum dynamics. By means of a time-dependent statistical operator $W(t)$, $t \in [o,T]$, a family of measures $\mu_{W(t)}$ can be set up which describes a stochastic process with state space $H^{[o,T]}$. As the measure can be chosen arbitrarily (up to the covariance operator) at each instant of time, this process contains much more information than that which empirically is relevant. From this we conclude that <u>it is impossible to associate a well defined stochastic process with quantum dynamics</u>.

7. CONNECTIONS, EXTENSIONS, RESTRICTIONS

The representation of quantum theory we have proposed here is similar to the <u>'causal quantum theory' of Wiener and Siegel</u> (cf.11) insofar as they define a representation of the expectation value in terms of integration in Hilbert space too. Their approach is discerned from the present one by a complete different construction of the measure and the expectation functional and is distinguished by the property that the expectation functional implicitly depends on the state of the system. Due to this defect this theory defines no hidden variables theory and is therefore inappropriate for a structural comparison of classical and quantum mechanics.

The formulation given here resembles that one which can be set up by means of a continuous representation by generalized coherent states (cf. 12) as the expectation value is defined in terms of diagonal elements which are continuously summed up. This analogy is not just by chance but, e.g., revealed by the fact that the representation of the relevant operators of a spin-1/2-particle in terms of coherent spin states[13] is - up to a factor - equivalent to the expectation functionals of these operators in the present representation on the Hilbert space $\mathbb{R}^4$.

Considering the general set up of continuous representations as proposed in[14], <u>the formulation by means of integration in</u>

Hilbert space can be regarded as an infinite-dimensional continuous representation which is distinguished by the fact that it allows for a complete disentangling of the operator product WA. The latter fact constitutes a neccessary requirement of a (formal) hidden variables theory which is not met by the usual coherent state representation.

With respect to quantum dynamics the Feynman path-integral representation and the formulation given here have the property in common that both of them do not define a stochastic process for a quantum mechanical evolution. Whereas the latter approach is not apt to determine the process uniquely the former one cannot define a process at all.

We remark that besides the obvious applications of the present formalism to quantum statistical mechanics a representation of the partition function Z can be obtained. The canonical distribution, $\rho = \exp(-\beta \mathcal{H})$, has the properties which permit the definition of a measure μ_0 (no probability measure) from which the formula

$$Z = \mathrm{tr}(\rho) = \frac{1}{2} \int_H d\mu_\rho(\phi) \tag{33}$$

can be derived.

Our representation is restricted to observables which are represented by operators $A \in \mathfrak{A}(H)$, hence to bounded operators. For unbounded self-adjoint operators A with dense domain D(A) in H the expectation functional f_A diverges on the (uncountable) complement of D(A). In this situation the concept of rigged Hilbert spaces is useful in quantum theory. We expect that it may be appropriate for the integral representation, especially as there exists a theory of integration[15] which specializes the general set up of abstract Wiener spaces in this case (cf.16).

8. THE INTERPRETATION OF QUANTUM THEORY (cf.6)

Already the reference to hidden variables constitutes a mandatory reason to reflect the implications of the new representation with respect to the interpretation of quantum theory. The formalism of quantum theory is open to interpretation as it contains a theoretical term (i.e. a term without empirical counterpart), namely the wave-function. It is the meaning of this quantity which discernes the Copenhagen interpretation and the statistical interpretation (cf.6) insofar as the latter declares that the wave-function refers to an individual system whereas the former one states that the wave-function describes a statistical situation which empirically is realized by an ensemble.

As we have shown there exists a representation of quantum

theory which structurally is analogous to the formulation of classical statistical mechanics. This, in our opinion, supports the statistical interpretation and Einstein's point of view (cf. 17). On the other hand, the incompleteness of the conventional representation of quantum theory which is revealed by the present formalism is a formal property. The fact that the hidden variables have no empirical meaning shows that these properties imply no empirical incompleteness.

The impossibility to associate uniquely a probability measure with a quantum mechanical state reveals that the description of quantum phenomena involves two stages of indeterminacy: classical probability and an additional degree of indeterminateness which is connected with the non-uniqueness of the measures. This shows that - in contrast to classical statistical mechanics - probability in quantum theory is an inherent property (cf.18). Formally, probability in quantum theory as expressed by the present set up by means of classical probability theory, is a theoretical term. On the other hand, the indeterminism itself is empirical.

Considering the fact that the hidden variables have no empirical meaning, the given formulation may indicate that the representation of the quantum mechanical system of propositions by means of a Hilbert space utilizes an unneccessary complicated structure which should be replaced by some other with an empirical state space. Nontheless, the representation of quantum theory by means of integration in Hilbert space restores the structural unity of classical and quantum mechanics and provides fundamental insight into the difference between these theories.

REFERENCES

1. "Feynman Path Integrals", S. Albeverio, Ph. Combe, R. Hoegh-Krohn et al. eds., Springer, Berlin (1979).
2. D. Dürr and A. Bach, The Onsager-Machlup Function as the Most Probable Path of a Diffusion Process, Comm. math. Phys. 60:153 (1978).
3. A. Bach, Quantum Mechanics and Integration in Hilbert Space, Phys. Lett. 73A:287 (1979).
4. A. V. Skorohod, "Integration in Hilbert Space", Springer, Berlin (1974).
5. H.-H. Kuo, "Gaussian Measures in Banach Spaces", Springer, Berlin (1975).
6. M. Jammer, "The Philosophy of Quantum Mechanics", Wiley, New York (1974)
7. J. v. Neumann, "Die mathematischen Grundlagen der Quantenmechanik", Springer, Berlin (1968).
8. A. M. Gleason, Measures on the Closed Subspaces of a Hilbert Space, J. Math. and Mech. 6:885 (1957).

9. S. Kochen and E. P. Specker, The Problem of Hidden Variables in Quantum Mechanics, J. Math. and Mech. 17:59 (1967).
10. J. S. Bell, On the Einstein Podolsky Rosen Paradox, Physics 1:195 (1964).
11. J. Schwartz, The Wiener-Siegel Causal Theory of Quantum Mechanics, in: "Integration of Functionals", K. O. Friedrichs and H. N. Shapiro, eds., Courant Institute, New York (1957).
12. J. R. Klauder and E. C. G. Sudarshan, "Fundamentals of Quantum Optics", Benjamin, New York (1968).
13. Y. Takahashi and F. Shibata, Spin Coherent State Representation in Non-Equilibrium Statistical Mechanics, J. Phys. Soc. Japan 38:656 (1975).
14. J. M. Radcliffe, Some Properties of Coherent Spin States, J. Phys. A4:313 (1971).
15. I. M. Gelfand und N. J. Wilenkin, "Verallgemeinerte Funktionen (Distributionen)", Band 4, VEB Deutscher Verlag der Wissenschaften, Berlin (1964).
16. D. Kölzow, A Survey of Abstract Wiener Spaces, in: "Proceedings of the Summer Research Institute on Statistical Interference for Stochastic Processes", Vol. 1, Madan Lal Puri, ed., Academic Press, Bloomington (1975).
17. A. Einstein, Physik und Realität, in: A. Einstein, "Aus meinen späteren Jahren", Deutsche Verlags-Anstalt, Stuttgart (1952).
18. K. Popper, Quantum Mechanics without Observer, in: "Quantum Theory and Reality", M. Bunge, ed., Springer, Berlin (1967).

PATH INTEGRALS FOR AFFINE VARIABLES

John R. Klauder

Bell Laboratories
Murray Hill, NJ 07974 USA

ABSTRACT

The phase-space path-integral quantization of systems subject to $p > 0$ is studied. The nonexistence of a q representation is circumvented by adopting affine variables rather than canonical ones, and the phase-space path integral attains a meaningful interpretation in terms of affine coherent states. A Lagrangian path-integral quantization finds its proper interpretation in terms of a two-dimensional system rather than an obvious one-dimensional one. Throughout, the formalism is applied to an elementary model of quantum gravity; nonetheless, the results for this model may have implications for the full theory of quantum gravity.

I. INTRODUCTION

In a formal sense the canonical form of the path integral symbolically represented as

$$\mathcal{N}\int \exp\{i \int_{t'}^{t''} [p\dot{q}-H(p,q)]dt\}\mathcal{D}p\mathcal{D}q \tag{1}$$

provides for quantization under a widely diverse set of circumstances. We wish to study such expressions and their proper interpretation for systems constrained in such a way that

$$p(t) > 0 \tag{2}$$

for all time t while q is unconstrained. For such systems

$$H(p,q) = pq^2 \tag{3a}$$

$$= pq^2+K/p, \quad K > 0 , \tag{3b}$$

$$= p^2+p^3+q^2 , \tag{3c}$$

etc. all provide examples of nonnegative classical Hamiltonians, the first two of which will be of special interest to us. Our motivation to study such systems stems from the fact that the choices (3a) and (3b) correspond to one-dimensional analogues of the gravitational field and the restriction $p > 0$ is the remnant of the signature requirements on the metric $g_{\mu\nu}$. A discussion of this model system and its relation to gravity has been given elsewhere[1] and will not be repeated here. In this paper we concentrate on interpreting the meaning of path-integral quantization for systems subject to the constraint $p(t) > 0$ independently, for the most part, of their potential physical application.

It is a simple argument to determine that the interpretation of (1) is not at all straightforward under the requirement (2). For a pair of Heisenberg operators P,Q for which the spectrum of $P > 0$ and which satisfy $[Q,P] = i$, it follows that Q cannot be an observable and thus cannot be diagonalized. In other words there is no q representation and no Q eigenstates, $|q\rangle$, with which to interpret (1) as the propagator

$$\langle q'',t''|q',t'\rangle \equiv \langle q''|e^{-i(t''-t')\mathcal{H}}|q'\rangle \tag{4}$$

for some Hamiltonian operator $\mathcal{H}$. To see this let us realize P by multiplication by k, $0 < k < \infty$, on the space of functions $L^2(0,\infty)$. Then, since Q is realized as $i\partial/\partial k$,

$$e^{-iaQ}\psi(k) = e^{a\partial/\partial k}\psi(k) = \psi(k+a) , \tag{5}$$

which is not a unitary transformation on $L^2(0,\infty)$ for $a > 0$ as it must be if Q is to be an observable (self adjoint). Thus to interpret (1) as the propagator between sharp q states is not merely technically difficult, it is a manifest impossibility.

In order to resolve this problem we must first introduce affine variables and affine coherent states and study their properties, which we do in Sec. II. The use of this formalism to construct the phase-space path integral is the subject of Sec. III, with special emphasis being given to a highly simplified model of gravity[1] (a toy model to be sure!). The Lagrangian form of the path integral is treated in Sec. IV, particularly for the gravitational model which is shown to be closely connected with

the traditional path integral of a two-dimensional system. Associated stochastic processes are the subject of Sec. V where it is emphasized that the unexpected two- (rather than one-) dimensional nature of the traditional system is indeed appropriate. Section VI is devoted to a brief conclusion.

II. AFFINE VARIABLES AND THEIR PROPERTIES

Instead of the pair of canonical variables Q and P consider the pair of affine variables B and P which satisfy the affine commutation relation

$$[B,P] = iP \ . \tag{6}$$

There are two inequivalent, irreducible representations of this relation with self-adjoint B and P, one for which $P > 0$ and one for which $P < 0$.[2] We focus on the representation for which $P > 0$ and note that we can realize B as

$$B = \tfrac{1}{2}(QP+PQ) \ . \tag{7}$$

That such an operator can be self adjoint (although Q is not) follows from the fact that

$$\begin{aligned} e^{-i\alpha B}\psi(k) &= e^{\frac{1}{2}\alpha(k\partial/\partial k+\partial/\partial k\ k)}\psi(k) \\ &= e^{\frac{1}{2}\alpha}\psi(e^{\alpha}k) \ , \end{aligned} \tag{8}$$

which for all real α is a unitary transformation on $L^2(0,\infty)$ acting simply as a dilation or contraction on the half line. Consequently we are led to adopt the affine variables B and P (rather than the canonical variables Q and P) as basic kinematical variables.

As unitary operators of the affine group we choose

$$U[p,q] \equiv e^{-iqP}e^{i\ell np\ B} \tag{9}$$

where $-\infty < q < \infty$ and $p > 0$. The identity element of the group is $U[1,0] = I$, while the group composition law follows from

$$U[p,q]U[p',q'] = U[pp',q+p^{-1}q'] \ . \tag{10}$$

In particular

$$U^\dagger[p,q] = U^{-1}[p,q] = U[p^{-1},-pq] \ , \tag{11}$$

and it follows that

$$U^\dagger[p,q](\alpha P+\beta Q+\gamma B)U[p,q] = \alpha pP+\beta(p^{-1}Q+q)+\gamma(B+pqP) \ . \tag{12}$$

Affine Coherent States

We next introduce what we may call the affine coherent states. Let $|0\rangle$ be a normalized vector and define

$$|p,q\rangle \equiv U[p,q]\,|0\rangle \tag{13}$$

for all $p > 0$ and $-\infty < q < \infty$. These vectors form an overcomplete family of states and admit a resolution of unity in the form[3]

$$\int_0^\infty \int_{-\infty}^\infty |p,q\rangle \frac{dpdq}{M} \langle p,q| = 1 \tag{14}$$

provided $M < \infty$, where

$$M \equiv 2\pi\langle 0|P^{-1}|0\rangle \ . \tag{15}$$

We shall assume hereafter that $M < \infty$. In addition we shall frequently assume that $|0\rangle$ satisfies the physical requirements

$$\langle 0|P|0\rangle = 1 = \langle 0|0\rangle \tag{16a}$$

$$\langle 0|Q|0\rangle = 0 = \langle 0|B|0\rangle \tag{16b}$$

which will facilitate the interpretation of the affine coherent states. With these conditions it follows in particular that

$$\langle p,q|(\alpha P+\beta Q+\gamma B)|p,q\rangle = \alpha p+\beta q+\gamma(pq) \ . \tag{17}$$

The kind of requirements imposed on $|0\rangle$ above are quite modest, and further conditions may be adopted if desired. For example, let us examine the analogue of the uncertainty relation in the affine variables. It follows directly that

$$\begin{aligned} \langle P\rangle^2 &= |\langle [B,P-\langle P\rangle]\rangle|^2 \\ &\leq 4|\langle B(P-\langle P\rangle)\rangle|^2 \\ &\leq 4\langle B^2\rangle\langle (P-\langle P\rangle)^2\rangle \ . \end{aligned} \tag{18}$$

Equality between the first and last expressions here requires the two conditions

$$\langle B(P-\langle P\rangle)\rangle = -\langle (P-\langle P\rangle)B\rangle \ , \tag{19a}$$

$$B|\phi\rangle = -i\beta(P-\langle P\rangle)|\phi\rangle \tag{19b}$$

for some β. Given the second condition the first is satisfied provided β is real. In the k-space representation the solution to

(19b) requires $\beta > 0$ and is given by

$$\phi(k) = (2\beta)^{\beta\langle P\rangle}\Gamma^{-\frac{1}{2}}(2\beta\langle P\rangle)k^{\beta\langle P\rangle-\frac{1}{2}}e^{-\beta k} \quad . \tag{20}$$

For each $\langle P\rangle > 0$ and $\beta > 0$ these vectors are minimum uncertainty states as follows from the fact that

$$\langle(P-\langle P\rangle)^2\rangle = (2\beta)^{-1}\langle P\rangle \tag{21}$$

and thus [along with (19b)] satisfy

$$\langle P\rangle^2 = 4\langle B^2\rangle\langle(P-\langle P\rangle)^2\rangle \quad . \tag{22}$$

Note in addition that in each of these states $\langle Q\rangle = \langle B\rangle = 0$ (since ϕ is real), and moreover in order that $M = 2\pi\langle P^{-1}\rangle < \infty$ it is essential that $\langle P\rangle > (2\beta)^{-1}$ in which case $M = 2\pi[\langle P\rangle-(2\beta)^{-1}]^{-1}$. In what follows next we shall choose $\langle P\rangle = 1$.

The Affine Continuous Representation

Although the affine coherent states admit a resolution of unity for a general fiducial vector $|0\rangle$ it is useful to examine further the affine coherent states based on a minimum uncertainty state as a particular example and the continuous representation of Hilbert space they engender.[3] We now denote by $|0\rangle$ the minimum uncertainty state with $\langle P\rangle = 1$ and general $\beta > \frac{1}{2}$.

Let us first examine the vector representatives

$$\psi(p,q) = \langle p,q|\psi\rangle$$
$$= p^{-\frac{1}{2}} \int_0^\infty \phi_0^*(p^{-1}k)e^{ikq}\psi(k)dk \tag{23}$$

defined for each $\psi\epsilon L^2(0,\infty)$, and which in the case of the minimum uncertainty state becomes

$$\psi(p,q) = (2\beta)^{\beta}\Gamma^{-\frac{1}{2}}(2\beta)p^{-\beta} \int_0^\infty k^{\beta-\frac{1}{2}}e^{-k(\beta p^{-1}-iq)}\psi(k)dk \quad . \tag{24}$$

We note that apart from a common factor $p^{-\beta}$ every representative function $\psi(p,q)$ is actually a function of the complex variable $\zeta^* \equiv \beta p^{-1}-iq$ and is <u>analytic</u> <u>in</u> <u>the</u> <u>half</u> <u>plane</u> $\mathrm{Re}\zeta^* > 0$.

The Hilbert space of vector representatives admits a reproducing a kernel[4] which is given by

$$\begin{aligned}\langle p,q|p',q'\rangle &= (2\beta)^{2\beta}\Gamma^{-1}(2\beta)(pp')^{-\beta}\int_0^\infty k^{2\beta-1}e^{-k[\beta(p^{-1}+p'^{-1})+i(q'-q)]}dk \\ &= (2\beta)^{2\beta}(pp')^{-\beta}[\beta(p^{-1}+p'^{-1})+i(q'-q)]^{-2\beta} \\ &= \left[\tfrac{1}{2}\left(\sqrt{\frac{p}{p'}}+\sqrt{\frac{p'}{p}}\right)+\frac{i}{2}\beta^{-1}\sqrt{pp'}(q'-q)\right]^{-2\beta} .\end{aligned} \tag{25}$$

Observe that the parameter β enters in a nontrivial fashion other than solely as a dilation of a single state.

From the explicit expression given above it is straightforward to verify the general reproducing kernel composition law

$$\begin{aligned}&\langle p,q|p'',q''\rangle \\ &= \int_0^\infty\int_{-\infty}^\infty \langle p,q|p',q'\rangle\langle p',q'|p'',q''\rangle(dp'dq'/M) .\end{aligned} \tag{26}$$

Every vector representative fulfills the relations

$$\langle p,q|\psi\rangle = \int_0^\infty\int_{-\infty}^\infty \langle p,q|p',q'\rangle\langle p',q'|\psi\rangle(dp'dq'/M) , \tag{27}$$

and

$$\langle\psi|\psi\rangle = \int_0^\infty\int_{-\infty}^\infty |\langle p,q|\psi\rangle|^2(dpdq/M) . \tag{28}$$

Moreover every vector representative is given as the L^2 limit

$$\langle p,q|\psi\rangle = \underset{N\to\infty}{\ell.i.m.} \sum_{n=1}^{N} c_n\langle p,q|p_n,q_n\rangle \tag{29}$$

for suitable real p_n,q_n and complex $c_n, n=1,\ldots,N$.

Operator Matrix Elements

Of course the properties of the reproducing kernel and vector representatives indicated above hold for any choice of the fiducial vector $|0\rangle$ with finite M and not only the minimum uncertainty states. On the other hand, there is one additional feature of the representation based on the minimum uncertainty states worth emphasizing. Consider the matrix elements of a general operator $\mathcal{B}$ given by $\langle p,q|\mathcal{B}|p',q'\rangle$. According to the remarks made above this expression has the form

$$\langle p,q|\mathcal{B}|p',q'\rangle = (pp')^{-\beta}F(\beta p^{-1}-iq,\beta p'^{-1}+iq')$$
$$\equiv (pp')^{-\beta}F(\zeta^*,\zeta') \quad (30)$$

where $F(\zeta^*,\zeta')$ is analytic in the region $\mathrm{Re}\zeta^* > 0$, $\mathrm{Re}\zeta' > 0$. The diagonal matrix elements in turn are given by

$$B(p,q) \equiv \langle p,q|\mathcal{B}|p,q\rangle$$
$$= p^{-2\beta}F(\zeta^*,\zeta) \ . \quad (31a)$$

A theorem about complex variables assures us that the information in F on the diagonal uniquely determines F everywhere in its analytic domain.[5] In particular, one has only to reexpress the diagonal matrix element in the form

$$B(p,q) = p^{-2\beta}F(\beta p^{-1}-iq,\beta p^{-1}+iq) \quad (31b)$$

which then determines the off-diagonal form (30) quite directly. Thus we see that for affine coherent states (at least those based on minimum uncertainty states) the diagonal matrix elements of an operator uniquely determine the off-diagonal matrix elements. This property is identical to that of the canonical coherent states (based on the canonical minimum uncertainty states, among others).[6] Unlike the canonical coherent states, however, the affine coherent states are not in general eigenstates of any particular operator.

III. PHASE-SPACE PATH INTEGRAL

The construction of the phase-space path integral for affine variables follows the technique first used in the case of conventional canonical variables and coherent states.[7] With H denoting the self-adjoint Hamiltonian we examine the affine coherent-state representation for the propagator

$$\langle p'',q'',t''|p',q',t'\rangle$$
$$\equiv \langle p'',q''|e^{-i(t''-t')H}|p',q'\rangle$$
$$= \int\cdots\int \prod_{k=0}^{N} \langle p_{k+1},q_{k+1}|e^{-i\varepsilon H}|p_k,q_k\rangle \prod_{k=1}^{N} d\mu(p_k,q_k) \ , \quad (32)$$

where in the last expression we have inserted N resolutions of unity, $\varepsilon \equiv (t''-t')/(N+1)$, $d\mu(p,q) \equiv dpdq/M$, $p_0,q_0 \equiv p',q'$ and $p_{N+1},q_{N+1} \equiv p'',q''$. This factorization is exact for any N and thus holds in the limit $N \to \infty$ or $\varepsilon \to 0$. For small ε one makes the approximation that

$$\begin{aligned}&\langle p_{k+1},q_{k+1}|e^{-i\varepsilon H}|p_k,q_k\rangle\\ &\quad\approx \langle p_{k+1},q_{k+1}|(1-i\varepsilon H)|p_k,q_k\rangle\\ &\quad= \langle p_{k+1},q_{k+1}|p_k,q_k\rangle[1-i\varepsilon H(p_{k+1},q_{k+1};p_k,q_k)]\\ &\quad\approx \langle p_{k+1},q_{k+1}|p_k,q_k\rangle\exp[-i\varepsilon H(p_{k+1},q_{k+1};p_k,q_k)]\end{aligned} \tag{33}$$

valid to first order in ε, where

$$H(p_{k+1},q_{k+1};p_k,q_k) \equiv \frac{\langle p_{k+1},q_{k+1}|H|p_k,q_k\rangle}{\langle p_{k+1},q_{k+1}|p_k,q_k\rangle}\ . \tag{34}$$

Thus we are led to the lattice-space expression for the propagator given by

$$\begin{aligned}&\langle p'',q'',t''|p',q',t'\rangle\\ &\quad= \lim_{\varepsilon\to 0}\int\cdots\int \prod_{k=0}^{N}\{\langle p_{k+1},q_{k+1}|p_k,q_k\rangle e^{-i\varepsilon H(p_{k+1},q_{k+1};p_k,q_k)}\}\\ &\quad\times \prod_{k=1}^{N} d\mu(p_k,q_k)\end{aligned} \tag{35}$$

provided the integrals involved exist.

<u>Formal Path Integral</u>

It is tempting to interchange the order of the integrations and the limit $\varepsilon \to 0$ in order to get a formal path-integral expression. Preparatory to so doing let us note that

$$\begin{aligned}&\langle p_{k+1},q_{k+1}|p_k,q_k\rangle\\ &\quad= 1-\langle p_{k+1},q_{k+1}|(|p_{k+1},q_{k+1}\rangle-|p_k,q_k\rangle)\\ &\quad\approx \exp[-\langle p_{k+1},q_{k+1}|(|p_{k+1},q_{k+1}\rangle-|p_k,q_k\rangle)]\ ,\end{aligned} \tag{36}$$

which leads to the suggestive intermediate relation

$$\begin{aligned}&\lim_{\varepsilon\to 0}\int\cdots\int \exp\{\sum_{k=0}^{N}[-\langle p_{k+1},q_{k+1}|(|p_{k+1},q_{k+1}\rangle-|p_k,q_k\rangle)\\ &\quad- i\varepsilon H(p_{k+1},q_{k+1};p_k,q_k)]\}\prod_{k=1}^{N} d\mu(p_k,q_k)\ .\end{aligned} \tag{37}$$

This relation motivates the formal path-integral expression

$$\langle p'',q'',t''|p',q',t'\rangle$$

$$= \mathcal{N}\int\exp\{i\int_{t'}^{t''}\left[i\langle p,q|\frac{d}{dt}|p,q\rangle-\langle p,q|\mathcal{H}|p,q\rangle\right]dt\}\mathcal{D}p\mathcal{D}q \qquad (38)$$

where $\mathcal{N}$ is a formal normalization factor arising from the M factors, $\mathcal{D}p = \Pi_t dp(t)$ and $\mathcal{D}q = \Pi_t dq(t)$. The integrand in (38) is written, as customary, in the form that holds for continuous and differentiable paths. Such a formal expression holds for any set of affine coherent states, i.e., for any fiducial vector $|0\rangle$ with $M < \infty$.

Let us examine the two terms in the exponent separately. It follows that

$$i\,\frac{d}{dt}\,|p,q\rangle = \dot{q}P|p,q\rangle-\dot{p}p^{-1}U[p,q]B|0\rangle \qquad (39)$$

and thus

$$i\langle p,q|\frac{d}{dt}|p,q\rangle = \dot{q}\langle p,q|P|p,q\rangle-\dot{p}p^{-1}\langle 0|B|0\rangle$$
$$= p\dot{q}\langle 0|P|0\rangle-\dot{p}p^{-1}\langle 0|B|0\rangle\ , \qquad (40)$$

which according to the physical requirements placed on $|0\rangle$ in Eq. (16) simply becomes

$$i\langle p,q|\frac{d}{dt}|p,q\rangle = p\dot{q}\ . \qquad (41)$$

The second term may be adopted as the classical Hamiltonian and reads

$$H(p,q) \equiv \langle p,q|\mathcal{H}(P,Q,B)|p,q\rangle$$
$$= \langle 0|\mathcal{H}(pP,p^{-1}Q+q,B+pqP)|0\rangle \qquad (42)$$

where we have allowed for the possibility that $\mathcal{H}$ is expressed in terms of P and Q, P and B, or all three variables. For example, assume that

$$\mathcal{H} = QPQ+\mathcal{V}(P)\ , \qquad (43)$$

then it follows from (7) and (16) that

$$H(p,q) = \langle 0|(p^{-1}Q+q)pP(p^{-1}Q+q)|0\rangle+\langle 0|\mathcal{V}(pP)|0\rangle$$
$$= pq^2+(\Lambda/p)+v(p) \qquad (44)$$

where $\Lambda \equiv \langle 0|QPQ|0\rangle$ is a positive constant and $v(p) \equiv \langle 0|\mathcal{V}(pP)|0\rangle$.

Elsewhere we have argued for the plausibility of accepting the diagonal coherent-state Hamiltonian matrix elements as a candidate for the classical Hamiltonian.[8] In addition we have discussed how the auxiliary factor Λ/p suggested by the quantum theory in the above example removes singularities that otherwise attend the classical solutions in this toy model for gravity.[1] At any rate, by combining the indicated relations we are led to the formal path-integral expression for the affine coherent-state representation propagator given by

$$\langle p'',q'',t''|p',q',t'\rangle = \mathcal{N}\int \exp\{i \int_{t'}^{t''} [p\dot{q}-H(p,q)]dt\}\mathcal{D}p\mathcal{D}q \qquad (45)$$

integrated over paths subject to $p(t') = p'$, $q(t') = q'$, $p(t'') = p''$ and $q(t'') = q''$.

Thus in the sense described we have achieved the goal we set out initially to attain. Namely, we may interpret the formal path-integral expression above in which $p > 0$ and $-\infty < q < \infty$ is respected throughout as an expression for the propagator in the affine coherent-state representation which is to be properly interpreted in the sense of Eq. (35). Note, in this regard, if one adopts a minimum uncertainty state to define the affine coherent states, then the classical Hamiltonian (diagonal matrix elements) determines the quantum Hamiltonian (by way of its off-diagonal matrix elements). Moreover the expression for the overlap of two such affine coherent states appears in Eq. (25).

IV. LAGRANGIAN PATH INTEGRAL

Up to this point we have concentrated on the first-order action and phase-space form of the path integral. In the case of canonical variables, connection with the Lagrangian form of the path integral is possible under certain circumstances [notably when the canonical Hamiltonian $H(p,q) = \frac{1}{2}p^2+V(q)$]. We take up now the question of the connection to the Lagrangian form for affine variables.

Implicit in the Lagrangian form as compared to the phase-space form is the integration over only one set of histories, either those of p or those of q. Such a prescription can only lead to matrix elements depending on one variable (p or q) initially and the same variable (p or q) finally, and thus the representation in question is the representation in which P or Q is diagonalized. Since Q cannot be diagonalized for affine variables the only possibility is a Lagrangian in terms of p and a path integral over p histories.

To see what kind of Lagrangian may emerge let us examine as an example the classical action

$$I = \int [p\dot{q} - pq^2 - V(p)]dt \ . \tag{46}$$

It follows in this case that $q = -\dot{p}/(2p)$ is a universal equation of motion. Substituting this relation into (46) we learn that

$$I = \int [\dot{p}^2/(4p) - V(p) - \ddot{p}/2]dt \ . \tag{47}$$

The last term is a total derivative and does not affect the equations of motion; we thus adopt as the Lagrangian form of the action the expression

$$I = \int [\dot{p}^2/(4p) - V(p)]dt \ . \tag{48}$$

This is actually the appropriate form of the action for our toy model of gravity. The primary goal of this section is to analyze the path integral for such a classical action in which $p > 0$ is respected throughout. In fact, we shall concentrate our attention on this example because alternative choices for the Hamiltonian may be analyzed in analogous fashion.

Based on the foregoing discussion we are led to study the formal expression

$$\langle p'',t''|p',t'\rangle \equiv \langle p''|e^{-i(t''-t')\mathcal{H}}|p'\rangle$$

$$= \mathcal{N}\int \exp\{i \int_{t'}^{t''} [\dot{p}^2/(4p) - V(p)]dt\}\mathcal{D}p \tag{49}$$

integrated over paths $p > 0$ subject to the boundary conditions $p(t') = p'$ and $p(t'') = p''$. The integral in question is qualitatively similar to the usual path integral apart from the important restriction $p > 0$ and the modification of the kinetic energy term.

Construction of the Path Integral

In order to give proper sense to such a path integral we follow the procedure first used by Nelson for Schrödinger mechanics.[9] The Hamiltonian operator for the system under study has the form

$$\mathcal{H} = QPQ + V(P) \ . \tag{50}$$

We shall assume $V(P)$ is properly chosen to validate Trotter's product formula

$$e^{-i(t''-t')\mathcal{H}} = \lim_{\varepsilon\to 0}[e^{-i\varepsilon QPQ}e^{-i\varepsilon V(P)}]^{(N+1)} \tag{51}$$

where $\varepsilon \equiv (t''-t')/(N+1)$. Specifically, for this relation to hold it is sufficient if $\mathcal{H}$ is essentially self-adjoint on the intersection of the domain of the self-adjoint operators QPQ and V(P). In particular, if $V(P) \geq 0$ and is bounded for P away from zero and infinity, then (51) holds.

We next invoke properties of the formal eigenstates $|p\rangle$ of the P operator. In particular, it may be shown that

$$\langle p''|e^{-itQPQ}|p'\rangle = (it)^{-1}J_o(2\sqrt{p''p'}/t)e^{i(p''+p')/t} \tag{52}$$

valid for all t, where J_o is the usual zero-order Bessel function. Repeated insertion of a resolution of unity with respect to the $|p\rangle$ states thus leads to the expression

$$\langle p'',t''|p',t'\rangle = \lim_{\varepsilon\to 0} \int\cdots\int \times \prod_{\ell=0}^{N}\left[(i\varepsilon)^{-1}J_o(2\sqrt{p_{\ell+1}p_\ell}/\varepsilon)e^{i(p_{\ell+1}+p_\ell)/\varepsilon-i\varepsilon V(p_\ell)}\right] \times \prod_{\ell=1}^{N} dp_\ell \tag{53}$$

where $p_o \equiv p'$ and $p_{N+1} \equiv p''$, which is a valid (lattice-space) form for the desired path integral.

An interesting variation on this expression exists as well. Let us introduce the integral representation

$$J_o(w) = (2\pi)^{-1}\int_0^{2\pi} e^{-iw\cos\theta}d\theta \tag{54}$$

for the Bessel function throughout. In that case (53) becomes

$$\langle p'',t''|p',t'\rangle = \lim_{\varepsilon\to 0}\int\cdots\int (2\pi i\varepsilon)^{-(N+1)} \times \exp\{i\sum_{\ell=0}^{N}[\varepsilon^{-1}(p_{\ell+1}+p_\ell-2\sqrt{p_{\ell+1}p_\ell}\cos\theta_\ell)-\varepsilon V(p_\ell)]\}$$

$$\times \prod_{\ell=0}^{N} d\theta_\ell \prod_{\ell=1}^{N} dp_\ell \ . \tag{55}$$

Next we can readily make a change of angle variables so that

$$\langle p'',t''|p',t'\rangle$$
$$= \lim_{\varepsilon\to 0} \int\ldots\int (2\pi i\varepsilon)^{-(N+1)}$$
$$\times \exp\Big(i \sum_{\ell=0}^{N} \{\varepsilon^{-1}[p_{\ell+1}+p_\ell-2\sqrt{p_{\ell+1}p_\ell}\ \cos(\theta_{\ell+1}-\theta_\ell)]-\varepsilon V(p_\ell)\}\Big)$$
$$\times \prod_{\ell=0}^{N} d\theta_\ell \prod_{\ell=1}^{N} dp_\ell \tag{56}$$

where $\theta_{N+1} \equiv 0$. In this form the change of variables

$$p_\ell = \tfrac{1}{2}(y_{1\ell}^2+y_{2\ell}^2) \equiv \tfrac{1}{2}\vec{y}_\ell^{\,2} \equiv \tfrac{1}{2}y_\ell^2 \ , \tag{57a}$$

$$\tan\theta_\ell = y_{2\ell}/y_{1\ell} \ , \tag{57b}$$

suggests itself. Under this change

$$d\theta_\ell dp_\ell = d\theta_\ell y_\ell dy_\ell = dy_{1\ell}dy_{2\ell} \equiv d\vec{y}_\ell \ , \tag{58}$$

which amounts to passing from cylindrical to Euclidean coordinates. In terms of these variables

$$\langle p'',t''|p',t'\rangle$$
$$= \lim_{\varepsilon\to 0} \int\ldots\int (2\pi i\varepsilon)^{-(N+1)}$$
$$\times \exp\Big\{i \sum_{\ell=0}^{N} [\tfrac{1}{2}\varepsilon^{-1}(\vec{y}_{\ell+1}-\vec{y}_\ell)^2-\varepsilon V(\tfrac{1}{2}\vec{y}_\ell^{\,2})]\Big\} \prod_{\ell=1}^{N} d\vec{y}_\ell d\theta_o \tag{59}$$

where $p' = \tfrac{1}{2}\vec{y}_o^{\,2}$ and $p'' = \tfrac{1}{2}\vec{y}_{N+1}^{\,2} = \tfrac{1}{2}y_{1N+1}^2$ (since $\theta_{N+1} \equiv 0$). Thus we reach the important conclusion that the path integral in question has the form of that of a particle in <u>two</u> dimensions in the presence of a circularly symmetric potential, and which in addition is averaged over the initial angle θ_o.

In terms of the lattice-space formulation in (59) let us interchange the integrations and the limit $\varepsilon \to 0$ which yields the

formal path-integral expression

$$\langle p'',t''|p',t'\rangle$$

$$= (2\pi)^{-1} \int_0^{2\pi} \mathcal{N}\int \exp\{i \int_{t'}^{t''} [\tfrac{1}{2}\dot{\vec{y}}^2 - V(\tfrac{1}{2}\vec{y}^2)]dt\}\mathcal{D}\vec{y}\,d\theta_0 \qquad (60)$$

integrated over two-dimensional paths $\vec{y}$ such that $p' = \frac{1}{2}\vec{y}^2(t')$ and $p'' = \frac{1}{2}\vec{y}^2(t'') = \frac{1}{2}y_1^2(t'')$ (since $\theta_{N+1} \equiv 0$), followed by an integration over θ_0 (which could equally well be called θ'). The expression in (60) has the advantage over the one in (49) in that no positivity restriction is placed on the $\vec{y}$ variables and the kinetic energy expression is the standard one. In fact, as shown in our derivation, the simplest and most natural interpretation of (60) [as (59)] is the correct one.

We assert that a direct interpretation of (49) in the manner of (60) would be essentially impossible. Indeed, one might be tempted to introduce the change of variables $p = u^2/2$, for which it follows that $\dot{p} = u\dot{u}$ so that $\dot{p}^2/(4p) = \dot{u}^2/2$. This would be satisfactory in the classical theory. But in the quantum theory regarding u as a one-dimensional variable would be incorrect (as we have seen) and it would be very difficult to motivate the two-dimensional choice $p = \vec{y}^2/2$, $\vec{y} = (y_1,y_2)$, to which we have been led. In addition, as we shall see in the next section the two-dimensional parameterization is essential to ensure $p > 0$; the one-dimensional parameterization certainly implies that $p \geq 0$, but it fails to ensure $p > 0$, and this is simply not good enough.

V. ASSOCIATED STOCHASTIC PROCESSES

It is well known that the quantum mechanical path integral for the free particle is transformed to the path integral for Wiener measure by a change of the time $t \to -it$. In like manner we can formulate an associated stochastic process for the quantum model of the last section by a study of the Markoff transition element

$$\langle p|e^{-tQPQ}|p'\rangle = t^{-1}I_0(2\sqrt{pp'}/t)e^{-(p+p')/t} \qquad (61)$$

which follows directly from (52). We may be assured that there is an underlying probability measure μ_A on the path space of continuous functions $p(t) > 0$ that is generated by (61). Below, we shall relate the stochastic process characterized by this transition element to the so-called two-dimensional Bessel process.

Let us first exploit the transition element and the Trotter product formula to get an analogue of the Feynman-Kac formula, to wit (with $\tau \equiv t''-t'$)

$$\langle p''|e^{-\tau[QPQ+V(P)]}|p'\rangle$$

$$= \lim_{\varepsilon\to 0} \int\ldots\int \prod_{\ell=0}^{N} [\varepsilon^{-1} I_o(2\sqrt{p_{\ell+1}p_\ell}/\varepsilon) e^{-(p_{\ell+1}+p_\ell)/\varepsilon - \varepsilon V(p_\ell)}]$$

$$\times \prod_{\ell=1}^{N} dp_\ell \ , \tag{62}$$

where as before $p' = p_0$ and $p'' = p_{N+1}$. In the present case the interchange of integration and the limit $\varepsilon \to 0$ can rigorously be made by exploiting the measure μ_A. This leads to the path integral

$$\langle p''|e^{-\tau[QPQ+V(P)]}|p'\rangle = \int e^{-\int_{t'}^{t''} V(p(t))dt} d\mu_A(p) \ , \tag{63}$$

where we have implicitly assumed that μ_A is pinned so that $p(t') = p'$ and $p(t'') = p''$.

An alternative form may be given to these expressions through use of the integral representation

$$I_o(w) = (2\pi)^{-1} \int_0^{2\pi} e^{w\cos\theta} d\theta \ . \tag{64}$$

With this representation (62) becomes

$$\langle p''|e^{-\tau[QPQ+V(P)]}|p'\rangle$$

$$= \lim_{\varepsilon\to 0} \int\ldots\int (2\pi\varepsilon)^{-(N+1)}$$

$$\times \exp\{-\sum_{\ell=0}^{N} [\varepsilon^{-1}(p_{\ell+1}+p_\ell-2\sqrt{p_{\ell+1}p_\ell}\cos\theta_\ell)+\varepsilon V(p_\ell)]\}$$

$$\times \prod_{\ell=0}^{N} d\theta_\ell \prod_{\ell=1}^{N} dp_\ell \ , \tag{65}$$

while a change of angle variables brings it to the form

$$\langle p''|e^{-\tau[QPQ+V(P)]}|p'\rangle$$

$$= \lim_{\varepsilon\to 0} \int\ldots\int (2\pi\varepsilon)^{-(N+1)}$$

$$\times \exp\Big(-\sum_{\ell=0}^{N} \{\varepsilon^{-1}[p_{\ell+1}+p_\ell-2\sqrt{p_{\ell+1}p_\ell}\,\cos(\theta_{\ell+1}-\theta_\ell)]+\varepsilon V(p_\ell)\}\Big)$$

$$\times \prod_{\ell=0}^{N} d\theta_\ell \prod_{\ell=1}^{N} dp_\ell \ , \qquad (66)$$

where as before $\theta_{N+1} \equiv 0$. With the change of variables indicated in (57) and (58) it follows that

$$\langle p''|e^{-\tau[QPQ+V(P)]}|p'\rangle$$

$$= \lim_{\varepsilon\to 0} \int\ldots\int (2\pi\varepsilon)^{-(N+1)}$$

$$\times \exp\{-\sum_{\ell=0}^{N} [\tfrac{1}{2}\varepsilon^{-1}(\vec{y}_{\ell+1}-\vec{y}_\ell)^2+\varepsilon V(\tfrac{1}{2}\vec{y}_\ell^{\,2})]\} \prod_{\ell=1}^{N} d\vec{y}_\ell\, d\theta_o \ . \qquad (67)$$

In the present form we recognize the integrand as the lattice-space Feynman-Kac formula for a two-dimensional system. Consequently, by appealing to a two-dimensional Wiener measure we can take the limit under the integral sign and determine that

$$\langle p''|e^{-\tau[QPQ+V(P)]}|p'\rangle = (2\pi)^{-1} \int_0^{2\pi} \int e^{-\int_{t'}^{t''} V(\frac{1}{2}\vec{y}^{\,2}(t))dt}\, d\mu_W(\vec{y})\, d\theta_o \ , \qquad (68)$$

where we have implicitly assumed that the Wiener measure μ_W is pinned so that $p' = \frac{1}{2}\vec{y}^{\,2}(t')$ and $p'' = \frac{1}{2}\vec{y}^{\,2}(t'') = \frac{1}{2}y_1^2(t'')$. The preceding discussion indicates how a Euclidean formulation of the toy model for gravity, as an example, is to be formulated.

Stochastic Variables

In the case that $V(p) = 0$ it follows from the foregoing that we may set

$$p(t) = \tfrac{1}{2}[y_1^2(t)+y_2^2(t)] \qquad (69)$$

where the distribution of p as a stochastic variable follows from the fact that y_1 and y_2 are two, independent Wiener processes. Recall[10] that the stochastic process determined by r(t), where

$$r(t) = \sqrt{y_1^2(t)+y_2^2(t)} \ , \qquad (70)$$

is called the two-dimensional Bessel process; r is related to p

simply by $p = r^2/2$. Since we assume that $\vec{y}^2(t') = 2p' > 0$, then it follows from known results[10] that with probability one $p(t) > 0$ for all t. This desirable feature is a direct property of the two-dimensional representation of p. Suppose instead we assume that

$$p(t) = \tfrac{1}{2}u^2(t) \tag{71}$$

where (as suggested by the discussion in the preceding section) u(t) has the distribution of a one-dimensional Wiener process pinned to start at $u(t') = +\sqrt{2p(t')} > 0$ (say). Recall[11] that the local time at level x is (formally) defined by

$$t^*(x) = \int_{t'}^{t''} \delta(u(t)-x)dt , \tag{72}$$

and it represents a measure of the time the path spends at level x in the time interval $t''-t'(>0)$. Moreover, as a stochastic variable $t^*(x)$ is continuous in x and nonvanishing. Roughly speaking, this means that the visitation time for $x = e^{-137}$ (say) for which $p > 0$ is substantially no different than the visitation time for $x = 0$ for which $p = 0$. More explicitly, we note that a one-dimensional Wiener process pinned to start at $u(t') = +\sqrt{2p(t')}$ will, with a positive probability given by

$$1-\sqrt{2/\pi(t-t')} \int_{\sqrt{2p(t')}}^{\infty} e^{-x^2/2(t-t')}dx , \tag{73}$$

reach the level $u = 0$ in the time interval $t-t'$ (> 0). As a result the one-dimensional parameterization $p(t) = u^2(t)/2$ does not achieve the desired goal of ensuring $p(t) > 0$ with probability one. As noted above, this goal is successfully achieved with the two-dimensional parameterization (69).

It would be of interest in the present context to develop the associated stochastic differential equations that account for the presence of a nonvanishing potential V(p). However we shall not pursue that question here.

VI. CONCLUSION

In this paper we have studied the quantization of simple systems subject to the inequality $p > 0$. In large measure, we have been motivated in this endeavor by the positivity requirements that attend the metric of the gravitational field. Consequently, the example we have discussed almost exclusively is a toy model of gravity. Some of our results are special to that model, while others are not. For example, the absence of a q-representation is universal, and as a result affine variables and affine coherent states are basic in order to interpret the

phase-space path integral. On the other hand, the analysis of the Lagrangian formulation that we presented entails a specific model (or class of models) so as to yield a universal elimination of one of the canonical variables. The resultant process for the example studied was shown to be the square of a two-dimensional Bessel process rather than the obvious choice, the square of a one-dimensional Wiener process.

Finally, a few comments on field theory. It is important to recognize that the inapplicability of the obvious one-dimensional parameterization for the simple model problem has negative implications for the successful parameterization of the gravitational metric by the vierbein in the context of quantization. It is interesting in this respect to note that Pilati[12] has recently utilized affine field operators to study an ultralocal model of the gravitational field attempting to take into account the usual Hamiltonian constraints and thereby extending the analysis of quantum field models treated in the second article of Ref. 1. Yet another study of affine field operators is given in Ref. 13 which is devoted to the analysis of nonrenormalizable model scalar field theories. Hopefully, operator and path integral techniques can provide complementary information with which to improve our understanding of quantum field theories, the variables of which are restricted by one or another inequality.

REFERENCES

1. J. R. Klauder and E. W. Aslaksen, "Elementary Model for Quantum Gravity", Phys. Rev. D 2:272 (1970); see also J. R. Klauder, in Relativity, ed. by M. Carmeli, S. I. Fickler, and L. Witten (Plenum, 1970), p. 1.
2. I. M. Gel'fand and M. A. Naimark, Dokl. Akad. Nauk SSSR 55:570 (1947); E. W. Aslaksen and J. R. Klauder, "Unitary Representations of the Affine Group", J. Math. Phys. 9:206 (1968).
3. E. W. Aslaksen and J. R. Klauder, "Continuous Representation Theory Using the Affine Group", J. Math. Phys. 10:2267 (1969).
4. See, e.g., H. Meschkowski, Hilbertsche Räume mit Kernfunktion (Springer, 1962).
5. See, e.g., S. Bochner and W. T. Martin, Several Complex Variables (Princeton, 1948), Theorem 7, Chapter II.
6. J. R. Klauder and E. C. G. Sudarshan, Fundamentals of Quantum Optics (W. A. Benjamin, New York, 1968).
7. J. R. Klauder, Ann. Phys. (NY) 11:123 (1960); J. R. Klauder, in Path Integrals, ed. by G. J. Papadopoulos and J. T. Devreese (Plenum, 1978), p. 5.
8. J. R. Klauder, J. Math. Phys. 8:2392 (1967); see also Refs. 1 and 7.
9. E. Nelson, J. Math. Phys. 5:332 (1964).

10. H. P. McKean, Jr., Stochastic Integrals (Academic Press, 1969).
11. K. Itô and H. P. McKean, Jr., Diffusion Processes and Their Sample Paths (Academic Press, 1965).
12. M. Pilati, "The Canonical Formulation of Supergravity and the Quantization of the Ultralocal Theory of Gravity", Princeton University Thesis, 1979 (unpublished).
13. J. R. Klauder, J. Math. Phys. 18:1711 (1977).

PATH INTEGRALS OVER COHERENT STATES[¶]

Enrico Onofri

Istituto di Fisica, Università di Parma
and I.N.F.N., Sezione di Milano
Parma, Italy 43100

In the so-called "Reggeon Quantum Mechanics" one is faced with the problem of constructing the evolution operator $\exp\{-YH\}$ for $Y > 0$ and

$$H = \mu\, a^{\dagger}a + i\lambda\, a^{\dagger}(a+a^{\dagger})a + \lambda' a^{\dagger 2}a^{2} \qquad (1)$$

where μ, λ, λ' are positive constants and a, $a^{\dagger}$ are the usual boson creation and annihilation operators. This talk is devoted to the construction of $\exp\{-YH\}$ through a path-integral. I shall only sketch the main ideas, since a detailed presentation can be found in Ref.(1).

The most natural approach to formulate a path-integral representation for $\exp\{-YH\}$ seems to be the Klauder-Schweber phase-space path-integral in terms of (Glauber-Bargmann-Segal) coherent states. This is because H is given by a second order differential operator in Bargmann space B while it is a complicated fourth order differential operator in L_2. If $\{|z\rangle\}$ denotes the overcomplete basis of coherent states and $\langle z|\psi\rangle = \psi(z)$ is any entire function in B, one has

$$\langle z|H|\psi\rangle = (H\psi)(z) = A(z)\frac{d^2\psi}{dz^2} + B(z)\,\frac{d\psi}{dz} \qquad (2)$$

with

$$A(z) = iz(\lambda - i\lambda' z) \quad , \quad B(z) = z(i\lambda z - \mu) \qquad (3)$$

The usual prescription[2] for constructing a path integral is the following: start from the identity

---

¶ Work done in collaboration with M.Ciafaloni (S.N.S., Pisa)

$$<z|e^{-YH}|\psi> = <z|\left(e^{-YH/N}\right)^N|\psi> =$$

$$= \prod_1^N \int \frac{dz_k \wedge d\bar{z}_k}{2\pi i} e^{(z_{k+1}-z_k)\bar{z}_k} K_{Y/N}(z_{k+1},\bar{z}_k)\ \psi(z_1) \qquad (4)$$

$(z_{N+1} \equiv z)$ where

$$K_\varepsilon(z,\bar{\zeta}) = \frac{<z|e^{-\varepsilon H}|\zeta>}{<z|\zeta>} \qquad (5)$$

Now one approximates K_ε by some $\mathcal{K}_\varepsilon$ such that

i) $K_\varepsilon - \mathcal{K}_\varepsilon = o(\varepsilon)$

ii) Eq.(4) is recovered in the limit $N\to\infty$.

The usual choice is the following

$$\mathcal{K}_\varepsilon(z,\bar{\zeta}) = e^{-\varepsilon h(z,\bar{\zeta})} \qquad (6)$$

where

$$h(z,\bar{\zeta}) = \frac{<z|H|\zeta>}{<z|\zeta>} \qquad (7)$$

$h(z,\bar{\zeta})$ is obtained by H under the substitution $a\to\bar{\zeta}$, $a^\dagger\to z$, provided H is in normal Wick form.

This choice, however, *does not work* when H contains powers of a and/or $a^\dagger$ higher than the first (as it happens for our model). This is because $\exp\{-\varepsilon h(z,\bar{\zeta})\}$ does not belong to $\mathcal{B}$; the first integration in Eq.(4) gives a singularity at some $z \simeq \sqrt{(N/Y)}$ and further integrations cannot be performed. In other words the approximation $\mathcal{K}_\varepsilon$ satisfies condition (i) only pointwise, but not in some strong (Banach norm) sense.

There are several ways to circumvent this difficulty. The first proposal is to split H into $H = H_1 + H_2$, with

$$H_1 = \mu a^\dagger a + \lambda' a^{\dagger 2} a^2 \qquad (8)$$

and define

$$\mathcal{K}_\varepsilon(z,\bar{\zeta}) = (1-\varepsilon h_2(z,\bar{\zeta}))\ \frac{<z|e^{-\varepsilon H_1}|\zeta>}{<z|\zeta>} \qquad (9)$$

The first factor is small w.r.t. H_1 and the second can be calculated in closed form

$$<z|e^{-\varepsilon H_1}|\zeta> = \int_\infty^\infty \frac{d\xi}{\sqrt{\pi}}\ e^{-\xi^2} \exp\{z\bar{\zeta}\ e^{(\mu+\lambda')\varepsilon}\ e^{2i\xi(\lambda'\varepsilon)^{\frac{1}{2}}}\} \qquad (10)$$

THEOREM (see Ref.1): with this new choice of $\mathcal{K}_\varepsilon$ every finite N approximation exists and the limit $N\to\infty$ gives the right result (in the strong limit sense).

A second possibility is to define the finite N approximations starting from the anti-normal ordering rule[3]

$$H = \int \frac{dz \wedge d\bar{z}}{2\pi i} e^{-z\bar{z}} \tilde{h}(z,\bar{z}) \; |z\rangle\langle z| \tag{11}$$

where

$$\tilde{h}(z,\bar{z}) = \exp\{-\frac{\partial^2}{\partial z\, \partial \bar{z}}\} h(z,\bar{z}) \tag{12}$$

and approximating

$$e^{-\varepsilon H} \simeq \int \frac{dz \wedge d\bar{z}}{2\pi i} e^{-z\bar{z} - \varepsilon\tilde{h}(z,\bar{z})} \; |z\rangle\langle z| \tag{13}$$

Since $\tilde{h}(z,\bar{z})$ is evaluated at the same point, the factor $e^{-\varepsilon\tilde{h}}$ does not give rise to any singularity. It is shown in Ref.(1) that this prescription gives the same result as the first one (Eq.9).

CONCLUDING REMARKS

The point we wanted to stress here is that the usual approach to path integrals over coherent states is rather formal and it leads to undefined expressions. This is also true for *generalized coherent states*[4,5]. In general one has a classical phase space with fundamental (Kaehler) two-form

$$\omega = i\bar{\partial}\partial f \equiv i \sum \frac{\partial^2 f}{\partial \bar{z}_k \partial z_h} d\bar{z}_k \wedge dz_h \tag{14}$$

and a Hilbert space of holomorphic functions (sections) $\langle z|\psi\rangle$ where the coherent states satisfy

$$\langle z|\zeta\rangle = e^{f(z,\bar{\zeta})} \quad , \quad \int \omega^n e^{-f} |z\rangle\langle z| = I \tag{15}$$

One can still define (formally)

$$(e^{-\varepsilon H}\psi)(z) \simeq \int \omega^n e^{f(z,\bar{\zeta}) - f(\zeta,\bar{\zeta}) - \varepsilon h(z,\bar{\zeta})} \psi(\zeta) \tag{16}$$

with the same definition (7), but in general $\exp\{-\varepsilon h\}$ does not belong to the Hilbert space of holomorphic functions. For example, take

$$f = 2j \ln(1+z\bar{z}) \tag{17}$$

which corresponds to spin coherent states. $\langle z|e^{-\varepsilon H}|\zeta\rangle$ is a polynomial in z and ζ times $\langle z|\zeta\rangle$ and it is badly approximated by $\langle z|\zeta\rangle \exp\{-\varepsilon h(z,\bar{\zeta})\}$. Whereever possible, a definition in terms of anti-normal ordering plus Eq.(13) should give a meaningful expression.

References

1. M.Ciafaloni and E.Onofri, Nucl.Phys.B151 (1979) 118-146.
2. J.R.Klauder, Thesis (Princeton University); S.Schweber, J.Math.Phys.3 (1962) 831.
3. See for instance: K.E.Cahill and R.J.Glauber, Phys.Rev.177 (1969) 1857.
4. For a general review see: A.M.Perelomov, Sov.Phys.Usp.20 (1977) 703-720.
5. E.Onofri, J.Math.Phys.16 (1975) 1087-1089.

PATH INTEGRALS, COHERENT STATES, AND GEOMETRIC QUANTIZATION

H.P. Berg and Jan Tarski

Institut für Theoretische Physik
Technische Universität Clausthal
D-3392 Clausthal-Zellerfeld, F.R. Germany

ABSTRACT: The connections between path integrals and geometric quantization are discussed. Complex polarizations and coherent states are emphasized. The resulting set-up differs in several ways from the coordinate representation, and in particular two kinds of action are encountered.

1. INTRODUCTION

The derivation of the Feynman path integral from the premises of geometric quantization, at least at the level of formal manipulations, has become a familiar procedure [1],[2]. However, the presentations of this derivation in loc. cit. were confined to the elementary example, where one has a Schrödinger particle under the influence of a potential (without derivatives), and where the integral is over paths on the coordinate space.

In the present article we consider this derivation for some other examples. We discuss in particular path integrals which refer to coherent states and analytic function spaces. Such integrals are usually expressed in a form like the following:

$$\int \mathcal{D}(\alpha^*)\,\mathcal{D}(\alpha)\; e^{iS(\alpha^*,\alpha)}\; F(\alpha^*,\alpha) \quad , \qquad (1.1a)$$

$$S(\alpha^*,\alpha) = \int_0^t d\tau \left\{ \tfrac{1}{2} i \left[\alpha^* \dot{\alpha} - (\alpha^*)^{\cdot} \alpha \right] - H(\alpha^*,\alpha) \right\} . \qquad (1.1b)$$

We recall that path integrals of this general kind are encountered in statistical mechanics, see e.g. [3],§6. Some other applications of such integrals can be found in [4],[5]. A construction of such integrals, which is based on normal ordering of the Hamiltonian,

has been given by Schweber [6].

We felt it would be worthwile to elucidate the structure of integrals as in (1.1) by investigating them with the help of procedures of geometric quantization. At the same time, such an investigation would provide some examples of complex polarizations, the experience with which is still rather limited. We have made small steps in these directions.

Our contribution lies not so much in a central result, but rather, in having indicated some geometric features related to such path integrals, features which have been largely unappreciated. For instance, in this article we are led to consider three different reference one-forms. Moreover, the problem of factor ordering and of deriving the equations of motion differs somewhat from the corresponding problem in the coordinate representation.

Furthermore, two different notions of action arise. The action S in (1.1b), in particular, differs in general from an action S_{cl}, associated with a classical path, even in the case of quadratic Hamiltonians. We discuss a connection between S and S_{cl} [cf. eq. (4.18) below], but we have not found an interpretation for S which would be primarily geometric.

We present our arguments at the level of formal manipulations, as is also done in the works cited above. Moreover, even at this level, we can give a reasonably satisfactory discussion of the path integral of (1.1) only for quadratic Hamiltonians. (The same limitation applies to [6].) Justification of details, however, should not bring about serious problems. E.g., one could rely on explicit calculations for quadratic Hamiltonians, and on available results on convergence of iterated short-time approximations, as summarized in [7].

For the sake of brevity in writing, we restrict our considerations to a particle on R^1, and to time-independent interactions.

In sec. 2 we summarize the derivations of the path integral, as given in [1], [2]. In sec. 3 we adapt the arguments of sec. 2 to complex polarizations and to coherent states, but we find that a direct adaption does not suffice to obtain the path integral of interest. Section 4 discusses time evolution and Green's functions (for complex polarizations), and connections with path integrals are indicated. In sec. 5 we discuss briefly the ordering problem.

We are grateful to Profs. D.J. Simms and J. Śniatycki for helpful discussions. One of us (J.T.) thanks Prof. H.D. Doebner for his hospitality at T.U. Clausthal.

2. DERIVATION OF PATH INTEGRALS OVER COORDINATE SPACE

We start by reviewing some notions from geometric quantization. We introduce the reference section σ_1 and the reference one-form θ_1 on the phase space $M=R^2$ by

$$\sigma_1((p,q)) = ((p,q),1) \quad , \quad \theta_1 = p\,dq \quad . \tag{2.1a}$$

The pair (σ_1,θ_1) defines a connection for sections on M, such that the covariant derivative becomes

$$\nabla_\xi^{(1)}(f\sigma_1) = (\xi f)\sigma_1 - i(\xi \lrcorner \theta_1)(f\sigma_1) \quad . \tag{2.1b}$$

The choice of constants corresponds to setting $\hbar=1$ in quantum-mechanical applications. The index (1) in $\nabla_\xi^{(1)}$ will distinguish this derivative from another which will be introduced below.

To the polarization (∂_p) correspond sections of the form $\psi(q)\sigma_1$, i.e.

$$\nabla_{\partial_p}^{(1)}(\psi(q)\sigma_1) = 0 \quad . \tag{2.2}$$

However, to the polarization (∂_q) correspond sections which contain a q-dependent factor:

$$\nabla_{\partial_q}^{(1)}(\varphi(p)\sigma') = 0 \quad \text{where} \quad \sigma' = e^{ipq}\sigma_1 \quad . \tag{2.3}$$

One may verify that σ' is associated to $\theta'=-q\,dp$, in the sense that (2.1b) remains valid if we replace $\sigma_1 \to \sigma'$, $\theta_1 \to \theta'$. More generally, let $F:M \to C^1$ be nowhere-vanishing (and smooth), and let us introduce a new reference section σ_F and the corresponding one-form θ_F through

$$\sigma_F = F\sigma_1 \quad , \quad i\,dF/F = \theta_1 - \theta_F \quad . \tag{2.4a}$$

Then (2.1b) is equivalent to

$$\nabla_\xi^{(1)}(f\sigma_F) = (\xi f)\sigma_F - i(\xi \lrcorner \theta_F)(f\sigma_F) \quad . \tag{2.4b}$$

Consider next a nonrelativistic Hamiltonian,

$$H = p^2/2m + V(q) \quad , \tag{2.5a}$$

and the associated vector field,

$$\xi_H = (\partial_p H)\partial_q - (\partial_q H)\partial_p = (p/m)\partial_q - V'(q)\partial_p \quad . \tag{2.5b}$$

These determine the prequantized operator ,

$$P_H^{(1)} = i^{-1}\nabla_{\xi_H}^{(1)} + H \quad . \tag{2.5c}$$

The action of this operator on a section $\psi_o(q)\sigma_1$ is

$$P_H^{(1)}(\psi_o\sigma_1) = i^{-1}(p/m)\psi_o'(q)\sigma_1 - (p^2/m)(\psi_o\sigma_1) + H(\psi_o\sigma_1) \ . \qquad (2.6)$$

In the remainder of this section we consider the case of a short time t. Then (2.6) yields

$$\left[(\exp -itP_H^{(1)})(\psi_o\sigma_1)\right](p,q) = \psi_o(q-tp/m)\ \exp(it\left[p^2/2m - V(q)\right])\sigma_1 + o(t) \ . \qquad (2.7)$$

We set

$$q_{-t} := q - t\xi_H q = q - tp/m \qquad (2.8a)$$

$$\lambda_{-t} := \exp(i\left[\tfrac{1}{2}m(q - q_{-t})^2/t - tV(q)\right])\sigma_1 \ . \qquad (2.8b)$$

Then $\lambda_0=\sigma_1$, and

$$\left[(\exp -itP_H^{(1)})(\psi_o\sigma_1)\right](p,q) = \psi_o(q_{-t})\lambda_{-t} + o(t) \ . \qquad (2.9)$$

The section $\psi_o(q_{-t})\lambda_{-t}$ does not satisfy (2.2), but rather,

$$\nabla_\zeta^{(1)}(\psi_o(q_{-t})\lambda_{-t}) = o(t) \ , \quad \zeta = \partial_p + (t/m)\partial_q \ . \qquad (2.1o)$$

The last operator can be obtained by applying the Lie derivative,

$$\zeta = (1 - tL_{\xi_H})(\partial_p) = \partial_p - t[\xi_H,\partial_p] \ , \qquad (2.11)$$

and it agrees with $\partial_{p_{-t}}$ (at constant q_{-t}, and up to o(t)), where $p_{-t} = p - t\xi_H p$. We see that up to a term o(t), $\psi_o(q_{-t})\lambda_{-t}$ corresponds to the polarization $(\partial_{p_{-t}})$. Now, to this section we may associate in a canonical way the section $\psi_t(q)\sigma_1$ corresponding to the polarization (∂_p). Transforms which link different polarizations are the BKS transforms. All the ingredients for applying such a transform are now available, except for the pairing of the associated half-forms ν, which provides the proper normalization. (We refer to [2],[8] for full details.) We have, with $\omega(\xi_1,\xi_2) = \xi_1\lrcorner\xi_2\lrcorner\omega$,

$$(\nu_{-t},\nu_o) = \left[\omega(\zeta,\partial_p)/i\right]^{\frac{1}{2}} = (t/mi)^{\frac{1}{2}} \ . \qquad (2.12)$$

The transform $\psi\mapsto\psi_t$ is now determined by

$$\langle\chi^*,\psi_t\rangle = (2\pi)^{-\frac{1}{2}}(t/mi)^{\frac{1}{2}}\int dpdq\,\chi^*(q)\psi_o(q_{-t}) \times \exp(i\left[\tfrac{1}{2}m(q-q_{-t})^2/t - tV(q)\right]) + o(t) \qquad (2.13)$$

where $\chi\in L_2$ is arbitrary. The factor $(2\pi)^{-\frac{1}{2}}$ is determined by the limit $t\searrow 0$. The last relation implies

$$\psi_t(q)\sigma_1 = (2\pi)^{-\frac{1}{2}}(t/mi)^{\frac{1}{2}} \int_{-\infty}^{\infty} dp\psi_0(q_{-t})\lambda_{-t} + o(t) \quad , \qquad (2.14a)$$

and, in view of (2.8a),

$$\psi_t(q)\sigma_1 = (m/2\pi it)^{\frac{1}{2}} \int_{-\infty}^{\infty} dq_{-t}\, \psi_0(q_{-t})\lambda_{-t} + o(t) \quad . \qquad (2.14b)$$

One may now verify, as in[9], that this ψ_t satisfies the Schrödinger equation. A standard Calculation also shows that $\psi_t \to \psi_0$ as $t \searrow 0$.

The last equation describes the evolution of the quantized particle over a short time interval . If we have an arbitrary time interval $[0,T]$, we may proceed as usual by subdividing the interval into n parts, by iterating (2.14) n times, and by letting $n \to \infty$. (cf. also secs. 4 and 5 .)

The foregoing expressions also show how various relations of classical mechanics enter into the short-time approximation. We note e.g. $q_{-t}=q-tp/m$, which we may also write as $q_{-t}=q-t\dot{q}$, where p (and $\dot{q}$) refer to $t=0$ and where the potential provides a correction $o(t)$. Moreover, a basic equation for the Hamiltonian vector field (which is related to (2.5b) through Hamilton's equations) and the corresponding contribution for the Lagrangian,

$$\xi_H = \dot{q}\partial_q + \dot{p}\partial_p \quad , \qquad \xi_H \rfloor \theta_1 = p\dot{q} \quad , \qquad (2.15)$$

allow us to express the quantity $p^2/2m - V(q)$ of (2.7) in a form which is familiar in path integrals, namely $p\dot{q} - H$.

In the foregoing we emphasized the dependence of the connection, or of ∇, on the pair (σ_1, θ_1). We should therefore like to consider also the connection defined by

$$\sigma_0 := \sigma_1 \quad , \quad \theta_0 := \frac{1}{2}(pdq - qdp) = \theta_1 - \frac{1}{2}d(pq) \quad . \qquad (2.16)$$

Since eqs. (2.4a) are not fulfilled, $\nabla^{(0)} \neq \nabla^{(1)}$. In fact, in the present case the sections corresponding to the polarization (∂_p) must have an extra factor $\exp(-ipq/2)$:

$$\nabla_{\partial_p}^{(0)} \left[\psi(q)\exp(-ipq/2)\sigma_1\right] = 0 \qquad (2.17)$$

The Lagrangian and the action depend on the reference one-form. If θ_1 is replaced by θ_0, then we should also replace $p\dot{q}$ by $(p\dot{q}-q\dot{p})/2$ etc. In particular, for a free particle, $p\dot{q} - H$ would become $pq/2 - p^2/2m = 0$. These observations raise the questions: Is the path-integral formalism modified when the reference one-form is changed? Does anything particular happen for the free particle, when S=0 along a classical path, and when the classical paths fully determine the quantum behavior?

To answer these questions for the case at hand, we decompose the (integrated) action defined by θ_o as follows,

$$S_o = S_1 - \frac{1}{2}(pq)_{\tau=0} + \frac{1}{2}(pq)_{\tau=-t} \quad , \quad S_1 = \int(pdq - Hd\tau) \quad . \qquad (2.18)$$

When we form e^{iS_o}, we see that the two endpoint terms in (2.18) are responsible for the time evolution of the factor $\exp(-ipq/2)$, while $\exp(iS_1)$ governs the time evolution of Ψ, as before. Nothing special happens for the free particle, when $S_o=0$.

We conclude with the following remark: The possibility of changing the Lagrangian by a total differential and of modifying the wave function by the corresponding phase is of course familiar. Less familiar is the content of eq.(2.17), namely, that this phase factor is also implied by geometric quantization. This circumstance allows the preceding derivation of path integrals to go through in the present case.

3. COMPLEX POLARIZATIONS

The representation of quantum states in terms of entire functions, often called the Bargmann-Segal representation [10], [11], is familiar. We now summarize its main properties. Further details can be found e.g. in loc. cit. and in [2],[6].

We consider q and p as coordinates on M, and we set

$$a := 2^{-\frac{1}{2}}(q + ip) \quad , \quad a^* := 2^{-\frac{1}{2}}(q - ip) \quad . \qquad (3.1)$$

These variables are natural ones for the harmonic oscillator with unit constants, for which

$$H_1 = \frac{1}{2}(p^2 + q^2) = a^* a \quad . \qquad (3.2)$$

A quantum state corresponds to an entire function $f(a^*)$ of a not-too-fast increase, multiplied by a reference section σ_A (see (3.15) below). We introduce scalar products of quantum states and of corresponding entire functions in the following way,

$$\langle f_2\sigma_A, f_1\sigma_A\rangle = \langle f_2, f_1\rangle = \int d\mu(a)\ f_2^*(a^*)\ f_1(a^*) \quad . \qquad (3.3a)$$

The section σ_A determines the measure μ, and one has

$$d\mu(a) = \pi^{-1} d(\mathrm{Re}\ a)\ d(\mathrm{Im}\ a)\ \exp(-|a|^2)$$
$$= \pi^{-1}\ d^2a\ \exp(-|a|^2) \quad . \qquad (3.3b)$$

The correspondence between this representation and the usual q-repretation can be described as follows: $f\sigma_A \leftrightarrow \Psi\sigma_1$, or $f \leftrightarrow \Psi$, where

$$f(a^*) = \int dq\, A(a^*,q)\,\Psi(q) \quad , \tag{3.4a}$$

$$\Psi(q) = \int d\mu(a)\, A^*(a^*,q)\, f(a^*) \quad , \tag{3.4b}$$

$$A(a^*,q) = \pi^{-\frac{1}{4}} \exp\left[-\tfrac{1}{2}(a^{*2} + q^2) + \sqrt{2}a^*q\right] . \tag{3.4c}$$

In particular, $f=1$ corresponds to $\Psi(q)=\pi^{-\frac{1}{4}} e^{-\frac{1}{2}q^2}$, i.e. to the ground state of the harmonic oscillator with the Hamiltonian H_1.

We make the following notational convention: Upon writing $F(a^*)$ we imply an entire function of a^*. However, $F(a)$ could indicate a nonanalytic function, also a measure, etc.

For reference we note the following three properties of the Bargmann-Segal representation. First, such f's constitute a reproducing-kernel Hilbert space, and explicit ly,

$$f(a^*) = \int d\mu(b)\, k_b(a^*)\, f(b^*) \quad , \tag{3.5a}$$

where

$$k_b(a^*) = \exp\,(\,ba^*\,) \quad . \tag{3.5b}$$

This kernel in fact defines the unnormalized state $k_b\sigma_A$ for any $b \in C^1$. Equation (3.5a) can also be written as

$$f(b^*) = \langle k_b, f\rangle \quad . \tag{3.5c}$$

The corresponding normalized functions are given by:

$$k_b(a^*)\, \exp(-\tfrac{1}{2}|b|^2) \;, \quad \text{so that} \quad \langle k_b, k_b\rangle e^{-|b|^2} = 1 \; . \tag{3.6}$$

Second, the k_b's allow a resolution of the identity in the following way:

$$\langle \varphi, f\rangle = \int d^2b\, \pi^{-1}\, e^{-|b|^2} \langle \varphi, k_b\rangle \langle k_b, f\rangle \quad . \tag{3.7}$$

Third, let us define the quantum-mechanical operators $\hat{a}$, $\hat{a}^*$in terms of the usual operators $\hat{q}$, $\hat{p}$ through equations analogous to (3.1). Then these satisfy $[\hat{a}, \hat{a}^*]=1$, and upon transfering their action to the states $f(a^*)\sigma_A$ the following is obtained:

$$\hat{a}^*\, f(a^*)\sigma_A = a^* f(a^*)\sigma_A \quad , \quad \hat{a}\, f(a^*)\sigma_A = (df(a^*)/da^*)\sigma_A \; . \tag{3.8}$$

Note that (at least formally) $\widehat{a^*} = \hat{a}^*$. For convenience we will use the notation $\hat{a}^*$.

We next want to correlate this representation with geometric quantization. It is convenient to utilize here the connection defined by (σ_0, θ_0) of (2.16). We note the following alternative

expressions for θ_o:

$$\theta_o = \frac{1}{2}i(a^*da - ada^*) = -iada^* + \frac{1}{2}id(a^*a) \ . \qquad (3.9)$$

Let us introduce also

$$\theta_2 := -iada^* \ , \qquad \sigma_2 := \sigma_1 = \sigma_o \ . \qquad (3.10)$$

In view of the relations

$$\partial_a \lrcorner\, da = \partial_{a^*} \lrcorner\, da^* = 1 \ , \quad \partial_a \lrcorner\, da^* = \partial_{a^*} \lrcorner\, da = 0 \ , \qquad (3.11)$$

where ∂_a, ∂_{a^*} can be obtained from (3.1),

$$\partial_a = 2^{-\frac{1}{2}}(\partial_q - i\partial_p) \ , \quad \partial_{a^*} = 2^{-\frac{1}{2}}(\partial_q + i\partial_p) \ , \qquad (3.12)$$

there follows

$$\nabla^{(2)}_{\partial_a} f(a^*)\sigma_1 = 0 \ . \qquad (3.13)$$

However, θ_2 is not real, and the derivative $\nabla^{(2)}$ violates the following basic relation in geometric quantization ([2],§3.2; [8], p.26):

$$\xi\langle\lambda_1,\lambda_2\rangle = \langle\nabla_\xi\lambda_1, \lambda_2\rangle + \langle\lambda_1, \nabla_\xi\lambda_2\rangle \ , \qquad (3.14)$$

which must hold for any real vector field ξ.

We will therefore utilize the pair (σ_o,θ_o) and the derivative $\nabla^{(0)}$. One may verify that

$$\nabla^{(0)}_{\partial_a} f(a^*)\sigma_A = 0 \quad \text{where} \quad \sigma_A = e^{-\frac{1}{2}|a|^2}\sigma_1 \ . \qquad (3.15)$$

This conclusion is also expected on the basis of the above relations and (2.16) - (2.18).

We next turn to the problem of time evolution. We assume a Hamiltonian $H(a^*,a)$, whose associated vector field can be expressed as

$$\xi_H = i\left[(\partial_a H)\partial_{a^*} - (\partial_{a^*}H)\partial_a\right] \ . \qquad (3.16)$$

From this relation we read off Hamilton's equations,

$$\dot{a} = -i\partial_{a^*}H \ , \qquad (a^*)^{\cdot} = i\partial_a H \ . \qquad (3.17)$$

The prequantized Hamiltonian for the connection defined by (σ_o,θ_o) is

$$P^{(0)}_H = i^{-1}\nabla^{(0)}_{\xi_H} + H \ . \qquad (3.18)$$

Moreover the prequantized operators $P^{(0)}_a$, $P^{(0)}_{a^*}$, if restricted to

sections such as in (3.15), yield $\hat{a}$ and $\hat{a}^*$ respectively.

We consider the case of a short time t, and we follow the discussion of sec. 2. We introduce the time-translated independent variables,

$$a_{-t} := a - t\xi_H a = a + it(\partial_{a^*}H) = a - t\dot{a} \quad , \tag{3.19a}$$

$$(a_{-t})^* = (a^*)_{-t} = a^* - t\xi_H a^* = a^* - it(\partial_a H) = a^* - t\dot{a}^* . \tag{3.19b}$$

Then for any (smooth) function $F(a^*,a)$,

$$\left[(1 - t\xi_H)F\right](a^*,a) = F(a^*_{-t},a_{-t}) + o(t) \quad , \tag{3.20}$$

and, for f entire in a^*,

$$\left[\exp(-itP_H^{(0)})(f\sigma_A)\right](a^*,a) = f(a^*_{-t})\lambda_{A;-t} + o(t) \quad , \tag{3.21}$$

where

$$\lambda_{A;-t} = e^{-\frac{1}{2}|a_{-t}|^2} e^{itL} \sigma_A \tag{3.22a}$$

$$L = \frac{1}{2}i(a^*\dot{a} - \dot{a}^* a) - H \tag{3.22b}$$

The section in (3.21) corresponds (up to a term $o(t)$) to the polarization (η), where

$$\eta = \partial_a - t[\xi_H,\partial_a] = \partial_a + it(\partial_a{}^2 H)\partial_{a^*} - it(\partial_a\partial_{a^*}H)\partial_a \ . \tag{3.23}$$

We have now all the ingredients to construct a scalar product $\langle\varphi,f_t\rangle$ in the same way as in (2.13) [12],[13]. This scalar product will then determine the map $f \to f_t$. We write this as

$$\langle\varphi,f_t\rangle = \int d^2a\,\pi^{-1} e^{-\frac{1}{2}|a|^2} e^{-\frac{1}{2}|a_{-t}|^2} e^{itL} \varphi(a^*) f(a_{-t}) \tag{3.24}$$
$$\times \left[\omega(\eta,\partial_a^*)/i\right]^{\frac{1}{2}} + o(t) \quad .$$

We see that here the variables do not separate, and so this equation does not easily give the map $f \to f_t$, in contrast to the situation encountered in sec. 2.

To conclude, we observe the following. In the above $a_{-t} = (q_{-t} + ip_{-t})/\sqrt{2}$, and q_{-t}, p_{-t} constitute a canonical pair (up to terms $o(t)$). Therefore there is a unitary map (up to $o(t)$) between the functions $f(a_{-t})$ and $\psi(q_{-t})$, which is given by eqs. (3.4), aside from a relabeling of variables. In particular, the factor $\exp(itL)$ above, or the corresponding factor in (2.8b), has no effect on this map.

4. TIME EVOLUTION AND GREEN'S FUNCTIONS

A familiar method of deriving path-integral expressions depends on iterating short-time propagators, as follows: We start with $\langle \chi, \exp(-itH)\psi_o \rangle$, we subdivide the time interval so as to obtain $\langle \chi, \exp(-itH/n),,,\exp(-itH/n)\psi_o \rangle$, and we insert resolutions of the identity. In case of the Bargmann-Segal representation, the appropriate resolution of the identity is given in (3.8), and

$$\langle F, e^{-itH} f \rangle = \int d\mu(b_n)\ldots d\mu(b_o) \langle F, k_{b_n} \rangle \langle k_{b_n}, e^{-itH/n} k_{b_{n-1}} \rangle \ldots$$
$$\ldots \langle k_{b_1}, e^{-itH/n} k_{b_o} \rangle \langle k_{b_o}, f \rangle \quad . \qquad (4.1)$$

This decomposition was utilized by Schweber in [6].

The next step is to approximate the short-time propagators $\langle k_{b''}, \exp(-i(\Delta t)H)\, k_{b'} \rangle$ in such a way as to arrive at the form (1.1) of the path integral as $n \to \infty$. Now, approximate short-time propagators are given by eq. (3.24), but as we already remarked, it is not easy to extract useful information from this equation. In particular, this equation does not show a simple relation between the propagator and the action S.

Since useful approximations for these propagators have already been obtained by an operational (or algebraic) approach, cf. [6], we will not insist on rederiving these approximations geometrically. Rather, we confine ourselves to discussing some examples and properties of these propagators, especially those properties which relate to geometric quantization.

We now define, without limitation to small t,

$$g(t;b'',b') = \langle k_{b''}, e^{-itH} k_{b'} \rangle \quad . \qquad (4.2)$$

In some cases g is in fact entire in b''^* (also in b'), and then we may write $g(t;b''^*,b')$. The time evolution implied by the Hamiltonian H can be analyzed in terms of the composition

$$f_o(a_{-t}^*) \to \psi_o(q_{-t}) \to \psi_t(q) \to f_t(a^*) \quad , \qquad (4.3a)$$

where we indicated general wave functions. This composition yields (G being the Green's function in the q-representation),

$$f_t(a^*) = \int dq\, A(a^*,q) \int dq_{-t}\, G(t;q,q_{-t}) \int d\mu(a_{-t})\, A^*(a_{-t}^*,q_{-t}) f(a_{-t}^*)$$
$$(4.3b)$$

A further study of the functions g requires some manipulations whose validity may be questioned, especially those of interchanges of integrations (and of other limiting processes). The approximation

$g \approx \exp(iS)$, cf. (4.12) below, suggests that such interchanges are valid for quadratic Hamiltonians and for small times but not otherwise. If we assume that these interchanges are valid, then the above relations and the properties of the kernel k_b imply

$$f_t(a^*) = \int d\mu(a_{-t})\, g(t;a^*,a_{-t})\, f_0(a_{-t}^*) \quad , \tag{4.4a}$$

$$g(t;a^*,a_{-t}) = \int dq dq_{-t}\, A(a^*,q)\, G(t;q,q_{-t})\, A^*(a_{-t}^*,q_{-t}) \ . \tag{4.4b}$$

One may verify that if $G \in \mathcal{S}'\otimes\mathcal{S}'$ (in the dependence on q, q_{-t}), then the r.h.s. of (4.4b) is entire in a^* and in a_{-t}. However, analyticity of the propagators in (4.2) is in general less clear.

A comment about the notation: In sec. 2 the variables q and q_{-t} were related by the flow of the Hamiltonian vector field ξ_H. The same applies to a and a_{-t} (also to a^*, a_{-t}^*) in sec. 3. Here we will also use a_τ to denote the variables that are transformed by ξ_H, e.g. $(1 - t\xi_H): a_0 \to a_{-t}$. In the present section a will be a variable independent of the a_τ. In particular, a and a_0 both refer to the same time, but are independent.

(We note that in general, compositions of the BKS transformations may lead to a discrepancy of phase, $\exp(iN\pi)$, as specified by the Maslov index, cf. [14]. This discrepancy does not arise here, since N is an integer, clearly $N = 0$ for $t = 0$, and N depends continuously on t.)

Let us give two examples of g. The first is the harmonic oscillator with $H_1 = a^*a$ (i.e. $\omega = 1$), cf. (3.2). In this case the Hamiltonian vector field ξ_{H_1} leaves the polarization (∂_a) invariant, and the time evolution is given by

$$e^{-itH_1}: f(a^*) \to e^{-\frac{1}{2}it} f(e^{it}a^*) \quad . \tag{4.5}$$

The factor $e^{-\frac{1}{2}it}$ corresponds to the ground-state energy $\frac{1}{2}$, which is also implied by geometric quantization [2]. We see that, with reference to the previous notation, $f_t = \exp(-\frac{1}{2}it)f_0$, $a_0^* = \exp(it)a_{-t}^*$. The corresponding function g_1 therefore must reduce essentially to a reproducing kernel,

$$g_1(t;a^*,a_{-t}) = e^{-\frac{1}{2}it} \exp(e^{it}a^*a_{-t}) \ . \tag{4.6}$$

Second example, that of a free particle ($V = 0$), is less trivial in the Bargmann-Segal representation. The Hamiltonian here becomes

$$H_0 = p^2/2m = -(4m)^{-1}(a - a^*)^2 \quad . \tag{4.7}$$

Since H_0 involves a^2, ξ_{H_0} does not leave the polarization (∂_a) invariant, and analyticity in $a_{\tau_1}{}^*$ and in $a_{\tau_2}{}^*$ are different notions for $\tau_1 \neq \tau_2$.

Equation (3.19b) shows in fact that

$$a_{\tau_2}^{\ *} = a_{\tau_1}^{\ *} + i(\tau_1 - \tau_2)(2m)^{-1}(a_{\tau_1} - a_{\tau_1}^{\ *}) \quad . \tag{4.8}$$

The function g_0 can be obtained from (4.4), with A given in (3.4c) and with G as implied by (2.13) - (2.14). The calculations can readily carried out with the help of the following formula:

$$\int_{-\infty}^{\infty} du \exp\left[-B(u - v)^2\right]\exp\left[-C(u - w)^2\right] = \pi^{\frac{1}{2}}(B + C)^{-\frac{1}{2}}$$
$$\times \quad \exp\left[-(v - w)^2 BC(B + C)^{-1}\right] \quad . \tag{4.9}$$

One finds

$$g_0(t; a^*, a_{-t}) = (1 + it/2m)^{-\frac{1}{2}} \exp(\tfrac{1}{2}a^{*2} + \tfrac{1}{2}a_{-t}^{\ 2})$$
$$\times \quad \exp\left[-\tfrac{1}{2}(a^* - a_{-t})^2(1 + it/2m)^{-1}\right]. \tag{4.10}$$

Note that g_0 and g_1 are entire in a^* and a_{-t}, of order two or one. Moreover, for $t = 0$ they reduce to $\exp(a^* a_0)$, as required by (4.4a).

We will now make a few remarks relating to the function g.

First. Let us write the Hamiltonian operator H in (4.2) in normal-ordered form ($\hat{a}^*$ to the left of $\hat{a}$). Inparticular, for the above two examples we have

$$\hat{p}^2/2m = -(4m)^{-1}(\hat{a}^{*2} + \hat{a}^2 - 2\hat{a}^*\hat{a} - 1) = H_0(\hat{a}^*, \hat{a}) \ , \tag{4.11a}$$
$$\tfrac{1}{2}(\hat{p}^2 + \hat{q}^2) = \hat{a}^*\hat{a} + \tfrac{1}{2} = H_1(\hat{a}^*, \hat{a}) \quad . \tag{4.11b}$$

Let us also include in (4.2) the normalizing factors $e^{-\frac{1}{2}|b''|^2}$, $e^{-\frac{1}{2}|b'|^2}$. Then the discussion of [6] shows (at least formally) that

$$e^{-\frac{1}{2}|b''|^2 - \frac{1}{2}|b'|^2} g(t; b'', b') =$$
$$= \exp\left\{ i\cdot\tfrac{1}{2}i\left[b''^*(b'' - b') - (b''^* - b'^*)b'\right] - itH(b''^*, b')\right\} +$$
$$+ \ o(t) \quad . \tag{4.12}$$

Here the exponent can be considered as $iS = itL$, with $L = -i(b''\dot{b} - \dot{b}\, b') - H$ and $\dot{b} = (b'' - b')/t$. The Hamiltonian function H is defined by the condition that it have the same functional form as the corresponding normal-ordered operator, e.g. $H = b''^* b' + 1/2$ for the harmonic oscillator.

The relation (4.12) can be readily confirmed for g_0 and g_1. Note that the normalizing factor of g_0, cf. (4.10), satisfies

$$(1 + it/2m)^{-\frac{1}{2}} = e^{-it/4m} + o(t) .$$

<u>Second</u>. In the above we encountered in effect two different interpretations of the functions g: Namely, in (4.2) b'' and b' are indices of the kernel functions k_b, while in (4.4) a^* and a_{-t} are points of the phase space. (The indices can of course be identified with points of the phase space, but nonetheless it is sometimes convenient to make the distinction.) From (4.2) and (4.4) we obtain the following equation, which combines the two interpretations:

$$g(t;b''^*,b') = \int d\mu(a_1)\, d\mu(a_2)\, k_{b''}^*(a_1^*) g(t;a_1^*,a_2) k_{b'}(a_2^*) . \quad (4.13)$$

This last equation applies also to the approximations e^{iS} of (4.12), if $\exp(iS)$ is an entire function of a not-too-fast increase. One is limited by this condition to Hamiltonians which are quadratic in p and q jointly. Moreover, if we approximate g by $\exp(iS)$ in (4.13), then this equation has the following suggestive interpretation: The quantity $\exp(iS)$, evaluated on the index space, is a superposition, or an average, of the quantities $\exp(iS)$ evaluated on the phase space.

We observe also that for such Hamiltonians, with the approximations $g \approx \exp(iS)$, the b-integrations in (4.1) go through directly. Thus as $n \to \infty$, the form (1.1) results.

<u>Third</u>. Let us return to eq. (3.24). If we set $f = k_{b'}$, $\varphi = k_{b''}$ we obtain a different kind of expression for the short-time propagators g. For the case of g_0 and g_1 we have verified agreement to $o(t)$, and we should like to give a few details of the calculation for g_0.

The Lagrangian is

$$L = \tfrac{1}{2}i(a^*\dot{a} - a^{*\cdot}a) - H = -ia^{*\cdot}a + \tfrac{1}{2}i(d/d\tau)(a^*a) - H . \quad (4.14)$$

Here we can identify a with a_0, and we can replace the approximation itL by the exact expression:

$$i\int_{-t}^{0} d\tau\, L = a^{*\cdot}\int_{-t}^{0} d\tau\, a(\tau) - \tfrac{1}{2}(a_0^* a_0) + \tfrac{1}{2}(a_{-t}^* a_{-t}) - itH , \quad (4.15)$$

where we used H = constant, and also (4.8):

$$a^{*\cdot} = \text{const.} = -i(2m)^{-1}(a_0 - a_0^*) . \quad (4.16)$$

The integral of $a(\tau)$ can be done in closed form, but it reduces to $ta_0 + o(t)$. The calculations then proceed easily by expanding $\exp(t..) = 1 + t.. + o(t)$ and by using the reproducing kernel property.

Fourth. In the preceding remarks the action $S = \int d\tau\, L$ had two different meanings. In thethird, the action is the integral along the classical path in phase space, as usual. In the first two, on the other hand, iS was in effect defined by the expression $\{\ldots\}$ of (4.12). Moreover, the arguments of S here are (primarily) the indices b rather than points of the phase space. It appears indeed fortuitous that the normalizing factors $\exp(-|b|^2/2)$ of the k_b combine with the other terms in just the right way to yield an expression resembling a Lagrangian.

One can also say that the function S in (4.12) was evaluated for a straight-line path, but in general this path does not correspond to a classical motion, even approximately. Indeed, there is the difficulty (noted in [4]) that in general there is no classical path joining a_{-t} and a. For the free particle, e.g., one has a classical path only if p = const., i.e. only if $\operatorname{Im} a_{-t} = \operatorname{Im} a$.

An alternative way of expressing the same idea is as follows: The classical action S_{cl} is determined by the time t and by the initial point a_{-t}, so that it is meaningless to speak of S_{cl} as a function $S_{cl}(t; a^*, a_{-t})$. Attempts to force S_{cl} into such a form may lead to anomalies, like the following: For the harmonic oscillator with $H_1 = a^*a$, the implied time evolution is $a \to \exp(-i\tau)a$, $a^* \to \exp(i\tau)a^*$, and

$$S_{cl} = \int_{-t}^{0} d\tau \left[\tfrac{1}{2} i(a^*\dot{a} - \dot{a}^* a) - a^*a\right] = 0 \quad . \tag{4.17}$$

If a_{-t} and a lie along a classical path, then $iS_{cl} = 0$, and this differs from the exponent of g_1 in (4.6).

The two kinds of action are combined in the following equation, which follows form (3.24) and from the approximation $g = \exp(iS) + o(t)$, and whose interpretation is not clear:

$$e^{iS(t;b'',b')} = \int d^2a\, \pi^{-1} e^{-\frac{1}{2}|a|^2}\, e^{-\frac{1}{2}|a_{-t}|^2}\, k_{b''}{}^*(a^*) e^{iS_{cl}(t;a_{-t})}$$
$$\times\ k_{b'}(a_{-t}{}^*)\left[\omega(\eta, \partial_{a^*})/i\right]^{\frac{1}{2}} + o(t) \tag{4.18}$$

Fifth. We now consider the time evolution $f_o \to f_t$, defined by the free Hamiltonian H_o, and without regard to the action. We should like to point out, that we may interpret this evolution as a BKS transform, between functions analytic in $a_{-t}{}^*$ and in a^*, respectively (the two variables being related by (4.8)). This interpretation can be justified e.g. with the help of the chain (4.3a) and the interpretation of $\psi_o \to \psi_t$ as an analogous BKS transform.

The BKS transform for $f_o \to f_t$ is therefore the integral transform defined by the kernel function g_o. For reference we note the extensive study in [15] of similar transforms between analytic

function spaces. This study, however, is by methods independent of geometric quantization.

5. THE ORDERING OF FACTORS AND STOCHASTIC PROPERTIES

The action may contain products of factors whose quantum-mechanical representatives do not commute. Then in the path-integral formulation the corresponding factors have to be ordered chronologically. This problem has been much discussed in literature, but not in conjunction with geometric quantization. We devote the present section to two simple examples which illustrate the ordering problem in the present context.

As a preliminary, let us consider again the case of the q-representation, with a potential $V(q)$, as in sec. 2. In this case the weight $\exp[im(q - q_{-t})^2/2t]$ determines the normalization, and there follows the order-of-magnitude estimate $(q - q_{-t})^2 \sim t$. Therefore, in $\int_{-t}^{0} d\tau\, V(q(\tau))$, the variation of V over $-t \leq \tau \leq 0$ is $O(t^{1/2})$, and the value of the integral differs from $tV(q)$ and from $tV(q_{-t})$ by $O(t^{3/2})$, which is $o(t)$. These rough estimates provide the basis for the approximations made in sec. 2, and also show how to proceed in other situations.

For our first example we take a Hamiltonian modeled on the interaction with a magnetic field, but in one dimension:

$$H = \frac{1}{2}(p - A(q))^2 \quad . \tag{5.1}$$

This Hamiltonian can be reduced to $p^2/2$ by a canonical transformation (in the classical case) or by an unitary one (in the quantum case). Thus this Hamiltonian provides an especially simple example of factor ordering.

The discussion of sec. 2. adapts easily to the above Hamiltonian, and we indicate only the main differences. In the present situation we have

$$\dot{q} = \partial H/\partial p = p - A(q) = \text{const.} = (q - q_{-t})/t \quad . \tag{5.2}$$

In particualr, $\dot{q} = \pm (2H)^{\frac{1}{2}}$, $H = \frac{1}{2}\dot{q}^2$. Also

$$\begin{aligned}((1 - t\xi_H)\psi_0)(p,q) &= (e^{-t\xi_H}\psi_0)(p,q) = \psi_0(q - t[p - A(q)]) \\ &= \psi_0(q_{-t}) \ , \end{aligned} \tag{5.3}$$

$$\begin{aligned}(1 - itP_H^{(1)})\sigma_1 &= (1 + it(\dot{q}p - \tfrac{1}{2}\dot{q}^2))\sigma_1 \\ &= (1 + it[\tfrac{1}{2}\dot{q}^2 - \dot{q}A(q)])\sigma_1 \quad . \end{aligned} \tag{5.4}$$

An integrated form of the last equation is

$$(e^{-itP_H^{(1)}}\sigma_1)(p_o,q_o) = \exp\left[\tfrac{1}{2}it\dot{q}^2 - i\dot{q}\int_{-t}^{o} d\tau\, A(q(\tau))\right]\sigma_1, \quad (5.5)$$

where $(p(\tau),q(\tau))$ follows a classical path, and $p_o = p(0)$, $q_o = q(0)$. (We used here $\dot{q}$ = Const.; cf. the discussion of [2], chap. 7.)

We now make order-of-magnitude estimates such as before. Again we have $(q - q_{-t})^2 \sim t$, $\dot{q} \sim t^{-1/2}$. Thus $\dot{q}\int d\tau A \sim O(t^{1/2})$, in contrast to $\int d\tau V \sim O(t)$ that we had before, and variations in $A(q(\tau))$ can no longer be neglected. However, it is easy to verify (at the formal level) the intuitively expected relation,

$$\dot{q}\int_{-t}^{o} d\tau\, A(q(\tau)) = (q - q_{-t})\frac{1}{2}\left[A(q) + A(q_{-t})\right] + O(t^{\frac{3}{2}}) \quad .(5.6)$$

This form of the ordering prescription is natural, when one constructs the approximations $\int dq_{-t}\,\psi_o(q_{-t})\ldots$ A more familiar form results from replacing $1/2\,[\ldots]$ in (5.6) by $A(\frac{1}{2}(q + q_{-t}))$ [16], [17].

In transcribing (5.6) to the operator language, $(q - q_{-t})/t$ becomes $p/m \sim (im)^{-1}\partial_q$, and factor ordering is determined by chronological ordering, so that (5.6) corresponds to the symmetrized product $(\hat{p}A + A\hat{p})/2$. In order to justify this conclusion in detail, we may replace $q_{-t} = q - u$ and expand in u, so in particular $A(q) = 1 - u\partial_q A + \ldots$ Then $\partial_q A$ can be combined with terms involving $A\partial_q$ to yield the symmetrized product. We also note that the symmetrization rule was obtained in [2], sec.6, for a situation where p^2 does not occur.

Our second example is the free particle, described in terms of the variables a^*,a. The Hamiltonian H_o then contains the product a^*a, cf. (4.10), while the Lagrangian also contains $a^{*\cdot}a$. We expect that again symmetrized products such as in (5.6) will occur, but here detailed evaluations such as in (5.6) can be bypassed, for the following reason: In $a^{*\cdot}a$ symmetrization is not necessary, as it would introduce a correction of $o(t)$, cf. the sentences which follow eq. (4.16). With regard to a^*a, this product occurs in the time-independent Hamiltonian, and the time-dependence of individual terms and their factors need not to be considered separately.

The symmetrization rule, however, continues to apply. One way to check its validity depends on verifying that the Green's function g_o satisfies the following symmetrized Schrödinger equation:

$$-i^{-1}\partial_t \Phi = -(4m)^{-1}(\hat{a} - \hat{a}^*)^2 \Phi$$
$$= -(4m)^{-1}(\partial_a{}^2 + a^{*2} - \partial_{a^*}a^* - a^*\partial_{a^*})\Phi \ . \qquad (5.7)$$

The calculations are straightforward.

It is also instructive to verify that this equation is satisfied by a function f_t given by $\int d\mu(a_{-t})\exp(iS)f_0 + o(t)$, in accordance with eqs. (4.4a), (4.12). In this case symmetrization is assured by the structure of the Hamiltonian in S, i.e. by normal ordering with a compensating term, as in (4.11a).

Let us indicate a few more details. We set $a_{-t} = a - c$, in analogy to $q_{-t} = q - u$ used above, and we expand $f(a^* - c^*)$ and $\exp(iS)$, except for the weight $\exp(-|c|^2)$. In particular,

$$f(a^* - c^*) = f(a^*) - c^*f'(a^*) + \tfrac{1}{2}c^{*2}f''(a^*) -+ \ldots \ . \qquad (5.8)$$

Upon integrating with $d\mu(c)a^*$, only $f(a^*)$ will contribute, and thus a^* acts multiplicatively. (A more concise argument, depending on properties of integrals of harmonic functions, could be given here. See e.g. [18].) The factor a in the integrand, on the other hand, occurs in conjunction with c, and an integration with $d\mu(c)c$ will select the term $c^*f'(a^*)$ from (5.8), etc. We conclude that $a \sim \partial_{a^*}$, and the present argument for this relation differs from that mentioned in sec. 3.

Let us return to order-of-magnitude estimates. We recall the conclusion $(q - q_{-t})^2 \sim t$ for small t. This means (heuristically) that $q - q_{-t} \to 0$ as $t \to 0$, and that the corresponding Feynman integral is over continuous paths. On the other hand, in dealing with the Bargmann-Segal representation we encounter the weight $\exp(-|a - a_{-t}|^2)$, without an explicit t-dependence. Thus $a - a_{-t} \sim 1$, and the paths are not expected to be continuous. An independent argument for non-continuity can in fact be given [19].

REFERENCES

1. D.J. Simms, in: Differential geometrical methods in mathematical physics II—proc., Bonn 1977, edited by K. Bleuler, H.R. Petry, and A. Reetz (Springer-Verlag, Berlin-Heidelberg-New York 1978; Lecture notes in mathematics 676), p.351; in: Feynman path integrals—proc., Marseille 1978, edited by S. Albeverio, Ph. Combe, R. Høegh-Krohn, G. Rideau, M. Sirugue-Collin, M. Sirugue, and R. Stora (Springer, as above, 1979; Lecture notes in physics 106), p. 220; and to be published in other conference proceedings.

2. J. Śniatycki, Geometric quantization and quantum mechanics, to be published.
3. V.N. Popov, Continual integrals in quantum field theory and statistical mechanics (in Russian; Atomizdat, Moscow, 1976).
4. J.R. Klauder, in: Path integrals—proc., Antwerpen 1977, edited by G.J. Papadopoulos and J.T. Devreese (Plenun Press, New York 1978), p.5; Phys. Rev. D 19, 2349 (1979).
5. M. Ciafaloni and E. Onofri, Nucl.Phys. B-151,118 (1979); E. Onofri, in these proceedings.
6. S.S. Schweber, J. Math. Phys. 3, 831 (1962)
7. E. Nelson, J. Math. Phys. 5, 332 (1964)
8. D.J. Simms and N.M.J. Woodhouse, Lectures on geometric quantization (Springer, as in ref. 1, 1976; Lecture notes in physics 53).
9. R.P. Feynman, Rev. Mod. Phys. 20, 367 (1948).
10. V. Bargmann, Comm. Pure Appl. Math. 14, 187 (1961).
11. I.E. Segal, Ill. J. Math. 6, 500 (1962).
12. R.J. Blattner, in: Differential geometrical methods in mathematical physics—proc., Bonn 1975, edited by K. Bleuler and A. Reetz (Springer, as in ref. 1, 1977; Lecture notes in mathematics 570), p. 11.
13. J.H. Rawnsley, Comm. Math. Phys. 58, 1 (1978).
14. J.M. Souriau, in: Group theoretical methods in physics—proc., Nijmegen 1975, edited by A. Janner, T. Janssen, and M. Boon (Springer, as in ref. 1, 1976; Lecture notes in physics 50), p. 117.
15. I. Satake, Adv. in Math. 7, 83 (1971).
16. D.W. McLaughlin and L.S. Schulman, J. Math. Phys. 12, 2520 (1971)
17. W. Garczyński, in these proceedings.
18. I.I. Priwalow, Randeigenschaften analytischer Funktionen, 2nd edition (VEB Deutscher Verlag der Wissenschaften, Berlin, 1956), Teil II.
19. J. Tarski, Acta Phys. Austr. 44, 89 (1976), especially pp. 101 - 102.

TRANSLATIONAL INVARIANCE IN FEYNMAN-TYPE INTEGRALS

Jan Tarski

Institut für Theoretische Physik
Technische Universität Clausthal
3392 Clausthal-Zellerfeld, F.R. Germany

Abstract : Examples are constructed, which show how translational invariance in Feynman-type integrals may be violated. The consequences for the action principle are noted. Furthermore, a new definition of Feynman-type integrals, based on analytic continuation, is suggested.

1. INTRODUCTION

Translational invariance in Feynman-type integrals is one of the basic ingredients in the foundation of the subject. Indeed, the characterization of such integrals as $\int \mathcal{D}(\eta)\ e^{iS(\eta)} \ldots$ is meamingless unless some condition is imposed on the generalized measure $\mathcal{D}(\eta)$, as e.g. $\mathcal{D}(\eta) = \mathcal{D}(\eta+\beta)$. Also, the connection between this invariance and the action principle has been brought forth in a number of heuristic discussions (e.g. in [1]).

In the rigorous approaches to Feynman-type integrals, however, this invariance has often been neglected. Itô was apparently the first to handle this invariance in a satisfactory way [2] . Itô's device depends on using approximating Gaussian measures with arbitrary mean vectors α . This device was subsequently utilized in only a few works. We cite in particular two of our articles, an exposition on Itô's theory [3] and a presentation based on a modified definition [4] .

In [4] the following question was raised : Do there exist examples where the limits defining a Feynman-type integral are indeed dependent on α , so that translational invariance does not hold, or is this invariance a consequence of the other conditions ? (We recall that the limits in question are those as the covariance operator or

the variance parameter $\to \infty$.) We will give examples to show that α-dependent limits in fact exist.

Before describing these examples in detail in the next section, we should like to comment on their significance for the action principle. (See also [1] , [3].)
We consider a Feynman path integral, with translational invariance and with associated expectation values, as follows (the condition $\eta(0)=0$ and the time interval $[0,t]$ are understood :

$$\langle F\rangle = \int \mathcal{D}(\eta)e^{iS(\eta)}F(\eta) = \int \mathcal{D}(\eta)e^{iS(\eta+c\alpha)}F(\eta+c\alpha) \qquad (1)$$

where we wrote the arbitrary vector as $c\alpha$, $c \in R^1$. We apply $D_\alpha := (d/dc)_{c=0}$, and we proceed formally and interchange D_α with Feynman integration. We obtain in this way a special case of the action principle

$$\int\mathcal{D}(\eta)\; e^{iS}\left[i(D_\alpha S)F + D_\alpha F\right] = i\langle(D_\alpha S)F\rangle + \langle D_\alpha F\rangle = 0 \qquad (2)$$

Now, for our counterexample to (2) we take a free particle in one dimension, so that

$$S(\eta) = \frac{1}{2}\, m \int_0^t d\tau(d\eta/d\tau)^2 = \frac{1}{2}\, m \langle\dot\eta,\dot\eta\rangle \qquad (3)$$

and this scalar product and the condition $\eta(0) = 0$ determine the (real) Hilbert space H for integration. Moreover, we let

$$F_0(\eta) = [\exp(-\tfrac{1}{2}im\langle\dot\eta,\dot\phi\rangle^2)\; \varepsilon(\langle\dot\eta,\dot\phi\rangle)]\;\; \delta(y-\eta(t)) \qquad (4)$$

where $\varepsilon(u) = \pm 1$ for $u \gtrless 0$, and where $\phi \in H$ is arbitrary, subject to $\phi(t) = 0$, $\langle\dot\phi,\dot\phi\rangle = 1$. The δ-function in (4) is a usual factor in path integrals for propagators, but this function plays no particular role for us.

We now select an $\alpha \in H$, and the path integral of F_0, or of $F_0(\cdot + c\alpha)$, can be reduced to a one-dimensional integral. The conclusions of sec. 2 then show that, if $\langle\dot\alpha,\dot\phi\rangle \neq 0$,

$$\langle i(D_\alpha S)F_o + D_\alpha F_o\rangle = 2(-im/2\pi)^{1/2}\langle\dot\alpha,\dot\phi\rangle \quad G^{(0)}(t;y,o) \neq 0 \qquad (5)$$

where $G^{(0)}$ is the free-particle propagator. This equation also follows from a formal handling of derivatives in the one-dimensional integral, since the effective action becomes $S = 0$, and $(d/du)\,\varepsilon(u) = 2\delta(u)$.

A systematic way to calculate the path integral in question depends on factorizing it into an integral over the linear span (ϕ) and one over $(\phi)^\perp$. The integral over $(\phi)^\perp$ can be handled as in [2], [3] or in [4], and yields $G^{(0)}$. To determine the integral over (ϕ), we include the convergence factor $\exp(-\frac{1}{2}bu^2)$ and then let $b\to 0$

We conclude this article with an appendix containing a new definition of the (usual) Feynman-type integral. This definition is based on analytic continuation in variance parameters, and it ensures translational invariance.

The author thanks Professor H.D. Doebner for his hospitality at T.U. Clausthal.

2. THE EXAMPLES

In this section we will consider Feynman integrals over R^1. The definitions of the Feynman integral as given in [2] - [4] then reduce to the following : Let $f \in L_1$ (du exp $(-1/2b'u^2)$) for $\forall\, b'>0$, let $b \in C^1$ be such that Re $b>0$, let $\alpha \in R^1$, and we set

$$I^{b,\alpha}(f) = [(b-i\kappa)/2\pi]^{1/2} \int_{-\infty}^{\infty} du\, e^{-\frac{1}{2}b(u-\alpha)^2} e^{\frac{1}{2}i\kappa u^2} f(u), \tag{6a}$$

$$I(f) = \lim_{b\to 0} I^{b,\alpha}(f) \tag{6b}$$

with the provision that the limit be independent of α . Here and below, $b\to 0$ refers to a nontangential limit from the half-plane {Re $b>0$} , cf. [4] , [5] . The parameter κ is a fixed constant satisfying Im $\kappa \geq 0$, $\kappa \neq 0$. The square root is determined by $|\arg(b-i\kappa)^{1/2}| < 1/2\,\pi$. The quantity I(f) is then the Feynman integral of interest.

Obviously every $f \in L_1(du)$ is Feynman-integrable.

Consider now the following function :

$$g_o(u) = \varepsilon(u) e^{-\frac{1}{2}i\kappa u^2} \tag{7}$$

where $\varepsilon(u)$ is as above. We suppose for definiteness that $\alpha>0$, and we observe that

$$I^{b,\alpha}(g_o) = [(b-i\kappa)/2\pi]^{1/2} \int_{-\infty}^{\infty} du\, e^{-\frac{1}{2}b(u-\alpha)^2} \{\varepsilon(u-\alpha) + [\varepsilon(u) - \varepsilon(u-\alpha)]\}$$

$$= 2[(b-i\kappa)/2\pi]^{1/2} \int_0^{\alpha} du\, e^{-\frac{1}{2}b\,(u-\alpha)^2}, \tag{8}$$

since the integral of $\varepsilon(u-\alpha)$ vanishes, and $\varepsilon(u) - \varepsilon(u-\alpha) = 2$ for $0<u<\alpha$, $= 0$ for $u<0$ or $u > \alpha$. Therefore

$$\lim_{b\to 0} I^{b,\alpha}(g_o) = 2\alpha(-i\kappa/2\,\pi)^{1/2} \tag{9}$$

and the provision that the limit be independent of α is not fulfilled.

The preceding example can be put into a slightly more general form. Since changing g_0 on a finite interval amounts to adding to g_0 a function $f_0 \varepsilon L_1(du)$, which is Feynman-integrable, we conclude :

Proposition 1. Let $f \varepsilon L_1(du \exp(-\frac{1}{2}b' u^2))$ for $\forall b'>0$, and we suppose $\exists\, v \geqslant 0$ and $a\, \varepsilon C^1$ such that

$$f(u) = -ae^{-\frac{1}{2}i\kappa u^2} \text{ for } u< -v, \quad = ae^{-\frac{1}{2}i\kappa u^2} \text{ for } u> v . \tag{10a}$$

Then

$$\lim_{b\to 0} I^{b,\alpha}(f) = c(f) + 2\alpha a\,(-i\kappa/2\pi)^{1/2} \tag{10b}$$

where $c(f)$ is a quantity depending on f but not on α.

A more striking example of an α-dependent limit is given by $g_1(u) = u \exp(-\frac{1}{2} i\kappa u^2)$. Here

$$I^{b,\alpha}(g_1) = [(b-i\kappa)/2\pi]^{1/2} \int_{-\infty}^{\infty} du\, e^{-\frac{1}{2} b(u-\alpha)^2} [(u-\alpha) + \alpha] \tag{11}$$
$$= \alpha[(b-i\kappa)/2\pi]^{1/2} \int_{-\infty}^{\infty} du\, e^{-\frac{1}{2}b(u-\alpha)^2}$$

Thus $\lim_{b\to 0} I^{b,\alpha}(g_1) = 0$ for $\alpha = 0$, and the limit is undefined (or infinite) for $\alpha \neq 0$.

It is instructive to interprete these anomalies from the point of view of analyticity. We consider the integrals $I^{b,\alpha}(f)$, and we decompose the convergence factor :

$$e^{-\frac{1}{2}b(u-\alpha)^2} = e^{-\frac{1}{2} bu^2} e^{(b,\alpha)u} e^{-\frac{1}{2}b\alpha^2} . \tag{12}$$

As $b\to 0$, the last factor $\to 1$, and it can be ignored. We see that, in essence, $I^{b,\alpha}(f)$ is a function of the independent variables b and $(b\alpha)$. Moreover, $I^{b,\alpha}(f)$ is (clearly) analytic in {Re b>0} , and for such b's it is entire in $(b\alpha)$. Therefore we may write,

$$I^{b,\alpha}(f)\, [(b-i\kappa)/2\pi]^{-1/2} e^{\frac{1}{2}b\alpha^2} = \phi_0(b) + (b\alpha)\, \phi_1(b) + \ldots . \tag{13}$$

As $b\to 0$, we expect that $I^{b,\alpha}(f) \to (-i\kappa/2\pi)^{1/2}\, \phi_0(0)$, the last quantity being the indicated boundary value. An exception may occur, however, if some ϕ_j's have sufficiently strong singularities at b=0. Let us verify that for $f=g_0$, $\phi_1(b)$ has a simple pole at b=0, while the other ϕ_k do not contribute in the limit :

$$I^{b,\alpha}(g_0)[(b-i\kappa)/2\pi]^{-1/2} e^{\frac{1}{2}b\alpha^2} = \int_{-\infty}^{\infty} du\, e^{-\frac{1}{2}bu^2} \varepsilon(u)\, [1 + (b\alpha)u + \\ + \frac{1}{2}(b\alpha)^2 u^2 \ \ldots\ ] , \tag{14}$$

$$\phi_{2j+1}(b) = 2\int_0^\infty du\, e^{-\frac{1}{2}bu^2} u^{2j+1} = (2/b)^{j+1} j! \tag{14b}$$

and $\phi_{2j}(b)=0$. Therefore $b\alpha\phi_1(b) \to 2\alpha$ as $b\to 0$, while the other ϕ_k yield

$$\Sigma_{k\geq 0, k\neq 1} (k!)^{-1}(b\alpha)^k \phi_k(b) = \tag{15}$$

$$= \Sigma_{j\geq 1} [j!/(2j+1)!] \ (b\alpha)^{2j+1}(2/b)^{j+1} \to 0$$

With the help of the preceding analysis we also obtain :

Proposition 2. Let f be odd, $f \in L_1$ $(du \exp(-\frac{1}{2}b'u^2))$ for $\forall\, b'>0$, and suppose that for some $v\geq 0$, $\delta>0$,

$$|f(u)| \leq (\text{const.})u^{-\delta} \quad \text{whenever } u \geq v. \tag{16}$$

Then f is Feynman-integrable (and obviously $I(f) = 0$).

Note that the function $\varepsilon(u)$ corresponds to the limit $\delta \downarrow 0$.

Proof : We use the expansion (13), and $\phi_{2j} = 0$ as before. The integrals of f over $[-v,v]$ can be ignored since $f \in L_1(du)$ when restricted to this interval. The contribution of the ϕ_{2j+1}, $j\geq 1$, from $(-\infty,-v]$ and $[v,\infty)$ can be majorized by the second sum in (15) times a constant, if $b\alpha > 0$. [Otherwise replace $(b\alpha)$ in this sum by $|b\alpha|$, and $(2/b)$ by $(2/(\text{Re}\, b))$.] Moreover, we may suppose $\delta<1$, and then we can easily majorize the contribution of these infinite intervals to ϕ_1 by $(\text{Re}\, b)^{-1+1/2\delta}$ times a constant.
Thus $b\alpha\, \phi_1(b) \to 0$, independently of α, and it follows also that $I^{b,\alpha}(f) \to 0$.

□

APPENDIX. A DEFINITION BASED ON ANALYTICITY

In discussing the Feynman path integral, a recurring suggestion is to define it as follows : Start with the Wiener integral, establish analyticity in the variance parameter, and continue analytically in the variance to the desired boundary value (e.g. to the imaginary value which is associated with the physical mass). Procedures of this kind can be found for instance in [5] , [6] .

Two objections may be raised against such a definition of the integral. The first is of conceptual nature : One likes to think of the Feynman integral and of quantum theory as having an intrinsic existence, and not merely as analytic continuations of some diffusion processes. The second objection related to the preceding examples : An integral which is defined as we outlined would not be translationally invariant.

We can meet the second objection by employing a more sophisticated continuation procedure. Moreover, the first objection would lose its force if the definition by continuation is intended as an auxiliary definition, which should supplement rather than replace a more direct one.

We suggest therefore the following definition as a supplement to that of [4]. — Let κ be a parameter satisfying $\mathrm{Im}\ \kappa \geq 0$, $\kappa \neq 0$ (as before), let $\mathcal{H}$ be a real Hilbert space, and let $f : \mathcal{H} \to C^1$ be a (sufficiently regular) function under consideration.

Let $b_1, b_2 > 0$, and consider the following (normalized) Gaussian integral of f:

$$\int \mathcal{D}(\xi) \exp\left[-\frac{1}{2}(b_1 + b_2) \langle \xi, \xi \rangle\right] f(\xi) \quad . \tag{17a}$$

This integral can be based on a measure, constructed on a suitable extension of $\mathcal{H}$. We use this measure to define the following function, where $\alpha \in \mathcal{H}$:

$$J(b_1, \alpha, b_2; f) = \int \mathcal{D}(\xi) \exp\left[-\frac{1}{2} b_1 \langle \xi - \alpha, \xi - \alpha \rangle - \frac{1}{2} b_2 \langle \xi, \xi \rangle\right] f(\xi). \tag{17b}$$

<u>Definition 3.</u> Suppose that $J(b_1, \alpha, b_2, f)$ is analytic in (b_1, b_2) when $b_1, b_2 > 0$, and that it can be continued analytically to a region which includes $\{(b_1, b_2): \mathrm{Re}\ b_1 > 0,\ \mathrm{Re}\ b_2 > 0\}$. If the nontangential limit of $J(b_1, \alpha, -i\kappa, f)$ (as $b_1 \to 0$) exists and is independent of α , we call this limit the Feynman integral of f in the sense of analytic continuation (abbreviation : s.a.c.).

We will use here the notation $J(f)$ for the integral just defined, the dependence on κ being suppressed.

The region of analyticity does not need to be as large as specified. However, in the examples which are known from [4] one has analyticity when $\mathrm{Re}\ (b_1 + b_2) > 0$.

Much (perhaps all) of the discussion in [4] could be adapted to the integral J. We confine ourselves here to stating three simple properties of this integral. The first two relate J to the integral I of <u>loc. cit.</u>

<u>Proposition 4</u>. The functions F described in propositions 5-7, 14 and theorem 25, of [4] are Feynman-integrable s.a.c., and for these F's, $J(F) = I(F)$. Furthermore, if $H = H_o + V$ is self-adjoint, and if V is continuous on the complement of a set of capacity zero, then the corresponding Green's function has a representation by a Feynman integral s.a.c.

The second part of this proposition is covered by propositions 15,16 of [4] and their proofs. The ingredients needed for the first part are likewise available in [4] , but they are not localized there in a compact way. —
The functions F in question are the familiar elementary examples : Gaussians, polynomials, etc., also integrands in representation of Green's functions for certain potentials. We recall also, that in case of a general self-adjoint $H_o + V$, with V continuous as prescribed, the corresponding Feynman integral I(f) for the Green's function has not been shown to converge.

<u>Proposition 5.</u> Let dim $\mathcal{H}<\infty$. Then J(f) = I(f), where the existence of either side implies that of the other and the equality.

This proposition follows from the fact that if dim $\mathcal{H}<\infty$, then J(f) and I(f) are both approximated by the same finite-dimensional integrals.

<u>Proposition 6.</u> The integral J is translationally invariant, i.e. : If $\beta\varepsilon\mathcal{H}$ and if F and f_β are related by

$$f_\beta(\xi)\, e^{\frac{1}{2}i\kappa\,\langle\xi,\xi\rangle} = F(\xi-\beta)\, e^{\frac{1}{2}i\kappa\,\langle\xi-\beta,\xi-\beta\rangle} \tag{18}$$

then $J(f_\beta) = J(F)$. Here the existence of either integral J implies the existence of the other and the equality. Furthermore, if $\zeta\varepsilon\mathcal{H}$ and if J(f), $J(\langle\cdot,\zeta\rangle f)$, and $J(D_\zeta f)$ all exist, then

$$i\kappa\, J(\langle\cdot,\zeta\rangle f) + J(D_\zeta f) = 0 \quad . \tag{19}$$

The last equation relates of course to the action principle. Note that J(f) does not occur there, and the hypothesis that J(f) exists can be greatly weakened.
—— The proof can be easily constructed by adapting the proofs of propositions 4 and 11 of [4].

NOTE

After completing this paper, the author learned of the articles of Cameron and Storvick [7], [8], which deal with questions related to translational invariance. In particular, these authors use a definition of the Feynman integral which is essentially lim $J(0,0,b_2,f)$ as $b_2\to -i\kappa$, and they give some sufficient conditions for the equality of the integrals of f_β and F, with reference to eq. (18).

REFERENCES

1. R. P. Feynman and A.R. Hibbs, Quantum mechanics and path integrals (McGraw Hill Book Co., New York etc., 1965), especially sec. 7-2.

2. K. Itô, in : Proc. 5th Berkeley symposium on mathematical statistics and probability, vol. II part I (Univ. California Press, Berkeley, 1966), p. 145.

3. J. Tarski, in : Complex analysis and its applications, vol. III (IAEA, Vienna, 1976), p. 193.

4. J. Tarski, in : Feynman path integrals —proc. , Marseille 1978, edited by S. Albeverio, Ph. Combe, R. Høegh-Krohn, G. Rideau, M. Sirugue-Collin, M. Sirugue, and R. Stora (Springer-Verlag, Berlin-Heidelberg-New York, 1979, Lecture notes in physics 106), p. 254.

5. E. Nelson, J. Math. Phys. 5, 332 (1964).

6. R.H. Cameron, J. anal. Math. 10, 287 (1962).

7. R.H. Cameron and D.A. Storvick, Trans. Amer. Math. Soc. 125, 1 (1966); see also ibid., p. 7.

8. R.H. Cameron and D.A. Storvick, in: Entire functions and related parts of analysis, edited by J. Korevaar, S.S. Chern, L. Ehrenpreis W.H.J. Fuchs, and L.A. Rubel (Amer. Math. Soc., Providence, R.I., 1968; Proc. symposia in pure math., vol. XI), p. 149.

CANONICAL VERSUS FUNCTIONAL METHODS IN QUANTUM MECHANICS AND FIELD THEORY

A.C. Hirshfeld, H. Leschke*, and T. Suzuki

Institut für Physik, der Universität
D-4600 Dortmund 50, West Germany
Department of Physics, Kanazawa University
J-920 Kanazawa, Japan

INTRODUCTION : Some Applications of Functional Integral and Canonical Operator Methods

We list in Table I some of the topics which have been, during the years, treated by both operator and path integral methods.

Remarks:

1) The canonical operator formalism of quantum mechanics was set down by Dirac[11]. Dirac[25] also first proposed the functional integral representation of the propagator. The systematic development of quantum mechanics in this formalism is due to Feynman[1].

2) Schwinger[12] and Feynman[2] used different methods to calculate the Lamb shift in quantum electrodynamics. Feynman's calculation is far simpler, in part because his method maintains Lorentz covariance at every stage. A covariant quantization scheme in the canonical framework was given later by Gupta[13] and Bleuler[14].

3) The attempts to formulate chiral dynamics as a field theory of hadron interactions first focussed the attention of elementary particle theorists on the quantization of nonlinear dynamical systems. Early calculations involving dynamical variables related by a nonlinear transformation yielded different answers, until it was realized that the symmetry with

*Present address : Institut für Theoretische Physik der Universität Düsseldorf, D-4000 Düsseldorf 1, West Germany

TABLE I

	Path Integral Formalism	Canonical Operator Formalism
1) Non-relativistic Quantum mechanics	1948 Feynman[1]	1930 Dirac[11]
2) Quantum Electrodynamics	1949 Feynman[2]	1948 Schwinger[12] 1950 Gupta,[13] Bleuler[14]
3) Chiral Dynamics	1971 Charap,[3] Honerkamp and Meetz,[4] Gerstein, Jackiw, Lee and Weinberg[5]	1972 Suzuki and Hattori,[15] Kvitky and Mouton[16] 1973 Charap[17]
4) Yang-Mills Theory	1967 Faddeev and Popov[6] 1972 Lee and Zinn-Justin,[7] 't Hooft and Veltman[8]	1962 Schwinger[18] 1976 Frey[19] 1978 Kugo and Ojima[20]
5) Soliton Quantization	1975 Gervais, Jevicki and Sakita[9] 1976 Gervais and Jevicki[10]	1975 Tomboulis,[21] Creutz[22] 1977 Baacke and Rothe[23] 1978 Baacke and Koch[24]

respect to such coordinate transformations had not been correctly implemented. In the path integral formalism inclusion of the factor $\sqrt{g}$ (where g is the determinant of the metric tensor) in the invariant functional integration measure lead to consistent results. In the operator formalism it was found that the Lee-Yang term, relating different chronological products, and factor-ordering terms played an essential role. The field-theoretic methods developed in this context later played a key role in the quantization of gauge theories; see e.g. B. Lee[26].

4) The quantization of Yang-Mills theories was made possible by Faddeev and Popov[6], who showed how the constraints arising from the singular nature of the Lagrangian can be incorporated into the quantum theory in the framework of the path integral formalism. This formalism again played an essential role in

Slavnov's derivation[27] of the generalized Ward-Takahashi identities, which express the invariance of the theory with respect to gauge transformations. The program of quantization in the Coulomb gauge in the operator formalism was begun by Schwinger,[28] but because of the cumbersome nature of this method could be completed only recently by Frey[19]. A covariant canonical quantization scheme, generalizing the Gupta-Bleuler method for quantum electrodynamics, was formulated by Kugo and Ojima[20]. J. Kubo[29] has demonstrated that the perturbation expansion for the S-matrix in this formalism agrees with that derived using path integral methods.

5) Soliton quantization involving collective coordinates presented a challenge to theorists' ingenuity. Gervais, Jevicki and Sakita[9] utilized the path integral method to handle the zero frequency modes and the complicated nonlinear Hamiltonian. In the operator approach special care was again necessary with respect to the factor-ordering problem. Gervais and Jevicki[10] called attention to the relation between the factor-ordering problem and the discretization ambiguity of the path integral in this context, and the effect of these on the terms of the perturbation series. The general relation between operator ordering for nonlinear Hamiltonians and the appropriate form of the perturbation expansion was worked out by Leschke, Hirshfeld and Suzuki[30,31] in the canonical formalism, by Langouche, Roekaerts and Tirapegui[32] in the functional integral context.

In the course of the developments outlined above, it became clear that the main advantages of the path integral formalism are (i) the possibility to incorporate constraints in a simple manner, (ii) the direct implementation of the symmetries of the theory. Other good points, such as the convenience of WKB approximations, or the possibility to 'integrate out' some of the dynamical variables (e.g. in the polaron problem), are discussed by other speakers at this meeting. In the light of these advantages, and in view of the many successful applications, and remembering that a rigorous mathematical definition of the path integral for the general case remains to be given, the question arises: how can we justify the use of path integral techniques (in the context of perturbation theory) without recourse to a measure-theoretic definition? The answer to this question is the subject of the following section.

FORMAL MANIPULATION OF FUNCTIONAL INTEGRALS AND THE PERTURBATION EXPANSION

In order to discuss the question raised above in a quantitative manner we set down below three representations of the generating functional of a general system, from which the Green's functions of the theory are derived:

a) Functional Integral Representation:

$$Z[\eta] = \int D\varphi\, e^{i\int dt[\varphi_2(t)\varphi_1(t)-h^0(\varphi(t))+\eta(t)\varphi(t)]}\, e^{-i\int dt\; h^I(\varphi(t))}$$

b) Canonical (Dyson-Wick) Representation:

$$Z[\eta] = e^{-i\int dt\; h^I\left(\frac{\delta}{i\delta\eta(t)}\right)}\, e^{-\frac{i}{2}\int dt\int dt'\eta(t)\Delta(t-t')\eta(t')}$$

$$= e^{\frac{i}{2}\int dt\int dt'\frac{\delta}{\delta\varphi(t)}\Delta(t-t')\frac{\delta}{\delta\varphi(t')}}\, e^{i\int dt[\eta(t)\varphi(t)-\; h^I(\varphi(t))]}\Big|_{\varphi=0}$$

c) Diagrammatic Representation:

$$Z[\eta] = Z[0]+\int \frac{\delta Z[\eta]}{\delta\eta(t)}\Big|_{\eta=0}\eta(t)dt+\frac{1}{2}\int\int\frac{\delta^2 Z[\eta]}{\delta\eta(t)\delta\eta(t')}\Big|_{\eta=0}\eta(t)\eta(t')dtdt'+\ldots$$

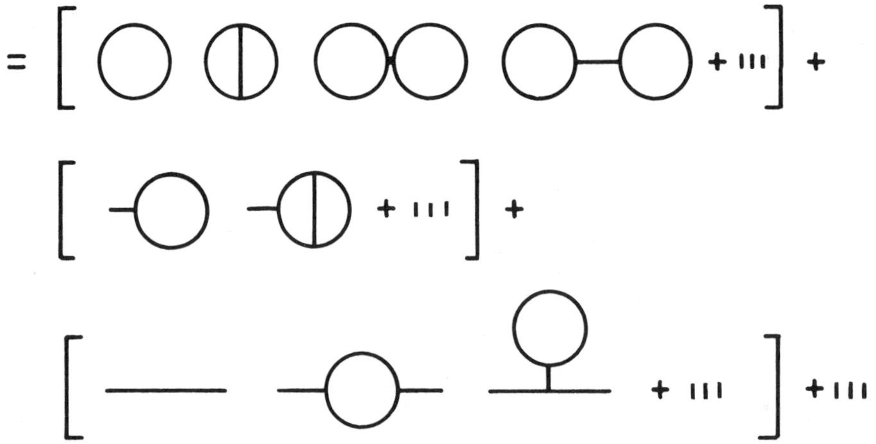

The above expressions are written somewhat schematically: $\varphi(t)\equiv(\varphi_1(t),\ \varphi_2(t))\equiv(q(t),\ p(t))$ is to be understood as a two-component vector, as is $\eta\equiv(\eta_1,\ \eta_2)$, and in (a) the functional integration is over the phase-space variables. $h^0(\varphi)$ is the quadratic part of the Hamiltonian $h^0(\varphi)=\frac{1}{2}\varphi^2$. The time variable t, which is appropiate for quantum mechanics, is to be replaced by (x^0,x^1,x^2,x^3) in the field theoretic context.

The generating functional in the canonical operator formalism is cast into the Dyson-Wick form (b), of which (c) is just a graphical representation, by use of the Wick theorem in the standard fashion. The functional integral form (a) is equivalent to (b) if we assume

i) Functional integration may be interchanged with functional differentiation with respect to the source field: then

$$Z[\eta]=e^{-i\int dt\, h^I\left(\frac{\delta}{i\delta\eta(t)}\right)}\int D\varphi\, e^{i\int dt[\varphi_2(t)\dot{\varphi}_1(t)-\frac{1}{2}\varphi^2(t)+\eta(t)\varphi(t)]}$$

ii) The functional integral satisfies the Gaussian formula:

$$\int D\varphi\, e^{i\int dt[\varphi_2(t)\dot{\varphi}_1(t)-\frac{1}{2}\varphi^2(t)+\eta(t)\varphi(t)]}$$

$$= e^{-\frac{i}{2}\int dt\int dt'\eta(t)\Delta(t-t')\eta(t')}$$

where the symmetric 2x2 propagator matrix $\Delta(t)$ arises as the inverse kernel of the unperturbed action.

From the assumptions (i) and (ii) it is hence obvious that the equivalence of the functional integral representation (a) with the canonical or diagrammatic forms (b) and (c) follows. For the purposes of perturbation theory no further properties of the functional integration symbol are required. Slavnov[33] takes the formula (ii) as the <u>definition</u> of functional integration. One would expect it to be fulfilled in any reasonable measure-theoretic definition of the functional integral.

Alternatively, it is sufficient to assume that the functional integration is a linear operation, which satisfies the integration-by-parts lemma (with neglect of boundary terms). From this it follows that the quantity defined in (a) satisfies the Schwinger functional differential equation, which is characteristic of the generating functional in the canonical formalism (see e.g. Katz[34]). Since it also satisfies the same boundary conditions the equivalence is again established.

From such considerations it becomes clear, as demonstrated in detail by Slavnov[33] and Zinn-Justin,[35] that the usual manipulations performed on functional integrals, such as the change of variables formula used for example in deriving Ward-Takahashi identities, stand in a one-to-one correspondence with manipulations of the perturbation series, and therefore the former are just as rigorous - or non-rigorous - as the latter, independent of the details of a measure-theoretic definition of the path integral. Unfortunately, neither the functional integral formula (a) nor the canonical definition (b) are sufficient to give a well-defined meaning to the terms of the perturbation expansion (c) in the cases of quantum field theory or nonlinear quantum mechanics. In the following section we turn to a discussion of these questions.

PERTURBATION EXPANSIONS AND FUNCTIONAL INTEGRALS IN NONLINEAR QUANTUM MECHANICS AND FIELD THEORY

In the context of quantum field theory it is well known that it is necessary to prescribe a regularization and renormalization procedure in order to assign definite values to the diagrams of the perturbation series, and that such procedures are not unique. In fact a similar ambiguity is already present for the perturbation expansion of a general quantum mechanical system, and this ambiguity has a direct bearing on the correct definition of path integrals in this context. We first describe below the situation in quantum mechanics, and afterwards discuss the comparison to field theory.

In quantum mechanics the root of the ambiguity may be traced back to the indefiniteness of the time-ordering prescription used in the Dyson-Wick expansion for equal-time contractions. That is, this prescription does not give us the values of the propagators

$$\Delta^{\nu\nu'}(t) = -i \langle T\{\Phi_\nu(t)\Phi_{\nu'}(0)\}\rangle \qquad (1)$$

for t=0. We are using here the notation $(\Phi_1,\Phi_2)\equiv(Q,P)$, $\langle\ \rangle$ denotes the expectation value with respect to the ground state of the free Hamiltonian of the system, and the time dependence of the operators is determined by the free Hamiltonian. For some simple systems only the contractions of commuting operators occur in the perturbation expansion; in general also contractions of non-commuting operators occur, in which case we refer to the system as "nonlinear". In this case we see that the closed-loop diagrams in the perturbation expansion (c) of the previous section, and correspondingly the Dyson-Wick representation (b), are not well-defined.

In Ref.30 we showed that if one takes for the equal-time contractions the values

$$\Delta_{\lambda}^{\nu\nu'}(0) \equiv \frac{1}{2i}(\delta_{\nu\nu'} - \lambda_{\nu\nu'}) \tag{2}$$

with $\lambda_{\nu\nu'} = \lambda_{\nu'\nu}$ arbitrary, and correspondingly associates with the interaction Hamiltonian operator the c-number function

$$h_{\lambda}^{I}(\varphi) \equiv \Lambda\left(\frac{\partial}{\partial\varphi_1}, \frac{\partial}{\partial\varphi_2}\right) h_0^{I}(\varphi) \tag{3}$$

where

$$\Lambda(\theta_1,\theta_2) \equiv e^{(1/4)\lambda_{\nu\nu'}\theta_{\nu}\theta_{\nu'}} \tag{4}$$

and $h_0^I(\varphi)$ is the Weyl-Wigner transform of H^I,

$$h_0^I(p,q) \equiv \int_{-\infty}^{\infty} dr\, e^{ipr} \langle q - \frac{r}{2} | H^I | q + \frac{r}{2} \rangle \tag{5}$$

then the generating functional

$$Z[\eta] = e^{\frac{i}{2}\int dt \int dt' \frac{\delta}{\delta\varphi(t)} \Delta_{\lambda}(t-t') \frac{\delta}{\delta\varphi(t')}} e^{i\int dt (\eta(t)\varphi(t) - h_{\lambda}^{I}(\varphi(t)))} \Big|_{\varphi=0} \tag{6}$$

is independent of λ.

The prescription (2) is equivalent to prescribing a <u>time-ordering operation</u> valid for all values of the argument (compare Ref. 31), so that eqs. (1,2) may be written as

$$\Delta_{\lambda}^{\nu\nu'}(t) = - i \langle T_{\lambda}\{\Phi_{\nu}(t)\Phi_{\nu'}(0)\} \rangle \tag{7}$$

Correspondingly, eq.(3) chooses a definite c-number function from the infinite class of such functions which may in principle be chosen to represent a given operator. In a c-number formalism such as the generating functional or functional integral method the reason for the ambiguity may be seen as the non-unique correspondence between the Abelian algebra of c-number observables and the non-Abelian algebra of quantum operators. In an operator formalism it corresponds to the non-unique <u>factor-ordering</u> of the interaction Hamiltonian.

The choice $\lambda_{\nu\nu'}=\delta_{\nu\nu'}$ corresponds to normal -, $\lambda_{\nu\nu'}=0$ to Weyl-ordering.

The λ-ordering described above is the most general scheme which allows a Dyson-Wick expansion with pair contractions. The diagrammatic technique which results for nonlinear systems involves λ-dependent interaction vertices and closed loops, so that individual diagrams are λ-dependent. Their sum is nevertheless prescription-independent.

It is remarkable that the perturbation series as described above, with definite values for the closed-loop graphs, may be obtained directly from the functional integral representations (a) if one uses a λ-dependent lattice definiton of the integral:

$$Z[\eta] = \lim_{N\to\infty} \int d^{(N)}\varphi \; e^{iS_\lambda^{(N)}(\varphi,\eta)} , \tag{8}$$

with

$$d^{(N)}\varphi \equiv \frac{dp_N}{(2\pi)} \prod_{j=1}^{N-1} \frac{dq_j dp_j}{(2\pi)} , \tag{9}$$

and

$$S_\lambda^{(N)} \equiv \sum_{j=1}^{N} \Delta_N \{p_j \frac{q_j - q_{j-1}}{\Delta_N} - h_\lambda(p_j, q_{j-1}, q_j) + \eta_{1j} q_j + \eta_{2j} p_j\} \tag{10}$$

where Δ_N is the (time-) lattice spacing, and

$$h_\lambda(p,q',q) \equiv \Lambda(i\frac{\partial}{\partial \bar{q}}, q'-q) h_\lambda(p,\bar{q}) \Big|_{\bar{q} = \frac{q+q'}{2}} \tag{11}$$

is the "λ-discretization" of the c-number function h_λ associated with the full Hamiltonian $H \equiv H^O + H^I$ via eqs. (3)-(5).

The consistency of the generalized Dyson-Wick formula (6) with the above lattice definition of the functional integral was pointed out by Leschke and Schmutz[36] for a one-parameter class of ordering schemes, the u-ordering ($\lambda_{11} = \lambda_{22} = 0$, $\lambda_{12} = i(1-2u)$, $0 \leq u \leq 1$). The general relation between Dyson-Wick expansions and dis-

cretization prescriptions for the functional integral has been given in the detailed and rather complete investigations by Langouche, Roekaerts and Tirapegui[32]. Within this context Suzuki[37] has shown that the privileged role played by u-ordering for "conventional" phase-space functional integrals is taken over by s-ordering ($\lambda_{11} = \lambda_{12} = s$, $\lambda_{12} = 0$, $-1 \leq s \leq 1$) for coherent-state functional integrals.

The formulas (6) and (8) for the generating functional contain a complete specification of the content of the quantum theory. One may verify, for example, that if the perturbation series is evaluated in terms of new dynamical variables, related to the original ones by a general nonlinear transformation, all expectation values remain invariant: see Ref.31 for an explicit demonstration. In the canonical formalism the correct Feynman rules for evaluating the new series involve vertices which arise from reordering non-commuting terms in the interaction Hamiltonian. All information concerning such "ordering terms" is lost in the formal expressions for the generating functional (a) and (b) of Sec. II. There is no λ-prescription in which all such ordering terms may be neglected. This is the reason that a change of variables in the "naive" expression for the functional integral (a) leads to an incorrect perturbation series in the nonlinear case, as noted by Gervais and Jevicki[10].

The discussion to this point has been concerned with systems with a finite number of degrees of freedom. We now turn to quantum field theory. Here one finds again that the chronological products of the perturbation expansion are prescription dependent: to different prescriptions correspond different interaction Hamiltonians, these differ from each other by so-called counterterms, which in a renormalizable theory are at most of the order of the original terms in the interaction Hamiltonian. The S-matrix is again prescription-independent; see for example G. Clément[38].

However, the amount of freedom available for choosing a prescription in field theory, which assigns a definite value to the chronological products, is larger than in quantum mechanics. For a comparison of field theory and quantum mechanics in this respect, see Suzuki, Hirshfeld and Leschke[39]. In field theory it is indeed possible in many cases to find a procedure which respects the symmetries of the classical theory. In this case the Ward identities for the unrenormalized Green's functions derived, for example, by manipulating the functional integral expression (a) in the manner of Slavnov, remain true for the finite regularized Green's functions. Such a procedure is called an invariant regularization and renormalization procedure.

The dimensional regularization procedure, reviewed by Leibbrandt[40], combined with 't Hooft's minimal subtraction scheme[41] implementing the renormalization, provides for a large class of theories an invariant regularization method. Vladimirov[42] has established the inverse result - a regularization scheme which satisfies the invariance requirements for a maximally large group of symmetry transformations turns out to be essentially identical with the dimensional regularization. That is, the Green's functions in an invariant scheme are the same as those obtained by dimensional regularization up to an immaterial finite renormalization.

OUTLOOK

In quantum mechanics we believe that our considerations provide a framework to which proposed measure-theoretic definitions for the functional integral, which are to be presumed applicable to the general nonlinear case, must conform. In particular, it must be possible to incorporate the multiplicity of possible discretizations, all of which lead to equally valid perturbation expansions, in such a definition.

In field theory renormalizable theories are known, such as those involving fermions and γ_5-matrices, in which dimensional regularization does not provide an invariant regularization scheme. This is because there is no generalization of the γ_5-matrix to n dimensions, which preserves all of the properties it possesses in the 4-dimensional Minkowski space. Hence it was believed that there is no regularization scheme for the Green's functions such that the "naive" Ward identity, generated by performing a chiral transformation on the integration variables of the functional integral, is fulfilled in perturbation theory.

Explicit calculation of the relevant Feynman diagrams shows the Ward identity to be violated because of the presence of the Adler anomaly term. Recently Fujikawa[43] has shown that by using a chiral invariant functional integration measure, calculated via a simple cut-off procedure, the correct Ward identity is generated in a completely natural fashion, including the Adler anomaly term. Roskies[44] has demonstrated that Fujikawa's method yields directly the photon mass due to dynamical symmetry breaking in the exactly soluble Schwinger model for QED in two dimensions. These efforts indicate that, even in theories in which an invariant regularization scheme of the usual kind is not possible, functional integral methods will continue to provide a valuable tool.

REFERENCES

1. R. P. Feynman, Rev. Mod. Phys. 20: 267 (1948).
2. R. P. Feynman, Phys. Rev. 76: 769 (1949).
3. J. M. Charap, Phys. Rev. D3: 1998 (1971).
4. J. Honerkamp and K. Meetz, Phys. Rev. D3: 1996 (1971).
5. I. S. Gerstein, R. Jackiw, B. W. Lee, and S. Weinberg, Phys. Rev. D3: 2486 (1971).
6. L. D. Faddeev and V. N. Popov, Phys. Lett. 25B: 29 (1967).
7. B. W. Lee and J. Zinn-Justin, Phys. Rev. D5: 3121, 3137 (1972).
8. G. 't Hooft and M. Veltmann, Nucl. Phys. B44: 189 (1972).
9. J.-L. Gervais, A. Jevicki, and B. Sakita, Phys. Rev. D12: 1038 (1975).
10. J.-L. Gervais and A. Jevicki, Nucl. Phys., B110: 93 (1976).
11. P. A. M. Dirac, "The Principles of Quantum Mechanics", Clarendon Press, Oxford (1930).
12. J. Schwinger, Phys. Rev. 73: 416 (1948).
13. S. N. Gupta, Proc. Phys. Soc. A63: 681 (1950).
14. K. Bleuler, Helv. Phys. Acta 23: 567 (1950).
15. T. Suzuki and C. Hattori, Prog. Theor. Phys. 47: 1722 (1972).
16. J. S. Kvitky and J. O. Mouton, Prog. Theor. Phys. 48: 1693 (1972).
17. J. M. Charap, Jour. Phys. A6: 393 (1973).
18. J. Schwinger, Phys. Rev. 125: 1043 (1962).
19. H. Frey, Jour. Math. Phys. 17: 322 (1976).
20. T. Kugo and I. Ojima, Phys. Lett. 73B: 459 (1978); Prog. Theor. 60: 1869 (1978) ibid 61: 294, 644 (1979).
21. E. Tomboulis, Phys. Rev. D12: 1678 (1975).
22. M. Creutz, Phys. Rev. D12, 3126 (1975).
23. J. Baacke and H. J. Rothe, Nucl. Phys. B118: 371 (1977).
24. J. Baacke and R. Koch, Nucl. Phys. B135: 304 (1978).
25. P. A. M. Dirac, Phys. Zeitschrift der Sowjetunion 3: Heft 1 (1933).
26. B. W. Lee, "Chiral Dynamics", Gordon and Breach, New York (1972).
27. A. A. Slavnov, Teor. Mat. Fiz. 10: 153 (1972).
28. See Ref. 18.
29. J. Kubo, Diplom Thesis, Dortmund University (1979).
30. H. Leschke, A. C. Hirshfeld, and T. Suzuki, Phys. Lett. 67A: 87 (1978).
31. H. Leschke, A. C. Hirshfeld, and T. Suzuki, Phys. Rev. D18: 2834 (1978).
32. F. Langouche, D. Roekaerts, and E. Tirapegui, Phys. Rev. D20: 419, 433 (1979).

33. A. A. Slavnov, Teor. Mat. Fiz. 22: 177 (1975).
34. A. Katz, "Classical Mechanics, Quantum Mechanics, Field Theory", Academic Press, New York (1972).
35. J. Zinn-Justin, in "Trends in Elementary Particle Theory", Lecture Notes in Physics 37, Springer-Verlag, Berlin-Heidelberg-New York (1975).
36. H. Leschke and M. Schmutz, Zeitschr. für Phys. B27: 85 (1977).
37. T. Suzuki, Kanazawa University preprint DPKU-7905 (1979).
38. G. Clément, Nucl. Phys. B121: 326 (1977).
39. T. Suzuki, A. C. Hirshfeld, and H. Leschke, Prog. Theor. Phys. 63: No. 1 (1980).
40. G. Leibbrandt, Rev. Mod. Phys. 47: 849 (1975).
41. G. 't Hooft, Nucl. Phys. B61: 455 (1973).
42. A. A. Vladimirov, Teor. Mat. Fiz. 35: 392 (1978).
43. K. Fujikawa, Phys. Rev. Lett. 42: 1195 (1979).
44. R. Roskies, University of Pittsburgh preprint Pit-217 (1979).

A STOCHASTIC DESCRIPTION OF TUNNELING IN QUANTUM MECHANICS

E. Etim

Laboratori Nazionali INFN
Frascati, Italy*

Quantum theory and classical probability theory have some structures in common from which the development of quantum theory has sometimes benefited. The best known connection between them is that Euclidean (i.e. imaginary time) quantum theory coincides with the theory of diffusion in real time. Hence by means of the Euclidicity postulate one can transform the characteristic differential equations of probability theory as well as the descriptions in terms of functional intengrals into quantum theory.[1]

The purpose of this lecture is to discuss an interesting area of overlap, namely tunneling phenomena, where the theory of stochastic processes offers some relief in the difficult problem of computing functional determinants.[2] In the standard method of recovering transition probabilities from the functional integral

* Permanent address; presently at Fakultät f. Physik Universität Gesamthochschule Siegen, W.Germany

one comes inevitably against this difficulty. There is in principle a different approach towards the recovery of transition probabilities from the generating functional which avoids Gaussian integrals. It consists in first defining out of the generating functional other functionals (sections) which, besides normalisation, are semi-continuous and positive-definite. These properties are sufficient to activate Böchner's theorem which then allows to obtain the transition probabilities as Fourier transforms of the sections. I will not follow this approach here. Our main observation is that tunneling phenomena in quantum theory, whether ot not one looks at them as transitions associated with instantons and anti-instantons[3] may be modeled by a birth and death counting (Poisson) process. The problem of computing the functional determinant is reduced, via this modeling, to the much simpler problem of finding the average waiting time of the counting process.[2] There is a simple formula connecting the two.

Let us start by considering the description of tunneling in quantum mechanics. From the Schrödinger equation

$$-\frac{\hbar^2}{2m}\frac{d^2\varphi(x)}{dx^2} + V(x)\varphi(x) = E\varphi(x) \qquad (1)$$

one obtains, by introducing the drift velocity

$$T(x) = \frac{\hbar}{m}\frac{d}{dx}\ell n\varphi(x) \qquad (2)$$

the Riccati equation

$$\frac{\hbar}{2}\frac{dT(x)}{dx} + \frac{m}{2}T^2(x) = V(x) - E \qquad (3)$$

The solution of the original Schrödinger equation is now sought by solving (3) by iteration:

$$T_0(x) = \pm \left[\frac{2}{m} (V(x) - E) \right]^{1/2} \tag{4}$$
$$= \pm \frac{i\hbar}{m} k(x) = \pm \frac{\hbar}{m} K(x)$$

K(x) is real where $V(x) > E$ and purely imaginary in those regions where $V(x) < E$. The n-th iterate is

$$T_n(x) = \left(T_0{}^2(x) - \frac{\hbar}{m} \frac{dT_{n-1}(x)}{dx}\right)^{1/2}$$
$$\simeq T_0(x) - \frac{\hbar}{2m} \frac{1}{T_0(x)} \frac{dT_{n-1}(x)}{dx} \tag{5}$$

The first iterate (the negative sign in eq (4) gives a normalisable wave function)

$$T_1(x) \simeq - \frac{\hbar}{m} K(x) - \frac{\hbar}{2m} \frac{d}{dx} m K(x) \tag{6}$$

gives the WKB approximation. Let $\psi(x)$, through eq (2), be the corresponding wave function. One finds the well known result.

$$\psi(x) = \frac{1}{\sqrt{K(x)}} \exp \left(- \int^{x} dyK(y) \right) \tag{7}$$

Contrary to quantum mechanics the theory of stochastic processes invests considerably more attention in the study of the consequences of the zeroth solution $T_0(x)$. It gives the so-called deterministic solution for the velocity, which in the Euclidean space description ($\tau = it$) is given by

$$\frac{dx(\tau)}{d\tau} = T_0(x) \tag{8}$$

$x(\tau)$ will always stand for the classical (i.e. deterministic) path. The reason for the special interest of stochastic mechanics in eq.(8) is that some of the equilibria of the physical system which is being described are the singular points of eq.(8). These are the zeros of $T_o(x)$; i.e. the points $x_n (n=1,2,...)$ with

$$T_o(x_n) = 0; \quad n = 1, 2, \ldots \tag{9}$$

Systems for which eq.(9) defines equilibrium are usually dissipative, dissipation occuring through the drift. The equilibria are absorptive, that is once the system relaxes into any one of these states it remains there indefinitely. Random fluctuations alone cannot drive the system into another equilibrium state. The problem of tunneling does not exist for such systems.

For conservative systems on the other hand, force does more than just impart a velocity; it produces acceleration so that equilibrium is not defined by eq.(9). For these systems equilibria are all orbits of uniform velocity (including zero velocity) i.e. the points x_n (n = 1,2, ...) where

$$\left(\frac{dT_o(x)}{dx}\right)_{x=x_n} = 0, \quad n = 1, 2, \ldots \tag{1o}$$

The absorptive equilibria (those x_n with $T_o(x_n) = 0$ in addition to (1o)) constitute therefore only a subset of all the equilibrium states. Nonabsorptive equilibria are called transients. Random fluctuations

alone can induce transitions between them, even when in Minkowski space - time these transitions are not deterministically possible.
Equilibrium sates which are so related are said to be communicating. Communication is an equivalence relation in the set of transient equilibria. An equivalence class is called a chain. The problem of tunneling in quantum mechanics has thus been transformed into one in stochastic mechanics.

Consider then the chain spanned by a countable number of states labelled by integers (both positive and negative for instance). Transitions in the chain consist then in a time-dependent step-up (birth) and step-down (death) of the integer coordinates. We shall assume that these are Poisson processes. What is the relationship between this description and the solutions of the Riccati equation through which one recovers the description in terms of wave functions? In other words, how does one measure the effect of the random fluctuations responsible for transitions in the chain?

Let $q(\tau)$ be the stochastic process with drift velocity $T(q)$ and diffusion coefficient $\nu = \hbar/2m$ for which the Riccati equation (eq.(3) constitutes the first integral of the action of the corresponding generator

$$(T(x) \frac{d}{dx} + \frac{\hbar}{2m} \frac{d^2}{dx^2}) \; T(x) = \frac{1}{m} \frac{dV(x)}{dx} \tag{11}$$

$q(\tau)$ satisfies the Langevin equation

$$dq(\tau) = T(q) \; d\tau + dw(\tau) \tag{12}$$

where $dw(\tau)$ is a Wiener process.

$$\langle dw(\tau)\rangle = 0$$
$$\langle dw(\tau_2)\, dw(\tau_1)\rangle = \frac{\hbar}{m}\,|\tau_2 - \tau_1| \qquad (13)$$

Any transient equilibrium perturbed by $dw(\tau)$ is rendered unstable after some (random) time. For vanishing diffusion coefficient, that is, for $\hbar \to 0$, the probability for the system to pass from a state $q(\tau_1) = x_1$ to $q(\tau_2) = x_2$ in the time $\tau = \tau_2 - \tau_1$ is measured by the function

$$w(\tau_2, x_2|\tau_1 x_1) = \exp(-E(\tau_2-\tau_1)/\hbar)\cdot$$
$$\cdot \exp\left[-\frac{m}{2\hbar}\int_{\tau_1}^{\tau_2} d\tau \left(\frac{d\acute{q}(\tau)}{d\tau} - T_0(q(\tau)\,\right)\right] \qquad (14)$$

Using eqs (2) and (3) in (14), $w(\tau_2, x_2|\tau_1 x_1)$ becomes

$$w(\tau_2, x_2|\tau_1, x_1) = \frac{\varphi_0(x_2)}{\varphi_0(x_1)}\ \exp\left(-\frac{1}{\hbar}\, S_E(\tau_1, \tau_2)\right) \qquad (15)$$

where $\varphi_0(x)$ is obtained from eq (2) with $T(x) \equiv T_0(x)$ and

$$S_E(\tau_2, \tau_1) = \int_{\tau_1}^{\tau_2} d\tau \left(\frac{m}{2}\left(\frac{dq}{d\tau}\right)^2 + V(q)\right) \qquad (16)$$
$$\equiv \int_{\tau_1}^{\tau_2} d\tau\ H\ (q(\tau), \dot{q}(\tau))$$

is the Euclidean action of the classical problem associated with the Schrödinger Hamiltonian in eq(1). $H\ (q(\tau), \dot{q}(\tau))$ is the corresponding Hamiltonian.

Now the characteristics of the distribution of random times at which transitions occur are those of the Poisson processes in the Markov chain. So let $P_{n,n+1}(\tau)$ be the probability of a birth (B) in time τ $P_{n,n-1}(\tau)$ the probability for death (D) and $P_{n,n}(\tau)$ the probability for permanence in the same state n after time τ . From the assumption that transition processes are Poissonian we have in a short time interval $\Delta\tau$

$$
\begin{aligned}
P_{n,n+1}(\Delta\tau) &= \lambda\Delta\tau + O[(\Delta\tau)^2] \\
P_{n,n-1}(\Delta\tau) &= \lambda\Delta\tau + O[(\Delta\tau)^2] \qquad (17) \\
P_{n,n}(\Delta\tau) &= 1 - 2\lambda\Delta\tau + O[(\Delta\tau)^2]
\end{aligned}
$$

For simplicity we have assumed the same rate λ for both birth and death. Birth and death processes are in competition in activating the chain. The probability for a transition in time τ from a given initial state n to a final state n + N is therefore given by the conditional probability

$$
\begin{aligned}
T_{n,n+N}(\tau) &= \frac{Pr(B(\tau)=n_+, D(\tau)=n_- \mid B(\tau)-D(\tau)=N)}{P_{n,n}(\tau)} \\
&\equiv \sum_{n_-,n_+=0}^{\infty} \delta((n_+-n_-)-N) \cdot \frac{P_{n,n+n_+}(\tau)P_{n,n-n_-}(\tau)}{P_{n,n}(\tau)} \qquad (18)
\end{aligned}
$$

From the integration of eq(17) we have the finite

probabilities

$$P_{n,n+n_+}(\tau) = \frac{(\lambda\tau)^{n_+}}{(n_+)!} e^{-\lambda\tau}$$

$$P_{n,n-n_-}(\tau) = \frac{(\lambda\tau)^{n_-}}{(n_-)!} e^{-\lambda\tau} \tag{19}$$

$$P_{n,n}(\tau) = e^{-2\lambda\tau}$$

Substituting (19) into (18) gives [3]

$$T_{n,n+N}(\tau) = \frac{1}{2\pi}\int_0^{2\pi} d\theta e^{-iN\theta} \exp(\lambda\tau\cos\theta)$$

$$\equiv \frac{1}{2\pi}\int_0^{2\pi} d\theta \langle n+N|\theta\rangle\langle\theta|e^{-H\tau/\hbar}|n\rangle \tag{20}$$

where the Hamiltonian H is the integrand of eq (16). Transitions from the discrete states $|n\rangle$ of the chain into the continuous set of intermediate states $|\theta\rangle$ are given by the matrix elements

$$\langle n+N|\theta\rangle = e^{-i(n+N)\theta}$$

$$\langle\theta|e^{-H\tau/\hbar}|n\rangle = e^{-E(\theta)\tau/\hbar} e^{in\theta} \tag{21}$$

$$E(\theta) = -\hbar\lambda\cos\theta$$

Eq (2o) contains the unknown parameter λ. Its physical meaning is, however, clear from both the point of view of the counting processes and that of the difference in energies between the perturbed states. We will now show how it may be related to a time average over the distribution $w(\tau_2,x_2|\tau_1,x_1)$. To this

end let σ be the first arrival time of the Poisson processes, i.e. the first time a birth or a death occurs. σ is exponentially distributed:

$$f\,(\sigma) \quad = \quad \lambda e^{-\lambda\sigma} \tag{22}$$

The probability for just <u>one</u> transition to occur is therefore proportional to the integral

$$I = \int_0^\infty d\sigma f(\sigma) \int_{\tau_1}^{\tau_1+\sigma} d\tau_2 \, \frac{dq(\tau_2)}{d\tau_2} \, w(\tau_2, q(\tau_2) \,|\, \tau_1, x_1) \tag{23}$$

$$= \int_0^\infty d\sigma f(\sigma) \int_0^\sigma d\tau \, \frac{dq(\tau)}{d\tau} \, w(\tau, q(\tau) \,|\, 0, x_1)$$

The constant of proportionality, N, is given by the normalisation

$$N \int_0^\infty d\tau \, \frac{dq(\tau)}{d\tau} \, w(\tau, q(\tau) \,|\, 0, x_1) = 1 \tag{24}$$

of the total transition probability out of the state x_1. The average waiting time at the state x_1 (i.e. its mean life time) is therefore given by

$$\frac{1}{\lambda} = \frac{\displaystyle\int_0^\infty d\sigma f(\sigma) \int_0^\sigma d\tau \, \tau \, \frac{dq(\tau)}{d\tau} \, w(\tau, q(\tau) \,|\, 0, x_1)}{\displaystyle\int_0^\infty d\tau \, \frac{dq(\tau)}{d\tau} \, w(\tau, q(\tau) \,|\, 0, x_1)} \tag{25}$$

The evaluation of the integrals in eq (25) is well

known; one uses eqs (15) and (16) for $w(\tau, q(\tau) \mid 0, x_1)$ and expands $S_E(\tau, 0)$ about a classical path. The classical path in the time interval $(0,\sigma)$ is just x_1. The mean value theorem is used to simplify the calculation. A Gaussian integral results from the use of eq (13) to replace $[\delta q(\tau)]^2$ by

$$\langle[\delta q(\tau)]^2\rangle = \frac{h}{m}\tau + O(\tau^2) \tag{26}$$

for small τ. The final result is

$$\left(\frac{\delta^2 H}{\delta x^2}\right)^{-1/2} = \left[\det\left(-\frac{md^2}{d\tau^2} + \frac{d^2V(x)}{dx^2}\right)\right]$$

$$= \frac{1}{\lambda}\left(\frac{\pi}{m}\right)^{1/2} e^{-S_E/h} \tag{27}$$

The functional determinant has thus been evaluated without encountering the problem of zero eigenvalues. The exact value of the rate λ is not required. It can be absorbed into a normalisation constant[3]. The reader can easily verify that eq (27) gives the familiar result for the harmonic oscillator. The classical action in this case is found by applying the ergodic theorem

$$S_E(T,0) = \int_0^T d\tau\left[\frac{m}{2}\left(\frac{dq}{d\tau}\right)^2 + \frac{m}{2}\omega^2 q^2\right]$$

$$= m\omega^2 T \lim_{T\to\infty} \frac{1}{T}\int_0^T d\tau\, q^2(\tau)$$

$$= m\omega^2 T \quad \langle q^2 \rangle$$

$$= \frac{\hbar\omega}{2} T \tag{28}$$

Although, we have considered here only the one dimensional Schrödinger equation the extension to more dimensions and to field theory is fairly straight - forward.

References:

1. J.Klauder; Schladming Lectures: Proc. of the 14th International Universitätswochen f. Kernphysik 1975 p. 581, ed. P. Urban

2. This approach was first considered by G. Jona-Lasinio. See University of Rome preprint No. 138, March 1979

3. S.Coleman: Lectures at the 1977 International Summer School "Ettore Majorana", ed. A Zichichi

DEPENDENCE OF THE FEYNMAN PATH INTEGRAL ON DISCRETIZATION

THE CASE OF A SPINLESS PARTICLE IN AN EXTERNAL ELECTROMAGNETIC FIELD

Włodzimierz Garczynski

Institute of Theoretical Physics
University of Wrocław, Poland

I. INTRODUCTION

The transition amplitude $(t,x;s,y)$ i.e., the probability amplitude for finding a particle at the point $X \varepsilon R^3$, at the time instant t, when it is known that at the time $s<t$ the particle was at $y \varepsilon R^3$, satisfies the conditions

$$(i\hbar\,\partial_t - \hat{H})\,(t,x;s,y) = 0$$

$$\lim_{t \downarrow s} (t,x;s,y) = \delta(x-y). \tag{1}$$

The Hamiltonian $\hat{H}$ depends crucially on the ordering of canonical variables $\hat{q},\hat{p}$ if the classical Hamilton functions $H(q,p)$ does depend on the products

$$q^m\,p^n \qquad m,n \geq 1 . \tag{2}$$

This fact we shall denote by attaching to H the index θ representing a given ordering applied when quantizing the theory

$$\hat{H} = H(\hat{q},\hat{p})_\theta \quad . \tag{3}$$

Correspondingly, the transition amplitude should depend on θ as a solution of the Cauchy problem (1). However, it is not a simple matter to see this θ-dependence from the transition amplitude

$$(t,x;s,y)_\theta = \int_{(s,y)}^{(t,x)} \mathcal{D}q\mathcal{D}p\; e^{\,i\int_s^t d\tau[p\dot{q} - H(q,p)]} \tag{4}$$

Here $\mathcal{D}q$ stands for the product

$$\prod_{s}^{t} dq(\tau) \quad , \tag{5}$$

where $q(\tau)$ is a trajectory connecting initial and final points $q(s) = y$, $q(t) = x$. Similarly, the integration $\mathcal{D}p$ is understood as

$$\prod_{s}^{t} dp(\tau) \tag{6}$$

where every $p(\tau)$ varies from $-\infty$ to $+\infty$, as it is symbolically indicated by limits of the integrations. [1]

The whole right hand side of the formula (4) is rather symbolic and formal indeed. The θ-dependence of it is not at all obvious. We shall present another, somewhat more precise expression for the Feynman path integral from which it will be clear how the θ-parameter enters. It is based on some stochastic concepts formulated in terms of probability amplitudes instead of probabilities [2]-[4]

2. STOCHASTIC PSEUDOPROCESSES - THE DANIEL TYPE SCHEME

As it is well known the transition amplitude satisfies the following conditions :

(i) $(t,x;s,y) = (s,y;t,x)^{*}$

(ii) $\lim_{t \downarrow s} (t,x;s,y) = \delta(x-y)$

(iii) $\int_{\mathfrak{X}} (t,x;\tau,z)\,(t,y;\tau,z)^{*} dz = \delta(x-y)$

(iv) $\int_{\mathfrak{X}} (t,x;\tau,z)\,(\tau,z;s,y)\,dz = (t,x;s,y) \quad s \lessgtr \tau \lessgtr t$

(v) $(t,x;s,y)$ - continuous function in $x,y \in \mathfrak{X}$, where $\mathfrak{X}$ is a set of states of a system i.e., $\mathfrak{X} = R^3$ for a single, spinless particle.

The fourth condition can be viewed as the Markov property of an underlying quantum process, (or pseudoprocess), which is analogous to the diffusion process. The conditions (ii) and (v) are also in common with usual processes of diffusion while the conditions (i) and (iii) (time reversiblity and unitarity) are specific.
They presume that the transition amplitude is complex. In fact for the simplest case of a spinless particle with a mass m, moving freely along the line $= R^1$, this is the well known function

$$\langle t,x;s,y\rangle_0 = \left(\frac{2\pi i\hbar(t-s)}{m}\right)^{1/2} \exp\left\{\frac{i\, m(x-y)^2}{2\hbar(t-s)}\right\} \tag{7}$$

One can provide quite a large variety of functions satisfying the conditions (i-v) and also conditions for a process to be diffusional (c.f. e.g. [2])

The differential equations for the transition amplitude may be derived in the same way as the Kolmogorov equations (backward and forward) are derived. The forward differential equation coincides with the Schrödinger equation. This circumstance, and also the fact that the notion of independence of events has the same form in terms of probability amplitudes as in the theory of prbability, hints strongly that some stochastic type scheme, in terms of probability amplitudes, can be developed. There is, however, a stumbling block on the standard way of constructing such a scheme. Namely, the standard construction of a set function corresponding to the transition amplitude (7) leeds to an object with an infinite total variation [5]. Therefore, it is not a measure in contradistinction to the Wiener measure, corresponding to the similar function in which $i.\hbar/m = \lambda$ is replaced by a positive parameter. The standard construction of an integral with respect to this object is not possible.

However, there exists another approach to the integration theory not requiring the existence of a measure. One has in mind the Daniel type scheme in which one deals with a functional, exclusively. Only if a domain of definition of the functional includes indicators of some sets one can find corresponding measures of them as values of the functional on these indicators. Such a scheme was outlined by the author (c.f. e.g. [3]), and we shall present here the most essential elements of it.

Let Ω be a set of elementary events, and $\mathcal{B}(\Omega)$ a selected σ- algebra of subsets of Ω. Let further $\mathcal{X}$ and $\mathcal{B}(\mathcal{X})$ be a set of possible states of a system and selected σ-algebra of its subsets. Let $\mathcal{B}(\Omega)/\mathcal{B}(\mathcal{X})$ be the set of all mappings X,Y,Z,... such that

$$X : \Omega \to \mathcal{X} \tag{8}$$

$$X^{-1}(A) \in \mathcal{B}(\Omega) \qquad \forall \; A \in \mathcal{B}(\mathcal{X})$$

Let finally $\gamma(\Gamma/\Gamma')$ be a subset of $\mathcal{B}(\Omega)/\mathcal{B}(\mathcal{X})$ with $\Gamma \in \mathcal{B}(\Omega)$, $\Gamma' \in \mathcal{B}(\mathcal{X})$, on which some complex valued average operation is defined

$$Q : \gamma \to \mathcal{X} + i\mathcal{X} \tag{9}$$

such that

$$Q\{\lambda X + \mu Y\} = \lambda Q\{X\} + \mu Q\{Y\} \tag{10}$$
$$Q\{X_\Omega\} = Q\{1\} = 1$$

If $X_A(\omega) \in \gamma$ then the probability amplitude $M\{A\}$ of the event A may be defined (χ_A -an indicator of the set $A \in \mathcal{B}(\Omega)$)

$$M\{A\} = Q\{\chi_A\} \tag{11}$$

and its probability

$$P\{A\} = |M\{A\}|^2 . \tag{12}$$

For a simple random variable X i.e. for

$$X(\omega) = \sum_{k=1}^{n} a_k \chi_{A_k}(\omega) , \quad \bigcup_{k=1}^{n} A_k = \Omega , \quad A_k \cap A_\ell = \phi , \; k \neq \ell$$

we have

$$Q\{\chi_A X\} = \sum_{k=1}^{n} a_k M\{A_k \cap A\} \overset{df}{=} \int_A X(\omega) M(d\omega) . \tag{13}$$

We assume, that for any $X \varepsilon \gamma$ (Γ/Γ') there exists a sequence $\{X_n\}$ of simple functions convergent to X in the sense (Q-convergence)

$$\text{(a)} \lim_{n\to\infty} |X_n(\omega) - X(\omega)| = 0, \quad \omega\varepsilon\Omega$$

$$\text{(b)} \lim_{n\to\infty} |Q\{\chi_A(X_n - X)\}| = 0 \tag{14}$$

for any $A\varepsilon\Gamma$.

Therefore, if $X = Q - \lim_{n\to\infty} X_n$ we may write

$$Q\{\chi_A X\} = \lim_{n\to\infty} Q\{\chi_A X_n\} \overset{df}{=} \int_A X(\omega) M(d\omega) . \tag{15}$$

We shall not distinguish two variables X and Y if

$$Q\{\chi_A (X-Y)\} = 0 \text{ for all } A\varepsilon\Gamma. \tag{16}$$

We call them Q-equivalent since they replace each other under the Q-operation sign.
Every random variable X induces another quantum average q_X defined on functions on the space of states $\mathfrak{X}$

$$q_X\{\chi_A f\} = Q\{\chi_{X^{-1}(A)} f \circ X\}, \; A\varepsilon\mathcal{B}(\mathfrak{X}) \tag{17}$$

or

$$\int_A f(x)\, m_X(dx) = \int_{X^{-1}(A)} f \circ X(\omega)\, M(d\omega)$$

$$m_X(dx) = M\{X\varepsilon[x, x + dx]\} = Q\{\chi_{X\varepsilon[x,x+dx]}\} . \tag{18}$$

We also assume that for any $X \varepsilon \gamma(\Gamma/\Gamma')$ and every σ-algebra $\mathcal{C} \subseteq \Gamma$ there exists a variable

$$Y \overset{df}{=} Q\{X|\mathcal{C}\} \ \varepsilon\ \gamma\ (\mathcal{C}/\Gamma') \quad \text{such that}$$

$$Q\ \{\chi_A(X-Y)\} = 0 \text{ for any } A \varepsilon \mathcal{C} \tag{19}$$

$$= Q\{\chi_A(X-Q\{X|\mathcal{C}\})\}\ .$$

It is called the conditional quantum average of X with respect to the σ-algebra $\mathcal{C} \subset \Gamma$. The quantum conditional averages enjoy the same main properties as the classical conditional average operations.

We say that random variables X and Y are conditionally independent with respect to a σ-algebra $\mathcal{C}$ if

$$Q\{XY|\mathcal{C}\} = Q\{X|\mathcal{C}\}\ Q\{Y|\mathcal{C}\}. \tag{20}$$

The necessary and sufficient condition for this is the equality

$$Q\{X|\mathcal{C}\ ,Y\} = Q\{X|\mathcal{C}\} \tag{21}$$

where $\mathcal{C}$,Y conditioning means a conditioning on a minimal σ-algebra generated by $\mathcal{C}$ and events $Y^{-1}(A)$, $A\ \varepsilon \mathcal{B}(\mathcal{X})$, together.
In particular, the conditional quantum average

$$Q\{X|Z\} \equiv Q\{X|\sigma\{Z\}\} = F \circ Z \tag{22}$$

is a Borel function F of the variable Z. Here

$$\sigma\{Z\} = \sigma\ \{Z^{-1}(A)\ ;\ A \varepsilon\ \mathcal{B}(\mathcal{X})\} \tag{23}$$

is a minimal σ-algebra generated by variable Z.

We say that a process

$$X = \{X(t);\ t \varepsilon T\}$$

$$X(t) : \Omega \rightarrow \mathcal{X}\ ,\ \forall\ t\ \varepsilon T \tag{24}$$

$$X(t) \varepsilon\ \gamma\ (\Gamma/\Gamma')$$

is Markovian if the following equalities hold

$$Q_{s,y}\ \{f \circ X(t)|F_\tau\} = Q_{\tau,X(\tau)}\ \{f \circ X(t)\} \tag{25}$$

$$Q^{t,x}\ \{g \circ X(s)|\ G_\tau\} = Q^{\tau,X(\tau)}\{g \circ X(s)\} \qquad s< \tau<t\ . \tag{26}$$

Here $F_\tau = \sigma\{X(s),\ s \leqslant \tau\}$ -a history of the process up to the time τ, $F_{\tau'} \supset F_\tau \quad \tau' > \tau$.

$G_\tau = \sigma\{X(t);\ t \geqslant \tau$ - a future of the process from the time τ and further , $G_{\tau'} \subset G_\tau$, $\tau' > \tau$

$$
\begin{aligned}
Q_{s,X(s)}\{\ldots\ldots\} &= Q\ \{\ldots\ldots\ |X(s)\} \\
Q^{t,X(t)}\{\ldots\ldots\} &= Q\ \{\ldots\ldots\ |X(t)\}\ .
\end{aligned}
\tag{27}
$$

The Markovian requirements (25), (26) mean that the history and the future of a process are conditionally independent with respect to the present time.
Introducing the transition amplitudes

$$
\begin{aligned}
M_{s,y}\{X(t)\,\varepsilon A\} &= (t,A;s,y] = Q_{s,y}\{\chi_A \circ X(t)\} \\
M^{t,x}\{X(s)\,\varepsilon B\} &= [t,x;s,B) = Q^{t,x}\{\chi_B \circ X(s)\}
\end{aligned}
\tag{28}
$$

and assuming that they do have densities

$$
\begin{aligned}
(t,A;s,y] &= \int_A dx\ (t,x;s,y] \\
[t,x;s,B) &= \int_B dy\ [t,x;s,y)
\end{aligned}
\tag{29}
$$

one obtains Chapman-Kolmogorov equations from (25) and (26), respectively

$$
\begin{aligned}
(t,x;s,y] &= \int_{\mathcal{X}} dz\ (t,x;\tau,z]\ (\tau,z;s,y] \\
[t,x;s,y) &= \int_{\mathcal{X}} dz\ [t,x;\tau,z)\ [\tau,z;s,y)\ .
\end{aligned}
\qquad s < \tau < t
\tag{30}
$$

The straight brackets indicate the place where conditioning was applied (at initial or at final states).
For the reversible processes one has

$$
(t,x;s,y] = [t,x;s,y) = (t,x;s,y)\ . \tag{31}
$$

Using the relations

$$
Q_{s,y}\{f \circ X(t)\} = \int_{\mathcal{X}} dx\ f(x)\ (t,x;s,y) = \varphi\ (s,y) \tag{32}
$$

$$
Q^{t,x}\{g \circ X(s)\} = \int_{\mathcal{X}} dy\ g(y)\ (t,x;s,y) = \psi\ (t,x) \tag{33}
$$

one may translate the conditions (i-v), for the transition amplitudes in corresponding properties of the conditional quantum averages. The Markov character of the process permits the extension of these relations to the following basic formulae :

$$Q_{s,y}\{\prod_{k=1}^{n} f_k \circ X(t_k)\} = \underset{\ast}{\int} dy_1 \;....\; \underset{\ast}{\int} dy_n \; f_1(y_1) \;....f_n(y_n)\cdot$$
$$\cdot(t_n,y_n;t_{n-1},y_{n-1}) \;.....\; (t_1,y_1;s,y) \tag{34}$$

and

$$Q^{t,x}\{\prod_{k=1}^{n} g_k \circ X(t_k)\} = \underset{\ast}{\int} dx_n \;....\; \underset{\ast}{\int} dx_1 \; g_1(x_1) \;....g_n(x_n)\cdot$$
$$\cdot(t,x;t_n,x_n) \;....\; (t_2,x_2;t_1,x_1) \text{ for } s < t_1 < \;.....< t_n < t. \tag{35}$$

These formulae permit to express the averaging operations $Q_{s,y}$ and $Q^{t,x}$ by the transition amplitude, which is a familiar object.

EXAMPLE : QUANTUM BROWNIAN MOTION (WIENER PSEUDOPROCESS)

A process Z(t) is called the quantum Brownian motion on a line if

1° $Z(t)\varepsilon R$ for all $t\varepsilon[0,\infty)$, $Z(0) = 0$

$$Q\{Z(t)\} = 0,\; Q\{Z^2(t)\} = \lambda t \;,\quad \lambda = i\,\frac{\hbar}{m} \tag{36}$$

2° Z(t) has independent increments in disjoint time intervals

3° Z(t) is stationary and its transition amplitude is

$$M\,\{Z(\tau)\varepsilon[a,b]\} = \int_a^b dx\;(\tau,x;0,0)_0$$
$$(\tau,x;0,0)_0 = (2\,\pi\lambda\tau\,)^{-1/2} \exp\,(-\,\frac{x^2}{2\lambda\tau}\,). \tag{37}$$

The property (36) gives rise to a new phenomenon, a mixing of

$$(\Delta Z)^2 = [Z(t_1) - Z(t_2)]^2 \quad \text{with } \lambda\,(t_1 - t_2)$$

under the Q-operation sign ! This is the place where the θ-dependence occurs.
Namely, if we define the following Q-limit

$$Q\text{-}\lim_{n\to\infty} \sum_{k=0}^{n-1} f\,[t_k,\, \theta X(t_k) + \mu X(t_{k+1})]\,[Z(t_{k+1}) - Z(t_k)]$$

$$\overset{df}{=} \int_a^b f[t,x(t)]\; d_\theta Z(t) \;,\; \theta + \mu = 1 \;,\; \theta,\mu \geqslant 0 \tag{38}$$

which is called the stochastic θ-integral of $f[t,x(t)]$ with respect to the Brownian process Z, then it does depend in general on a choice of θ-parameter.

Namely, if X(t) is a solution of the integral stochastic equations

$$X_k(t) = X_k(s) + \int_s^t d\tau\, a_k[\tau, X(\tau)] + \int_s^t \sigma_k^{\ i}[\tau, X(\tau)]\ d_\theta Z_i(\tau) \qquad (39)$$
$$k = 1,2,3\ ,\ X(t) \varepsilon\ R^3$$

then the following (Itô) formulae hold

$$\int_s^t \sigma_k^i[\tau, X(\tau)]\ d_{\theta_1} Z_i(\tau) - \int_s^t \sigma_k^{\ i}[\tau, X(\tau)]\ d_{\theta_2} Z_i(\tau) = \qquad (40)$$
$$= \lambda(\theta_2 - \theta_1) \int_s^t \sigma_j^i[\tau, X(\tau)]\ \partial^j \sigma_k^i[\tau, X(\tau)]\ d\tau$$

$$v[t, X(t)] - v[s, X(s)] \overset{Q}{=} \int_s^t d\tau\ [\partial_\tau + a_k \partial^k + \tfrac{1}{2}\lambda\ (2\theta - 1)\ \sigma_j^i \partial^j \sigma_k^i] v$$
$$+ \int \sigma_k^i \partial^k v\ \ dZ. \qquad (41)$$

Simplification occurs for θ= 1/2 (mid-point or Stratonovich integral [6])

$$v(t) - v(s) \overset{Q}{=} \int_s^t d\tau\ (\partial_\tau + a_k \partial^k)\ v(\tau) + \int_s^t \sigma_k^i \partial^k v\ dZ_{1/2}\ . \qquad (42)$$

For convenience we shall omit the subindex 1/2 for the midpoint integral, and we shall write R for θ= 0 and L for θ= 1 (right and left integrals respectively)

$$d_{1/2}Z = dZ$$
$$d_{\theta=0}Z = d_R Z \qquad (43)$$
$$d_{\theta=1}Z = d_L Z\ .$$

Solutions to the stochastic equation (39) are diffusion processes i.e. the following limits exist

$$\lim_{t \downarrow s} (t-s)^{-1}\ Q_{s,y}\{x_k(t) - y_k\} = \lim_{t \downarrow s} (t-s)^{-1} \int (x_k - y_k)\ \text{Ӿ}(t,x;s,y)dx =$$
$$= a_k(s,y) \qquad (44)$$

$$\lim_{t\downarrow s} (t-s)^{-1} Q_{s,y}\{[x_k(t)-y_k][x_j(t)-y_j]\} = \lim_{t\downarrow s} (t-s)^{-1} \int_{\mathcal{X}} (x_k-y_k)\,\cdot$$

$$\cdot (x_j-y_j)\ (t,x;s,y)\ dx = \lambda\ \sigma_k{}^i\ (s,y)\sigma_j{}^i(s,y)$$

and higher moments vanish in this limit.

The functions

$$\varphi\ (s,y) = Q_{s,y}\{f[t,x(t)]\ \exp\int_s^t C[\tau,x(\tau)]\ d\tau\ \} \qquad (45)$$

$$\psi\ (t,x) = Q^{t,x}\{g[s,x(s)]\ \exp\int_s^t C[\tau,x(\tau)]\ d\tau\ \} \qquad (46)$$

solve the following Cauchy problems

$$\left.\begin{aligned} &(\partial_s + a_k\partial^k + \frac{\lambda}{2}\ \sigma_j^i\partial^j\sigma_k{}^i\partial^k + C)\ \varphi(s,y) = 0 \\ &\varphi(t-0,y) = f(t,y) \end{aligned}\right\} \qquad (47)$$

$$\left.\begin{aligned} &(-\partial_t - \partial^k a_k + \frac{\lambda}{2}\ \partial^k\sigma_k{}^i\partial^j\sigma_j^i + C)\ \psi(t,x) = 0 \\ &\psi\ (s+0,x) = g(s,x). \end{aligned}\right\} \qquad (48)$$

Since they are Schrödinger equation for the backward and the forward wave functions respectively, the formulae (45) and (46) give the meaning to the Feynman path integrals representing those solutions. Let's illustrate it on the simplest example:

Let $\mathcal{X} = R$, $a = 0, \sigma = 1$, $x(s) = z(s)$ (49)

then $x(t) = z(t)$ $\quad t > s$ (50)

and $(t,x;s,y) = [2\pi\lambda\ (t-s)]^{-1/2}\ \exp\{-\frac{(y-x)^2}{2\lambda(t-s)}\} = (t,x;s,y)_0$.

The backward wave function may be written as follows

$$\varphi(s,y) = Q_{s,y}\{f[t,z(t)]\ \exp\int_s^t\ C[\tau,z(\tau)]\ d\tau\ \} = \qquad (51)$$

$$= \lim_{n\to\infty} Q_{s,y}\{f[t,z(t)]\ \exp\sum_{k=0}^{n-1}\ C[\tau_k,z(\tau_k)]\ \frac{t-s}{n}\ \}\ ,$$

$$\tau_k = s + k\,\frac{t-s}{n} \qquad k = 0,1,\ \ldots.,\ n.$$

Now, using the basic formula (34) we get

$$\varphi(s,y) = \lim_{n\to\infty} \int_{-\infty}^{\infty} dy_1 \ldots. \int_{-\infty}^{\infty} dy_n f(t,y_n)\ \exp\ [\sum_{k=0}^{n-1} \mathbf{C}(\tau_k,y_k)\ \frac{t-s}{n}]\cdot$$

$$\cdot(t,x;\tau_{n-1},y_{n-1})_0 \ldots.. (\tau_1,y_1;\ s,y)_0 = 0\ . \qquad (52)$$

Substituting the transition amplitude (50) we get

$$\varphi(s,y) = \lim_{n\to\infty} \int_{-\infty}^{\infty} \frac{dy_1}{A} \cdots\cdots \int_{-\infty}^{\infty} \frac{dy_n}{A} f(t,y_n) \exp\{\frac{i}{\hbar} \sum_{k=0}^{n-1} [\frac{m}{2} (\frac{y_{k+1}-y_k}{\Delta\tau})^2 - V(\tau_k,y_k)]\}\Big|_{y_0=y} = \tag{53}$$

$$= \int_{C[X(s)=y]} \mathcal{D}X\, f[t,X(t)] \exp \frac{i}{\hbar} \int_s^t d\tau \quad (\frac{m}{2}[\dot{X}(\tau)]^2 - V[\tau,X(\tau)])$$

where $\{X(\tau)\ ,\ \tau\varepsilon[s,t]\}$ is a path starting at the point y for $\tau = s$ and $C[X(s) = y]$ is the set of all continuous paths starting at $\tau = s$ from the point y,

$$A = (2\pi\lambda\Delta\tau\ )^{1/2}\ ,\quad \Delta\tau = \frac{t-s}{n} \qquad V = i\,\hbar C. \tag{54}$$

In this case we have no problem with the θ-dependence since there is no mixing term in the Lagrangian. The ordering problem in the canonical formulation is absent in this case. In general, however, the θ-parameter enters the Feynman integral, and its fixing corresponds to the fixing of some ordering of the canonical variables in a Hamiltonian.
Fixing the θ-parameter determines the rule of chosing interval points under the Riemannian sum for the stochastic integral [c.f. (38)] , and this in turn determines the structure of the discrete approximation to the path integral [c.f. a passage between (51) and (52)]. Therefore, fixing the θ-parameter is equivalent to the fixing of some discretization of the path integral. Hence, a given discretization corresponds to a given ordering of canonical variables in the operator formulation of Quantum Mechanics [7] . We shall demonstrate this on the example of a charged particle moving in an external electromagnetic field where we can give a complete discussion of the θ-dependence of the Feynman integral, [8] .

EXAMPLE : A PARTICLE IN AN EXTERNAL ELECTROMAGNETIC FIELD

Consider the wave functions

$$\varphi(s,y) = Q_{s,y}\{f[t,X(t)] \exp[\int_s^t C d\tau + \int_s^t \sigma_k{}^j e^k dZ_j]\} \tag{55}$$

and

$$\psi(t,x) = Q^{t,x}\{g[s,X(s)] \exp[\int_s^t C d\tau + \int_s^t \sigma_k{}^j e^k dZ_j]\} \tag{56}$$

where

$$e^k = \frac{iq}{\hbar c} A^k \tag{57}$$

$$C = C[0] - \frac{iq}{\hbar c} A^0 + \frac{iq}{\hbar c} a_k A^k$$

A^0, A^k electromagnetic potentials

q the electric charge of a particle

$C[0]$ a potential energy of other then electromagnetic interactions.

The functions φ and ψ satisfy the following Cauchy problems for the Schrödinger equations.

$$[\partial_s + a_k(\partial^k + e^k) + \frac{\lambda}{2} \sigma_j{}^{\ell}(\partial^j + e^j) \sigma_k{}^{\ell}(\partial^k + e^k) + C - a_k e^k] \cdot \varphi(s,y = 0) \tag{58}$$

$$\cdot \varphi(s = t-0,y) = f(t,y)$$

$$[- \partial_t - (\partial^k - e^k) a_k + \frac{\lambda}{2} (\partial^k - e^k) \sigma_k{}^{\ell}(\partial^j - e^j) \sigma_j{}^{\ell} + C - a_k e^k] \cdot \psi(t,x = 0)$$

$$\cdot \psi(t = s + 0, X) = g(s,x). \tag{59}$$

Notice that the mid-point prescription is used here, and at this choice of θ the coefficient $C[0]$ is identified with out potential. (More exactly $V = i\hbar C[0]$)

Upon the gauge transformation

$$A^k \to A^k + \partial^k \Lambda \, , \; A^0 \to A^0 - \partial^0 \Lambda \tag{60}$$

the following extra term appears under the exponents in (55), (56)

$$\int_s^t d\tau(\partial_\tau + a_k \partial^k)\Lambda + \int_s^t \sigma_k{}^j \partial^k \Lambda dZ_j \overset{Q}{=} \Lambda[t,X(t)] - \Lambda[s,X(s)]. \tag{61}$$

The last Q-equivalence follows from the formula (42). Therefore, the wave functions transform properly under this gauge transformation

$$\begin{aligned} \psi(t,x) &\to \psi(t,x) \exp\{\frac{iq}{\hbar c} \Lambda(t,x)\} \\ \varphi(s,y) &\to \varphi(s,y) \exp\{-\frac{iq}{\hbar c} \Lambda(s,y)\} \end{aligned} \tag{62}$$

and so the transition amplitude

$$(t,x;s,y)_{A'} = (t,x;s,y)_A \exp \frac{iq}{\hbar c} [\Lambda(t,x) - \Lambda(s,y)] \tag{63}$$

$$A^{k'} = A^k + \partial^k\Lambda$$

$$A^{o'} = A^o - \partial^o\Lambda$$

where

$$(t,x;s,y)_A = Q\Big(\delta\,[X(t)-x]\delta[X(s)-y] \exp \{ \int_s^t [C[0] + \frac{iq}{\hbar c} \cdot$$

$$\cdot (-A^o + a_k A^k)]\, d\tau + \frac{iq}{\hbar c} \int_s^t \sigma_k{}^j A^k dZ_j \}\Big). \tag{64}$$

If one wishes to switch from the mid-point prescription (corresponding to the Weyl ordering in canonical formulation) to some other θ-rule one should use the formula (40) which reeds in this case

$$\int_s^t \sigma_k{}^j A^k dZ_j = \int_s^t \sigma_k{}^j A^k d_\theta Z_j + \lambda(\theta - \frac{1}{2}) \int_s^t \sigma_j{}^i \partial^j \sigma_k{}^i A^k d\tau . \tag{65}$$

Therefore, if one corrects the potential $C[0]$ by the term depending on θ

$$C[0] \to C_\theta[0] = C[0] + \frac{q}{mc} (\frac{1}{2} - \theta)\ \sigma_j^i \partial^j \sigma_k^i A^k \tag{66}$$

the integral will not change. Passage from one discretization to another is harmless if we correct the interaction adding relevant compensating terms. Otherwise, omitting corection terms will result in θ-dependence of a path integral i.e. on the way of computing it by means of various discretization procedures, which is certainly wrong. A path integral remembers only its initial factor ordering when the potential is identified. In our case it was the mid-point discretization. Further changes of discretizations should be followed by including correcting terms to the potential in order to get meamingful results.

In the particular case we are considering here some simplification is possible by chosing a special gauge. Namely if we impose the condition on A^k

$$\sigma_j{}^\ell \partial^j \sigma_k^\ell A^k = 0 \tag{67}$$

then the correcting term vanishes and any discretization procedure will give the same unique answer for the path integral. This gauge reduces to the Coulomb gauge for the case of a constant diffusion coefficient (flat space)

$$\sigma_j{}^\ell = \delta_j{}^\ell , \quad \partial^k A^k = 0, \tag{68}$$

and goes over to the Lorentz gauge for the relativistic particle moving in an external electromagnetic field [9]. Incidently, the last case was first tackled by Feynman who got the right answer without using the mid-point stochastic integrals. Instead he used under the exponent sign the expression which goes after the discretization into the sum

$$\sum_{k=0}^{n-1} \frac{1}{2} [A_\mu (t_k, Z_k) + A_\mu (t_{k+1}, Z_{k+1})] \Delta Z^\mu \tag{69}$$

which is different from the mid-point prescription enforcing us to use the following sum

$$\sum_{k=0}^{n-1} A_\mu \left(t_k, \frac{Z_k + Z_{k+1}}{2}\right) \Delta Z^\mu . \tag{70}$$

In fact both expressions lead to the gauge invariant results and, what is more important here, to the same one. The reason is that they are in fact Q-equivalent random variables.
This follows from the following general relations between various stochastic integrals

$$\begin{aligned} \int_s^t f dZ &\overset{Q}{=} \int_s^t f d_L Z + \frac{\lambda}{2} \int_s^t \sigma \partial f \quad d\tau \\ \int_s^t f dZ &\overset{Q}{=} \int_s^t f d_R Z - \frac{\lambda}{2} \int_s^t \sigma \partial f \quad d\tau \overset{Q}{=} \int_s^t f \frac{1}{2} (d_L Z + d_R Z). \end{aligned} \tag{71}$$

The question of the dependence of the Feynman path integrals on their discretizations has attracted recently a great deal of attention [10] - [17] . Parallel, and equivalent, work was done also, in the canonical framework, on the so called ordering problem of noncommuting variables. Most of this work concentrates, however, on the case with mixing term lineair in $\hat{p}$ (in the Hamiltonian), out of which the case of a particle moving in an external electromagnetic field is the most interesting. Real novelty comes from the consideration of the problem in a curved space, when the diffusion coefficient is a function of space point (c.f. e.g. [16]).

ACKNOWLEDGMENTS

It is a pleasure to thank the Organizing Committee for the kind invitation to this workshop, and for the hospitality which I experienced here. In particular I shall thank Professor J.P. Antoine and F. Langouche and D. Roekaerts for their help in various situations.

REFERENCES

[1] R.F. Feynman and A.R. Hibbs, "Quantum Mechanics and Path Integrals", Mc Graw-Hill, New York 1965

[2] W. Garczynski, Quantum Mechanics as a Quantum Markovian Process, Acta Phys. Polon.,35 (1969) 479

[3] W. Garczynski, Quantum Stochastic Processes and the Feynman Path Integral for a Spinless Particle, Reports on Math. Phys. 4 (1973) 21

[4] W. Garczynski, Stochastic Pseudoprocesses and Quantum Theory, Proceedings of the XII-th Winter School of Theoretical Physics in Karpacz, Vol. 1, 241-325.
Acta Universitatis Wratislavienses nr. 368, Wroclaw 1976

[5] R. H. Cameron, A Family of Integrals Serving to Connect the Wiener and Feynman Integrals, Journ. Math. and Phys. 39 (1960) 126

[6] R. L. Stratonovich, "Conditional Markovian Processes and their Applications to the Theory of Optimization" (in Russian) University Press, Moscow 1966

[7] F.A. Berezin,"Nonwiener Continual Integrals"(in Russian) Teor. Math. Phys. 6 (1971), 194

[8] W. Garczynski, On Alternative Ways of Including of an External Electromagnetic Field, Bull. Acad. Polon. Sci., CL. III, 21 (1973), 355

[9] W. Garczynski, Relativistic Pseudoprocesses for Single Spinless Particle, Dubna report E2-7787 (1974)

[10] J. S. Dowker, J. Math. Phys. 17 (1976), 1873

[11] H. Leschke and M. Schmutz, Z. Phys. B27, (1977), 85

[12] H. Leschke, A.C. Hirshfeld and T. Suzuki, Phys. Rev. D18 (1978) 2834

[13] J. Bertrand and M. Irac, Lett. in Math. Phys. 3 (1979), 97

[14] M. M. Mizrahi, J. Math. Phys. 17 (1976), 490

[15] F. Langouche, D. Roekaerts and E. Tirapegui, Phys. Rev. D20 (1979),419 and D20 (1979), 433 and references to earlier work given there.

[16] F. Langouche, D. Roekaerts and E. Tirapegui, Lett. al Nuovo Cimento, 25 (1979), 307

[17] F. Langouche, D. Roekaerts and E. Tirapegui, Phys. Lett. 72A (1979), 413

SEMICLASSICAL EXPANSIONS ON RIEMANNIAN MANIFOLDS

F. Langouche★ , D. Roekaerts★★

Instituut voor Theoretische Fysica, Universiteit Leuven,
B-3030 Leuven, Belgium

E. Tirapegui

Institut de Physique Théorique, Université de Louvain,
B-1348 Louvain-la-Neuve, Belgium

I. INTRODUCTION

Given the differential equation ($Q = (Q^1,Q^2,\dots,Q^M)$, $\partial \equiv \partial/\partial Q$)

$$\frac{\partial}{\partial t} p(Q,t) = \mathcal{L}(Q,\partial,\eta)\, p(Q,t) \tag{1}$$

where $L(Q,\partial,\eta)$ contains at most second derivatives and η is a small parameter, one is interested in the propagator of (1), i.e. the solution $I(Q,t;Q_o,t_o)$ such that $I(Q,t_o;Q_o,t_o) = \delta(Q-Q_o)$.
The semiclassical expansion of I is of the form

$$I(Q,t;Q_o,t_o) = I_{WKB}(Q,t;Q_o,t_o).(1 + \sum_{k=1}^{\infty} I_{(k)}\eta^k) \tag{2}$$

where the WKB-approximation I_{WKB} is such that

$$I_{WKB}^{-1} \left(\frac{\partial}{\partial t} - \mathcal{L} \right) I_{WKB} = O(\eta). \tag{3}$$

The problem we address ourselves to here is the explicit computation of the higher order corrections $I_{(k)}$. We will give a unified treatment of the cases and methods we have studied earlier.[1-4]
For further information we also refer to the works of Elworthy and Truman [5], De Witt-Morette [6,7] and Mizrahi [8,9] .

★ Onderzoeker IIKW, Belgium
★★ Aspirant NFWO, Belgium

II. EXAMPLES

Let us first give two important examples.

In quantum mechanical applications $\eta=\hbar$. We will see that the general Schrödinger equation [10]

$$\frac{\partial}{\partial t} I = \frac{\hbar i}{2} \Delta_2 I + \frac{1}{2} [A^\alpha \nabla_\alpha + \nabla_\alpha A^\alpha] I + \frac{1}{\hbar i} [\frac{1}{2} A^\alpha A_\alpha + V] I \tag{1}$$

$$= \frac{\hbar i}{2} [\frac{1}{\sqrt{g}} \partial_\alpha \sqrt{g}\, g^{\alpha\beta} \partial_\beta] I + \frac{1}{2} [A^\alpha \partial_\alpha + \frac{1}{\sqrt{g}} \partial_\alpha \sqrt{g}\, A^\alpha] I + \frac{1}{\hbar i} [\frac{1}{2} A^\alpha A_\alpha + V] I$$

corresponds to the classical system with Lagrangian

$$L_{cl}(\dot{Q},Q) = \frac{1}{2} g_{\alpha\beta}(Q)\dot{Q}^\alpha \dot{Q}^\beta + A_\alpha(Q)\dot{Q}^\alpha - V(Q) . \tag{2}$$

(II.1) is of the form of (I.1) for

$$\mathcal{L}(Q,\partial,\hbar) = \frac{\hbar i}{2} \frac{1}{\sqrt{g}} \partial_\alpha \sqrt{g}\, g^{\alpha\beta} \partial_\beta + \frac{1}{2} [A^\alpha \partial_\alpha + \frac{1}{\sqrt{g}} \partial_\alpha \sqrt{g}\, A^\alpha] + \frac{1}{\hbar i} \cdot [\frac{1}{2} A^\alpha A_\alpha + V]. \tag{3}$$

In the case of Fokker-Planck dynamics η is a parameter measuring the strength of the fluctuations. Let $P(Q,t;Q_o,t_o)$ be the transition probability density of the Markovian process $Q(t)$ determined by the Langevin equation

$$\dot{Q}^\alpha(t) + a^\alpha(Q(t)) = \sqrt{\eta}\, \sigma_i^{\ \alpha} (Q(t))\, f_i(t), \quad \alpha = 1, \ldots, M, \tag{4}$$

where $f_i(t)$, $i = 1, \ldots, M' \geq M$, is a Gaussian white noise, and set

$$g^{\alpha\beta}(Q) = \sigma_i^{\ \alpha} (Q)\, \sigma_i^{\ \beta} (Q), \tag{5}$$

$$g(Q) = \det g_{\alpha\beta}(Q). \tag{6}$$

Then the invariant transition probability density [11]

$$I(Q,t;Q_o,t_o) = [g(Q)/g(Q_o)]^{1/2}\, \mathbf{P}(Q,t;Q_o,t_o) \tag{7}$$

satisfies

$$\frac{\partial}{\partial t} I = \frac{\eta}{2} \frac{1}{\sqrt{g}} \partial_\alpha \sigma_i^{\ \alpha} \partial_\beta \sqrt{g}\, \sigma_i^{\ \beta} I + \frac{1}{\sqrt{g}} \partial_\alpha \sqrt{g}\, a^\alpha I. \tag{8}$$

Again this is of the form (I.1), in this case

$$\mathcal{L}(Q,\partial,\eta) = \frac{\eta}{2}\frac{1}{\sqrt{g}}\,\partial_\alpha \sigma_i^{\ \alpha}\,\partial_\beta \sqrt{g}\,\sigma_i^{\ \beta}\, I + \frac{1}{\sqrt{g}}\,\partial_\alpha \sqrt{g}\, a^\alpha\, I. \tag{9}$$

We see then from (3) and (9) that we can put forward the following general expression for $\mathcal{L}(Q,\partial,\eta)$:

$$\mathcal{L}(Q,\partial,\eta) = \frac{\eta c}{2}\,\Sigma\; A(Q)\partial_\alpha\, B(Q)\partial_\beta\, C(Q) + \Sigma\, D(Q)\partial_\alpha\, E(Q) + \frac{1}{\eta c}\, F(Q). \tag{10}$$

where c=i in the quantum mechanical application and c=1 in the case of Fokker-Planck dynamics and where Σ indicates a sum of terms of the same form.

III. OPERATOR FORMALISM AND FUNCTIONAL INTEGRAL REPRESENTATIONS

The computation of the higher order corrections $I_{(k)}$ as it was done in 1-4 is based on discretization techniques of functional integrals that we have developed in 12-16. Also the operator formalism turns out to be a useful tool. Let us therefore review basic facts. The correspondence $\hat{Q} \leftrightarrow Q$, $\hat{P} \leftrightarrow -i\partial$ (hence $[\hat{Q}^\alpha,\hat{P}_\beta] = i\delta^\alpha_\beta$) allows to write (I.1) as

$$i\,\frac{\partial}{\partial t}\, I = \hat{H}(P,Q)\, I, \tag{1}$$

where

$$\hat{H}(P,Q) = i\,\mathcal{L}\,(\hat{Q},i\hat{P},\eta) \tag{2}$$

$$= -\,i\,\frac{\eta c}{2}\;\Sigma\, A(\hat{Q})\,\hat{P}_\alpha\, B(\hat{Q})\,\hat{P}_\beta\, C(\hat{Q}) - \Sigma\, D(\hat{Q})\,\hat{P}_\alpha\, E(\hat{Q}) + \frac{i}{\eta c}\, F(\hat{Q}),$$

and the propagator $I(Q,t;Q_o,t_o)$ can be written as

$$I(Q,t;Q_o,t_o) = \langle Q|U(t,t_o)|Q_o\rangle \tag{3}$$

where $U(t,t_o)$ is determined by

$$i\,\frac{\partial}{\partial t}\, U(t,t_o) = \hat{H}(\hat{P},\hat{Q})U(t,t_o),\quad U(t_o,t_o) = 1\,. \tag{4}$$

Owing to our choice of commutation relations (independent of η) all η-dependence of the operator $\hat{H}(\hat{P},\hat{Q})$ (we will call it the "Hamiltonian" also in the non-quantum case) is explicit.

One has for I functional integral representations in phase space :[14-16]

$$I(Q,t;Q_o,t_o) = \int_\gamma \mathcal{D}Q\mathcal{D}P \exp i \int_{t_o}^{t} [P.\dot{Q} - H^\gamma(P,Q)]d\tau.\delta(Q(t)-Q). \quad (5)$$

$$.\delta(Q(t_o)-Q_o),$$

where γ stands for the discretization and H^γ depends on it.[12–22] Knowledge of γ means that one is given one of the many functions $h^\gamma(P_j,Q_j,Q_{j-1})$ satisfying

$$<Q_j|\hat{H}(\hat{P},\hat{Q})|Q_{j-1}> = \int \frac{dP_j}{(2\pi)^M} \exp[iP_j.\Delta Q_j]\, h^\gamma(P_j,Q_j,Q_{j-1}). \quad (6)$$

Then (5) is defined as $I = \lim I_N$, $N\to\infty$, where

$$I_N = \int \prod_{i=1}^{N} dQ_i \prod_{j=1}^{N+1} \frac{dP_j}{(2\pi)^M} \exp i\varepsilon \sum_{j=1}^{N+1} [P_j.\frac{\Delta Q_j}{\varepsilon} - h^\gamma(P_j,Q_j,Q_{j-1})] \quad (7)$$

and

$$H^\gamma(P,Q) = h^\gamma(P,Q',Q)\Big|_{Q'=Q} \quad (8)$$

IV. THE SEMICLASSICAL EXPANSION

Let us first pay some attention to the WKB-approximation. The standard procedure for its determination consists in imposing the condition (I.3) on a trial solution. It is of the form

$$I_{WKB} = \eta^{-M/2}.\bar{N}.\exp[\frac{i}{\eta} A_{cl}] \quad (1)$$

where A_{cl} is the classical action for the Hamiltonian

$$H_{cl}(P,Q) = - i\frac{c}{2} \Sigma\, ABC(Q)P_\alpha P_\beta - \Sigma\, DE(Q)P_\alpha + \frac{i}{c} F(Q) \quad (2)$$

and boundary conditions $Q(t) = Q$, $Q(t_o) = Q_o$, and the factor $\bar{N}$ essentially contains the Van Vleck determinant.

The correspondence rule

$$H_{cl}(P,Q) = \hat{H}(\hat{P}\to P, \hat{Q}\to Q)\Big|_{\eta=1} \quad (3)$$

is a direct consequence of the way powers of η appear in the original differential operator $\mathcal{L}(Q,\partial,\eta)$, i.e. the term quadratic in ∂ is proportional to η, the term linear in ∂ is independent of η and the term without ∂ is proportional to η^{-1}.

Let $(y(\tau),x(\tau))$ be the solution of the Hamilton's equations of motion of H_{cl} for $x(t_o) = Q_o$, $x(t) = Q$.

By making in (5),(6) an expansion of the paths (P,Q) around (y,x), one can generate the semiclassical expansion starting from any discretization γ. In 1-4 we used a path integral representation of the form (III.5) for a discretization $\bar{\gamma}$ such that

$$H^{\bar{\gamma}}(P,Q) = \hat{H}(\hat{P}\to P,\hat{Q}\to Q). \tag{4}$$

In Appendix A of 4 we showed by explicit construction of $h^{\bar{\gamma}}(P_j,Q_j,Q_{j-1})$ that such discretizations exist in all cases. We will first explain this method and in the next section show how to proceed when starting from a different discretization.

We do in (III.7) the change of variables $(y_j = y(t_j),\ x_j = x(t_j))$

$$P_j = y_j/\eta + p_j/\sqrt{\eta}\ ,\ Q_j = x_j + \sqrt{\eta}q_j \tag{5}$$

setting $\Delta x_j \equiv x_j - x_{j-1}$, $\Delta q_j \equiv q_j - q_{j-1}$ one has

$$P_j\cdot \Delta Q_j = \eta^{-1}\, y_j\cdot\Delta x_j + \eta^{-1/2}(p_j\cdot\Delta x_j + y_j\cdot\Delta q_j) + p_j\cdot\Delta q_j . \tag{6}$$

Let z_j stand for either p_j, q_j or q_{j-1} and let us expand the argument of the exponential in (III.7) in powers of z_j. We need to retain only terms up to order ε.[13-16]
In counting the order in ε one has that effectively $p_j \sim \Delta q_j/\varepsilon = O(\varepsilon^{-1/2})$ since $\Delta q_j = O(\varepsilon^{1/2})$,[13-16] and in $h^{\gamma}(y_j/\eta + p_j/\sqrt{\eta}\ , x_j + \sqrt{\eta}q_j,\ x_{j-1} + \sqrt{\eta}q_{j-1})$ one can replace x_{j-1} by x_j, since this is only a change in the discretization of the explicit time dependence.[4] One has then that

$$h^{\bar{\gamma}}(P_j,Q_j,Q_{j-1}) = \eta^{-1}\ H_{cl}(y_j,x_j) + \bar{h} + h_o + h_1 \tag{7}$$

where $\bar{h}$, h_o, h_1 are functions of $(y_j,\ x_j,\ p_j,\ q_j,\ q_{j-1})$ respectively linear, quadratic, and of order three or more in z_j.

The linear terms combined with $\eta^{-1/2}\ (p_j\cdot\Delta x_j + y_j\cdot\Delta q_j)$ coming from $P_j\cdot\Delta q_j$ vanish owing to the equations of motion of $(y(\tau),\ x(\tau))$, (this is a consequence of using $\bar{\gamma}$) and since

$$\prod_{i=1}^{N} dQ_i \prod_{j=1}^{N} dP_j = \eta^{-M/2} \prod_{i=1}^{N} dq_i \prod_{j=1}^{N+1} dp_j \tag{8}$$

one has

$$I_N = \eta^{-M/2}\ \exp \frac{i}{\eta}\ \varepsilon \sum_{j=1}^{N+1} [y_j\cdot\frac{\Delta x_j}{\varepsilon} - H_{cl}(y_j,x_j)]\ . \tag{9}$$

$$\cdot\ \int \prod_{i=1}^{N} dq_i \prod_{j=1}^{N+1} \frac{dp_j}{(2\pi)^M}\ \exp i\varepsilon \sum_{j=1}^{N+1} [p_j\cdot\frac{\Delta q_j}{\varepsilon} - h_o - h_1]$$

In the limit $N\to\infty$ $(\varepsilon\to 0)$ one has

$$I = \eta^{-M/2} \exp [\frac{i}{\eta} A_{cl}] \cdot \tilde{I} \tag{10}$$

with

$$A_{cl} = \int_{t_o}^{t} d\tau \, [y(\tau).\dot{x}(\tau) - H_{cl}(y(\tau),x(\tau))] \tag{11}$$

and

$$\tilde{I} = \int_{\bar{\gamma}'} \mathcal{D}q\mathcal{D}p \exp \{i \int_{t_o}^{t} d\tau[p.\dot{q} - H_o(\tau,p,q) - H_1(\tau,p,q)]\delta(q(t)) \cdot \delta(q(t_o)) \tag{12}$$

with

$$H_o(\tau,p,q) = h_o(y(\tau),x(\tau);\ p,q,q) \tag{13}$$

$$H_1(\tau,p,q) = h_1(y(\tau),x(\tau);\ p,q,q)$$

and where the discretization $\bar{\gamma}'$ is determined by the known functions h_o and h_1.

We remark that H_o and H_1 can also be obtained from a formal development of H^{γ} in the continuum expression (III.5). Then however the link with the discretization is lost and so is the meaning of the expansion since undefined terms (tadpoles) appear.[14]

It is convenient now to change from the discretization $\bar{\gamma}'$ to another, more simple, one. This we will do through a corresponding change of ordering of operators in the associated operator formalism where

$$\hat{q} \leftrightarrow q, \ \hat{p} \leftrightarrow -i \frac{\partial}{\partial q} \ .$$

$\tilde{I}$ can be interpreted as

$$\tilde{I} = \langle q = 0 | U_1(t,t_o) | q_o = 0 \rangle \tag{14}$$

with

$$i \frac{\partial}{\partial t} U_1(t,t_o) = (\hat{H}_o(t) + \hat{H}_1(t)) \, U_1(t,t_o), \ U_1(t_o,t_o) = 1 \tag{15}$$

and the time dependent "Hamiltonian" can be explicitly computed from (10) and (12). (see section on the inverse problem in 14). Alternatively one can obtain the operators $\hat{H}_o(t)$ and $\hat{H}_1(t)$ directly from $\hat{H}(P,Q)$ as given by (III.2) replacing formally there

$$P = y(t)/\eta + \hat{p}/\sqrt{\eta} \ , \ Q(t) = x(t) + \sqrt{\eta}\, \hat{q} \ , \ ([Q^{\alpha},P_{\beta}] = [\hat{q}^{\alpha},\hat{p}_{\beta}] = i\delta^{\alpha}_{\beta}$$

and developing in powers of $\hat{p}$ and $\hat{q}$.

The quadratic terms in $(\hat{p},\hat{q})$ are $\hat{H}_o$ and the terms of order three or more in $(\hat{p},\hat{q})$ are $\hat{H}_1$. The proof of this can be found in Appendix B of 4 and uses the existence and the form of $\bar{\gamma}$.

We then rewrite $\hat{H}_o$ in Weylordered way and $\hat{H}_1$ in standard ordered way. Since $\hat{H}_o$ is quadratic in $(\hat{p},\hat{q})$ the former just means that the terms in $\hat{p}\,\hat{q}$ or $\hat{q}\,\hat{p}$ have to be symmetrized by adding and subtracting the right amount of $[\hat{q}\,,\hat{p}\,] = i\,\delta$. Thus

$$\hat{H}_o(t) = \hat{H}_{OW}(t) + G(t) \tag{16}$$

where $\hat{H}_{OW}(t)$ is Weylordered and quadratic in $(\hat{q},\hat{p})$ and $G(\tau)$ is the remaining commutator term, and

$$\hat{H}_1(t) = \hat{\Lambda}\,(t) \tag{17}$$

where $\hat{\Lambda}(t)$ is in standard order. ($\hat{p}$ at the RHS)

One has then for $\tilde{I}$ the path integral representation[1,14]

$$\tilde{I} = \exp\,[-i \int_{t_o}^{t} G(\tau)d\tau]\;.\int_{\gamma_c} \mathcal{D}q\mathcal{D}p \,\exp\, i \int_{t_o}^{t} [p.\dot{q} - H_{OW}(\tau,p,q) - \tag{18}$$

$$- \Lambda(\tau,p,q)]\; d\tau \;\; .\delta(q(t))\;\delta(q(t_o))$$

where H_{OW} and Λ are the functions obtained frow $\hat{H}_{OW}$ and $\hat{\Lambda}$ replacing $\hat{p}\to p$, $\hat{q}\to q$, and the discretization γ_c indicates that H_{OW} is discretized in the midpoint $1/2(q_{j-1}+q_j)$ and Λ^c in the postpoint q_j.
From (18) one has now

$$\tilde{I} = \exp\,[-i \int_{t_o}^{t} G(\tau)d\tau]\;.\;\exp\,[-i \int_{t_o}^{t} d\tau\; \Lambda(\tau,\frac{1}{i}\frac{\delta}{\delta L^\star},\frac{1}{i}\frac{\delta}{\delta L})]\;. \tag{19}$$

$$.\; Z_o[L,L^\star]\;\Big|_{L\,=\,L^\star\,=\,0}$$

with

$$Z_o[L,L^\star] = \int_{\gamma_{1(1/2)}} \mathcal{D}q\mathcal{D}p\,\exp\,\{i \int_{t_o}^{t} d\tau[p.q - H_{OW}(\tau,p,q) + L(\tau). \tag{20}$$

$$.\; q(\tau) + L\,(\tau).p(\tau)]\}\;.\;\delta(q(t))\delta(q(t_o))$$

($\gamma_1(1/2)$) stands for the midpoint discretization , 13)
The calculation of $\hat{H}_o(t)$ and $\hat{H}_1(t)$ (see Appendix) shows that $\hat{H}_o(t)$ is independent of η and that

$$\Lambda(\tau) = \sum_{n=1}^{\infty} \sqrt{\eta}^{\;\eta}\; \Lambda_{(n)}(\tau,p(\tau),q(\tau)).$$

The Gaussian functional integral (20) can be computed and has the value (21)

$$Z_o[L,L^\star] = Z_o[o,o] \exp \{- \int_{t_o}^{t} dt'\, dt'' \, [\tfrac{1}{2} L_\alpha(t') G^{\alpha\beta}(t',t'') L_\beta(t'') +$$

$$+ L^{\star\alpha}(t') S_\alpha{}^\beta (t',t'') L_\beta(t'') +$$

$$+ \frac{1}{2} L^{\star\alpha}(t') \Delta_{\alpha\beta}(t',t'') L^{\star\beta}(t'')]\} ,$$

where $G^{\alpha\beta}(t',t'')$ satisfies the Jacobi equation for the action $A_{cl}[x(\tau)]$ with $G^{\alpha\beta}(t,t'_o) = G^{\alpha\beta}(t',t_o) = 0$ and $S_\alpha{}^\beta$ and $\Delta_{\alpha\beta}$ are determined in terms of $G^{\alpha\beta}$. (See 1-4). Setting

$$\bar{N}(Q,t;Q_o,t_o) = \exp [-i \int_{t_o}^{t} G(\tau).d\tau] \,.\, Z_o[o,o] \tag{22}$$

one finally obtains from (10) and (19) that

$$(\bar{Z}_o[L,L^\star] = Z_o[o,o]^{-1} Z_o[L,L^\star])$$

$$I = \eta^{-M/2} \bar{N}(Q,t;Q_o,t_o) \exp \frac{i}{\eta} A_{cl}[x(\tau)] \,. \tag{23}$$

$$\exp[-i \int_{t_o}^{t} d\tau \sum_{n=1}^{\infty} \sqrt{\eta}^{\,n} \Lambda_{(n)}(\tau, \frac{1}{i}\frac{\delta}{\delta L^\star(\tau)} \frac{1}{i}\frac{\delta}{\delta L(\tau)})].\bar{Z}_o[L,L^\star]\Big|_{L=L^\star=0}$$

In (23) all the η-dependence is explicit, since $\bar{N}$, A_{cl}, $\bar{Z}_o$ and the $\Lambda_{(n)}$ are independent of η. Due to the form of $\bar{Z}_o$ (see (21)) when one develops $\exp[-i \int d\tau \, \Lambda(\tau)]$ only entire powers of η give a nonvanishing result when applied to $\bar{Z}_o$ and taken at zero sources.

There is one important remark here : the expression $\exp[-i \, d\tau \Lambda(\tau)$ applied to $Z_o[L,L^\star]$ is ambiguous since in (21) the function $S_\alpha{}^\beta(t',t'')$ has a jump at $t'=t''$, and consequently

$$\frac{\delta}{\delta L^{\star\alpha}(\tau)} \frac{\delta}{\delta L_\beta(\tau)} \bar{Z}_o$$

is not defined.[12,14,15,23-25] But, because the discretization γ_c tells us that $\Lambda(\tau)$ is discretized in the post-point one has to replace $\int d\tau \; \Lambda(\tau)$ in (19) by[12,14]

$$\lim_{\varepsilon \to 0^+} \int_{t_o}^{t} d\tau \, \Lambda(\tau \,, \frac{1}{i}\frac{\delta}{\delta L^\star(\tau)} \,, \frac{1}{i}\frac{\delta}{\delta L(\tau+\varepsilon)}) \,. \tag{24}$$

Now all terms in (23) are well-defined and one obtains an expansion of the form (I.2) with I_{WKB} given by (1) and (22).

The value of $Z_o[o,o]$, appearing in (22), can be read from the known expression for the WKB-approximation or also be computed from (20) as we did in 3. It is given by

$$Z_o[o,o] = [2\pi i]^{-1/2} \, [\overline{M}\,(Q,t;Q_o,t_o)]^{1/2} \tag{25}$$

with $\overline{M}$ the Van Vleck determinant.

So far this outline of the methods used in 1-4. In the appendix we present the explicit expressions for the operators $\hat{H}_o$ and $\hat{H}_1$ and the functions H_{OW}, G and Λ in the general case (II.10).

V. ALTERNATIVE METHOD

Although the discretization $\overline{\gamma}$ is appropriate in the sense that each order in the expansion around the classical solution is in one to one correspondence with a definite power of $\sqrt{\eta}$, one can freely choose any other discretization in the path integral representation (III.5) as a starting point for the derivation of the semiclassical expansion. In order to illustrate this we will treat here the Schrödinger equation for the free particle on a Riemannian manifold (II.1) for $A_\alpha \equiv 0$ and $V \equiv 0$) working from the beginning in the post-point discretization.

We write the Hamiltonian operator $\hat{H}(P,Q)$ in standard order :

$$\hat{H}(P,Q) = \frac{1}{2}\,\eta\, g^{\alpha\beta}(\hat{Q})\hat{P}_\alpha \hat{P}_\beta - \frac{i}{2}\,\eta\Big[\frac{1}{\sqrt{g}}\,\partial_\alpha\sqrt{g}\; g^{\alpha\beta}\Big]\,(\hat{Q})\;\hat{P}_\beta \tag{1}$$

and have for I the path integral representation in the post-point or $\gamma_1(1)$ discretization [13]

$$I(Q,t;Q_o,t_o) = \int_{\gamma_1(1)} \mathcal{D}Q\mathcal{D}P \,\exp i\int_{t_o}^{t} d\tau\,[P.\dot{Q} - H^{\gamma_1(1)}(P,Q)] \;. \tag{2}$$

$$.\; \delta(Q(t) - Q) \;.\; \delta(Q(t_o) - Q_o)$$

where $H^{\gamma_1(1)}(P,Q)$ is obtained from (1) replacing there $\hat{P}\to P$ and $\hat{Q}\to Q$, and

$$h^{\gamma_1(1)}(P_j,Q_j,Q_{j-1}) = \frac{1}{2}\,\eta g^{\alpha\beta}(Q_j)\,P_{j\alpha}P_{j\beta} - \frac{i}{2}\,\eta\Big[\frac{1}{\sqrt{g}}\,\partial_\alpha\sqrt{g}\,g^{\alpha\beta}\Big](Q_j)P_{j\beta}\,. \tag{3}$$

As before we make in the discretized version of (2) the expansion around $(y(\tau),x(\tau))$, the solution of the Hamilton's equations of motion of the classical Hamiltonian

$$H_{cl}(P,Q) = \frac{1}{2} P_\alpha P_\beta \; g^{\alpha\beta}(Q) \tag{4}$$

for the boundary conditions $Q(t) = Q$, $Q(t_o) = Q_o$. (Remember that H_{cl} followed in a unique way from $\mathcal{L}$, see after (IV.3)), and collect terms of equal power in z_j (which is either p_j, q_j or q_{j-1}. We have then that

$$i\varepsilon \left[P_j \cdot \frac{\Delta Q_j}{\varepsilon} - h^{\gamma_1(1)} (P_j, Q_j, Q_{j-1})\right] = E_j^{[0]} + E_j^{[1]} + E_j^{[2]} + E_j^{[3]} \tag{5}$$

where

$E_j^{[k]}$, $k = 0, 1, 2$ is of order k in z_j and $E_j^{[3]}$ of order 3 or more, explicitly :

$$E_j^{[0]} = i\,\varepsilon \frac{1}{\eta} \left[y_j \cdot \frac{\Delta x_j}{\varepsilon} - \frac{1}{2} y_{j\alpha} y_{j\beta} g^{\alpha\beta}(x_j)\right] + i\varepsilon \frac{i}{2} \cdot \left[\frac{1}{\sqrt{g}} \partial_\alpha \sqrt{g}\, g^{\alpha\beta}\right]\Big|_{x_j} y_{j\beta}, \tag{6}$$

$$E_j^{[1]} = i\,\varepsilon\Big[\frac{1}{\sqrt{\eta}} y_j \cdot \frac{\Delta q_j}{\varepsilon} + p_j \cdot \frac{\Delta x_j}{\varepsilon} - \frac{1}{2} y_{j\alpha} y_{j\beta} q_j^\rho (\partial_\rho g^{\alpha\beta})\Big|_{x_j} y_{j\beta} - p_{j\alpha} y_{j\beta} g^{\alpha\beta}(x_j)\Big] + i\varepsilon \frac{i}{2}\sqrt{\eta}\Big[\Big(\frac{1}{\sqrt{g}} \partial_\alpha \sqrt{g}\, g^{\alpha\beta}\Big)\Big|_{x_j} p_{j\beta} + \partial_\rho \Big(\frac{1}{\sqrt{g}} \partial_\alpha \sqrt{g}\, g^{\alpha\beta}\Big) q_j^\rho\, y_{j\beta}\Big], \tag{7}$$

$$E_j^{[2]} = i\varepsilon \Big[p_j \cdot \frac{\Delta q_j}{\varepsilon} - \frac{1}{4} y_{j\alpha} y_{j\beta}\, q_j{}^\rho q_j{}^\sigma (\partial_{\rho\sigma} g^{\alpha\beta})\Big|_{x_j} - p_{j\alpha} y_{j\beta}\, q_j^\rho (\partial_\rho\, g^{\alpha\beta})\Big|_{x_j} - \frac{1}{2} p_{j\alpha} p_{j\beta}\, g^{\alpha\beta}(x_j)\Big] + i\varepsilon \frac{i}{2} \eta \Big[\partial_\rho \Big(\frac{1}{\sqrt{g}} \partial_\alpha \sqrt{g}\, g^{\alpha\beta}\Big)\Big|_{x_j} q_j^\rho\, p_{j\beta} + \frac{1}{2}\partial_{\rho\sigma}\Big(\frac{1}{\sqrt{g}}\partial_\alpha \sqrt{g}\, g^{\alpha\beta}\Big)\Big|_{x_j} \cdot q_j^\rho\, q_j^\sigma\, y_{j\beta}\Big]. \tag{8}$$

and (the notation $\overline{A}_{(m)}$ is explained in the Appendix)

$$E_j^{[3]} = i\varepsilon \left[-\frac{1}{2\eta} \overline{y_{j\alpha} y_{j\beta} g^{\alpha\beta}}_{(3)} - \frac{1}{\sqrt{\eta}} \overline{p_{j\alpha} y_{j\beta} g^{\alpha\beta}}_{(2)} - \frac{1}{2} \overline{p_{j\alpha} p_{j\beta} g^{\alpha\beta}}_{(1)} \right]$$
$$+ i\varepsilon \left[\frac{i}{2} \overline{y_{j\beta} \left(\frac{1}{\sqrt{g}} \partial_\alpha \sqrt{g}\, g^{\alpha\beta} \right)}_{(3)} + \sqrt{\eta}\, \overline{p_{j\beta} \left(\frac{1}{\sqrt{g}} \partial_\alpha \sqrt{g}\, g^{\alpha\beta} \right)}_{(2)} \right]. \tag{9}$$

We see that the term of order $(z_j)^k$ has a part in $\sqrt{\eta}^{k-2}$ and a part in $\sqrt{\eta}^k$ and we can write

$$E_j^{[k]} = i\varepsilon \left[\eta^{(k-2)/2} R_j^{[k]} + \eta^{k/2} S_j^{[k]} \right], \; k = 0,1,2,3. \tag{10}$$

$\Sigma R_j^{[0]}$ gives the classical action and $\Sigma R_j^{[1]}$ vanishes owing to the equations of motion of $(y(\tau),x(\tau))$. We will use $R_j^{[2]}$ to define the free generating functional Z_o, but as before (section IV) we change to midpoint discretization

$$\left(\bar{q}_j = \frac{1}{2} (q_{j-1} + q_j) = q_j - \frac{1}{2} \Delta q_j \right).$$

Keeping terms up to order ε and making use of the fact that

$$\varepsilon p_{j\alpha} \Delta q_j^\rho \doteq i\varepsilon\, \delta_\alpha{}^\rho ,$$ [16] we obtain

$$R_j^{[2]} = \Big[p_j \cdot \frac{\Delta q_j}{\varepsilon} - \frac{1}{4} y_{j\alpha} y_{j\beta} \bar{q}_j^\rho \bar{q}_j^\sigma (\partial_{\rho\sigma} g^{\alpha\beta})\big|_{x_j} - \tag{11}$$
$$- p_{j\alpha} y_{j\beta} \bar{q}_j^\rho (\partial_\rho g^{\alpha\beta})\big|_{x_j} - \frac{1}{2} p_{j\alpha} p_{j\beta} g^{\alpha\beta} (x_j) \Big] -$$
$$- \frac{i}{2} y_{j\beta} (\partial_\alpha g^{\alpha\beta})\big|_{x_j} .$$

The last term combines with $S_j^{[0]}$ to give the normalization factor $\exp [-i \int G(\tau)\, d\tau]$ (see (III.18) and appendix)

$$\exp i\varepsilon \sum_{j=1}^{N+1} \left[\frac{1}{\sqrt{g}} (\partial_\alpha \sqrt{g}\,) g^{\alpha\beta} \right]\Big|_{x_j} y_{j\beta} \to [g(Q)/g(Q_o)]^{-1/4} . \tag{13}$$

Putting all this together we arrive at the expansion formula for $I(Q,t;Q_o,t_o)$:

$$I(Q,t;Q_o,t_o) = \eta^{-M/2} \cdot \exp \left[\frac{i}{\eta} A_{cl} \right] \left[\frac{g(Q)}{g(Q_o)} \right]^{-1/4} \cdot \bar{I}(Q,t;Q_o,t_o) \tag{14}$$

with (γ_c was defined in (III.18))

$$\bar{I}(Q,t;Q_o,t_o) = \int_{\gamma_c} \mathcal{D}q\mathcal{D}p \exp i \int_{t_o}^{t} [p.\dot{q} - H_{OW}(\tau,p,q) - \Lambda(\tau,p,q)]d\tau . \; . \; \delta(q(t)) \, \delta(q(t_o)) \tag{14}$$

where $[p.\dot{q} - H_{OW}(\tau,p,q)]$ comes from $R_j^{[2]}$ in (11) minus the last term :

$$H_{OW}(\tau,p,q) = \frac{1}{4} y_\alpha y_\beta q^\rho q^\sigma (\partial_{\rho\sigma} g^{\alpha\beta}) + p_\alpha y_\beta q^\rho (\partial_\rho g^{\alpha\beta}) + \frac{1}{2} p_\alpha p_\beta g^{\alpha\beta} \tag{15}$$

and $\Lambda(\tau,p,q)$ comes from $S_j^{[1]}$, $S_j^{[2]}$ and $E_j^{[3]}$ which we have put all together in the interaction Hamiltonian :

$$\Lambda(\tau,p,q) = \frac{1}{2\eta} y_\alpha y_\beta \overline{g^{\alpha\beta}}_{(3)} + \frac{1}{\sqrt{\eta}} \overline{g^{\alpha\beta}}_{(2)} p_\alpha y_\beta + \tag{16}$$

$$+ \frac{1}{2} p_\alpha p_\beta \overline{g^{\alpha\beta}}_{(1)} - \frac{i}{2}\sqrt{\eta}\, \overline{\left(\frac{1}{\sqrt{g}} \partial_\alpha \sqrt{g}\, g^{\alpha\beta}\right)}_{(0)} p_\beta -$$

$$- \frac{i}{2} \overline{\left(\frac{1}{\sqrt{g}} \partial_\alpha \sqrt{g}\, g^{\alpha\beta}\right)}_{(1)} y_\beta .$$

Comparing (14-16) with the formulae (11) and (13) of Ref. 1 we verify that we obtain the same expansion. (Set in (1 ,(13)) c=i and remark that(1/2)K≡ Λ).

A drawback of the present method is that it is not step by step covariant, consequently the scalar character of all higher order corrections is not explicitly displayed. In a forthcoming paper[26] we will obtain a covariant expansion performing a transformation to normal coordinates around the classical path.

APPENDIX

In section III we showed how to generate the semiclassical expansion of the propagator $I(Q,t;Q_o,t_o)$ for the differential equation (I.1). Here we present explicit expressions for the relevant quantities in the general case where $\mathcal{L}$ is given by (II.10) and $\hat{H}(\hat{P},\hat{Q})$ by (III.2). We will use the following notations. For any operator $A(\hat{Q})$ we write its Taylor expansion as

$$A(\hat{Q}) = A(x + \sqrt{\eta}\hat{q}) = \sum_{n=o}^{\infty} A_{(n)}(x,\hat{q}) \tag{A1}$$

$$A_{(n)} \equiv A_{(n)}(x,\hat{q}) = \frac{1}{n!} \sqrt{\eta}^{\,n}\, \hat{q}^{\alpha_1} \ldots\ldots \hat{q}^{\alpha_n}\, \partial_{\alpha_1 \ldots\ldots \alpha_n} A(x) \tag{A2}$$

We also define

$$\overline{A}_{(k)} \equiv \overline{A}_{(k)}(x,\hat{q}) = \sum_{n=k}^{\infty} A_{(n)}(x,\hat{q}) \tag{A3}$$

By the procedure explained after formula (III.15) one obtains from $\mathcal{H}(P,Q)$ as given by (III.2) the following operators $\mathcal{H}_0(\tau,\hat{p},\hat{q})$ and $\mathcal{H}_1(\tau,\hat{p},\hat{q})$:

$$\begin{aligned}\mathcal{H}_0(\tau,p,q) = -\frac{1}{2}\, ic\, \{ (ABC)_{(o)}\hat{p}_\alpha\hat{p}_\beta &+ \frac{1}{\sqrt{\eta}}\sum_{k+\ell=1} A_{(k)}\hat{p}_\alpha (BC)_{(\ell)} y_\beta + \\ &+ \frac{1}{\sqrt{\eta}}\sum_{k+\ell=1} (AB)_{(k)}\hat{p}_\beta C_{(\ell)} y_\alpha + \frac{1}{\eta}(ABC)_{(2)} y_\alpha y_\beta \} - \\ &- \{\frac{1}{\sqrt{\eta}}\sum_{k+\ell=1} D_{(k)}\hat{p}_\alpha E_{(\ell)} + \frac{1}{\eta}(DE)_{(2)} y_\alpha\} + \frac{i}{\eta c} F_{(2)}\end{aligned} \tag{A4}$$

$$\begin{aligned}\mathcal{H}_1(\tau,\hat{p},\hat{q}) = -\frac{1}{2}\, ic\, \{\sum_{k+\ell+m>1} & A_{(k)}\hat{p}_\alpha B_{(\ell)}\hat{p}_\beta C_{(m)} + \\ &+ \frac{1}{\sqrt{\eta}}\sum_{k+\ell>2} A_{(k)}\hat{p}_\alpha (BC)_{(\ell)} y_\beta + \frac{1}{\sqrt{\eta}}\sum_{k+\ell>2} (AB)_{(k)}\hat{p}_\beta C_{(\ell)} \cdot \\ &\cdot y_\alpha + \frac{1}{\eta}\overline{(ABC)}_{(3)} y_\alpha y_\beta\} - \{\frac{1}{\sqrt{\eta}}\sum_{k+\ell>2} D_{(k)}\hat{p}_\alpha E_{(\ell)} + \\ &+ \frac{1}{\eta}\overline{(DE)}_{(3)}\, y_\alpha\} + \frac{i}{\eta c}\overline{F}_{(3)} .\end{aligned} \tag{A5}$$

$\mathcal{H}_0(\tau,\hat{p},\hat{q})$ can be written in Weyl ordered way as $\mathcal{H}_0(\tau,\hat{p},\hat{q}) = \mathcal{H}_{OW}(\tau,\hat{p},\hat{q}) + G(t)$ where

$$\begin{aligned}\mathcal{H}_{OW}(\tau,\hat{p},\hat{q}) = -\frac{1}{2}\, ic\{ & (ABC)_{(o)}\hat{p}_\alpha\hat{p}_\beta + \frac{1}{2\sqrt{\eta}}[(ABC)_{(1)}\hat{p}_\alpha + \hat{p}_\alpha(ABC)_{(1)}] \cdot \\ &\cdot y_\beta + \frac{1}{2\sqrt{\eta}}[(ABC)_{(1)}\hat{p}_\beta + \hat{p}_\beta(ABC)_{(1)}]\, y_\alpha + \frac{1}{\eta}(ABC)_{(2)} \cdot \\ & y_\alpha y_\beta\} - \frac{1}{2\sqrt{\eta}}[(DE)_{(1)}\hat{p}_\alpha + \hat{p}_\alpha(DE)_{(1)}] + \frac{i}{\eta c}F_{(2)}\end{aligned} \tag{A6}$$

and

$$\begin{aligned}\mathcal{G}(t) = \frac{1}{4}\, c[(\partial_\alpha A)BC - A(\partial_\alpha BC)]_{(o)} y_\beta &+ \frac{1}{4}\, c[(\partial_\beta AB)C - AB(\partial_\beta C)]_{(o)} y_\alpha - \\ &- \frac{1}{2}\, i\, [(\partial_\alpha D)E - D(\partial_\alpha E)]_{(o)}\end{aligned} \tag{A7}$$

$\mathcal{H}_1(\tau,p,q)$ written in standard order is :

$$\hat{H}_1(\tau,p,q) = -\frac{1}{2}\, ic\{\overline{(ABC)}_{(1)}\hat{p}_\alpha\hat{p}_\beta + \frac{1}{\sqrt{\eta}}\overline{(ABC)}_{(2)}(\hat{p}_\alpha y_\beta + \hat{p}_\beta y_\alpha) + \quad \text{(A8)}$$
$$+ \frac{1}{\eta}\overline{(ABC)}_{(3)}y_\alpha y_\beta - i\sqrt{\eta}\,\overline{[A(\partial_\alpha B)C]}_{(0)}\hat{p}_\beta - i\sqrt{\eta}\,\cdot$$
$$\cdot\ \overline{[AB(\partial_\beta C)]}_{(0)}\hat{p}_\alpha - i\sqrt{\eta}\overline{[AB(\partial_\alpha C)]}_{(0)}\hat{p}_\beta -$$
$$- \eta\overline{[A(\partial_\alpha B)(\partial_\beta C)]}_{(0)} - \eta\overline{[AB(\partial_\alpha\partial_\beta C)]}_{(0)}\} -$$
$$- \{\frac{1}{\sqrt{\eta}}\overline{(DE)}_{(2)}\hat{p}_\alpha + \frac{1}{\eta}\overline{(DE)}_{(3)}y_\alpha - i\overline{[D(\partial_\alpha E)]}_{(2)}\} +$$
$$+ \frac{i}{\eta c}\overline{F}_{(3)}.$$

In deriving (A6) - (A8) we used that

$$[\hat{p}_\alpha, A_{(k)}] = \begin{cases} -i\sqrt{\eta}\,(\partial_\alpha A)_{(k-1)}, & k>0 \\ 0, & k=0 \end{cases} \quad \text{(A9)}$$

$$[\hat{p}_\alpha\hat{p}_\beta, A_{(k)}] = \begin{cases} -i\sqrt{\eta}(\partial_\alpha A)_{(k-1)}\hat{p}_\beta - i\sqrt{\eta}(\partial_\beta A)_{(k-1)}\hat{p}_\alpha - \eta(\partial_\alpha\partial_\beta A)_{(k-2)} & ,k>1 \\ -i\sqrt{\eta}(\partial_\alpha A)_{(k-1)}\hat{p}_\beta - i\sqrt{\eta}(\partial_\alpha A)_{(k-1)}\hat{p}_\alpha & ,k=1 \\ 0 & ,k=0 \end{cases} \quad \text{(A10)}$$

We have then finally that the functions $H_{OW}(\tau,p,q)$ and $\Lambda(\tau,p,q)$ are obtained by replacing in (A6) and (A8) $\hat{q}\to q$ and $\hat{p}\to p$.

A last remark is in order about the factor $\exp[-i\int G(\tau)d\tau]$ (See (III.19),(III.22)). If

$$A(Q) = D(Q) = \frac{1}{\sqrt{g(Q)}} \quad \text{(A11)}$$

which is the case in the examples of section II, one has that

$$\exp\,[-i\int_{t_0}^{t} G(\tau)\,d\tau] = [\frac{g(Q)}{g(Q_0)}]^{-1/4} \cdot \exp\,[-i\int_{t_0}^{t}\tilde{G}(\tau)d\tau] \quad \text{(A12)}$$

where

$$\tilde{G}(\tau) = -\frac{1}{4}\, c\,\frac{1}{\sqrt{g}}\,[(\partial_\alpha BC)y_\beta - (\partial_\beta B)Cy_\alpha + B(\partial_\beta C)y_\alpha] + \frac{i}{2\sqrt{g}}(\partial_\alpha E). \quad \text{(A13)}$$

In the case of the Schrödinger equation $\tilde{G}(\tau) \equiv 0$ and $\exp[-i\int G(\tau)d\tau]$ reduces to the wellknown factor

$$[g(Q)/g(Q_0)]^{-1/4} .$$

For the Fokker-Planck-equation $\tilde{G}(\tau) = -\frac{1}{2} y_\alpha \sigma^\alpha \nabla_\beta \sigma^\beta + \frac{i}{2} \nabla_\alpha a^\alpha$.

REFERENCES

1. F. Langouche, D. Roekaerts, E. Tirapegui, Lett. Nuov. Lim. 25, 307 (1979)
2. F. Langouche, D. Roekaerts, E. Tirapegui, Phys. Lett. 72A, 413 (1979)
3. F. Langouche, D. Roekaerts, E. Tirapegui, *Lecture Notes* (KUL-TF-79/028)
4. F. Langouche, D. Roekaerts, E. Tirapegui, *WKB-type Expansions for Langevin Equations*, Physica (to appear)
5. K.D. Elworthy, A.J. Truman, *Classical Mechanics, the Diffusion (Heat) Equation, and the Schrödinger Equation on Riemannian manifolds)*, preprint and talk given by A.J. Truman at the present Workshop on Functional Integration, Theory and Applications, Louvain-la-Neuve, November 6-9, 1979.
6. C. De Witt-Morette, Ann.Phys. 97, 367 (1976)
7. C. De Witt-Morette, A. Maheshwari, B. Nelson, Phys. Rep. 50, 257 (1979)
8. M.M. Mizrahi, J. Math. Phys. 18, 786 (1977)
9. M.M. Mizrahi, J. Math. Phys. 19, 298 (1978)
10. B.S. De Witt, Rev. Mod. Phys. 29, 377 (1957)
11. R. Graham, Z. Phys. B26, 397 (1977)
12. F. Langouche, D. Roekaerts, E. Tirapegui, Physica 95A, 252 (1979)
13. F. Langouche, D. Roekaerts, E. Tirapegui, Nuov. Cim. B53, 135 (1979)
14. F. Langouche, D. Roekaerts, E. Tirapegui, Phys. Rev. D20, 429 (1979)
15. F. Langouche, D. Roekaerts, E. Tirapegui, Phys. Rev. D20, 433 (1979)
16. F. Langouche, D. Roekaerts, E. Tirapegui, *Functional Integrals in Phase Space* (to appear)
17. F. A. Berezin, Theor. Math. Phys. 6, 194 (1971)
18. I.W. Mayes, J.S. Dowker, Proc. Roy. Soc. Lond. A327, 131 (1972)
19. J.S. Dowker, J. Math. Phys. 17, 1873 (1976)
20. H. Leschke and M. Schmutz, Z. Phys. B27, 85 (1977)
21. J. Bertrand, M. Irac, Lett. Math. Phys. 3, 97 (1979)
22. W. Garczynski, Rep. Math. Phys. 4, 21 (1973)
23. H. Leschke, A.C. Hirshfeld, T. Suzuki, Phys. Rev. D18, 2834 (1978)
24. H. Leschke, A.C. Hirshfeld, T. Suzuki, Phys. Lett. 67A, 87 (1978)
25. Talk by A.C. Hirshfeld at the present Workshop on Functional Integration, Theory and Applications, Louvain-la-Neuve, November 6-9, 1979.
26. F. Langouche, D. Roekaerts, E. Tirapegui, *Covariant WKB-expansions in Riemannian Space*, preprint KUL-TF-80/3.

QUANTIZATION IN CURVED SPACES

Functional Integration and the Quantum Action Principle in Riemannian Geometries

H. Dekker

Physics Laboratory TNO
Den Haag
P.O. Box 96864
The Netherlands

ABSTRACT

Feynman's path integral representation of the covariant quantum mechanical propagator entails Schwinger's dynamical variational principle as shown by DeWitt. On one hand we discuss the covariant quantum Hamiltonian obtained from Schwinger's principle in curved space, following Kawai. On the other hand we present a novel Fourier series analysis of the path integral itself. The resulting Hamiltonian is identical to Kawai's. For the 'free particle' the Hamiltonian involves a quantum mechanical curvature scalar potential $v=-\hbar^2R/8$.

1. INTRODUCTION

The conceptually appealing concept of a weighted summing over all possible trajectories in order to obtain the transition probability between a specified initial and final situation, known in the theory of classical stochastic processes since the original work of Wiener around 1930 (e.g. ref. 1, and references contained therein), was introduced into quantum theory by Feynman in 1948[2]. Some ten years later DeWitt presented a first discussion of Feynman quantization in curved spaces[3].
Like any procedure, path integral quantization involves the question of operator ordering. However, as already known since Podolski's 1928-paper[4], such ambiguities are resolved by the requirement of covariance.

The path integral quantization was expected to lead to exactly the same covariant Schrödinger equation as obtained from the conventional Lagrange-Hamilton-Dirac quantization, replacing Poisson brackets by commutators. But DeWitt observed the curious phenomenon that the two results were slightly different. The classical covariant

'free particle' Lagrangian

$$L^{(0)}(x,\dot{x})=\tfrac{1}{2}g_{\mu\nu}(x)\dot{x}^{\mu}\dot{x}^{\nu} \quad , \qquad (1.1)$$

where $g_{\mu\nu}(x)$ represents the covariant metric tensor, leads via the classical action principle to a Hamiltonian $\tilde{H}^{(0)}(x,\dot{x})\equiv L^{(0)}(x,\dot{x})$. Defining the usual canonical momentum and $H^{(0)}(x,p)\equiv\tilde{H}^{(0)}(x,\dot{x})$, one obtains

$$H^{(0)}(x,p)=\tfrac{1}{2}g^{\mu\nu}(x)p_{\mu}p_{\nu} \quad , \qquad (1.2)$$

where the contravariant tensor $g^{\mu\nu}(x)$ is the inverse of $g_{\mu\nu}(x)$. Following Podolski, inserting the appropriate factors into (1.2) so as to ultimately guarantee covariance, the resulting quantum Hamiltonian reads

$$\mathcal{H}^{(0)}_{o}(\hat{x},\hat{p})=\tfrac{1}{2}g^{-\frac{1}{4}}(\hat{x})\hat{p}_{\mu}g^{\frac{1}{2}}(\hat{x})g^{\mu\nu}(\hat{x})\hat{p}_{\nu}g^{-\frac{1}{4}}(\hat{x}) \quad , \qquad (1.3)$$

where $g=\|g_{\mu\nu}\|$ is the determinant of the metric tensor. We have purposely added (1.3) the subscript zero, a notion that will become clear later on. Using the c-number Lagrangian (1.1) in the covariant propagator, however, DeWitt found the Hamiltonian $\hat{\mathcal{H}}^{(0)}_{--}=\hat{\mathcal{H}}^{(0)}_{o}-\hbar^2R/6$, where R is the curvature scalar with Weinberg's[5] sign convention (and hence is the negative of DeWitt's R, so that the above $\hat{\mathcal{H}}_{--}$ corresponds to his $\hat{\mathcal{H}}_{++}$).

In the present paper we resolve this problem. On the one hand it is noted that the quantization procedure by means of the classical action principle and subsequent canonical quantization is not in any precise sense (i.e. on the quantum level) related to the path integral. Rather, the path integral is intimately connected with Schwinger's quantum action principle[6], as has been shown by DeWitt. On the other hand it is recognized that DeWitt's evaluation of the path integral involves an adhoc requirement in order to put the continuous time action integral on a lattice. Rather than postulating that the short time action be calculated merely along the true classical (i.e. extremal) trajectory, we hold that the paths must remain in principle fully arbitrary a priori, no matter how short the time interval. This important notion quite naturally leads to a spectral analysis of these trajectories[7,8] in order to obtain a skeletonized form for the short time propagator. It intrinsically involves a functional averaging.

There has been some doubt whether Schwinger's principle could be extended in a consistent manner into curved spaces. Indeed, this is a highly nontrivial matter involving the subtle problem of invariance of the Lagrangian operator at the quantum level. The actual possibility of a consistent formulation of the quantum action principle in Riemannian geometries has been shown only rather recently by Kawai (ref. 9, and references therein).

Even more recently the Fourier series analysis of stochastic trajectories, which has been employed succesfully in flat spaces, was applied to the evaluation of the path integral in Riemannian

geometries[10], primarily from the point of view of classical diffusion processes in order to determine the curved space Onsager-Machlup Lagrangian. In[10] the path integral was first transformed to local Cartesian frames where the spectral analysis was done. Afterwards the skeletonized short time propagator was transformed back to the globally Riemannian coordinates and the associated differential equation (be it the diffusion or the Schrödinger equation) was calculated. The result agreed with DeWitt's. However, since it turns out that the definition of the Cartesian local frames in fact can not be made precise enough within the path integral if space is essentially curved, the result of[10] is actually believed to be of value in flat spaces only[11]. Therefore, in this paper we present a novel analysis, directly in Riemannian coordinates.

In section 2 we briefly recall the most relevant features of the classical action principle and canonical quantization. The covariant path integral representation of the quantum mechanical propagator will be introduced in section 3, and the quantum action principle will be derived. In section 4 we discuss Kawai's theory and show that for the 'free particle' it leads to the Hamiltonian $\hat{H}^{(0)}=\hat{H}_o^{(0)}-\hbar^2R/8$. Then, in section 5, the short time path integral will be evaluated using the Fourier series analysis of smooth paths. It will be seen that this leads to exactly the same quantum dynamics as the Schwinger-Kawai principle, which is the essential outcome of this article. Section 6 finally contains a summary and some concluding remarks.

2. THE CLASSICAL ACTION PRINCIPLE

The Lagrange-Hamilton-Dirac quantization scheme in fact separates into two parts: the classical action principle and the quantum-classical correspondence principle. The classical action principle asserts that the true classical trajectory between a fixed initial point x_i^μ at time t_i and a fixed final point x_f^μ at time t_f is the particular trajectory that makes the action functional

$$S(\{x(t)\}) = \int_{t_i}^{t_f} L(x(t),\, \dot{x}(t))dt \tag{2.1}$$

stationary. That is, if we let $\delta x^\mu(t)=x'^\mu(t)-x^\mu(t)$ be an arbitrary instantaneous infinitesemal variation in the continuous and at least twice differentiable function $x(t)$, then

$$[\delta S]_{(x_i,t_i)}^{(x_f,t_f)}=0. \tag{2.2}$$

This principle leads in the familiar manner (see e.g. ref. 12) to the Euler-Lagrange equations for the stationary or extremal trajectory,

$$\frac{d}{dt}\frac{\partial L}{\partial \dot{x}^{\mu}} - \frac{\partial L}{\partial x^{\mu}} = 0. \tag{2.3}$$

For simple conservative systems the Lagrangian $L(x,\dot{x})$is the difference between the kinetic and potential energy. The Euler-Lagrange equations contain all information concerning the classical motion.

Having the extremal trajectory available we define Hamilton's principle function

$$\overline{S}(x_f,t_f|x_i,t_i)=[S(\{x(t)\})]_{x(t)\,\mathrm{extremal}} \tag{2.4}$$

In words, Hamilton's principle function is the action functional computed for the true classical trajectory. Now let $\delta x^{\mu}(t)$ be the variation in the true classical trajectory caused by infinitesemal alterations δx_i^{μ}, δt_i and δx_f^{μ}, δt_f in its end points. The associated change in the value of Hamilton's principle function becomes

$$\delta\overline{S}(x_f,t_f|x_i,t_i)=\delta[\int_{t_i}^{t_f} L(x,\dot{x})dt]_{x(t)\,\mathrm{extr.}}$$

$$=L_f\delta t_f-L_i\delta t_i+\int_{t_i}^{t_f} \frac{d}{dt}[\frac{\partial L}{\partial \dot{x}^{\mu}}\,\delta x^{\mu}(t)]dt$$

$$=\frac{\partial L}{\partial \dot{x}_f^{\mu}}\,\delta x^{\mu}(t_f)+L_f\delta t_f - \frac{\partial L}{\partial \dot{x}_i^{\mu}}\,\delta x^{\mu}(t_i)-L_i\delta t_i, \tag{2.5}$$

where we have used (2.3). Since $\delta x^{\mu}(t_i)=\delta x_i^{\mu}-\dot{x}_i^{\mu}\delta t_i$, and similarly at t_f, one may write the result of this end point variation as

$$\delta\overline{S}(x_f,t_f|x_i,t_i)=G_f-G_i, \tag{2.6}$$

where we have introduced the classical generator

$$G=p_{\mu}\delta x^{\mu}-H\delta t. \tag{2.7}$$

The momenta and the Hamiltonian are conventionally defined as

$$p_{\mu} = \frac{\partial L}{\partial \dot{x}^{\mu}}, \tag{2.8}$$

$$H(x,p)=\tilde{H}(x,\dot{x})=p_{\mu}\dot{x}^{\mu}-L(x,\dot{x}). \tag{2.9}$$

Eq. (2.6) implies the usual Hamilton-Jacobi equations. Completely changing to the independent dynamical variables x^{μ} and p_{μ}, one derives in a well-known manner the Hamilton equations

$$\dot{p}_{\mu}=-\frac{\partial H}{\partial x^{\mu}}\ ,\ \dot{x}^{\mu}=\frac{\partial H}{\partial p_{\mu}}\ . \tag{2.10}$$

These can be considered as special cases of the general dynamical equation obeyed by an arbitrary function $F(x,p)$,

$$\dot{F}=\{F,H\}_- \ , \tag{2.11}$$

where we have introduced the Poisson brackets

$$\{A,B\}_- = \frac{\partial A}{\partial x^\mu}\frac{\partial B}{\partial p_\mu} - \frac{\partial B}{\partial x^\mu}\frac{\partial A}{\partial p_\mu} \ . \tag{2.12}$$

Quantization within this framework now follows by Diracs correspondence procedure, replacing Poisson brackets by commutator brackets (divided by ih). This leads to the Heisenberg equations of motion

$$\dot{\hat{p}}_\mu = -\frac{i}{\hbar}[\hat{p}_\mu,\hat{H}]_- \ , \ \dot{\hat{x}}^\mu = -\frac{i}{\hbar}[\hat{x}^\mu,\hat{H}]_- . \tag{2.13}$$

The position and momentum operator obey an algebra, where

$$[\hat{p}_\mu,\hat{F}]_- = -i\hbar\frac{\partial \hat{F}}{\partial \hat{x}^\mu} \ . \tag{2.14}$$

A particular case of (2.14) is the fundamental commutator

$$[\hat{p}_\mu,\hat{x}^\nu]_- = -i\hbar\delta^\nu_\mu \ . \tag{2.15}$$

For the classical Lagrangian $L=L^{(0)}-v(x)$, the canonical procedure leads to the Hamiltonian $H=L+2v(x)=H^{(0)}+v(x)$, where by definition $L^{(0)}\equiv H^{(0)}$ are the 'free particle' quantities. Confining ourselves to this 'free particle', and resolving operator ordering ambiguities by the requirement of covariance, we thus obtain the result (1.3) for the Hamiltonian operator. Transforming from the Heisenberg representation to the Schrödinger coordinate representation, we introduce the scalar wave function $\varphi(x,t)$, which is normalized as

$$\int|\varphi(x,t)|^2 g^{\frac{1}{2}}dx=1 \ . \tag{2.16}$$

The coordinate representation of the momentum operator reads (see e.g. ref. 3).

$$\hat{p}_\mu=-i\hbar g^{-\frac{1}{4}}\frac{\partial}{\partial x^\mu}g^{\frac{1}{4}} , \tag{2.17}$$

so that the covariant Schrödinger equation becomes

$$i\hbar\frac{\partial\varphi(x,t)}{\partial t} = -\tfrac{1}{2}\hbar^2 g^{-\frac{1}{2}}\frac{\partial}{\partial x^\mu}g^{\frac{1}{2}}g^{\mu\nu}\frac{\partial}{\partial x^\nu}\varphi(x,t) \ . \tag{2.18}$$

This may be written shorthand as

$$i\hbar\varphi_{,t} = -\tfrac{1}{2}\hbar^2(g^{\mu\nu}\varphi_{;\nu})_{;\mu} \ , \tag{2.19}$$

where $;\nu$ denotes covariant differentiation[5]. Comparison with the occasionally used formulation in terms of the conventional proba-

bility amplitude $\psi(x,t)$, which is normalized as

$$\int|\psi(x,t)|^2 dx=1 \quad , \tag{2.20}$$

is obtained setting $\varphi=g^{-\frac{1}{4}}\psi$ and leads to

$$i\hbar\frac{\partial\psi(x,t)}{\partial t}=-\tfrac{1}{2}\hbar^2 g^{-\frac{1}{4}}\frac{\partial}{\partial x^{\mu}}g^{\frac{1}{4}}g^{\mu\nu}g^{\frac{1}{4}}\frac{\partial}{\partial x^{\nu}}g^{-\frac{1}{4}}\psi(x,t) \quad . \tag{2.21}$$

Of course, the normalization does not influence possible potential terms $v(x)$[10,13]. In summary of this section: separate use of the classical action principle and subsequent quantization leads to (2.19) for the 'free particle'.

3. THE COVARIANT PATH INTEGRAL

Let us reconsider the quantization postulate, originally put forward by Feyman, in curved spaces. The quantum mechanical transformation function or scalar propagator is given as

$$<x_f,t_f|x_i,t_i>=\iint\mathcal{D}\{x(t)\}\exp[\tfrac{i}{\hbar}\,S(\{x(t)\})] \quad , \tag{3.1}$$

where $S(\{x(t)\}$ represents a c-number (classical) action functional. The pertinent Lagrangian has been defined by (2.1). It should be noted that $S(\{x(t)\})$ in (3.1) is indeed, in principle, the action and not Hamilton's principle function (see section 2).
The formal scalar measure in (3.1) reads

$$\mathcal{D}\{x(t)\}=\lim_{N\to\infty} \mathcal{N}_N \prod_{k=1}^{2N} dx_k \quad , \tag{3.2}$$

where $\mathcal{N}_N$ indicates the appropriate normalization factors. In (3.2) we have introduced $dx_k=g_k^{\frac{1}{2}}dx_k$ for the invariant scalar volume element, with $dx_k=dx_k^0 dx_k^1\ldots dx_k^{M-1}$, M being the space dimension. Further $x_k^{\mu}=x^{\mu}(t_k)$, $x_i^{\mu}=x_0^{\mu}$, and $x_f^{\mu}=x_{2N+1}^{\mu}$. The operational content of (3.1) is that we must sample an arbitray trajectory, connecting fixed end points $x_i=x(t_i)$ and $x_f=x(t_f)$, at an infinity of times $t_k \in (t_i,t_f)$ and integrate over all possible values of the intermediate points $\{x_k=x(t_k)\}$. The transition function obeys the integral equation (group property)

$$<x_k,t_k|x_m,t_m>=\int<x_k,t_k|x_\ell,t_\ell>dx_\ell<x_\ell,t_\ell|x_m,t_m> \quad , \tag{3.3}$$

which implies the resolution of unity

$$\int|x_k,t_k>dx_k<x_k,t_k|=1 \quad , \tag{3.4}$$

expressing the assumed completeness of the position operators. By (3.4) we have

$$|\varphi>=\int|x,t>dx<x,t|\varphi> \tag{3.5}$$

for an arbitrary ket vector. With $\langle x,t|\varphi\rangle=\varphi(x,t)$ denoting the scalar wave function, one obtains

$$\varphi(x,t)=\int\langle x,t|x',t-\tau\rangle\varphi(x',t-\tau)dx' \quad . \tag{3.6}$$

Clearly, relating the path integral (3.1) to the Schrödinger equation requires the computation of the short time ($\tau\downarrow 0$) propagator. DeWitt's evaluation of (3.1) amounts to considering, at least on a very short time interval, the action functional as Hamilton's principle function (2.4). For the c-number 'free particle' Lagrangian (1.1) this leads to the Schrödinger equation

$$i\hbar\varphi_{,t}=-\tfrac{1}{2}\hbar^2(g^{\mu\nu}\varphi_{;\nu})_{;\mu}-\tfrac{1}{6}\hbar^2R\varphi \; . \tag{3.7}$$

Here R is the curvature scalar of Riemannian geometry, defined as[5]

$$R=g^{\lambda\nu}g^{\mu\kappa}R_{\lambda\mu\nu\kappa} \quad , \tag{3.8}$$

where $R_{\lambda\mu\nu\kappa}$ is the fully covariant Riemann-Christoffel tensor

$$R_{\lambda\mu\nu\kappa}=\tfrac{1}{2}(g_{\lambda\nu,\mu\kappa}-g_{\kappa\lambda,\nu\mu}+g_{\mu\kappa,\lambda\nu}-g_{\nu\mu,\kappa\lambda})+g_{\eta\sigma}(\Gamma^{\eta}_{\lambda\nu}\Gamma^{\sigma}_{\mu\kappa}-\Gamma^{\eta}_{\kappa\lambda}\Gamma^{\sigma}_{\nu\mu}) \; . \tag{3.9}$$

The affine connection $\Gamma^{\lambda}_{\mu\nu}$ is expressed in terms of the metric tensor as

$$\Gamma^{\lambda}_{\mu\nu}=\tfrac{1}{2}g^{\lambda\kappa}(g_{\kappa\mu,\nu}-g_{\mu\nu,\kappa}+g_{\nu\kappa,\mu}) \quad . \tag{3.10}$$

Obviously, (3.7) differs from (2.19). Incidentally, it also differs from Graham's result[14]; he found a curvature scalar potential $v=-\hbar^2R/12$, using a fixed point prescription. In brief, he considers that particular solution of (3.3) that exactly preserves its form over the short time interval. However, from a point of view of observable physics there is no reason why the fixed point short time propagator should have priority over any other. It is well-known that the discrete expression for the short time propagator is not unique. Both the extremal path and the fixed point evaluation of the path integral seem to depend on rather arbitrary ad hoc prescriptions.

Now let $\delta\langle x_k,t_k|x_\ell,t_\ell\rangle$ and $\delta\langle x_\ell,t_\ell|x_m,t_m\rangle$ be any conceivable infinitesemal c-number alteration of the corresponding transition function. By (3.3) the implied variation of $\langle x_k,t_k|x_m,t_m\rangle$ reads

$$\delta\langle x_k,t_k|x_m,t_m\rangle=\int dx_\ell\{\delta\langle x_k,t_k|x_\ell,t_\ell\rangle\langle x_\ell,t_\ell|x_m,t_m\rangle$$
$$+\langle x_k,t_k|x_\ell,t_\ell\rangle\delta\langle x_\ell,t_\ell|x_m,t_m\rangle\} \; . \tag{3.11}$$

Continuing this procedure ad infinitum and using the path integral representation (3.1) of the transition function, one formally obtains[3]

$$\delta\langle x_f,t_f|x_i,t_i\rangle=\frac{i}{\hbar}\iint\mathcal{D}\{x(t)\}\ \delta\int_{t_i}^{t_f} L\ dt\ \exp[\frac{i}{\hbar}\int_{t_i}^{t_f} Ldt]$$

$$=\frac{i}{\hbar}\langle x_f,t_f|\delta\int_{t_i}^{t_f}\hat{L}\ dt|x_i,t_i\rangle\ , \tag{3.12}$$

with $\hat{L}$ being the operator Lagrangian. The quantum principle of stationary action now stems from the fact that changes in the transformation function can be produced actually only by explicit alterations in the pertinent initial and final states. That is,

$$\delta\langle x_f,t_f|x_i,t_i\rangle=\frac{i}{\hbar}\langle x_f,t_f|\delta\hat{J}|x_i,t_i\rangle$$

$$=\frac{i}{\hbar}\langle x_f,t_f|\hat{G}_f-\hat{G}_i|x_i,t_i\rangle\ , \tag{3.13}$$

where we have introduced the action operator $\hat{J}$ and the generator $\hat{G}$. Formula (3.13) may be compared with the classical principle (2.6). If we keep the end points fixed, we have

$$[\delta\hat{J}]\Big|_{|x_i,t_i\rangle}^{|x_f,t_f\rangle}=0\ , \tag{3.14}$$

which is the operator version of (2.2). The quantum action principle implies equations of motion for the dynamical variables and will be explicated further on. Summarising this section: we have observed the relation between the covariant path integral representation of the quantum mechanical propagator and the operator principle of stationary action in curved spaces.

4. QUANTUM DYNAMICS AND THE ACTION PRINCIPLE

The determination of the operator Lagrangian is a highly nontrivial matter. It must fulfill two requirements. First, it must be covariant at the quantum level. Second, it must be consistent within the framework of the variational principle. The latter condition means that there must be consistency between the Euler-Lagrange and Hamilton equations at the quantum level.

Following Kawai[9] we begin considering the flat space free particle Lagrangian operator in Cartesian coordinates,

$$L^{(0)}(\hat{\xi},\hat{\dot{\xi}})=\tfrac{1}{2}\eta_{\mu\nu}\hat{\dot{\xi}}^{\mu}\hat{\dot{\xi}}^{\nu} \tag{4.1}$$

and derive its covariant form in general coordinates $\hat{x}^{\mu}$ by introducing the nonlinear point transformation $\hat{\xi}^{\mu}=\hat{\xi}^{\mu}(\hat{x})$. It will be convenient to anticipate the outcome where

$$\left.\begin{aligned} &L^{(0)}(\hat{x},\hat{\dot{x}})=\tfrac{1}{2}\hat{\dot{x}}^{\mu}g_{\mu\nu}(\hat{x})\hat{\dot{x}}^{\nu}+\ell(\hat{x},\hat{\dot{x}}) \ , \\ &\frac{\partial\ell(\hat{x},\hat{\dot{x}})}{\partial\hat{\dot{x}}^{\mu}} = 0 \ , \end{aligned}\right\} \tag{4.2}$$

and where the fundamental commutator (2.15) will hold. In view of (4.2) the canonical momentum reads

$$\hat{p}_{\mu}=\frac{\partial\hat{L}}{\partial\hat{\dot{x}}^{\mu}}=\tfrac{1}{2}[\hat{g}_{\mu\nu},\hat{\dot{x}}^{\nu}]_{+} \ . \tag{4.3}$$

By means of (2.15) one then finds:

$$[\hat{\dot{x}}^{\mu},\hat{x}^{\nu}]_{-}=-i\hbar\hat{g}^{\mu\nu} \ . \tag{4.4}$$

Of course, one should refrain from using (4.4) itself in rewriting the Lagrangian. However, (4.4) implies that in the Lagrange equations of motion

$$[[\hat{\dot{x}}^{\mu},\hat{x}^{\nu}]_{-},\hat{x}^{\lambda}]_{-}=0 \ . \tag{4.5}$$

This allows us to write (4.1) as

$$L^{(0)}(\hat{x},\hat{\dot{x}})=\tfrac{1}{8}\eta_{\mu\nu}(\hat{v}_{\lambda}{}^{\mu}\hat{\dot{x}}^{\lambda}+\hat{\dot{x}}^{\lambda}\hat{v}_{\lambda}{}^{\mu})(\hat{v}_{\sigma}{}^{\nu}\hat{\dot{x}}^{\sigma}+\hat{\dot{x}}^{\sigma}\hat{v}_{\sigma}{}^{\nu}) \ , \tag{4.6}$$

where (see also[10])

$$\hat{v}_{\lambda}{}^{\mu}=v_{\lambda}{}^{\mu}(\hat{x})=\frac{\partial\hat{\xi}^{\mu}}{\partial\hat{x}^{\lambda}} \tag{4.7}$$

From (4.6) it is straightforward to obtain

$$\begin{aligned} L^{(0)}(\hat{x},\hat{\dot{x}})=&\tfrac{1}{2}\hat{\dot{x}}^{\lambda}\hat{g}_{\lambda\sigma}\hat{\dot{x}}^{\sigma}-\tfrac{1}{4}\eta_{\mu\nu}[\hat{\dot{x}}^{\lambda},\hat{v}_{\lambda}{}^{\mu}]_{-}\hat{v}_{\sigma}{}^{\nu}\hat{\dot{x}}^{\sigma} \\ &+\tfrac{1}{4}\eta_{\mu\nu}\hat{\dot{x}}^{\lambda}\hat{v}_{\lambda}{}^{\mu}[\hat{\dot{x}}^{\sigma},\hat{v}_{\sigma}{}^{\nu}]_{-}-\tfrac{1}{8}\eta_{\mu\nu}[\hat{\dot{x}}^{\lambda},\hat{v}_{\lambda}{}^{\mu}]_{-}[\hat{\dot{x}}^{\sigma},\hat{v}_{\sigma}{}^{\nu}]_{-} \ . \end{aligned} \tag{4.8}$$

Further progress is made noting that by virtue of (4.4) the Lagrange equations are invariant under

$$[\hat{\dot{x}}^{\mu},F(\hat{x})]_{-}=[\hat{\dot{x}}^{\mu},\hat{x}^{\nu}]_{-}F_{,\nu}(\hat{x}) \ , \tag{4.9}$$

where $F(\hat{x})$ is an arbitrary operator function. Using the relation[10]

$$\hat{v}_{\mu}{}^{\lambda}{}_{,\nu}=\hat{v}_{\kappa}{}^{\lambda}\hat{\Gamma}^{\kappa}_{\mu\nu} \ , \tag{4.10}$$

$\hat{\Gamma}^{\kappa}_{\mu\nu}$ being the operator affine connection, one finds

$$L^{(0)}(\hat{x},\hat{\dot{x}})=\tfrac{1}{2}\hat{\dot{x}}^{\lambda}\hat{g}_{\lambda\sigma}\hat{\dot{x}}^{\sigma}-\tfrac{1}{4}[\hat{\dot{x}}^{\lambda},\hat{x}^{\kappa}]_{-}\hat{g}_{\sigma\mu}\hat{\Gamma}^{\mu}_{\lambda\kappa}\hat{\dot{x}}^{\sigma}+\tfrac{1}{4}\hat{\dot{x}}^{\sigma}[\hat{\dot{x}}^{\lambda},\hat{x}^{\kappa}]_{-}\hat{g}_{\sigma\mu}\hat{\Gamma}^{\mu}_{\lambda\kappa}$$
$$-\tfrac{1}{8}[\hat{\dot{x}}^{\lambda},\hat{x}^{\kappa}]_{-}\hat{g}_{\mu\nu}\hat{\Gamma}^{\mu}_{\lambda\kappa}\hat{\Gamma}^{\nu}_{\sigma\rho}[\hat{\dot{x}}^{\sigma},\hat{x}^{\rho}]_{-} \quad . \qquad (4.11)$$

This is easily further evaluated into

$$L^{(0)}(\hat{x},\hat{\dot{x}})=\tfrac{1}{2}\hat{\dot{x}}^{\lambda}\hat{g}_{\lambda\sigma}\hat{\dot{x}}^{\sigma}+\tfrac{1}{4}[\hat{\dot{x}}^{\lambda},\hat{x}^{\kappa}]_{-}\{(\hat{g}_{\sigma\mu}\hat{\Gamma}^{\mu}_{\lambda\kappa})_{,\rho}-\tfrac{1}{2}\hat{g}_{\mu\nu}\hat{\Gamma}^{\mu}_{\lambda\kappa}\hat{\Gamma}^{\nu}_{\sigma\rho}\}[\hat{\dot{x}}^{\sigma},\hat{x}^{\rho}]_{-}$$
$$+\tfrac{1}{8}[[\hat{\dot{x}}^{\sigma},[\hat{\dot{x}}^{\lambda},\hat{x}^{\kappa}]_{-}]_{-},\hat{g}_{\sigma\mu}\hat{\Gamma}^{\mu}_{\lambda\kappa}]_{+} \quad . \qquad (4.12)$$

In view of (4.9) one has

$$[\hat{\dot{x}}^{\lambda},\hat{x}^{\kappa}]_{-}(\hat{g}_{\sigma\mu}\hat{\Gamma}^{\mu}_{\lambda\kappa})_{,\rho}[\hat{\dot{x}}^{\sigma},\hat{x}^{\rho}]_{-}=[\hat{\dot{x}}^{\lambda},\hat{x}^{\kappa}]_{-}(\hat{g}_{\lambda\nu}\hat{\Gamma}^{\nu}_{\sigma\rho})_{,\kappa}[\hat{\dot{x}}^{\sigma},\hat{x}^{\rho}]_{-} \quad .(4.13)$$

Invoking (4.13), using (3.10) for $\hat{\Gamma}^{\lambda}_{\mu\nu}$ and employing (3.9) for $\hat{R}_{\mu\lambda\nu\kappa}=0$, one obtains from (4.12) the result:

$$\left.\begin{aligned} L^{(0)}(\hat{x},\hat{\dot{x}})&=\tfrac{1}{2}\hat{\dot{x}}^{\mu}\hat{g}_{\mu\nu}\hat{\dot{x}}^{\nu}+[\hat{\dot{x}}^{\mu},\hat{x}^{\lambda}]_{-}A_{\mu\nu\lambda\sigma}(\hat{x})[\hat{\dot{x}}^{\nu},\hat{x}^{\sigma}]_{-}\\ &\quad+\tfrac{1}{2}[[\hat{\dot{x}}^{\lambda},[\hat{\dot{x}}^{\mu},\hat{x}^{\nu}]_{-}]_{-},B_{\mu\lambda\nu}(\hat{x})]_{+} \quad ,\\ A_{\mu\nu\lambda\sigma}(\hat{x})&=\tfrac{1}{8}(\hat{g}_{\mu\nu,\lambda\sigma}+\hat{g}_{\kappa\rho}\hat{\Gamma}^{\kappa}_{\mu\sigma}\hat{\Gamma}^{\rho}_{\nu\lambda});\ B_{\mu\lambda\nu}(\hat{x})=\tfrac{1}{4}\hat{g}_{\lambda\sigma}\hat{\Gamma}^{\sigma}_{\mu\nu} \quad . \end{aligned}\right\} \qquad (4.14)$$

This is Kawai's 'free particle' Lagrangian operator. It is covariant at the quantum level and consistent within the quantum action principle[9]. Note that (4.14) is in agreement with the Ansatz (4.2).

Two additions to (4.14) can be made. First, of course it is possible to add simple scalar potential terms $v(\hat{x})$, for example $v(\hat{x})=\alpha\hbar^2R(\hat{x})$ with arbitrary α. Second, the quantum action principle allows for so-called Ohtani-terms (see[9] for details). Taking these additions together, the general Lagrangian reads

$$L(\hat{x},\hat{\dot{x}})=L^{(0)}(\hat{x},\hat{\dot{x}})-v(\hat{x})+\beta[\hat{\dot{x}}^{\mu},\hat{x}^{\lambda}]_{-}\hat{R}_{\mu\nu\lambda\sigma}[\hat{\dot{x}}^{\nu},\hat{x}^{\sigma}]_{-}$$
$$+i\beta\hbar[[\hat{\dot{x}}^{\mu},\hat{x}^{\nu}]_{-},\hat{R}_{\mu\nu}]_{+} \quad , \qquad (4.15)$$

β being arbitrary. Within the action principle the Ohtani-terms behave effectively as scalar potential terms (actually of the type just mentioned) as they accordingly change the definition of the Hamiltonian in terms of the Lagrangian.

Now let $\delta t(\tau)=t'(\tau)-t(\tau)$ be an arbitrary infinitesemal alteration in the function $t(\tau)$, τ being an auxillary variable; $t_k=t(\tau_k)$, and τ_i and τ_f are kept fixed. And let $\delta x^{\mu}(t(\tau))=\hat{x}'^{\mu}(t'(\tau))-\hat{x}^{\mu}(t(\tau))$ be an arbitrary inifinitesemal c-number variation in the function $\hat{x}(t)$. This procedure places the time variable on somewhat the same footing as the dynamical

variables[6], and handles inner point and end point variations at once. The variational formula (3.13) is now explicited as

$$\langle x_f,t_f|\delta J(\{\hat{x}(t)\})|x_i,t_i\rangle=\langle x_f,t_f|\int_{\tau_i}^{\tau_f} L(\hat{x}',\frac{d\hat{x}'}{dt'})\frac{dt'}{d\tau}d\tau - \int_{\tau_i}^{\tau_f} L(\hat{x},\frac{d\hat{x}}{dt})\frac{dt}{d\tau}d\tau|x_i,t_i\rangle \; . \tag{4.16}$$

Using (i) that the Lagrangian is quadratic in $\dot{x}^{\mu}$, (ii) that the variations are c-numbers and (iii) a partial integration, one obtains

$$\langle x_f,t_f|\delta\hat{J}|x_i,t_i\rangle=\langle x_f,t_f|\int_{t_i}^{t_f}\{\frac{\partial\hat{L}}{\partial\hat{x}^{\mu}}-\frac{d}{dt}\frac{\partial\hat{L}}{\partial\hat{\dot{x}}^{\mu}}\}\delta x^{\mu}dt + \int_{t_i}^{t_f}\frac{d\hat{\tilde{H}}}{dt}\delta t dt+\hat{G}\Big|_{t_i}^{t_f}|x_i,t_i\rangle \quad , \tag{4.17}$$

where

$$\tilde{H}(\hat{x},\hat{\dot{x}})=L(\hat{x},\hat{\dot{x}})+2v(\hat{x})-i\beta\hbar[[\hat{\dot{x}}^{\mu},\hat{x}^{\nu}]_-,\hat{R}_{\mu\nu}]_+ \quad , \tag{4.18}$$

$$G(\hat{x},\hat{\dot{x}})=\hat{p}_{\mu}\delta x^{\mu}-\hat{\tilde{H}}\delta t \tag{4.19}$$

and where $\hat{p}_{\mu}$ is defined by (4.3). The operator principle of stationary action implies the Lagrange equations of motion. Further, expressing $\hat{\dot{x}}^{\mu}$ in terms of $\hat{p}_{\nu}$, and defining $H(\hat{x},\hat{p})\equiv\tilde{H}(\hat{x},\hat{\dot{x}})$, it leads to the Hamilton-Heisenberg dynamics[6,9]. Since the Lagrangian has been assumed not to depend explicity on time, the Hamiltonian is found to be a constant of the motion.

Let us again confine ourselves to the 'free particle' with $\hat{H}\equiv\hat{L}$, i.e. with $\hat{H}^{(0)}\equiv\hat{L}^{(0)}$. Since $\hat{L}$ is covariant, it can be conveniently transformed to the origin $y^{\mu}=0$ of Riemannian normal coordinates (see e.g.[15]), where

$$\hat{g}_{\mu\nu,\lambda}\Big|_o=0, \; \hat{g}_{\mu\nu,\lambda\sigma}\Big|_o=\tfrac{1}{3}(\hat{R}_{\mu\lambda\nu\sigma}+\hat{R}_{\nu\lambda\mu\sigma})\Big|_o \; . \tag{4.20}$$

Hence, $\hat{\Gamma}^{\lambda}_{\mu\nu}\Big|_o=0$ and $\hat{g}_{,\mu\nu}\Big|_o=\tfrac{2}{3}\hat{g}\hat{R}_{\mu\nu}\Big|_o$. Using (4.4), (4.20), the inverted version of (4.3) in order to express $\hat{\dot{x}}^{\mu}$ in terms of $\hat{p}_{\nu}$, the definition (3.8) of the curvature scalar and the general properties

$$\hat{g}^{\mu\lambda}\hat{g}^{\nu\sigma}\hat{R}_{\mu\lambda\nu\sigma}=0,\quad \hat{g}^{\mu\lambda}\hat{g}^{\nu\sigma}\hat{R}_{\nu\lambda\mu\sigma}=-\hat{R}\quad , \tag{4.21}$$

one obtains

$$\hat{H}^{(0)}=\tfrac{1}{8}[\hat{g}^{\lambda\mu},\hat{p}_\mu]_+\hat{g}_{\lambda\sigma}[\hat{g}^{\sigma\nu},\hat{p}_\nu]_+ + \frac{1}{24}\hbar^2\hat{R}\Big|_0 \quad . \tag{4.22}$$

Using the coordinate representation (2.17) and writing (4.22) in covariant form, one finally obtains the 'free particle' Schrödinger equation

$$i\hbar\varphi_{,t}=-\tfrac{1}{2}\hbar^2(g^{\mu\nu}\varphi_{;\nu})_{;\mu}-\tfrac{1}{8}\hbar^2R\varphi \quad . \tag{4.23}$$

5. QUANTUM DYNAMICS AND THE PATH INTEGRAL

The variational principle exploited in section 4 has been derived from the functional integral in section 3. In the present section we shall evaluate (3.1), and compare the outcome with (4.23), confining ourselves for simplicity again to the 'free particle'. In that case $\hat{L}^{(0)}\equiv\hat{H}^{(0)}$ are the operators corresponding to the c-number functions $L^{(0)}\equiv H^{(0)}$, so that we consider

$$<x_f,t_f|x_i,t_i>=\iint\mathcal{D}\{x(t)\}\exp[\frac{i}{\hbar}\int_{t_i}^{t_f}\tfrac{1}{2}g_{\mu\nu}(x)\dot{x}^\mu\dot{x}^\nu dt] \quad . \tag{5.1}$$

For reasons qualified earlier, neither DeWitt's (3.7) nor Graham's evaluation of this expression agrees with (4.23). Now note that in (5.1) there is no restriction whatsoever on the time interval $t_f-t_i=\tau$. This simply means that in (5.1) we must integrate over an infinite number of intermediate sample points, no matter how small τ may be. This requires a priori full arbitrariness of the trajectories connecting fixed end points, even on the shortest conceivable time lapses τ. There does not seem to be the slightest reason to evaluate (5.1) as $\tau\downarrow 0$ merely along the extremal short time path, although in flat spaces this leads in effect to the same result as more general techniques. So, if R=0 DeWitt's extremal 'classical' path evaluation appears to be justified a posteriori. However, if it is used in an a priori sense, it amounts to an ad hoc discretization prescription which has no foundation in general.

In order to overcome the difficulties we will invoke a Fourier series representation of the short time trajectories[7,8]. Such a spectral analysis of smooth paths allows for the usual interpretation of velocities $\dot{x}^\mu$, but does not at forehand disregard the possibility of 'almost non differentiable paths'[8,16]. In particular from a physical point of view such an analysis seems quite natural, and in line with the variational principle treatment which involves smooth operator functions.

As mentioned in the introduction, it is meaningless to trans-

form the path integral to locally Cartesian frames if space is essentially curved. However, like done in the evaluation of the action principle, we may attach the postpoint x_f^μ to the origin $y^\mu=0$ of a Riemannian normal coordinate system[12,13]. This considerably simplifies the calculations. Doing so, we shall evaluate the propagator $\langle 0,0|y_i,-\tau\rangle$ as $\tau\downarrow 0$ by setting

$$y^\mu(t)= - y_i^\mu s+z^\mu(s) \quad , \tag{5.2}$$

where $s=t/\tau$, where the first term on the r.h.s. represents the geodesic part of the trajectory and where $z^\mu(s)$ is an arbitrary remainder connecting $z^\mu(-1)=0$ with $z^\mu(0)=0$. The latter part is written as

$$z^\mu(s)= \sum_{n=1}^{N} a_n^\mu \sin 2\pi ns + \sum_{n=1}^{N} b_n^\mu(1-\cos 2\pi ns) \quad , \tag{5.3}$$

where finally $N\to\infty$. The representation (5.3) leads to more simple algebra than the earlier used pure sine series[8,10]. Nevertheless, we have verified that both representations do lead to the same final result. One now expands $g_{\mu\nu}(y)$ in the Lagrangian and $g(y)$ in the measure about the origin as (see also 4.20))

$$g_{\mu\nu}(y)=g_{\mu\nu}(0)+\tfrac{1}{6}[R_{\mu\lambda\nu\sigma}(0)+R_{\nu\lambda\mu\sigma}(0)]y^\lambda y^\sigma+\dots \quad , \tag{5.4}$$

$$g(y)=g(0)[1+\tfrac{1}{3}R_{\mu\nu}(0)y^\mu y^\nu+\dots] \quad . \tag{5.5}$$

More terms will not be needed since, as usual, we only have to keep track of terms of order τ in the short time integral; as will be seen in a minute, y^μ is of order $\tau^{\frac{1}{2}}$. By (5.4) the action separates in two obvious parts which are denoted as S_0 and S_2. Inserting (5.2) and (5.3) into

$$S_0=\frac{1}{2\tau}g_{\mu\nu}(0)\int_{-1}^{0}\dot{y}^\mu(s)\dot{y}^\nu(s)ds \quad , \tag{5.6}$$

and evaluating some simple goniometric integrals, the immediate result for the dominant part of the action reads

$$S_0=\frac{1}{2\tau}g_{\mu\nu}(0)y_i^\mu y_i^\nu+\frac{1}{\tau}g_{\mu\nu}(0)\sum_{n=1}^{N}\pi^2 n^2(a_n^\mu a_n^\nu+b_n^\mu b_n^\nu) \quad . \tag{5.7}$$

This leads to the usual calculation of Gaussian integrals over the Fourier coefficients (i.e. over the intermediate points). On has

$$\langle a_n^\mu a_m^\nu\rangle_o=\langle b_n^\mu b_m^\nu\rangle_o=i\hbar\tau g^{\mu\nu}(0)\delta_{nm}/2\pi^2n^2 \quad . \tag{5.8}$$

Higher moments easily follow by means of the Gaussian theorem. Further, in the end we must also perform an integration over the

prepoint y_i^μ. In contributions which are of order τ we may therefore directly use

$$\langle y_i^\mu y_i^\nu \rangle_o = i\hbar\tau g^{\mu\nu}(0) \quad . \tag{5.9}$$

The second part of the action becomes

$$S_2 = \frac{1}{6\tau} R_{\mu\lambda\nu\sigma}(0) \int_{-1}^{0} \langle y^\lambda y^\sigma \dot{y}^\mu \dot{y}^\nu \rangle_o ds \quad . \tag{5.10}$$

In view of (5.8) and (5.9) it is readily clear that S_2 is of order τ. Using (5.2) and (5.3), the Gaussian theorem, (5.9), the fact that by (5.8) $\langle z^\mu z^\nu \rangle_o \sim \langle \dot{z}^\mu \dot{z}^\nu \rangle_o \sim \tau g^{\mu\nu}(0)$, and the properties (3.8) connected with the curvature tensor, it is straightforward to split S_2 into four separate contributions, the first of which reads

$$S_2^{(1)} \underset{=}{<>} \frac{i\hbar}{6} R_{\mu\nu}(0) \int_{-1}^{0} \langle z^\mu z^\nu \rangle_o ds \quad , \tag{5.11}$$

where $\underset{=}{<>}$ denotes equivalence within the functional integral. Inserting (5.3) gives

$$S_2^{(1)} \underset{=}{<>} \frac{i\hbar}{6} R_{\mu\nu}(0) \sum_{n=1}^{N} \sum_{m=1}^{N} \Big[\langle a_n^\mu a_m^\nu \rangle_o \int_{-1}^{0} \sin 2\pi ns \, \sin 2\pi ms \, ds$$
$$+ \langle b_n^\mu b_m^\nu \rangle_o \int_{-1}^{0} (1-\cos 2\pi ns)(1-\cos 2\pi ms) ds \Big] . \tag{5.12}$$

Using (5.8) this leads to

$$S_2^{(1)} \underset{=}{<>} -\frac{\tau}{6} \hbar^2 R(0) \sum_{n=1}^{N} \frac{1}{\pi^2 n^2} \int_{-1}^{0} (1-\cos 2\pi ns) ds \quad . \tag{5.13}$$

Performing the integration and invoking the outcome $\pi^2/6$ for the sum of the inverse squares of all natural numbers (see e.g. ref. 17), one finds the result

$$S_2^{(1)} \underset{=}{<>} -\frac{\tau}{36} \hbar^2 R(0) \quad . \tag{5.14}$$

The next part $S_2^{(2)}$ reads

$$S_2^{(2)} \underset{=}{<>} -\frac{i\hbar}{3} R_{\mu\nu}(0) \int_{-1}^{0} \langle z^\nu \dot{z}^\mu \rangle_o s ds \quad . \tag{5.15}$$

Inserting (5.3), using (5.8), evaluating the integral and again using the mentioned result for the occurring sum, one obtains

$$S_2^{(2)} \overset{<>}{=} -\frac{\tau}{36}\hbar^2 R(0) \quad . \tag{5.16}$$

The following contribution $S_2^{(3)}$ reads

$$S_2^{(3)} \overset{<>}{=} \frac{i\hbar}{6} R_{\mu\nu}(0) \int_{-1}^{0} \langle \dot{z}^{\mu} \dot{z}^{\nu} \rangle_o \, s^2 ds \quad . \tag{5.17}$$

By the same procedure as above, one finds the singular result

$$S_2^{(3)} \overset{<>}{=} -\frac{\tau}{9} N\hbar^2 R(0) \quad . \tag{5.18}$$

The remaining $S_2^{(4)}$ is similarly found to be

$$S_2^{(4)} \overset{<>}{=} -\frac{\tau}{18} N\hbar^2 R(0) + \frac{\tau}{72}\hbar^2 R(0) \quad . \tag{5.19}$$

Adding up $S_2^{(1)}$ through $S_2^{(4)}$ one obtains

$$S_2 \overset{<>}{=} -\frac{\tau}{6} N\hbar^2 R(0) - \frac{\tau}{24}\hbar^2 R(0) \quad . \tag{5.20}$$

This suffices as far as the original action is concerned. By means of (5.5) the measure (3.2) separates into its dominant part (that goes into the normalization of the Gaussian integrations with S_o) and a remainder that can be exponentiated so as to effectively add a term Ξ to the action. Namely,

$$\Xi \overset{<>}{=} -i\hbar \,\ell n \prod_{k=1}^{2N} \langle [g(y_k)/g(0)]^{\frac{1}{2}} \rangle_o \quad . \tag{5.21}$$

Hence, we must evaluate

$$\Xi \overset{<>}{=} -\frac{i\hbar}{6} R_{\mu\nu}(0) \sum_{k=1}^{2N} \langle y^{\mu}(-\tfrac{k}{2N+1}) y^{\nu}(-\tfrac{k}{2N+1}) \rangle_o \quad . \tag{5.22}$$

Inserting (5.2) and (5.3) one finds

$$\Xi \overset{<>}{=} \frac{\tau}{6}\hbar^2 R(0) \sum_{k=1}^{2N} \left[\frac{1}{6} + \frac{k^2}{(2N+1)^2} - \sum_{n=1}^{N} \frac{1}{\pi^2 n^2} \cos\left(\frac{2\pi nk}{2N+1}\right)\right] \quad . \tag{5.23}$$

Interchanging the summations over k and n, and using some elementary formula (see e.g. ref. 17), one easily obtains the outcome

$$\Xi \overset{<>}{=} \frac{\tau}{6} N\hbar^2 R(0) \quad , \tag{5.24}$$

which thus precisely cancels the singular term in S_2, i.e. (5.20). Therefore, the skeletonized short time propagator is singularity free:

$$\langle 0,0 | y_i, -\tau \rangle \overset{<>}{=} N \exp\frac{i}{\hbar} \left[\frac{1}{2\tau} g_{\mu\nu}(0) y_i^{\mu} y_i^{\nu} - \frac{\tau}{24}\hbar^2 R(0)\right] \quad . \tag{5.25}$$

The appropriate normalization factor is $N=(2\pi i\hbar\tau)^{-M/2}$. It should be noted that the additional $-\tau\hbar^2R/24$ in (5.25) essentially stems from the fact that we have not a priori restricted restricted ourselves to the extremal trajectory. In order to derive the Schrödinger equation, the transition kernel (5.25) must now be inserted into the integral equation (3.6). At the origin of normal coordinates (3.6) reads

$$\varphi(0,0)=\int_{-\infty}^{\infty} \langle 0,0|y_i,-\tau\rangle\varphi(y_i,-\tau)g^{\frac{1}{2}}(y_i)dy_i \quad . \tag{5.26}$$

By means of Feyman's original technique involving integration over the prepoint (e.g. refs. 2, 7, 13 and 18), one readily obtains

$$i\hbar\frac{\partial\varphi}{\partial t}=-\tfrac{1}{2}\hbar^2 g^{-\frac{1}{2}}g^{\mu\nu}\frac{\partial^2}{\partial y^\mu\partial y^\nu}\varphi g^{\frac{1}{2}}+\frac{1}{24}\hbar^2R\varphi\Big|_0 \tag{5.27}$$

Casting this into covariant form using the properties of the metric tensor at the origin of normal coordinates, and then transforming back to the general coordinates one arrives at the result

$$i\hbar\varphi_{,t}=-\tfrac{1}{2}\hbar^2(g^{\mu\nu}\varphi_{;\nu})_{;\mu}-\tfrac{1}{8}\hbar^2R\varphi \quad , \tag{5.28}$$

which fully agrees with the variational principle result (4.23).

6. SUMMARY AND CONCLUDING REMARKS

We have considered the functional integral representation of the quantum mechanical transformation function as a quantization postulate. The purpose of our investigation has been twofold. First, to make clear that there is no precise relation at the quantum level between the path integral quantization postulate on the one hand, and the usual procedure using the classical action principle with subsequent canonical quantization on the other hand. On the contrary, there is an intimate connection between the path integral and the quantum action principle. The second purpose has been to show how the formal functional integral must be evaluated in order to find the corresponding Hamiltonian operator. This leads to precisely the same quantum dynamics as obtained from the variational principle.

Let us oncemore confine ourselves to the 'free particle'. For the 'classical free particle' one has $L^{(0)}\equiv H^{(0)}$; $L^{(0)}$ is given in (1.1); $H^{(0)}$ is defined within the framework of the classical action principle and explicited in (1.2). Similarly, for the 'quantal free particle' one has $\hat{\mathcal{L}}^{(0)}\equiv\hat{\mathcal{H}}^{(0)}$; $\hat{\mathcal{L}}^{(0)}$ is given in (4.14); $\hat{\mathcal{H}}^{(0)}$ is defined by the quantum action principle. In view of the connection between the covariant path integral and the variational principle, $L^{(0)}$ is the c-number function corresponding to $\hat{\mathcal{L}}^{(0)}$. Noticing that the quantum action principle essentially involves smooth operator functions, we have evaluated the path integral by smooth c-number

functions. Such trajectories have been represented by means of a Fourier series analysis in Riemannian normal coordinates. In this manner both the covariant action principle and the covariant funcional integral lead to one and the same quantum dynamics. In representation free operator form the 'free particle' Hamiltonian may be read from either (4.23) or (5.28) to be

$$\hat{H}^{(0)} = \tfrac{1}{2}\hat{g}^{-\frac{1}{4}}\hat{p}_\mu \hat{g}^{\frac{1}{2}}\hat{g}^{\mu\nu}\hat{p}_\nu \hat{g}^{-\frac{1}{4}} - \tfrac{1}{8}\hbar^2\hat{R} \quad . \tag{6.1}$$

Thus we have obtained the following scheme:

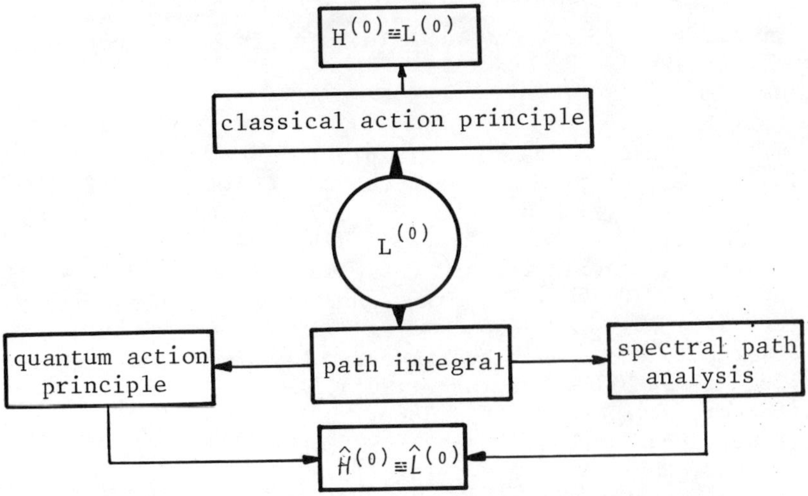

Incidentically, there is no special physical meaning to the term 'free particle' in a curved space where the particle is necessarily subject to gravitational forces. In order to avoid any confusion, the restriction in the preceding to the 'free particle' should be given a further comment because it is in no way essential. To put it firm, there is not the slightest reason to consider (6.1) as the unique quantum Hamiltonian corresponding to the classical 'free particle' (1.2). There exists an infinite number of quantum Hamiltonians that reduce to the classical free particle one as $\hbar \downarrow 0$. Typical examples are (1.3) and (3.7). As also mentioned in section 4, one may add in this sense any potential term with the property $\lim_{\hbar \to 0} v(x,\hbar) = 0$. The Ohtani-terms are of this type.
Of course, one could also consider a particle in a true classical potential. Such potentials play precisely the same role both in classical and in quantum dynamics. In any case, the essential outcome of our investigation is that the spectral path analysis and the quantum action principle lead to identical results.

Without going into the details, one final remark must be made concerning classical stochastic processes (see e.g. refs. 1, 8, 10 and 14). In view of the formal analogy between the Schrödinger

equation of quantum mechanics and the Fokker-Planck equation of Markovian diffusion processes, the so-called Onsager-Machlup Lagrangian occurring in the path integral representation of the covariant transition probability in curved phase space reads

$$L=\tfrac{1}{2}g_{\mu\nu}(\dot{x}^{\mu}-\alpha^{\mu})(\dot{x}^{\nu}-\alpha^{\nu})+\tfrac{1}{2}\alpha^{\mu}{}_{;\mu}+\tfrac{1}{8}R \quad , \tag{6.2}$$

where $\alpha^{\mu}(x)$ is the contravariant drift vector of the pertinent diffusion process.

ACKNOWLEDGEMENT

I am indebted to Dr. T. Kawai for a useful correspondence.

REFERENCES

1. H. Dekker, Physica 85A, 363 (1976).
2. R.P. Feynman, Revs. Mod. Phys. 20, 327 (1948).
3. B.S. DeWitt, Revs. Mod. Phys. 29, 377 (1957).
4. B. Podolski, Phys. Rev. 32, 812 (1928).
5. S. Weinberg, Gravitation and Cosmology, Wiley, New York (1972).
6. J. Schwinger, Quantum Kinematics and Dynamics, Benjamin, New York (1970).
7. R.P. Feynman and A.R. Hibbs, Quantum Mechanics and Path Integrals, McGraw-Hill, New York (1965).
8. H. Dekker, Phys. Lett. 65A, 388 (1978).
9. T. Kawai, Found. Phys. 5, 143 (1975).
10. H. Dekker, Phys. Rev. A19, 2102 (1979).
11. F. Langouche, D. Roekaerts and E. Tirapegui, preprint KUL-TF-78/027(Leuven), to appear in Phys.Rev.A.
12. C. Lanczos, The Variational Principles of Mechanics, Univ. Press, Toronto (1970).
13. G.A. Ringwood, J. Phys. A9, 1253 (1976).
14. U. Deininghaus and R. Graham, Z.Phys. B34, 211 (1979).
15. O. Veblen, Invariants of Quadratic Differential Forms, Univ. Press, Cambridge (1952).
16. C. Lanczos, Discourse on Fourier Series, Oliver and Boyd, Edinburgh (1966).
17. I.S. Gradshteyn and I.W. Ryzhik, Table of Integrals, Series and Products, Academic, New York (1965).
18. H. Dekker, Physica 84A, 205 (1976).

INTRINSIC PATH INTEGRAL SOLUTION TO THE FOKKER-PLANCK EQUATION

Luis Garrido and Josep Llosa

Departamento de Fisica Teórica
Universidad de Barcelona
Diagonal 647
Barcelona, 28 (Spain)

1. INTRODUCTION

In studying physical reality by tensor methods, one is invariably restricted to the natural frames associated with a local coordinate system. From the physical point of view it must be possible to express physical reality in any reference system. Therefore, we should be able to write all laws of physics in a way independent of the coordinates used to describe such a physical reality.

The aim of this paper is to present an intrinsic formulation of the Fokker-Planck equation, i.e., a formulation of the latter that is completely independent of the gross variables used to describe a general diffusion process. We also wish to solve such an intrinsic Fokker-Planck equation by means of a path integral that is itself deduced in an intrinsic way.

To achieve our aim we will use the theory of exterior differential forms. It has been argued before by one of us[1] that exterior differential calculus could be an appropriate tool to study the behaviour of the Fokker-Planck equation under general gross variable transformations. Since we concluded that Riemann differential geometry is not the most "economical" mathematical algorithm, we will try in this paper to avoid the concept of affine connection.

The main mathematical tools[2] that we use here to find an intrinsic expression for the Fokker-Planck equation are the exterior derivative operation, d, and the (Hodge) star operator, $\star$.
Both are operators that are independent of the gross variables, i.e., they are intrinsic operators.

In general, exterior differential calculus allows us to arrive at compact mathematical expressions for our equations. Besides the physical meaning of these is immediate since all local relations arise one way or another from Poincaré's lemma and all global relations arise from Stoke's theorem. Finally, once we learn how to handle the intrinsic operators d and ⋆ , we only need the boundary values of the gross variables of our problem in order to arrive at physical conclusions from our intrinsic equations.

We do not claim here to be completely rigorous from a mathematical point of view; we simply try to present a new representation for the Fokker-Planck equation and a method to solve it by path integrals. Our mathematical techniques are midway between purely formal and totally rigorous.

In section 2 of this work we present, for the sake of completeness, a short introduction to the covariant Fokker-Planck equation. Section 3 develops the intrinsic formulation of the latter by means of exterior calculus. The path integral solution is defined in section 4.

We wish to maintain our exposition coherent and never loose the intrinsic character of our equations. Consequently, we introduce in section 5 a definition of Fourier transform that is independent of the gross variables. Such a definition opens up the possibility of developing an intrinsic perturbation theory. Later on, in section 5, we integrate the Fokker-Planck equation and the Lagrangian obtained is presented in section 7. We end up our work with the conclusions and outlook.

2. COVARIANT FOKKER-PLANCK EQUATION

A Fokker-Planck equation is said to be covariant under general gross variable transformations if the form of the equation is left unchanged by the transformations. The principle of covariance imposes no restrictions on its physical content but only on the form in which it is written.

We study in this section the covariance of the Fokker-Planck equation by means of Riemann differential geometry using an affine connection $\Gamma^{\rho}_{\mu\nu}$ unsymmetric in its lower indices.

We write the Fokker-Planck equation as

$$\frac{\partial p(q,t)}{\partial t} \equiv \dot{p}(q,t) = \{ - \frac{\partial}{\partial q^{\nu}} f^{\nu}(q) + \frac{1}{2} \frac{\partial^2}{\partial q^{\nu} \partial q^{\mu}} D^{\nu\mu}(q) \} \cdot P(q,t) \qquad (2.$$

where the Greek indices denote the gross variables, $q^{\nu}(t), \nu = 1,..n$; $P(q,t)$ is the probability density to observe the phase space point $q = \{q^{\nu}\}$ at time t; $f^{\nu}(q)$ is the drift and $D^{\nu\mu}(q)$ is the non-constant diffusion matrix. Under a general transformation of the gross variables, $q' = q'(q)$, $f^{\nu}(q)$ does not behave like a contravariant vector neither is $P(q,t)$ a scalar, while , indeed, $D^{\nu\mu}(q)$ transforms like a contravariant tensor. It is convenient to rewrite the above equation in terms of a scalar probability density that, in the present case, is given by

$$S(q,t) = P(q,t) \cdot \sqrt{D(q)} \quad , \quad D \equiv |D^{\nu\mu}| \tag{2.2}$$

where D is the determinant of the tensor $D^{\nu\mu}$. The Fokker-Planck equation becomes

$$\dot{S} = - \sqrt{D} \left\{ \frac{1}{\sqrt{D}} (h^{\nu}.S - \frac{1}{2} D^{\nu\mu} \cdot S_{,\mu}) \right\}_{,\nu} \tag{2.3}$$

where we have written

$$h^{\nu} \equiv f^{\nu} - \frac{1}{2} \sqrt{D} \left(\frac{D^{\mu\nu}}{\sqrt{D}} \right)_{,\mu} \tag{2.4}$$

that behaves like a contravariant drift vector. Use has been made of the notation $A_{,\nu} \equiv \frac{\partial A}{\partial q^{\nu}}$ for any quantity A.

Now we write down the connection between any nonsingular contravariant symmetric tensor - in particular we will use the diffusion matrix $D^{\mu\nu}(q)$ -, the corresponding covariant tensor $D_{\mu\nu}$, defined by

$$D^{\lambda\mu} D_{\mu\nu} = D_{\nu\mu} D^{\nu\lambda} = \delta^{\lambda}_{\nu} \tag{2.5}$$

the covariant and ordinary derivatives of those, and the affine connection $\Gamma^{\rho}_{\mu\lambda}$ that connects them all. We easily arrive at

$$\Gamma^{\rho}_{\lambda\nu} = \overset{R}{\Gamma}{}^{\rho}_{\lambda\nu} - \frac{1}{2} D^{\rho\mu} (D_{\mu\nu;\lambda} + D_{\mu\lambda;\nu} - D_{\lambda\nu;\mu}) + \frac{1}{2} D^{\rho\mu} ({}_{\nu}T_{\lambda\mu} + {}_{\lambda}T_{\nu\mu}) + \\ + \frac{1}{2} T^{\rho}_{\lambda\nu} \tag{2.6}$$

where $\overset{R}{\Gamma}{}^{\rho}_{\lambda\nu}$, called here the Riemann affine connection, is defined by

$$\overset{R}{\Gamma}{}^{\rho}_{\lambda\nu} \equiv \frac{1}{2} D^{\rho\mu} (D_{\mu\nu,\lambda} + D_{\mu\lambda,\nu} - D_{\lambda\nu,\mu}) \tag{2.7}$$

$D_{\mu\nu;\lambda}$ represents the covariant derivative of $D_{\mu\nu}$ and the torsion tensor $T^{\rho}_{\mu\nu}$ is

$$T^{\rho}_{\mu\nu} = \Gamma^{\rho}_{\mu\nu} - \Gamma^{\rho}_{\nu\mu} \, , \qquad {}_{\rho}T_{\mu\nu} = D_{\rho\lambda} \; T^{\lambda}_{\mu\nu} \tag{2.8}$$

An important observation that we want to emphasize now is that to study the covariance of the Fokker-Planck equation we do not need all the components of the affine connection, $\Gamma^{\rho}_{\lambda\nu}$. Indeed, it is sufficient to consider the sum $\Gamma^{\rho}_{\rho\nu}$ that depends explicitly only on the index ν since all other indices are contracted. And so, we immediately have

$$\Gamma^{\rho}_{\rho\nu} = \overset{R}{\Gamma}{}^{\rho}_{\rho\nu} - \frac{1}{2} D^{\mu\rho} D_{\mu\rho;\nu} \tag{2.9}$$

where

$$\overset{R}{\Gamma}{}^{\rho}_{\rho\nu} = - \frac{1}{2} (\ln D)_{,\nu} \tag{2.10}$$

These expressions are valid quite generally without any restriction upon the value of the torsion tensor. Thus, we arrive at the covariant expression of the Fokker-Planck equation

$$\dot{S} = - (h^{\nu}S - \frac{1}{2} D^{\mu\nu} S_{;\mu})_{;\nu} - \frac{1}{2} D^{\sigma\tau} D_{\tau\sigma;\nu} (h^{\nu}S - \frac{1}{2} D^{\mu\nu} S_{;\mu}) \tag{2.11}$$

obtained without any condition on the value of the covariant derivative of the diffusion matrix.

Therefore, to study the covariant formulation of the physical problems related to the Fokker-Planck equation we only need the value of the contraction $\Gamma^{\rho}_{\rho\nu}$, leaving the rest of the components of the affine connection completely undetermined. With only the knowledge of the contraction $\Gamma^{\rho}_{\rho\nu}$ the covariant derivative of many tensors will not even be defined.

We may conclude from what has been said that Riemann differentia geometry is not the most "economical" mathematical algorithm to study the covariance of Fokker-Planck equation under general gross variable transformations. Indeed, in order to obtain such a covariance it is sufficient to evaluate the covariance of antisymmetric tensors. But antisymmetric tensors and their antisymmetrized derivatives possess certain remarkably simple and useful properties, that mathematicians have developed in a unified way, creating the general formalism known as the theory of exterior differential calculus.

In studying the covariance of an equation one is invariably restricted to the natural frames associated with local coordinate systems. In what follows we try to present an intrinsic formulation for the Fokker-Planck equation that is completely independent of the system of gross variables selected.

3. INTRINSIC FOKKER-PLANCK EQUATIONS

Gross variables are convenient crutches for describing the physical content of the Fokker-Planck equation. But such a physical content is independent of the gross variables one uses and this independence can, indeed, find its mathematical expression in the requirement that the Fokker-Planck equation be formulated in an intrinsic way. An intrinsic formulation does have a body of substantial or deep results established once and for all within the subject and then available for application.

We call M the manifold formed by the states of the physical system. To identify mathematically these states we select one among several systems of gross variables related by general transformations that are smooth and preserve their number. We consider also the infinitesimal variations dq^{ν}, of the gross variables; their ensemble, starting from a given state $q = \{q^{\nu}\}_{\nu}$ $\nu = 1,\dots.n$, constitute the cotangent vector space at q, and $\{dq^{\nu}, \nu = 1, \dots n\}$, form a base. Such a vector space is denoted in this work by $\Lambda^1_q M$ and its elements are called 1-forms. In general, the space $\Lambda^1_q M$ consists of all sums

$$A_{h_1,\dots,h_r} \, dq^{h_1} \wedge dq^{h_2} \wedge \dots \wedge dq^{h_r} \tag{3.1}$$

which we call r-forms, where $dq^{h_1} \wedge dq^{h_2}$ indicates the exterior product of two 1-forms dq^{h_1} and dq^{h_2}.

The ensemble of all differential r-forms - for any value of q - will be denoted by $\Lambda^r M$, $r > 0$. As an extension of this definition we will call $\Lambda^0 M$ the set of all smooth scalar functions on M.

Concretely, our manifold M is a Riemannian manifold in which a Euclidean geometry has been imposed in each cotangent space. Any Riemannian geometry allows us to define scalar products between differential 1-forms. A scalar product is a mapping that assigns to each pair α, β of differential 1-forms, a 0-form $\langle\alpha, \beta\rangle$ which is symmetric, bilinear, non degenerate and positive definite. In a concrete system of gross variables a scalar product is determined by the invertible diffusion tensor (2.5). Our main mathematical tools are the exterior differential operator d and the star operator $\star$[2]. The operator d exists ans is unique if it is axiomatized by

a) If $\omega \varepsilon \Lambda^{\tau} M$, then $d\omega \, \varepsilon \Lambda^{r+1} M$

b) $d(\omega + \lambda) = d\,\omega + d\,\lambda$

c) $d(\omega \wedge \lambda) = d\,\omega \wedge \lambda + (-1)^r \, \omega \wedge d\lambda$

d) For any form ω , $d(d\omega) = 0$

e) For each function $A = A(q) \varepsilon \Lambda^{\circ} M$

$$d A = \frac{\partial A}{\partial q^{\nu}} d q^{\nu} = A_{,\nu} \, dq^{\nu} \tag{3.2}$$

In addition we will assume that our manifold M is contractible, which guarantees the converse of property d) above (in other words, Poincaré's lemma holds on M) :

f) Given any r-form ω such that $d\omega = 0$, there exists an (r-1)-form λ such that $\omega = d\lambda$.

The space of n-forms $\Lambda^n M$ - which is one-dimensional - admits the orthogonal basis σ defined by

$$\sigma = \frac{1}{\sqrt{D(q)}} d q^1 \Lambda \dots \Lambda dq^n \tag{3.3}$$

The star operator $\star$ is a mapping that assigns to each r-form, $\omega \varepsilon \Lambda^r M$, an (n-r)-form $\star\omega \varepsilon \Lambda^{n-r} M$ in such a way that for any $\mu \varepsilon \Lambda^{n-r} M$ we have

$$\omega \Lambda \mu = \langle \star\omega \; \mu \rangle \sigma \tag{3.4}$$

After this short mathematical introduction we try to write eq. (2.1) in the intrinsic language of exterior differential calculus. To achieve our aim we introduce the time dependent (n-1)-form κ defined by

$$\kappa \equiv \left[P(q,t) f^{\nu}(q) - \frac{1}{2} \{D^{\mu\nu}(q) P(q,t)\}_{,\mu} \right] . (-1)^{(\nu)-1} dq^1 \Lambda \dots \Lambda \widehat{dq^{\nu}} \Lambda \dots \Lambda dq^n \tag{3.5}$$

where summation upon repeated indices ν is assumed, except when an index is within a parenthesis (ν).

We also suppose throughout this paper that the upper indices are always written in increasing order $1 < 2 < \dots < \nu < \dots < n$. By $\widehat{dq^{\nu}}$ we mean that the infinitesimal vector dq^{ν} is missing at the place ν.

The intrinsic drift, η, is a 1-form defined by

$$\eta \equiv h_{\nu} \, dq^{\nu} \qquad \eta \varepsilon \Lambda^1 M \tag{3.6}$$

$$h_{\mu} = D_{\mu\nu} \, h^{\nu} \tag{3.7}$$

where the contravariant drift vector h^{ν} was introduced in eq. (2.4)

We easily obtain

$$\kappa = \frac{1}{\sqrt{D}} \left(S\, h^{\nu} - \frac{1}{2} D^{\nu\mu} S,_{\mu}\right) (-1)^{(\nu)-1} dq^{1} \Lambda \,\ldots\, \Lambda dq^{\nu} \Lambda \,\ldots\, \Lambda dq^{n}$$

$$= \star\left(S\eta - \frac{1}{2} d\, S\right) \;; \quad \kappa \varepsilon \Lambda^{n-1} M \qquad (3.8)$$

where use has been made of the expression

$$\star\, dq^{\mu} = \frac{(-1)^{(\nu)-1} D^{\mu\nu}(q)}{\sqrt{D(q)}} dq^{1}\Lambda \,\ldots\, \Lambda dq^{\nu}\Lambda \ldots \Lambda dq^{n} \qquad (3.9)$$

that can be deduced easily from the definition of $\star$ operator.

The exterior derivative of κ is

$$d\kappa = \left(P\, f^{\nu} - \frac{1}{2}(D^{\mu\nu} P),_{\mu}\right),_{\nu} \; dq^{1}\Lambda \ldots \Lambda dq^{n} = d\star\left(S\eta - \frac{1}{2} dS\right) \qquad (3.10)$$

where, evidently, $d\kappa \varepsilon\, \Lambda^{n} M$.

We immediately arrive at the following expression equivalent to the Fokker-Planck equation (2.1) :

$$\dot{S}\, \sigma + d\kappa = 0 \qquad (3.11)$$

where $S \equiv S(q,t)$ is the time dependent scalar defined in eq. (2,2).

But remembering that

$$\star\sigma = 1 \qquad (3.12)$$

we get the following expression for the Fokker-Planck equation :

$$\dot{S} + \star\, d\, \star \left(S\eta - \frac{1}{2} d\, S\right) = 0 \qquad (3.13)$$

that is an intrinsic equation since both the exterior derivative, d, and the $\star$ operator are completely independent of the concrete set of gross variables that describe the physical reality up to general gross variable transformations.

We would like to find out the physical meaning of the (n-1) form κ . We have associated with each r-form, ω , an r+1-form, $d\omega$, the exterior derivative of ω. Its definition is given in such a way that the general Stokes' theorem holds :

$$\int_{\partial\Sigma} \omega = \int_{\Sigma} d\, \omega \qquad (3.14)$$

where Σ is an r+1 dimensional oriented manifold and $\partial\Sigma$ is its boundary. Global physical relations will arise from this theorem.

The physical meaning of κ is deduced from eqs. (3.11) and (3.14)

$$\int_{\Sigma} \dot{S}\, \sigma = -\int_{\Sigma} d\,\kappa = -\int_{\partial\Sigma} \kappa \qquad (3.15)$$

which is the conservation law of probability for the Fokker-Planck equation. Therefore, the form κ is the intrinsic probability current.

We want to study now the gauge freedom of eq. (3.13). Such an equation is invariant to a change Δ of the intrinsic drift

$$\eta \rightarrow \eta' = \eta + \Delta \ , \quad \Delta \in \Lambda^1 M \qquad (3.16)$$

provided that

$$d \star (S\Delta) = 0 \qquad (3.17)$$

Then, by axiom f), there exists an (n-2) form λ such that :

$$\star\ (S\Delta) = d\,\lambda \qquad (3.18)$$

From here we arrive at the expression for the intrinsic drift gauge freedom of eq. (3.13)

$$\Delta = (-1)^{n-1}\, S \star d\,\lambda \ , \ \forall\, \lambda \in \Lambda^{n-2} M \qquad (3.19)$$

Though the Fokker-Planck equation (3.13) is not modified by the gauge change $\eta \rightarrow \eta'$, the probability current κ is altered by the gauge change as follows : $\kappa \rightarrow \kappa'$

where

$$\kappa' \equiv \star(S\,\eta' - \frac{1}{2}\, d\, S) = \kappa + d\,\lambda \qquad (3.20)$$

Hereafter, in order to shorten the notation, we will call

$$M_q^{\star} = \Lambda^1_q M . \qquad (3.21)$$

4. THE PATH INTEGRAL REPRESENTATION

The solution of the Fokker-Planck equation (3.13) satisfying a given initial condition $S(q\, t_o) = S_o(q)$ can be expressed in terms of this boundary condition and the conditional probability $S(qt|q_o t_o)$, as follows

$$S(qt) = \int_M \sigma_{q'} \cdot S(qt|q't_o) \cdot S_o(q') \qquad (4.1)$$

The conditional probability is a solution of eq. (3.13) with the boundary condition : $S(qt_o|q_ot_o) = \delta\,(q;q_o)$ where $\delta\,(q;q_o)$ is a distribution defined by

$$\int_M \sigma_q \cdot \delta(q;q_o) \cdot f(q) = f(q_o) \qquad (4.2)$$

As a consequence of eq. (4.1) the continuous Markov property

$$\int_M \sigma_{q'} \cdot S(qt|q't')\, S(q't'|q_ot_o) = S(qt|q_ot_o)\ , \quad t_o<t'<t \qquad (4.3)$$

is satisfied.

Let t_o and t be the end points of a finite time interval and let us divide it into N equal parts of length $\varepsilon = (t-t_o)/N$:

$$t_o<t_1<t_2\ ,\ldots\ldots < t_N = t \quad ;\ t_j-t_{j-1} = \varepsilon\ . \qquad (4.4)$$

Using eq. (4.3) N-1 times we can write :

$$S(q_Nt_N|q_ot_o) = \int \prod_{j=1}^{N-1}\{\sigma_{q_j} . S(q_{j+1}t_{j+1}|q_jt_j)\}\ \ S(q_1t_1|q_ot_o) \qquad (4.5)$$

and considering this expression in the limit $\varepsilon \to 0$, we have :

$$S(qt|q_ot_o) = \lim_{\varepsilon\to 0} \int \prod_{j=1}^{N=1} \{\ \sigma\, q_j\ \cdot S(q_{j+1}t_{j+1}|q_jt_j)\}\ S(q_1t_1|q_ot_o) \qquad (4.6)$$

As it is well known, the expression on the right hand side is used to define the path integral. Therefore, we shall first study the term $S(q_{j+1}t_{j+1}|q_jt_j)$ for infinitesimal time intervals $t_{j+1}-t_j = \varepsilon$.

Let us mark that it is not possible at all to introduce the normal order in terms of the operators ★ and d appearing on the right hand side of eq. (3.13). Thus, we will describe here a method to obtain the conditional probability for infinitesimal time intervals which will be based in the concept of intrinsic Fourier transform on a Riemannian manifold.

5. THE INTRINSIC FOURIER TRANSFORM

In this section we shall define a kind of Fourier Transform for functions on a Riemannian manifold M. It is a generalization of the usual Fourier transform in R^n and it is also coordinate independent, i.e., intrinsic.

Let us define the world fuction W on M :

$$W : M \times M \rightarrow R$$

$$(q_1,q_2) \rightarrow W(q_1,q_2) = \frac{1}{2} \int_0^1 \langle T_\gamma, T_\gamma \rangle .dt \qquad (5.1)$$

where $\gamma: [0,1] \rightarrow M$ is the geodesic joining q_1 and q_2 - i.e. $\gamma(0)=q_1$ and $\gamma(1) = q_2$ - and T_γ is the vector field tangent to γ .
The concept of world function is common in General Relativity (see Synge 4, Chap. 2). We should remember that the world function is a two-point scalar, i.e. it depends on two points $q_1,q_2 \in M$ and it behaves like a scalar on both points. Similarly we shall deal here with two-point tensors, which are functions depending on two points $q_1,q_2 \in M$ and behaving like a tensor in q_1 and as another tensor in q_2.

The world function $W(q_1,q_2)$ is only well defined for pairs of points $q_1,q_2 \in M$ for which there is one and only one geodesic joining them.

As an illustrative example let us see what is the world function in the Euclidean manifold R^n :

$$W : R^n \times R^n \rightarrow R$$

$$(\vec{a},\vec{b}) \rightarrow \frac{1}{2} ||\vec{a},\vec{b}||^2 \qquad (5.2)$$

If we take the gradient in the variables $\vec{a}$ we arrive at :

$$- \text{grad}_{\vec{a}} W(\vec{a},\vec{b}) = \vec{b}-\vec{a}, \text{ i.e. : the position of } \vec{b} \text{ related to } \vec{a} .$$

In general case, by differentiation of $W(q_1,q_2)$ with respect to q_1 we obtain the 1-form $d_1W(q_1,q_2) \in M^\star_{q_1}$. Hence, analogously to the Euclidean case we can define the mapping :

$$Q_{q_1} : M \rightarrow M^\star_{q_1}$$

$$q \rightarrow Q_{q_1}(q) \equiv - d_1W(q_1,q) \qquad (5.3)$$

We shall call this mapping : "the position related to q_1". We have to realize that $d_1W(q_1,q_2)$ is a two point tensor which behaves as a scalar in q_2 and as a 1-form in q_1.

As we have pointed out above, in general the mapping Q_{q_1} is well defined only in a neighbourhood of q_1, whose size depends on the scalar curvative $R(q_1)$. For the sake of simplicity we shall assume that Q_{q_1} is a bijective mapping. This is a very restrictive assumption about the Riemannian structure of M. Nevertheless, we believe that it will not influence the validity of the results we derive in this paper, especially taking into account that we shall deal with very sharp Gaussian functions centered in q_1. (On the other hand, let us note that an assumption of this kind is implicit in Ref. 5). We suppose that the pullback converts functions summable on M into functions summable on M_{q_1}.

As Q_{q_1} is bijective, it allows us to identify M with $M^\star_{q_1}$ which is a Euclidean vector space with the metric $D(q_1) \equiv \langle\ ,\ \rangle_{q_1}$

Given any function S(q) on M, we can pull it back to $M^\star_{q_1}$ by means of $Q^{-1}_{q_1}$ and we obtain a new function δ_{q_1} on $M^\star_{q_1}$ defined by :

$$\delta_{q_1} \equiv S \circ Q^{-1}_{q_1} \tag{5.4}$$

Then, for any $q \varepsilon M$, we have

$$S(q) = \delta_{q_1} (-d_1 \omega(q_1, q)) \qquad (5,4')$$

As $M^\star_{q_1}$ is a Euclidean space we can define the Fourier transform of any square summable function $f \in L^2(M^\star_{q_1})$, as :

$$(\mathcal{F}f)(x) \equiv (2\pi)^{-n/2} \int_{M^\star_{q_1}} \sigma_{q_1}(Q) \cdot f(Q)\, e^{i\langle Q,x\rangle_{q_1}},\ x \varepsilon M^\star_{q_1} \tag{5.5}$$

where $\sigma_{q_1}(Q)$ is the volume element associated to the Euclidean metric $D(q_1)$ on $M^\star_{q_1}$.

Similarly we can define the inverse Fourier transform of any $g \varepsilon L^2(M^\star_{q_1})$:

$$(\overline{\mathcal{F}}g)(Q) = (2\pi)^{-n/2} \int_{M^\star_{q_1}} \sigma_{q_1}(x) \cdot g(x) \cdot e^{-i\langle x,Q\rangle_{q_1}} \tag{5.6}$$

These definitions, (5.5) and (5.6) are straightforward generalizations of those valid for functions on R^n and it is easy to show that the same properties that in that case hold now. We use here the property that successive application of $\mathcal{F}$ and $\overline{\mathcal{F}}$ in any order yield the identity.

6. INTEGRATION OF THE FOKKER-PLANCK EQUATION FOR INFINITESMAL TIME INTERVALS

We start from the Fokker-Planck equation (3.13). Let $S(q,t)$ be the unknown function and $q_1 \varepsilon M$. Let δ_{q_1} be the pull back of $S(q,t)$ by $Q_{q_1}^{-1}$ and $\tilde{\delta}_{q_1} = F\delta_{q_1}$ its Fourier transform, as we have defined in eq. (5.4). Using eq. (5.4) we have :

$$S(q,t) = (2\pi)^{-n/2} \int_{M_{q_1}} \sigma_{q_1}(x) . e^{-i<x,id_1 W(q_1,q)>_{q_1}} . \tilde{\delta}_{q_1}(x,t) \qquad (6.1)$$

Introducing this expression in (3.13) and taking the Fourier transform of the resulting equation, we obtain the Fokker-Planck equation in terms of $\tilde{\delta}_{q_1}$:

$$\partial_t \tilde{\delta}_{q_1}(Z,t) = - (2\pi)^{-n} \int_{M^{\star}_{q_1}} \sigma_{q_1}(Q) . \int_{M^{\star}_{q_1}} \sigma_{q_1}(X) .$$

$$. e^{i<Z-X,Q>_{q_1}} . \delta_{q_1}(X,t) . a_{q_1}(X,Q) \qquad (6.2)$$

where

$$a_{q_1}(X,Q) \equiv \frac{1}{2} G(Q,X) + i<A(Q),X>_{q_1} + B(Q) \qquad (6.3)$$

$$A(Q) \equiv <\eta(q),dd_1 W(q_1,q)>_q - \frac{1}{2} d_1 \star d \star dW(q_1,q) \varepsilon M^{\star}_{q_1} \qquad (6.4)$$

$$B(Q) = \star d \star \eta(q) = \text{div } \eta(q) \varepsilon R \qquad (6.5)$$

$G(Q,X)$ is the quadratic form in X defined by :

$$G(Q,X) = << X,d_1 d\, W(q_1,q)>_{q_1}, <X,d_1 d\, W(q_1,q) >_{q_1} >_q \qquad (6.6)$$

and $q \varepsilon M$ is such that

$$Q = Q_{q_1}(q) \qquad (6.7)$$

Before we continue we will comment on the last expressions. In most o them we find the two point 1-form $d_1 d\, W(q_1 q)$. Thus, in eq. (6.4) it appears within a scalar product $<,>_q$ that behaves like a scalar in q and as a 1-form in q_1. Also in eq. (6.4) we find $d_1 \star d \star d\, W$: the operators $\star$ and d act on the tensor character in q and therefore both of them commute with d_1 which operates on the tensor character in q_1. The two point tensor $d_1 \star d \star d\, W$ behaves as a 1-form in q_1 and as a

scalar in q, because the generalized Laplace operator in q ($\star d \star d$) acts on scalar functions in q.

We can write eq. (6.6) in another way :

$$G(Q,X) = G(Q)\ (X,X) \tag{6.6'}$$

where G(Q) is the 2-covariant tensor function defined by :

$$G(Q) = \langle d_1 dW(q_1,q),\ d_1 d\ W(q_1,q)\ \rangle_q \tag{6.8}$$

i.e. : the result of contracting the tensor product of $d_1 d\ W$ by itself with the metric D(q) in such a way that only the covariant indices in q_1 remain free.

Expressions for G(Q) and A(Q) are given in Appendix A.

Now we decompose G(Q), A(Q) and B(Q) as :

$$\begin{aligned} G(Q) &= G(0) + \overset{1}{G}(Q) \\ A(Q) &= A(0) + \overset{1}{A}(Q) \\ B(Q) &= B(0) + \overset{1}{B}(Q) \end{aligned} \tag{6.9}$$

and, similarly, for the function $a_{q_1}(X,Q)$ appearing on the right hand side of eq. (6.2) :

$$a_{q_1}(X,Q) = a_{q_1}(X,0) + \overset{1}{a}_{q_1}(X,Q) \tag{6.9'}$$

Then, using eqs. (6,4), (6.5), (6.6) and taking into account that $Q_{q_1}^{-1}(0) = q_1$, we have

$$\begin{aligned} G(0) &= \langle dd_1 W(q_1,q_1),\ dd_1 W(q_1,q_1)\rangle_{q_1} \\ B(0) &= \text{div}\ \eta(q_1) \\ A(0) &= \langle \eta(q_1),\ dd_1 W(q_1,q_1)\rangle_{q_1} - \frac{1}{2} d_1 \star d \star d\ W(q_1,q_1) \end{aligned} \tag{6.10}$$

Taking the coincidence limits for the world function derivatives [4] we can write :

$$\begin{aligned} G(0) &= D(q_1) \\ A(0) &= -\ \eta(q_1) \\ B(0) &= (\text{div}\ \eta)\ (q_1) \end{aligned} \tag{6.11}$$

and therefore :

$$a_{q_1}(X,0) = \frac{1}{2} \langle X,X\rangle_{q_1} - i \langle \eta(q_1),X\rangle_{q_1} + \text{div}\, \eta(q_1) \tag{6.12}$$

Introducing (6.9') in the integral on the right hand side of eq. (6.2) and carrying on the integration, we obtain :

$$\partial_t \tilde{\delta}_{q_1}(Z,t) + a_{q_1}(Z,0) \cdot \tilde{\delta}_{q_1}(Z,t) =$$

$$= -(2\pi)^{-n} \int_{M^\star_{q_1}} \sigma_{q_1}(Q) \int_{M^\star_{q_1}} \sigma_{q_1}(X).e^{i\langle Z-X,Q\rangle_{q_1}} .\tilde{\delta}_{q_1}(X,t).$$

$$\cdot\, a^{1}_{q_1}(X,Q) \tag{6.13}$$

Since we are interested in the conditional probability $S(qt|q_o0)$, which is the solution of eq. (3.13) with the initial condition $S(q0|q_o0) = \delta(q,q_o)$, we must integrate eq. (6.13) with the boundary condition :

$$\tilde{\delta}_{q_1}(Z,0) = (2\pi)^{-n/2} \cdot e^{i\langle Z,Q_o\rangle_{q_1}} \tag{6.14}$$

$$Q_o = Q_{q_1}(q_o)$$

i.e. : the FOurier transform of the pull back of $\delta(q,q_o)$.

Let $Y(t)$ be the Heaviside distribution and let us define :

$$V_{q_1}(Z,t) \equiv Y(t).\tilde{\delta}_{q_1}(Z,t) \tag{6.15}$$

Writing eq. (6.13)[6] in terms of V_{q_1} and using the covolution in t with Z fixed, we have

$$\{\partial_t\delta(t) + a_{q_1}(Z,0).\delta(t)\}\ C\ V_{q_1}(Z,t) =$$

$$= \rho(Z,t;\, [V_{q_1}]\,) + (2\pi)^{-n/2} \cdot e^{i\langle Z,Q_o\rangle_{q_1}} \cdot \delta(t) \tag{6.16}$$

In this paper we use the symbol C to indicate the convolution, and we define

$$\rho(Z,t;[\tilde{V}_{q_1}]) \equiv -(2\pi)^{-n} \int_{M^\star_{q_1}} \sigma_{q_1}(Q) \,.\, \int_{M^\star_{q_1}} \sigma_{q_1}(X) \,.$$

$$.\, e^{i\langle Z-X,Q\rangle_{q_1}} \,.\, \tilde{\delta}_{q_1}(X,t) \,.\, a^{1}_{q_1}(X,Q) \qquad (6.17)$$

Then, since for the convolution in t :

$$\{\partial_t \delta(t) + a_{q_1}(Z,0) \,.\, \delta(t)\}^{-1} = Y(t).e^{-t.a_{q_1}(Z,0)} \qquad (6.18)$$

We can isolate $\tilde{V}^{1}_{q_1}(Z,t)$ from eq. (6.16). Taking into account eq. (6.15) we have, for t>0 :

$$\tilde{\delta}_{q_1}(Z,t) = \{Y(t).e^{-ta_{q_1}(Z,0)}\} \;C\; \{\rho(Z,t;[\tilde{V}_{q_1}]) + (2\pi)^{-n/2} \,.$$

$$.\, e^{i\langle Z,Q_o\rangle_{q_1}} \,\delta(t)\} =$$

$$= (2\pi)^{-n/2} \,.\, e^{-ta_{q_1}(Z,0) + i\langle Z,Q_o\rangle_{q_1}} \,.\{1 + (2\pi)^{-n/2} \,.$$

$$.\int_o^t d\tau \,.e^{\tau a_{q_1}(Z,o) - i\langle Z,Q_o\rangle_{q_1}} \,.\, \rho(Z,\tau,[\tilde{V}_{q_1}])\} \qquad (6.19)$$

Hereafter we write :

$$\tilde{\delta}_{q_1}(Z,t) = (2\pi)^{-n/2}\, e^{-ta_{q_1}(Z,0) + i\langle Z,Q_o\rangle_{q_1}} \,.\, \theta(Z,t) \qquad (6.20)$$

Substituting eq. (6.21) into eq. (6.19) we obtain :

$$\theta(Z,t) = 1 - (2\pi)^{-n} \int_o^t d\tau \int_{M^\star_{q_1}} \sigma_{q_1}(Q) \,.\int_{M^\star_{q_1}} \sigma_{q_1}(X) \,.\, a^{1}_{q_1}(X,Q).\theta(X,\tau) \,.$$

$$.\, \exp\{\tau.a_{q_1}(Z,0) + i\langle Z-X,Q-Q_o\rangle_{q_1} - \tau.a_{q_1}(X,0)\} \qquad (6.21)$$

Notice that :

$$\lim_{t\to o} \theta(Z,t) = 1 \qquad (6.22)$$

We plan to solve the integral equation (6.21) by iteration. Let us consider the series

$$\sum_{m=o}^{\infty} \phi_m(Z,t) \qquad \text{defined by :}$$

$$\phi_0(Z,t) = 1 \text{ and } \phi_{m+1}(Z,t) = -(2\pi)^{-n} \int_0^t d\tau \cdot \int_{M^\star_{q_1}} \sigma_{q_1}(Q) \cdot \int_{M^\star_{q_1}} \sigma_{q_1}(X) \cdot$$

$$\cdot \exp\{\ldots\} \cdot \phi_m(X,\tau) \cdot a^1_{q_1}(X,Q) \qquad (6.23)$$

If this series is convergent, its sum will be the required solution $\theta(Z,t)$ of eq. (6.21).

In fact, we are not interested in $\theta(Z,t)$ only but also in $S(qt|q_00)$ or, equivalently, in $\delta q_1(Q,t)$. Therefore, we will have to calculate the inverse Fourier transform of δ_{q_1} given by eq. (6.21).

Since this operation will involve some Gaussian integrals with variance t, the relation between the sizes of the term $\phi_m(Z,t)$ and the corresponding terms obtained after the inverse Fourier transform is evaluated, will be masked. This problem can be circumvented by means of the following change of variables :

$$Z = \hat{Z} \cdot t^{-\frac{1}{2}} \; ; \; X = \hat{X} \cdot \tau^{-\frac{1}{2}}$$

$$\hat{\phi}_m(\hat{Z},t) = \phi_m(\hat{Z} \cdot t^{-\frac{1}{2}}, t) \qquad (6.24)$$

$$\sigma_{q_1}(X) = \sigma_{q_1}(\hat{X}) \cdot \tau^{-n/2}$$

Let us now work out the first step of the iteration :

$$\phi_1(\hat{Z},t) = -(2\pi)^{-n} \cdot \int_0^t d\tau \cdot \tau^{-n/2} \cdot \int_{M^\star_{q_1}} \sigma_{q_1}(Q) \cdot \int_{M^\star_{q_1}} \sigma_{q_1}(\hat{X})$$

$$\cdot \exp\{\tau a_{q_1}(\hat{Z}t^{-\frac{1}{2}},0) + i \langle \hat{Z}t^{-\frac{1}{2}} - \hat{X} \cdot \tau^{-\frac{1}{2}}, Q-Q_0 \rangle_{q_1} - \tau a_{q_1}(\hat{X} \cdot \tau^{-\frac{1}{2}}, 0)\}$$

$$\cdot a^1_{q_1}(\hat{X} \cdot \tau^{-\frac{1}{2}}, Q) \qquad (6.25)$$

Carrying on the integration with respect to $\hat{X}$ we obtain :

$$\phi_1(\hat{Z},t) = -(2\pi)^{-n/2} \int_0^t d\tau \cdot \tau^{-n/2} \cdot \int \dot{\sigma}_{q_1}(Q) \cdot$$

$$\cdot \exp\{-\frac{1}{2\tau} \langle Q - Q_o + \tau(A + i \hat{Z} \cdot t^{-\frac{1}{2}} \rangle^2_{q_1})\} \cdot f(Q) \qquad (6.26)$$

where :

$$f(Q) = \overset{(o)}{f}(Q) + \frac{1}{\tau}\overset{(1)}{f}(Q) + \frac{1}{\tau^2}\overset{(2)}{f}(Q) \tag{6.27}$$

$$\overset{(o)}{f}(Q) = -\frac{1}{2}\overset{1}{G}(Q)\,(A(o),A(o)) + \langle \overset{1}{A}(Q),A(o)\rangle_{q_1} + \overset{1}{B}(Q) \tag{6.27a}$$

$$\overset{(1)}{f}(Q) = \frac{1}{2}\,\mathrm{tr}\,\overset{1}{G}(Q) - \overset{1}{G}(Q)\,(A(o),Q-Q_o) + \langle \overset{1}{A}(Q),\, Q-Q_o\rangle_{q_1} \tag{6.27b}$$

$$\overset{(2)}{f}(Q) = -\frac{1}{2}\overset{1}{G}(Q)\,(Q-Q_o,Q-Q_o) \tag{6.27c}$$

and

$$\langle C\rangle^2_{q_1} = \langle C,C\rangle_{q_1} \quad ; \quad C \in M^{\star}_{q_1}$$

We mean by $\mathrm{tr}\,\overset{1}{G}(Q)$ in (6.27b) the trace of the contraction of the 2-covariant tensor $G(Q)$ with the metric $D(q_1)$. The expressions for (6.28) in any fixed vector basis of $M^{\star}_{q_1}$ are given in Appendix B.

In order to integrate with respect to Q on the right hand side of eq. (6.26) we expand $f(Q)$ as a power series in $Q-Q_o$. Using the results given in Appendix C we have, in an arbitrary basis of $M^{\star}_{q_1}$:

$$\phi_1(Z,t) = -\sum_{r=o}^{2}\sum_{K=o}^{\infty}\sum_{j=o}^{2j\leqslant K} \frac{(-1)^K}{j!(K-2j)!2^j}\cdot t^{-\frac{K}{2}+j}\int_o^t d\tau.\tau^{K-j-r}\,.$$

$$\overset{(r)}{f}_{\mu_1\ldots\mu_K}(Q_o).\,D^{\mu_1\mu_2}(q_1)\ldots D^{\mu_{2j-1}\mu_{2j}}(q_1).(A(o).t^{\frac{1}{2}}+i\hat{Z})^{\mu_{2j+1}}\ldots$$

$$\ldots (A(o).t^{\frac{1}{2}} + i\hat{Z})^{\mu_K} \tag{6.28}$$

The integrals on the right hand side are divergent when $K<j+r$. This drawback can be avoided choosing a discretization in which the coefficients of the divergent terms[7] vanish. So, taking $q_1 = q_o$ - i.e. $Q_o = 0$, postpoint discretization - we get :

$$\overset{(r)}{f}_{\mu_1\ldots\ldots\mu_K}(0) = 0 \text{ if } K<j+r \text{ and } 2j\leqslant K$$

as can be seen in Appendix B.

Making $Q_o = 0$ and working out the integrals on eq. (6.28), we have :

$$\phi_1(\hat{Z},t) = - t \{ \overset{(1)}{f}_{\mu\nu}(0) . [\tfrac{1}{2} D^{\mu\nu}_{(q_o)} - \tfrac{1}{4} \hat{Z}^{\mu} \hat{Z}^{\nu}] +$$

$$+ \overset{(2)}{f}_{\mu\nu\rho\lambda}(o) . [\tfrac{1}{8} D^{\mu\nu}_{(q_o)} D^{\rho\lambda}_{(q_o)} - \tfrac{1}{8} D^{\mu\nu}_{(q_o)} . \hat{Z}^{\rho} . \hat{Z}^{\lambda} + \tfrac{1}{4!3} . \hat{Z}^{\mu} . \hat{Z}^{\nu} \hat{Z}^{\rho} \hat{Z}^{\lambda}]$$

$$+ 0 (t^{3/2}) \tag{6.29}$$

That ends the first step in the iteration process. In accordance with eq. (6.23), for $m \geqslant 2$, $\phi_m(Z,t)$ would be a sum of integrals like :

$$- (2\pi)^{-n} \int_o^t d\tau . \tau^{-n/2} \int \sigma_{q_o}(Q) \int \sigma_{q_o}(X).\exp\{\dots\}.a^{1}_{q_o}(\hat{X}.\tau^{-\frac{1}{2}},Q) .$$

$$.\tau^{\ell} \hat{X}^{\nu_1} \dots\dots \hat{X}^{\nu_r} \tag{6.30}$$

where $\ell > 1$. Carrying on the integrations exactly in the same way as we have made above, we observe that eq. (6.30) behaves as

$t^{\ell + \frac{1}{2}}$, because $G^1(0) = 0, A^1(0) = 0$ and $B^1(0) = 0$.

Therefore, provided that the series $\sum_{m=o}^{\infty} \phi_m(\hat{Z},t)$ converges to $\hat{\theta}(Z,t)$, the first and second terms are enough to approximate the sum up to order t :

$$\theta(Z,t) = 1 + \phi_1(Z,t) + 0(t^{3/2}) \tag{6.31}$$

Then, substituting eq. (6.31) and eq. (6.29) into eq. (6.20) and carrying on the inverse Fourier transform, we have

$$\delta_{q_o}(Q,t) = (2\pi t)^{-n/2} . e^{-\frac{t}{2}<\frac{Q}{t}+A(o)>^2_{q_o} - tB(o)}$$

$$.\{1-t [\tfrac{1}{4} \overset{(1)}{f}_{\mu\nu}(o).D^{\mu\nu}_{(q_o)} + \tfrac{1}{24} \overset{(2)}{f}_{\mu\nu\rho\lambda}(o).D^{\mu\nu}_{(q_o)}.D^{\rho\lambda}_{(q_o)}] +$$

$$+ 0(t^{3/2})\} \tag{6.32}$$

Making use of the results given in Appendix B and of eq. (6.11) we obtain :

$$\delta_{q_o}(Q,t) = (2\pi t)^{-n/2} \cdot e^{-\frac{t}{2}\langle \frac{Q}{t} - \eta \rangle^2_{q_o} - t.\mathrm{div}\,\eta(q_o)}$$

$$\cdot \{1 + t.[+ \frac{1}{2}\,\mathrm{div}\,\eta(q_o) - \frac{1}{12} R(q_o)] + O(t^{3/2})\} \qquad (6.33)$$

If we apply the pullback with $Q^{-1}_{q_o}$, we obtain the conditional probability $S(qt|q_o 0)$ for infinitesimal values of t

$$S(qt|q_o 0) = (2\pi t)^{-n/2} \cdot e^{-\frac{t}{2}\langle Q - \eta \rangle^2_{q_o} - t.\mathrm{div}\,\eta} \cdot \{1 + t \,.$$

$$\cdot [\frac{1}{2}\,\mathrm{div}\,\eta - \frac{1}{12} R] + O(t^{3/2})\} \qquad (6.34)$$

where : $\dot{Q} = -\frac{1}{t} d_1 W(q_o q)$

and all the quantities div η , η , R, are evaluated at q_o.

Finally, as eq. (3.12) does not depend on time explicitly, it is clear that

$$S(q\ t_o + \varepsilon|q_o t_o) = S(q\varepsilon|q_o 0) \qquad (6.35)$$

7. THE LAGRANGIAN

We use here the conditional probability for infinitesimal time intervals, eq. (6.34) , to rewrite the functional integral eq. (4.5) as

$$S(qt|q_o t_o) = \int \prod_{j=1}^{N-1} \sigma_{q_j} \cdot \prod_{j=0}^{N-1} [(2\pi\varepsilon)^{-n/2} . e^{-\frac{\varepsilon}{2}\langle Q_j - \eta_j, Q_j - \eta_j \rangle_{q_j} - \varepsilon \mathrm{div}\eta_j}$$

$$\cdot \{1 + \varepsilon(+ \frac{1}{2}\,\mathrm{div}\,\eta_j - \frac{1}{12} R_j) + O(\varepsilon^{3/2})\}] \qquad (7.1)$$

or

$$S(qt|q_o t_o) = \int \prod_{j=1}^{N-1} \sigma_{q_j} \cdot (2\pi\varepsilon)^{-\frac{nN}{2}} \cdot \exp\{-\varepsilon \sum_{j=0}^{N-1} (\frac{1}{2}\langle Q_j - \eta_j, Q_j - \eta_j \rangle_{q_j} +$$

$$+ \mathrm{div}\,\eta_j)\} . \{1 + \varepsilon \sum_{j=1}^{N-1} (+ \frac{1}{2}\mathrm{div}\,\eta_j - \frac{1}{12} R_j) + O(\varepsilon^{3/2})\} \qquad (7.2)$$

where :

$$\eta_j \equiv \eta(q_j)$$

$$R_j \equiv R(q_j) \quad \text{and}$$

$$Q_j \equiv -\frac{1}{\varepsilon} \cdot d_j\, W(q_j, q_{j+1}) \tag{7.3}$$

And in the limit $\varepsilon \to 0$ the expression on the right hand side of eq.(7.2) yields the well known path integral

$$S(qt|q_o t_o) = \int_{q(t_o)=q_o}^{q(t)=q} D\mu([q(\tau)]) . \exp\{-\int_{t_o}^{t} d\tau \, . \, L(\dot{q}(\tau), q(\tau))\} \tag{7.4}$$

with

$$D\mu(\,[q(\tau)]) \equiv \lim_{\varepsilon \to o} \prod_{j=1}^{N-1} \sigma_{q_j} \, . \, (2\pi\varepsilon)^{-\frac{nN}{2}} \tag{7.5}$$

and the following expression for the Lagrangian

$$L(\dot{q}, q) = \frac{1}{2} \langle \dot{q} - \eta(q), \dot{q} - \eta(q) \rangle_q + \frac{1}{2} \operatorname{div} \eta(q) + \frac{1}{12} R(q) \tag{7.6}$$

where

$$\dot{q}(\tau) = - \lim_{\varepsilon \to o} \{\frac{1}{\varepsilon} d_{q(\tau)} W(q(\tau), q(\tau+\varepsilon))\} \varepsilon \, M^{\star}_{q(\tau)} \tag{7.7}$$

8. CONCLUSIONS AND OUTLOOK

In a recent publication[1], it was shown that the Riemannian connection on the manifold spanned by the gross variables is too strong a tool to write the Fokker-Planck equation in a covariant form. We have continued here this idea and obtained an intrinsic expression for this equation by means of the star operator and the exterior derivative only. These operators imply a less restrictive structure than the Riemannian connnection.

We have also integrated here the Fokker-Planck equation in an intrinsic way. Although it is not explicit in the text, we have used

in the integration some aspects of the Riemannian connection : to define the world function we must use the concept of geodesic curve and, as it is well known [8], a given connection is fully determined by the family of all its geodesics plus its torsion tensor.

In order to develop an integration method for the Fokker-Planck equation we have defined an intrinsic generalization of the Fourier transform. When one tries to build a covariant theory of perturbation, a problem arises immediately : the usual Fourier transform is coördinate dependent because the diffusion matrix is not constant and this would make the perturbation theory non-covariant. The intrinsic Fourier transform introduced here will surely provide a simpe solution to the problem of developing an intrinsic perturbation theory.

We have intended as far as possible to work without fixing a particular discretization. We had to give up this requirement in eq. (6.29) where we have taken the post-point discretization, otherwise our results would contain some divergent integrals which would invalidate them. Nevertheless, we are convinced that it is possible to obtain similar results keeping the formalism discretization independent. We believe that starting from a different metric for M_q^* and a different decomposition for a(X,Q) would lead to the expected results. We plan to present this aspect in a future publication.

Finally, we have derived a path integral representation of the conditional probability for general diffusion processes. We obtain a Lagrangian which agrees with other well known results.

REFERENCES

1. L. Garrido, Physica 100 A (1980) 140.
2. H. Flanders, "Differential Forms", Academic Press, NY(1963).
3. C. Dewitt, Phys. Rep. 50 (1979)
4. J.L. Synge, "Relativity : The General Theory", North-Holland, Amsterdam (1960)
5. R. Graham, Z. Physik B26, (1977) 281
6. L. Schwartz, "Métodos matemáticos para las Ciencias Físicas" , Selecciones Científicas, Madrid (1969)
7. F.Langouche, D. Roekaerts, E. Tirapegui, "Lecture Notes in Physics", V.84 , Springer-Verlag, Berlin (1978)
8. N. J. Hicks, "Notes on Differential Geometry", Van Nostrand, Princeton (1965)

APPENDIX A

The derivatives of the world function $W(q_1 q)$ will be denoted by W with the necessary indices. Those corresponding to covariant derivatives in q will be written as $\mu, \nu, \ldots.$ and those corresponding to q_1 as $\mu_1, \nu_1, \ldots.$ A complete list of properties of the world function derivatives can be found in Ref. 4. In a given coordinate frame $\{\xi^\mu\}$ we can write :

$$G_{\mu_1\nu_1}(Q) = W_{\mu_1\rho}(q_1 q) . W_{\nu_1}{}^{\rho}(q_1, q) \qquad (A.1)$$

$$A_{\mu_1}(Q) = \eta^{\rho}(q) . W_{\mu_1\rho}(q_1 q) - \frac{1}{2} W^{\rho}{}_{\rho\mu_1}(q_1, q) \qquad (A.2)$$

where indices are raised andlowered by means of the matrices $D^{\rho\lambda}(q)$ and $D_{\rho\lambda}(q)$, respectively, as it is usual in tensor calculus.

$G_{\mu_1\nu_1}(Q)$ and $A_{\mu_1}(Q)$ are the components of the tensor functions G(Q) and A(Q) related to the vector basis

$$\{d\,\xi^1(q_1), \ldots\ldots, d\,\xi^n(q_1)\} \text{ of } M^{\star}_{q_1}$$

Taking into account the results given in Ref. 4 we have for the derivatives of $G_{\mu_1\nu_1}(Q)$ and $A_{\mu_1}(Q)$ with respect to Q^α :

$$Q = Q_\alpha \,.\, d\,\xi^\alpha(q_1) \qquad (A.3)$$

$$\left(\frac{\partial\, G_{\mu_1\nu_1}}{\partial\, Q^\alpha}\right)_{Q=o} = 0 \qquad (A.4)$$

$$\left(\frac{\partial^2 G_{\mu_1\nu_1}}{\partial Q^\alpha \,.\, \partial Q^\beta}\right)_{Q=o} = +\frac{1}{3}\left(R_{\nu\alpha\beta\mu}(q_1) + R_{\mu\alpha\beta\nu}(q_1)\right) \qquad (A.5)$$

where $R_{\nu\alpha\beta\mu}$ is the Riemann tensor.

$$\left(\frac{\partial A_{\mu_1}}{\partial Q^\alpha}\right)_{Q=o} = \frac{\partial}{\partial Q^\alpha}\left(\eta_\rho(q) . W^{\rho}{}_{\mu_1}(q_1 q)\right)_{Q=o} + $$

$$+ \frac{1}{3} Ric_{\mu\alpha}(q_1) \qquad (A.6)$$

Here $Ric_{\mu\alpha} = R^{\rho}{}_{\mu\rho\alpha}$ is the Ricci tensor.

APPENDIX B

We have the following expressions :

$$\overset{(o)}{f}(Q) = -\frac{1}{2}\overset{1}{G}_{\mu_1\nu_1}(Q).\overset{\mu_1}{A}(o).\overset{\nu_1}{A}(o) + \overset{\mu_1}{A}(o).\overset{1}{A}_{\mu_1}(Q) + \overset{1}{B}(Q) \qquad (B.1)$$

$$\overset{(1)}{f}(Q) = \frac{1}{2}\overset{1}{G}_{\mu_1\nu_1}(Q).D^{\mu_1\nu_1}(q_1) - \overset{1}{G}_{\mu_1\nu_1}(Q).(Q^{\nu_1} - Q_o^{\nu_1})\overset{\mu_1}{A}(o) + \overset{1}{A}_{\mu_1}(Q).(Q^{\mu_1} - Q_o^{\mu_1}) \qquad (B.2)$$

$$\overset{(2)}{f}(Q) = -\frac{1}{2}\overset{1}{G}_{\mu_1\nu_1}(Q).(Q^{\mu_1} - Q_o^{\mu_1}).(Q^{\nu_1} - Q_o^{\nu_1}) \qquad (B.3)$$

We make hereafter $Q_o = 0$ and $q_1 = q_o$.

$$\overset{(r)}{f}_{\mu_1\ldots\mu_K}(0) = \left(\frac{\partial^K \overset{(r)}{f}}{\partial Q^{\mu_1}\ldots\partial Q^{\mu_K}}\right)_{Q=o}, \qquad (B.4)$$

$\overset{(2)}{f}_{\mu\nu\rho\lambda}(o)$ is the total symmetrization of $\left(\frac{\partial^2 \overset{1}{G}_{\mu_1\nu_1}}{\partial Q^\rho . \partial Q^\lambda}\right)_{Q=o}$, modulo a multiplicative factor. Since eq. (A.5)

$$\overset{(2)}{f}_{\mu\nu\rho\lambda}(Q) = 0 \qquad (B.5)$$

$$\overset{(1)}{f}_{\mu\nu}(o) = \frac{1}{2}\left(\frac{\partial^2 \overset{1}{G}_{\rho_1\lambda_1}}{\partial Q^\mu . \partial Q^\nu}\right)_{Q=o} . D^{\rho_1\lambda_1}(q_o) + 2\left(\frac{\partial \overset{1}{A}_{\mu_1}}{\partial Q^\nu}\right)_{Q=o} \qquad (B.6)$$

and taking into account eq. (A.6) we obtain :

$$\overset{(1)}{f}_{\mu\nu}(o) . D^{\mu\nu}(q_o) = -2 \operatorname{div} \eta(q_o) + \frac{1}{3} R(q_o) \qquad (B.7)$$

where $R(q_o) = D^{\mu\nu}(q_o) . Ric_{\mu\nu}$ is the Riemann scalar curvature.

APPENDIX C

Let E be a vector space with a euclidean metric $< , >$ and let $X,P \in E$, and X_μ, P_μ be its components. We can write :

$$\int \sigma(X) \, . e^{-a<X,X>} . X_{\mu_1} . X_{\nu_1} \ldots\ldots X_{\mu_K} . X_{\nu_K} =$$

$$= (-1)^K \frac{\partial^{2K}}{\partial p^{\mu_1} \ldots\ldots \partial p^{\nu_K}} \{ \int \sigma(X) . e^{-a<X,X> - i<P,X>} \}_{P=0} \qquad (C.1)$$

which is the (2K)th-term in the Mac Laurin expansion of the function :

$$\int \sigma \, (X) . e^{-a<X,X>-i<P,X>} = \left(\frac{\pi}{a} \right)^{n/2} . e^{-\frac{1}{4a} . <P,P>} \qquad (C.2)$$

Therefore we have :

$$\int \sigma(X) . e^{-a<X,X>} . X_{\mu_1} . X_{\nu_1} \ldots . X_{\mu_K} . X_{\nu_K} =$$

$$= \left(\frac{\pi}{a} \right)^{n/2} \frac{(2K)!}{K!} \left(\frac{1}{4a} \right)^K . D_{(\mu_1 \nu_1} \ldots . D_{\mu_K \nu_K)} \qquad (C.3)$$

where $D_{\mu_1 \nu_1}$ is the matrix of $< , >$ in the basis in consideration and the round bracket means total symmetrization.

PATH INTEGRALS, COMPOSITE OPERATORS AND MODE COUPLING

Heinz Horner

Institut für Theoretische Physik
Universität Heidelberg
Philosophenweg 19
D-6900 Heidelberg

The dynamics of classical systems is governed in many examples by stochastic nonlinear differential equations of the type of a Langevin equation. Correlation functions of such systems have been calculated using mode coupling approximations or alternatively perturbation theory. Using path integrals the framework for perturbation theory is generalized such that it yields the mode coupling results in second order. In contrast to the original mode coupling scheme higher order corrections can now be found in a systematic fashion.

BACKGROUND

In the following we will be concerned with the dynamics of classical systems described by nonlinear stochastic differential equations of the Langevin type. The dynamics is supposed to be purely relaxational and the system should be in thermal equilibrium and fluctuation-dissipation theorems are assumed. The state of the system is described by a variable $s(t)$ which might be a scalar, vector or a field. In the latter case functions of s have to be understood as functionals. Examples can be found in many fields of classical statistical mechanics.

The basic equation of motion is the nonlinear Langevin equation

$$\dot{s} = \mathcal{K}(s) + \xi \qquad (1.1)$$

where

$$\mathcal{K}(s) = -L \frac{\delta \mathcal{H}(s)}{\delta s} . \tag{1.2}$$

The fluctuating forces are assumed to be Gauss correlated with zero mean and

$$\langle \xi(t)\, \xi(t') \rangle = 2L\, \delta(t-t'). \tag{1.3}$$

One of the simplest examples of this type of system is the van der Pol oscillator which is used as a model for a single mode laser[1,2]. It has been extensively studied by various techniques[3,4,5] and we use it as a demonstration. In this case s is an n-component vector where $n = 2$ for the laser and

$$\begin{aligned} \mathcal{H} &= \tfrac{1}{2} a \sum_{\alpha} s_\alpha^2 + \tfrac{1}{8} u \sum_{\alpha\beta} s_\alpha^2 s_\beta^2 \\ \mathcal{K}_\alpha &= -L a s_\alpha - \tfrac{1}{2} L u \sum_{\beta} s_\beta^2 s_\alpha \end{aligned} \tag{1.4}$$

Systems described by the nonlinear Langevin equation (1.1) can in general not be solved exactly and one has to rely on approximations. Among those the mode coupling approach[3] and renormalized perturbation theory[4] are frequently used. In both schemes the fluctuation-dissipation theorem is employed in order to incorporate equal time correlation functions into the equations of motions for the dynamic correlation functions. Otherwise the two methods are not related in an obvious way and in the following we address the question how the two are related and whether the mode coupling approach can be obtained from a suitable perturbation theory.

MODE COUPLING THEORY

Starting point for the mode coupling theory is the Liouville operator associated with the Langevin equation (1.1) and the ensemble of fluctuating forces (1.3)

$$\mathcal{L} = L\, \delta_s \delta_s + \mathcal{K}\, \delta_s \tag{2.1}$$

where $\delta_s = \delta/\delta s$. Time dependent correlation functions are

given by

$$\langle B(0)\, A(t) \rangle = \langle B\, e^{\mathcal{L}t} A \rangle_{St} \tag{2.2}$$

where

$$\langle \cdots \rangle_{St} = Z^{-1} \int \mathcal{D}s\, e^{-\mathcal{H}} \cdots \tag{2.3}$$

denotes the equilibrium expectation value. One proceeds further by defining a scalar product in the linear space of observables A, B··

$$(A|B) = \langle AB \rangle_{St} \tag{2.4}$$

and by choosing some incomplete orthogonal basis of observables $A_1 \cdots A_\nu$ and with those a projection operator

$$\mathcal{P} = \sum_{i=1}^{\nu} \frac{|A_i)(A_i|}{(A_i|A_i)} \qquad Q = 1 - \mathcal{P} \tag{2.5}$$

The idea is to treat the dynamics in the subspace spanned by the observables $A_1 \cdots A_\nu$ exactly and to make approximations in the complementary subspace. The quality of the approximation depends of course crucially on the set of observables $A_1 \cdots A_\nu$ chosen. In many cases where mode coupling theory has been applied one has good arguments which set to choose and this is certainly one of the most attractive features of this scheme.

Technically the separation of the dynamics is done by decomposing the Liouville operator

$$\mathcal{L} = \mathcal{L}_{PP} + \mathcal{L}_{PQ} + \mathcal{L}_{QP} + \mathcal{L}_{QQ} \tag{2.6}$$

where $\mathcal{L}_{PP} = \mathcal{P}\mathcal{L}\mathcal{P}$, $\mathcal{L}_{PQ} = \mathcal{P}\mathcal{L}Q$ and so on. This yields the following equations of motion

$$\frac{d}{dt}\langle A_i(t)A_j(0)\rangle = -\sum_k \Omega_{ik}\langle A_k(t)A_j(0)\rangle + \sum_k \int_0^t d\tau\, \mathcal{M}_{ik}(t-\tau)\langle A_k(\tau)A_j(0)\rangle \tag{2.7}$$

where

$$\Omega_{ik} = \frac{\langle A_i\, \mathcal{L}_{PP}\, A_k\rangle}{\langle A_k\, A_k\rangle} \tag{2.8}$$

and

$$\mathcal{M}_{ik}(t) = \frac{\langle A_i\, \mathcal{L}_{PQ}\, e^{\mathcal{L}_{QQ}t}\, \mathcal{L}_{QP}\, A_k\rangle}{\langle A_k\, A_k\rangle} \tag{2.9}$$

Approximations now have to be made on the memory kernel $\mathcal{M}_{ik}(t)$. There appears to be no systematic way of calculating this quantity like for instance a perturbation expansion. The common method is to expand

$$\mathcal{L}_{QP} A_k = \sum_{mn} V_{kmn} A_m A_n + \sum_{mno} V_{kmno} A_m A_n A_o + \cdots \tag{2.10}$$

and to factorize the resulting expectation values of the products of operators into products of correlation functions of pairs of operators $\langle A_m(t) A_{m'}(0)\rangle$. In doing so the dynamics in the complementary space ruled by $\mathcal{L}_{QQ}$ is replaced by the full dynamics such that the equation of motion becomes nonlinear but closed in the subset of pair correlation functions. In the expansion (2.10) one has omitted the fact that the products of operators $A_m A_n \cdots$ are not necessarily orthogonal on the operators A_i. On the other hand one would not be well advised if one would try to correct for this fact but still replace $\mathcal{L}_{QQ}$ by $\mathcal{L}$. Obviously this factorization is based on intuition and there is no obvious way to go beyond.

For the laser model (1.4) the set of operators $s_1 \cdots s_n$

and $J = \frac{1}{2} s^2$ has turned out to yield quite satisfactory results[3].

PATH INTEGRALS AND COMPOSITE OPERATORS

The second approximation scheme[4] is perturbation theory with respect to the nonlinearities in $\mathcal{K}$. In this approach the basic variables s are distinct and composite operators, for instance s^2, cannot be treated a priory on the same level. This is quite contrary to the mode coupling scheme. In the following we therefore develop a generalization of the perturbation theory where this can be done. This combines the advantages of the mode coupling theory with the possibility of generating higher order corrections in a more systematic fashion.

We select again an appropriate set of observables $A_1 \cdots A_\nu$ which might contain the basic variables s but also composed operators or polynomials in s. From the Langevin equation (1.1) we then obtain a set of stochastic differential equations

$$\dot{A}_i = \{ \mathcal{K} + \xi \} A'_i + L A''_i \tag{3.1}$$

where $A'_i = \delta A_i / \delta s$ and $A''_i = \delta A'_i / \delta s$. Assume we have found the solutions of these equations $A_i(t, \{\xi\})$ for a given realization of the fluctuating forces. We can then write time dependent correlation functions as path integrals over the fluctuating forces

$$\langle A_i(t) A_j(t') \cdots \rangle = \mathcal{N}_I \int \mathcal{D}\{\xi\}\, e^{J_I(\xi)} A_i(t) A_j(t') \cdots \tag{3.2}$$

where

$$J_I(\xi) = -\int dt\, \xi \frac{1}{4L} \xi \tag{3.3}$$

in accordance with the assumed Gaussian distribution of the fluctuating forces.

In the second step we introduce the observables A_i as independent variables in the path integral. In order to insure that the above stochastic equations (3.1) are fulfilled we introduce appropriate products of δ-functions and write those as integrals over exponentials with auxiliary variables $\tilde{A}_i$. This yields

$$\langle A_i(t)\cdots\rangle = \mathcal{N}_{II}\int \mathcal{D}\{\xi, A_i, i\tilde{A}_i\}\, e^{J_{II}}\, A_i(t)\cdots \tag{3.4}$$

where

$$J_{II} = J_I - \sum_i \int dt\, \tilde{A}_i\left[\dot{A}_i - \{\mathcal{K}+\xi\}A'_i - L A''_i\right]. \tag{3.5}$$

Finally the fluctuating forces are easily integrated out and one gets the desired form

$$\langle A_i(t)\cdots\rangle = \mathcal{N}\int \mathcal{D}\{A_i, i\tilde{A}_i\}\, e^{J}\, A_i(t)\cdots \tag{3.6}$$

with

$$J = \int dt\left[\sum_{ij}\tilde{A}_i A'_i L \tilde{A}_j A'_j - \sum_i \tilde{A}_i\{\dot{A}_i - \mathcal{K}A'_i - L A''_i\}\right] \tag{3.7}$$

The normalization $\mathcal{N}$ has to be chosen appropriately.

We assume that the set of observables has been chosen such that the action J can be written as a polynomial in the $A_1 \cdots A_\nu$ their time derivatives and the auxiliary variables $\tilde{A}_1 \cdots \tilde{A}_\nu$. Writing J as such a polynomial corresponds to the expansion (2.10) of the Liouville operator. It should be noted, however, that the observables have not to be chosen orthogonal in the sense of the previous section. The path integral may then be evaluated by perturbation theory or other means.

If only the basic variables ϕ are used, the auxiliary variables $\tilde{\phi}$ generate response functions[6,7]. This is, however, no longer the case if composite operators are introduced. Assume $\mathcal{H}$ is supplemented by external time dependent sources

$$\mathcal{H} \longrightarrow \mathcal{H} - \sum_i h_i A_i \tag{3.8}$$

then

$$\mathcal{K} \longrightarrow \mathcal{K} + L\sum_i h_i A'_i. \tag{3.9}$$

Response functions are defined as

$$\frac{\delta \langle A_i(t) \cdot\cdot \rangle}{\delta L h_k(\tau) \cdot\cdot} = \langle A_i(t) \cdot\cdot \hat{A}_k(\tau) \cdot\cdot \rangle \tag{3.10}$$

where the "response operators" are given by

$$\hat{A}_k = A'_k \sum_i A'_i \tilde{A}_i \tag{3.11}$$

and again sould be rewritten as polynomials in the chosen set A_i. In the case where the A_i are only the basic variables s_i, in other words where $A'_i = \delta s_i/\delta s_j = \delta_{ij}$, the response operators are equal to the auxiliary variables $\hat{s}_i = \tilde{s}_i$. For the laser-model with s_i and $J = \frac{1}{2}s^2$ as the chosen set $\hat{s}_i = \tilde{s}_i + \tilde{J} s_i$ and $\hat{J} = \tilde{s} s + 2\tilde{J} J$.

EQUATIONS OF MOTION, SELFENERGIES

The quantities of prime interest are the correlation functions of pairs of observables

$$C_{ij}(t) = \langle A_i(t)\, A_j(0) \rangle \tag{4.1}$$

and the response functions

$$\mathcal{R}_{ij}(t) = \langle A_i(t)\, \hat{A}_j(0) \rangle. \tag{4.2}$$

Imposing causal boundary conditions $\mathcal{R}_{ij}(t) = 0$ for $t \leq 0$. Furthermore we introduce

$$\tilde{\mathcal{R}}_{ij}(t) = \langle A_i(t)\, \tilde{A}_j(0) \rangle \tag{4.3}$$

and again causality requires $\tilde{\mathcal{R}}_{ij}(t) = 0$ for $t \leq 0$. The expectation values involving $\hat{A}_i$ and $\tilde{A}_i$ are the obvious generalizations of the average (3.6).

Equations of motion are easily derived from the fact that the integral over a differential vanishes. For instance

$$\mathcal{N}\int \mathcal{D}\{A_i, i\tilde{A}_i\} \frac{\delta}{\delta \tilde{A}_i(t)} \left[e^{J} \tilde{A}_j(0) \right] \tag{4.4}$$

yields

$$\langle \{ \dot{A}_i(t) - \mathcal{K}(t) A_i'(t) - L A_i''(t) - \sum_k A_i'(t) L \tilde{A}_k(t) A_k'(t) \} \tilde{A}_j(0) \rangle \tag{4.5}$$
$$= \delta_{ij} \; \delta(t-t').$$

The last term in the bracket gives no contribution because of causality and the rest can be written as

$$\frac{d}{dt} \tilde{\mathcal{R}}_{ij}(t) = \delta_{ij} \delta(t) - \sum_k \tilde{\Gamma}_{ik} \tilde{\mathcal{R}}_{kj}(t) - \int_0^t d\tau \sum_k \tilde{\Gamma}'_{ik}(t-\tau) \tilde{\mathcal{R}}_{kj}(\tau) \tag{4.6}$$

where $\tilde{\Gamma}_{ik}$ and $\tilde{\Gamma}'_{ik}(t)$ are the instantaneous and retarded parts of the selfenergy, respectively. They are as usual given in a perturbative sense as a sum of proper diagrams[4,6,7]. Similarly one obtains for the response function

$$\frac{d}{dt} \mathcal{R}_{ij}(t) = \mathcal{P}_{ij} \delta(t) - \sum_k \Gamma_{ik} \mathcal{R}_{kj}(t) - \int_0^t d\tau \sum_k \Gamma'_{ik}(t-\tau) \mathcal{R}_{kj}(\tau) \tag{4.7}$$

with

$$\mathcal{P}_{ij} = \langle A_i' A_j' \rangle \tag{4.8}$$

as obtained from (3.11). Γ_{ik} and $\Gamma'_{ik}(t)$ are again appropriate selfenergies given by proper diagrams. It is convenient to relate $\tilde{\mathcal{R}}$ and $\mathcal{R}$ via another selfenergy defined by

$$\mathcal{R}_{ij}(t) = \sum_k \tilde{\mathcal{R}}_{ik}(t) \mathcal{P}_{kj} + \int_0^t d\tau \sum_k \tilde{\mathcal{R}}_{ik}(t-\tau) \hat{\Gamma}_{kj}(\tau) \tag{4.9}$$

Finally the equation of motion obtained from (4.5) by replacing $\tilde{A}_j(0)$ by $A_j(0)$ and taking into account now the last term in the bracket can be brought into the form

$$\mathcal{C}_{ij}(t) = \int_{-\infty}^{t} d\tau \int_{-\infty}^{0} d\tau' \sum_{hl} \mathcal{R}_{ih}(t-\tau) \cdot \left\{ \Delta_{hl}\, \delta(\tau-\tau') + \Delta'_{hl}(\tau-\tau') \right\} \mathcal{R}_{jl}(-\tau') \tag{4.10}$$

where Δ_{ij} and $\Delta'_{ij}(t)$ are again appropriate selfenergies. Alternatively we might write (4.10) using $\tilde{\mathcal{R}}$ rather than $\mathcal{R}$ and the resulting selfenergies $\tilde{\Delta}_{ij}$ and $\tilde{\Delta}'_{ij}(t)$ are then related to the original ones by

$$\Gamma + \Gamma' = \{ \mathcal{P} + \hat{\Gamma} \}^{-1} \{ \mathcal{P}(\tilde{\Gamma} + \tilde{\Gamma}') - \dot{\hat{\Gamma}} \}$$

$$\Delta + \Delta' = \{ \mathcal{P} + \hat{\Gamma} \}^{-1} \{ \tilde{\Delta} + \tilde{\Delta}' \} \{ \mathcal{P} + \hat{\Gamma}^{+} \}^{-1} \tag{4.11}$$

where the dot denotes the time derivative and a symbolic matrix notation has been used implying sums over the indices $h\, l$ and integrations over the intermediate times. It should be reminded that causality requires $\Gamma'(t) = \tilde{\Gamma}'(t) = \hat{\Gamma}(t) = 0$ for $t \leq 0$ whereas $\mathcal{C}_{ij}(t) = \mathcal{C}_{ji}(-t)$ and similarly for Δ' and $\tilde{\Delta}'$.

A system of the type considered obeys fluctuation-dissipation theorems[4,7] relating correlation and response functions. Among those one has

$$\frac{d}{dt}\, \mathcal{C}_{ij}(t) = -L \left\{ \mathcal{R}_{ij}(t) - \mathcal{R}_{ji}(-t) \right\}. \tag{4.12}$$

From this relation one finds a corresponding one for the self-energies

$$\frac{d}{dt}\, \Delta'_{ij}(t) = L \sum_{h} \left\{ \mathcal{P}^{-1}_{ih}\, \Gamma'_{hj}(t) - \Gamma'_{ih}(-t)\, \mathcal{P}^{-1}_{hj} \right\} \tag{4.13}$$

Because of the existence of these theorems it is sufficient to calculate the correlation functions and because of the symmetry

$\tau_{ij}(t) = \tau_{ji}(-t)$ one has to compute the correlation functions for positive times only. For $t>0$ using the above relations and the original equations of motion (4.7, 4.10) one finds[4]

$$\frac{d}{dt}\tau_{ij}(t) = -\sum_k \Omega_{ik}\tau_{kj}(t) - \frac{1}{L}\sum_{kl}\mathcal{P}_{ik}\int_0^t d\tau\, \Delta'_{kl}(t-\tau)\frac{d}{d\tau}\tau_{lj}(\tau) \tag{4.14}$$

where

$$\Omega_{ij} = \Gamma_{ij} + \Gamma'_{ij}(\omega=0) = L\sum_k \mathcal{P}_{ik}\tau^{-1}_{kj}(t=0) . \tag{4.15}$$

This quantity is therefore determined by static expectation values only. If the observables A_i were chosen orthogonal with respect to the scalar product (2.4) the frequencies Ω_{ij} in (4.15) were identical to those in the mode coupling scheme (2.8) which is easily seen by applying the fluctuation-dissipation theorem to (2.8)

$$\langle A_i \mathcal{L}_{pp} A_j\rangle = -\langle \dot{A}_i A_j\rangle = L\,\mathcal{R}_{ij}(0^+) = L\,\mathcal{P}_{ij} . \tag{4.16}$$

The term involving the time integration in (4.14) still differs from the corresponding expression in (2.7) because of the time derivative in the integrand. We can, however, write it also in the previous form (2.7)

$$\frac{d}{dt}\tau_{ij}(t) = -\sum_k \Omega_{ik}\tau_{kj}(t) + \int_0^t d\tau \sum_k \mathcal{M}_{ik}(t-\tau)\tau_{kj}(\tau) \tag{4.17}$$

introducing the memory kernel as solution of

$$\mathcal{M}_{ij}(t) = \frac{1}{L}\sum_{kl}\mathcal{P}_{ik}\Delta'_{kl}(t)\Omega_{lj} - \frac{1}{L}\sum_{kl}\int_0^t d\tau\, \mathcal{P}_{ik}\Delta'_{kl}(t-\tau)\mathcal{M}_{lj}(\tau). \tag{4.18}$$

In contrast to the mode coupling scheme we now have a systematic procedure to design higher order approximations relying for instance on perturbation theory.

PERTURBATION THEORY

The selfenergies and with it the memory kernel can be evaluated using perturbation theory. As we shall see the second order yields the mode coupling result. In order to perform the expansion we re-write the action (3.7) in the form

$$\mathcal{J} = \mathcal{J}_0 + \mathcal{J}' \tag{5.1}$$

with

$$\mathcal{J}_0 = \int dt \left[-\sum_i \tilde{A}_i \dot{A}_i + \frac{1}{2}\sum_{ij} W_{ij} \tilde{A}_i \tilde{A}_j + \sum_{ij} V_{ij} \tilde{A}_i A_j \right] \tag{5.2}$$

and

$$\mathcal{J}' = \int dt \left[\frac{1}{2} \sum_{ijk} \left\{ W_{ijk} \tilde{A}_i \tilde{A}_j A_k + V_{ijk} \tilde{A}_i A_j A_k \right\} + \cdots \right]. \tag{5.3}$$

Such a form is obtained if the terms in (3.7) containing $\mathcal{K}$ or derivatives are expanded in polynomials in $A_1 \cdots A_\nu$ which is supposed to be possible with the A_i chosen. Comparison of (3.11) with the first term in (3.7) and the resulting terms in the expansion (5.2, 5.3) yields

$$2L\hat{A}_i = \sum_j W_{ij} \tilde{A}_j + \sum_{jk} W_{ijk} \tilde{A}_j A_k + \cdots . \tag{5.4}$$

Perturbation theory, this is expansion with respect to $\mathcal{J}'$ (5.3), is conveniently represented by diagrams[4,6,7]. Their elements are the propagators $\mathcal{C}_{ij}(t)$ and $\tilde{\mathcal{R}}_{ij}(t)$ calculated in lowest order, and vertices representing the various terms in (5.3). Assuming that $\mathcal{J}'$ contains only the cubic terms written explicitely, which might be achieved by a proper choice of the A_i, the self-energy Σ' is in second order represented by the diagrams

$\tilde{\Delta}' =$  (5.5)

and using (5.4)

$2L\hat{\Gamma} =$  (5.6)

The instantaneous part of the selfenergy $\tilde{\Delta}_{ij}$ can be read off from (3.7) and is

$$\tilde{\Delta}_{ij} = 2L \langle A'_i \, A'_j \rangle = 2L\,\mathcal{P}_{ij} \tag{5.7}$$

where the definition (4.8) of $\mathcal{P}_{ij}$ has been used.

We now can calculate the memory kernel in one loop order by disregarding the second term in (4.18), expanding (4.11) to this order and inserting the above result and (4.15). We find that the second and third diagram of (5.5) cancels against the terms linear in $\hat{\Gamma}$ in the expansion of (4.11) and find

$$\mathcal{M}_{ij}(t) = \frac{1}{2} \sum_{klmno} V_{ilm} V_{kno}\, \tau_{ln}(t)\, \tau_{mo}(t) \cdot \tag{5.8}$$

$$\cdot\, \tau^{-1}_{kj}(0) + \mathcal{O}\left(V_3^4,\, V_3^2 V_4,\, V_4^2\right)$$

which is exactly the mode coupling expression generalized to non-orthogonal observables. In writing this expression we have replaced the lowest order propagators by the corresponding renormalized quantities considering the diagrams in (5.5) and (5.6) as the lowest contribution in a skeleton expansion. The order of the next correction to (5.8) is also indicated where V_3 denotes the cubic, V_4 eventual quartic terms in (5.3).

For the example of the n-component van der Pol oscillator $A_1 \cdots A_\nu = \{ s_1 \cdots s_n,\ J = \frac{1}{2} s^2 \}$. By symmetry $\tau_{\mu\nu}(t) = \delta_{\mu\nu}\tau(t)$

with $\mu = 1 \cdots n$, $\tau_{\mu J}(t) = 0$ and $\tau_{JJ}(t) = \tau_J(t)$.
Furthermore the nonvanishing elements of $\mathcal{P}_{ij}$ are

$$\mathcal{P}_{\mu\nu} = \delta_{\mu\nu} \qquad \mathcal{P}_{JJ} = 2\langle J \rangle \tag{5.9}$$

and similarly

$$\Omega_{\mu\nu} = \frac{2L}{n\langle J \rangle}\,\delta_{\mu\nu} \tag{5.10}$$

$$\Omega_{JJ} = \frac{2L\langle J \rangle}{\langle J^2 \rangle - \langle J \rangle^2}\,.$$

The nonvanishing components of the vertices V_{ijk} are

$$V_{\mu J \nu} = V_{\mu\nu J} = L u\,\delta_{\mu\nu} \tag{5.11}$$

$$V_{JJJ} = 2Lu$$

which is easily found from (1.4) and (3.7).

REFERENCES

1. H. Haken, Handbuch der Physik, Vol. XXV/2c (Springer, Berlin, 1970).
2. H. Risken, Fortschr. Phys. 16, 161 (1968); Z. Physik 191, 302 (1966).
3. S. Grossmann, Phys. Rev. A17, 1123 (1978).
4. U. Deker and F. Haake, Phys. Rev. A12, 1629 (1975); H. King, U. Deker and F. Haake, Z. Physik B36, 205 (1979).
5. K. Ziegler and H. Horner, Z. Physik B (1980).
6. P. C. Martin, E. D. Siggia and H. A. Rose, Phys. Rev. A8, 423 (1973).
7. H. K. Janssen, Z. Physik B23, 377 (1976); R. Bausch, H. K. Janssen and H. Wagner, Z. Physik B24, 113 (1976).

ONSAGER-MACHLUP FUNCTION OF NONLINEAR NON-EQUILIBRIUM THERMODYNAMICS

Robert Graham

Universität Essen, GHS
Fachbereich Physik
W-Germany

Abstract

The path integral formulation of non-equilibrium thermodynamics is reviewed. Starting with the linear theory of Onsager and Machlup valid near thermodynamic equilibrium, the description is generalized in sucessive steps by allowing for nonlinearities, and removing the restriction to systems subject to a detailed balance condition.

1. Introduction

In present day physics we witness a great resurgence of interest in the properties of macroscopic systems, governed by macroscopic dynamical laws. Examples where such descriptions have proved to be a convenient starting point are the modern theory of critical phenomena and most of the work on the problem of self-organization in open systems. The latter work incorporates the investigation of systems in quantum optics, hydrodynamics and chemically reacting systems.

The general theoretical framework of the macroscopic description of systems in equilibrium is, of course, equilibrium thermodynamics or thermostatics. It owes its generality and success to the fact that

- it furnishes a macroscopic description without necessarily involving microscopic features,
- its laws (e.g. equations of state) can be formulated in terms of extremum principles,
- it furnishes a simple description of fluctuations,

- for sufficiently simple systems it can be derived from the microscopic description.

Non-equilibrium thermodynamics is the theory, which, by suitable generalization of equilibrium thermodynamics, tries to save these features.
A linear theory, which acchieves this goal, but is only valid in the vicinity of thermodynamic equilibrium, was formulated by Onsager [1] and Onsager and Machlup [2]. Their formulation exhibited the new dynamical extremum principles, and, by the use of Gaussian path integrals, their theory also incorporated a dynamical description of fluctuations in a way analogous to equilibrium thermodynamics.

The theory of Onsager and Machlup [2,3] has since been generalized considerably in two directions. Some of the numerous papers on the subject are [4] - [17]. The first generalization consists in admitting nonlinearities in the variables describing the deviations from equilibrium, but leaving unchanged the time reversal symmetries present in systems with equilibrium boundary conditions. This is, e.g., the situation one deals with in critical dynamics.

The generalized Onsager Machlup formulation has, in this case, proved to be a very useful starting point, e.g. for setting up a dynamical formulation of the renormalization group [18,19].

The second generalization consists in admitting departures from the time reversal or detailed balance property characteristic of a system subject to equilibrium boundary conditions. This is the typical situation one has to deal with if systems in non-equilibrium steady states are to be considered. Unfortunately, much less is known generally about such systems, as compared to systems subject to equilibrium boundary conditions. An improved understanding is certainly necessary before one can hope to gain much further theoretical insight into problems of self organization in non-equilibrium steady states or into the inverse problem of the appearance of chaotic or turbulent steady states. Not the least for this reason is it interesting to see how much of the structure of the original Onsager Machlup theory survives this second generalizing step.

The present paper reviews the Onsager Machlup theory and its successive generalizations. In order to exhibit the analogy to equilibrium thermodynamics we first introduce some concepts of thermostatics in the next section. This is followed by a description of the linear Onsager Machlup theory. Then the generalization to nonlinear dynamics is introduced. In the next step the requirement of detailed balance is dropped, first in the linear theory and finally in the nonlinear theory. The last section contains our conclusions.

2. Thermostatics

Let $q=(q^1, q^2, \ldots q^n)$, $-\infty<q^i<+\infty$, be a complete set of macroscopic variables of a given system. Here and throughout this paper the formulation will be presented in terms of discrete variables only, the necessary formal generalizations for the case of fields being understood. Let the system be subject to equilibrium boundary conditions. For systems described by discrete variables this means that the system may interact with various reservoirs which are in equilibrium among themselves. We begin by considering states of thermodynamic equilibrium, described by thermodynamic potentials. The latter generally depend on the constraints imposed. Let the equilibrium state, constrained by keeping the q fixed, then be described by the thermostatic potential $\Phi(q)$.
If the constraints on q are lifted, the variables q, if not exactly conserved, will undergo a fluctuating dynamics and relax to some state $\tilde{q}$ which minimizes $\Phi(q)$

$$\Phi(\tilde{q}) \quad = \quad \min \tag{2.1}$$

The variable q may still make excursions away from $\tilde{q}$ due to fluctuations, according to the probability distribution

$$W(q) \sim (\mathrm{Det}\, g^{\nu\mu}(q))^{-\frac{1}{2}} \exp(-\Phi(q)) \tag{2.2}$$

(We use units with $k_B=1$). $-\Phi(q)$ may be considered as the total entropy (i.e. the entropy of the system and the reservoirs) [20]. Here, $g^{\nu\mu}(q)$ is a metric tensor in the space spanned by the variables q. If, in particular, the variables q are the natural thermodynamic variables, then $g^{\nu\mu}(q)$ is a Euclidean metric [10]. Thus for natural variables, $\tilde{q}$ is the most probable value of q. More generally, $\tilde{q}$ determines the location of the most probable volume element $(dq/\sqrt{\mathrm{Det}\, g^{\nu\mu}(q)})$ in q-space. If fluctuations are very small one may approximate the average $\langle q\rangle$ by the most probable value $\tilde{q}$. However, if fluctuations are important, as e.g. near critical points, $\Phi(q)$ is not the adequate potential for deriving $\langle q\rangle$. Instead we have to compute from $\Phi(q)$ the complete partition function

$$Z(\lambda) \quad = \quad \int dq \exp[-\Phi(q) + \lambda q]\, g^{-\frac{1}{2}}(q) \tag{2.3}$$

with

$$g(q) \quad = \quad \mathrm{Det}\, g^{\nu\mu}(q); \quad \langle q\rangle \quad = \quad \left.\frac{\partial \ln Z(\lambda)}{\partial\lambda}\right|_{\lambda=0} \tag{2.4}$$

By the Legendre transformation

$$v \quad = \quad \frac{\partial \ln Z(\lambda)}{\partial\lambda}; \quad \Gamma(v) \quad = \quad \lambda v - \ln Z(\lambda) \tag{2.5}$$

one defines the true thermodynamic potential $\Gamma(v)$ (while $\Phi(q)$ is

often called course grained thermodynamic potential) with

$$\Gamma\ (\langle q\rangle) \quad = \quad \min \tag{2.6}$$

i.e.

$$\left.\frac{\partial\Gamma}{\partial v}\right|_{v=\langle q\rangle} = 0; \quad \left[\frac{\partial^2\Gamma}{\partial v^{\cdot}\partial v^{\cdot}}\right]^{-1\ \nu\mu} = \langle (q^\nu-\langle q^\nu\rangle)(q^\mu-\langle q^\mu\rangle)\rangle \tag{2.7}$$

For Gaussian $W(q)$ one has, in particular,

$$\Gamma(v) \quad = \quad \Phi(v) \tag{2.8}$$

For non-Gaussian $W(q)$, $\Gamma(v)$ gets renormalized by the higher than second-order terms in $\Phi(q)$.

3. Linear thermodynamics

We now review the essential points of the linear theory given by Onsager and Machlup [2] in 1953. The formulation we present here differs somewhat from the one originally given by Onsager and Machlup [see also 3] but it is completely equivalent and all essential points remain the same. Apart from the usual assumption necessary in order that a macroscopic thermodynamic description is adequate [2], the theory contains two additional assumptions:

i) The system is subject to equilibrium boundary conditions, i.e. interacts with reservoirs which are in equilibrium among themselves.
ii) The system is subject to linear Markovian equations of motion.

The second assumption implies that the dynamics may be described by a linear Langevin equation (which we always take in the Stratonovich representation [21])

$$\dot{q}^\nu \quad = \quad K^\nu(q) + f^\nu(t) \tag{3.1}$$

where $K^\nu(q)$ is linear in q and $f^\nu(t)$ represents Gaussian white noise.

$$\langle f^\nu(t)\rangle \quad = \quad 0; \ \langle f^\nu(t+\tau)f^\mu(t)\rangle \quad = \quad Q^{\nu\mu}\ \delta(\tau) \tag{3.2}$$

The first assumption implies that $K^\nu(q)$ and $f^\nu(t)$ both have a form consistent with detailed balance in the equilibrium state.

The detailed balance condition implies [22,5] that $K^\nu(q)$ splits into a reversible part $r^\nu(q)$ and a dissipative part $d^\nu(q)$

$$K^\nu(q) \quad = \quad r^\nu(q) + d^\nu(q) \tag{3.3}$$

with

$$d^\nu(q) \quad = \quad -\frac{1}{2}\, Q^{\nu\mu} \; \frac{\partial\Phi(q)}{\partial q^\mu} \tag{3.4}$$

Here $\Phi(q)$ is the coarse grained thermodynamic potential introduced in the preceding section. The metric tensor $g^{\nu\mu}$ in the present linear theory is independent of q. The linear relation between the dissipative fluxes $d^\nu(q)$ and the thermodynamic forces $\frac{\partial\Phi}{\partial q^\mu}$ are known as linear constitutive laws. As a further consequence of detailed balance the matrix of transport coefficients $Q^{\nu\mu}$ satisfies the Onsager-Casimir symmetry relations.

Finally, the reversible drift $r^\nu(q)$ in the linear theory satisfies, due to detailed balance,

$$r^\mu(q)\,\frac{\partial\Phi(q)}{\partial q^\mu} \quad = \quad 0; \qquad \frac{\partial r^\nu(q)}{\partial q^\nu} \quad = \quad 0 \tag{3.5}$$

i.e. $r^\nu(q)$ describes a drift on equipotential surfaces of $\Phi(q)$ and conserves the volume element in the space spanned by the variables q.

Having made these assumptions, the aim is now to cast the formulation of the dynamics into a form which parallels the thermostatic description given before.
A dynamical formulation of the probability density of fluctuations is most directly obtained [5] by making use of the known properties of the $f^\nu(t)$ to write down their Gaussian probability density functional [23]

$$W_f(\{f\}) \sim \exp\,[-\frac{1}{2} \int_{-\infty}^{+\infty} d\tau\; Q_{\nu\mu} \;\; f^\nu(\tau)\; f^\mu(\tau)] \tag{3.6}$$

where $Q_{\nu\mu}$ is defined as the inverse+) of $Q^{\nu\mu}$.

+) The inverse of $Q^{\nu\mu}$ does not exist in the case when some of the fluctuating forces f^λ vanish. (Note that then automatically $d^\lambda=0$ by eq. (3.4)). Since one is free to make linear transformations among the variables q, the vanishing of some f^λ is even the most general situation, if the inverse of $Q^{\nu\mu}$ does not exist. The sums in eq. (3.6) then run over the restricted class of indices for which $f^\nu \neq 0$.

Inserting eq. (3.1), solved for f^ν, we obtain the probability density functional $W(\{q(\tau)\})$. The Jacobian is independent of q because of the linearity of eq. (3.1) and may therefore be disregarded. The result may be written in the form+)

$$W(\{q\}) \sim \exp\left[-\int_{-\infty}^{+\infty} d\tau\, \mathcal{O}(\dot{q}(\tau), q(\tau))\right] \tag{3.7}$$

The most probable path between two given points satisfies

$$\int_{t_0,q_0}^{t_1,q_1} d\tau\, \mathcal{O}(\dot{q}(\tau), q(\tau)) = \min \tag{3.8}$$

i.e. the Onsager Machlup function $\mathcal{O}(\dot{q},q)$ acts as a coarse grained thermodynamic potential in dynamics, Because $W(\{q(\tau)\})$ in the present case is Gaussian, $\mathcal{O}(\dot{q},q)$ is also the potential for the average path between two given points. The growth of a fluctuation q at time t from $q=\tilde{q}$ at $t\to-\infty$ is described by

$$\int_{-\infty,\tilde{q}}^{t,q} d\tau\, \mathcal{O}(\dot{q}(\tau), q(\tau)) = \min \tag{3.9}$$

while the decay of a given fluctuation to $\tilde{q}$ satisfies

$$\int_{t,q}^{\infty,\tilde{q}} d\tau\, \mathcal{O}(\dot{q}(\tau), q(\tau)) = \min \tag{3.10}$$

Again, most probable paths and average paths coincide in these cases.
The explicit form of $\mathcal{O}(\dot{q},q)$ is given by++)

$$\mathcal{O}(\dot{q},q) = \frac{1}{2} Q_{\nu\mu} (\dot{q}^\nu - K^\nu(q)) (\dot{q}^\mu(q) - K^\mu(q)) \tag{3.11}$$

+) In the case of the preceding footnote, the probability density (3.7) includes additional δ-functional factors $\delta(\{\dot{q}^\lambda - K^\lambda(q)\})$ for each f^λ that vanishes. The extremum principles that follow are then all subject to the constraints $\dot{q}^\lambda = K^\lambda(q)$.

++) Note that $\dot{q}^\lambda = K^\lambda(q) = r^\lambda(q)$ if $f^\lambda(t)$ vanishes. Therefore the sums over ν,μ in eqs. (3.11), (3.13) are automatically only over those indices for which $f^\nu(t)$ does not vanish.

Using the relations implied by detailed balance it may be reexpressed in terms of the coarse grained potential $\Phi(q)$ and the reversible drift $r^{\nu}(q)$ in the form

$$\mathcal{O}(\dot{q},q) = \frac{1}{2}\left(\psi_1(\dot{q}-r,\dot{q}-r) + \psi_2\left(\frac{\partial\Phi}{\partial q}, \frac{\partial\Phi}{\partial q}\right) - P\left(\dot{q}, \frac{\partial\Phi}{\partial q}\right)\right) \qquad (3.12)$$

Here

$$\psi_1 = Q_{\nu\mu}(\dot{q}^{\nu}-r^{\nu})(\dot{q}^{\mu}-r^{\mu}) \qquad (3.13)$$

$$\psi_2 = \frac{1}{4} Q^{\nu\mu} \frac{\partial\Phi}{\partial q^{\nu}} \frac{\partial\Phi}{\partial q^{\mu}} \qquad (3.14)$$

are the two dissipative potentials, introduced by Onsager [1].

The potential $-\Phi(q)$ is the total entropy of subsystem and reservoirs expressed as function of q [20]. $\psi_1 + \psi_2$ express the positive definite entropy production rate within the subsystem along an arbitrary trajectory $q(\tau)$ as a function of the dissipative fluxes $\dot{q}-r$ and the thermodynamic forces $\frac{\partial\Phi}{\partial q}$. This production rate, generally, is not the time derivative of any function of q. $P(\dot{q},\frac{\partial\Phi}{\partial q})$ in eq. (3.12) is defined by

$$P = -\dot{q}^{\nu} \frac{\partial\Phi}{\partial q^{\nu}} = -\dot{\Phi} \qquad (3.15)$$

This expression is a total differential and must therefore represent the total entropy change along a given trajectory. Under time reversal ψ_1 and ψ_2 are invariant and thus remain positive, while P changes sign. The physical meaning of $\mathcal{O}(\dot{q},q)$ has therefore become clear: $\mathcal{O}(\dot{q},q)\,dt$ just represents one half of the difference of the entropy produced within the subsystem along any given trajectory during the time interval dt and the change of the total equilibrium entropy $-\Phi(q)$ along that same trajectory.

Along the most probable paths and the average paths, which concide in the present case, the entropy production $\psi_1 + \psi_2$ takes its minimal value

$$\int d\tau\,\left[\psi_1(\dot{q}-r,\ \dot{q}-r) + \psi_2\left(\frac{\partial\Phi}{\partial q}, \frac{\partial\Phi}{\partial q}\right)\right] = \min \qquad (3.16)$$

This is the principle of minimum dissipation [1,2] or the principle of minimum entropy production [24]. It is most easily derived from the fluctuation formula (3.7). Since P is a total differential, it may be eliminated from the fluctuation formula (3.7) by carrying out the time integral between two given end points, at $t \to \pm\infty$, say. We obtain

$$W(\{q\}) \sim \exp \left[-\frac{1}{2} \int_{-\infty}^{+\infty} d\tau \, (\psi_1 + \psi_2) \right] \tag{3.17}$$

This formula expresses the probability density of paths entirely in terms of the entropy production $\psi_1 + \psi_2$. The formula shows that the principle of minimum entropy production is here a consequence of maximizing the probability density for the most probable path and the average path. For the decay of a given fluctuation at t=0 to an unconstrained value at $t=\infty$ the principle of minimum entropy production merely gives back the original equations of motion averaged over the fluctuating forces f^ν. However, it is important to realize that the extremum principle is far more general than this result. E.g. it also describes the growth of a fluctuation from $t=-\infty$ to a given value at t=0 and the average path between two given points in q-space which are both beyond the averaged equations.

For the decay of a given fluctuation q at t=0 to an unconstrained value at $t=\infty$, the minimum value of $\psi_1 + \psi_2$ just equals $P(\dot{q}, \frac{\partial \Phi}{\partial q})$ along the same path. Thus

$$\min \int_{q(0)=q}^{t=\infty} d\tau \, (\psi_1 + \psi_2) = - \int_{q(0)=q}^{t=\infty} d\tau \, \dot{q}^\nu \frac{\partial \Phi}{\partial q^\nu}$$

$$= \Phi(q) - \text{const} \tag{3.18}$$

or, by using the time reversal transformation properties of detailed balance

$$\Phi(q) = \text{const} + \min \int_{t=-\infty}^{q(0)=q} d\tau \, (\psi_1 + \psi_2) \tag{3.19}$$

These properties of Φ and $\psi_1 + \psi_2$ show, how the thermostatic description is contained in the dynamic formulation. We simply have

$$W(q) \sim \max_{(q(0)=q)} \exp \left[-\frac{1}{2} \int_{-\infty}^{+\infty} d\tau \, (\psi_1 + \psi_2) \right] \tag{3.20}$$

Analogous formulae also hold for multi-time joint probability densities, e.g.

$$W(q_1 t_1, q_2 t_2) \sim \max_{(q(t_1)=q_1, q(t_2)=q_2)} \exp\left[-\frac{1}{2}\int_{-\infty}^{+\infty} d\tau \; (\psi_1 + \psi_2)\right] \tag{3.21}$$

4. Nonlinear Thermodynamics

We now describe a first generalization of the Onsager Machlup theory by allowing equations of motion which are nonlinear in the variables q. However, we still keep the other restriction of the original Onsager Machlup theory, confining ourselves to systems subject to equilibrium boundary conditions.
The most convenient way to formulate the dynamics of the system is now by means of a Fokker Planck equation, which we may write in a manner which is invariant under nonlinear point transformations of the variables q [25,10]

$$\frac{\partial P}{\partial t} = \frac{\partial}{\partial q^\mu}\left[-h^\mu_g(q)P + \frac{1}{2\sqrt{g(q)}}\, Q^{\mu\nu}(q)\,\frac{\partial}{\partial q^\nu}\left(\sqrt{g(q)}\; P\right)\right] \tag{4.1}$$

Here

$$g(q) = \mathrm{Det}\; g^{\nu\mu}(q) \tag{4.2}$$

The conditional probability density $P(q|q_0,\tau)$ to find q at time $t+\tau$ if q_0 at time t was realized is a scalar density of weight -1 in q-space. Furthermore the drift $h^\mu_g(q)$ is a contravariant vector and $Q^{\mu\lambda}(q)$ is a contravariant tensor.
The detailed balance conditions are again formulated by splitting h^μ_g into a reversible part r^μ and a dissipative part d^μ (which are both contravariant vectors).

In the presence of detailed balance they take the form

$$d^\mu = -\frac{1}{2}\, Q^{\mu\nu}\,\frac{\partial \Phi}{\partial q^\nu} \tag{4.3}$$

$$\sqrt{g}\,\frac{\partial}{\partial q^\nu}\,\frac{r^\nu}{\sqrt{g}} - r^\nu\,\frac{\partial \Phi}{\partial q^\nu} = 0 \tag{4.4}$$

The path integral description corresponding to the Fokker Planck equation (4.1) has been derived [7,8] and can again be cast into a covariant form

$$W(\{q\})\, Dq \sim \exp\left[-\int_{-\infty}^{+\infty} d\tau \;\; \mathcal{O}(\dot{q}(\tau), q(\tau))\right] D\mu(\{q\}) \tag{4.5}$$

The measure $D\mu(\{q\})$ can be written in the form [18, 26]

$$D\mu(\{q\}) = \lim \prod_{i=-\infty}^{+\infty} \Big[dq(\tau_i)$$

$$\prod_{(\lambda)}{}' \delta(q^\lambda(\tau_i)-q^\lambda(\tau_{i-1})-(\tau_i-\tau_{i-1})h^\lambda(q(\tau_{i-1})))\cdot$$

$$\cdot\left[\mathrm{Det}\left(-\frac{\partial^2 S_o(q(\tau_i),q(\tau_{i-1}))}{\partial q^\nu(\tau_i)\,\partial q^\mu(\tau_{i-1})}\right)\right]^{1/2}\Big] \tag{4.6}$$

with

$$S_o(q(t),q(t_o)) = \min \int_{t_o,q(t_o)}^{t,q(t)} d\tau\ \mathcal{O}(\dot{q}(\tau),\ q(\tau)) \tag{4.7}$$

$\prod'_{(\lambda)}$ is a product over all λ for which there are no fluctuations. We see that, as in the linear theory, the probability density functional is entirely determined by the Onsager Machlup function. In addition to the exponential weight factor, the Onsager Machlup function also determines the volume element $D\mu$ in function space.

The explicit form [7] of $\mathcal{O}(\dot{q},q)$ is given by+)

$$\mathcal{O} = \frac{1}{2} Q_{\nu\mu}(q)\ (\dot{q}^\nu-h^\nu(q))\ (\dot{q}^\mu-h^\mu(q)) + \frac{1}{2}\sqrt{Q(q)}\ \frac{\partial}{\partial q^\nu}\frac{h^\nu(q)}{\sqrt{Q(q)}} + \frac{1}{12} R\ (q) + \frac{1}{4}\dot{q}^\nu \frac{\partial}{\partial q^\nu} \ln Q(q) \tag{4.8}$$

where

$$Q(q) = \mathrm{Det}\ Q^{\nu\mu}(q) \tag{4.9}$$

+) Again, like in the linear case $Q_{\nu\mu}(q)$ represents the inverse of $Q^{\nu\mu}(q)$ in the subspace of variables q^ν in which $Q^{\nu\mu}(q)$ is non-singular. All λ in the orthogonal subspace have to be omitted from the sums over ν,μ in eq. (4.8).

Here $R(q)$ is the Riemann scalar derived from the tensor $Q^{\nu\mu}(q)$. For dynamical processes $Q^{\nu\mu}(q)$ therefore forms a natural metric tensor. Also the drift $h^\nu(q)$ appearing in O is expressed in terms of $Q^{\nu\mu}(q)$ as a metric. Its explicit relation to $h^\nu_g(q)$, the Fokker Planck drift with metric $g^{\nu\mu}(q)$, is

$$h^\nu(q) = h^\nu_g(q) + \frac{1}{4} Q^{\nu\mu}(q) \frac{\partial}{\partial q^\mu} \ln \frac{Q(q)}{g(q)} \tag{4.10}$$

i.e.

$$h^\nu(q) = h^\nu_Q(q)$$

By introducing again the entropy production $\frac{1}{2}(\psi_1+\psi_2)$ along an arbitrary trajectory, with

$$\psi_1 = Q_{\nu\mu}(q)\,(\dot{q}^\nu - r^\nu(q))\,(\dot{q}^\mu - r^\mu(q)) \tag{4.11}$$

$$\psi_2 = \frac{1}{4} Q^{\nu\mu}(q) \frac{\partial\Phi}{\partial q^\nu} \frac{\partial\Phi}{\partial q^\mu} \tag{4.12}$$

and the reversible entropy change

$$P(\dot{q}, \frac{\partial\Phi}{\partial q}) = -\dot{q}^\nu \frac{\partial\Phi}{\partial q^\nu} \tag{4.13}$$

we can reexpress $O(\dot{q},q)$ in the form

$$O(\dot{q},q) = \frac{1}{2}(\psi_1+\psi_2 + \sigma_{dyn} - P - P_{dyn}) \tag{4.14}$$

Apart from the terms σ_{dyn} and P_{dyn}, the relation of O to ψ_1, ψ_2 and P is the same as in the original linear theory. The new terms σ_{dyn}, P_{dyn} have their origin in the more complicated geometries of nonlinear flows in q-space. They may be interpreted as an additional, dynamical, irreversible and reversible entropy production, respectively. σ_{dyn} is a scalar and consists of two physically distinct parts

$$\sigma_{dyn} = \sigma^{drift}_{dyn} + \sigma^{diff}_{dyn} \tag{4.15}$$

with

$$\sigma^{drift}_{dyn} = \sqrt{g(q)} \frac{\partial}{\partial q^\nu} \frac{d^\nu(q)}{\sqrt{g(q)}} \tag{4.16}$$

This part of σ_{dyn} is a dynamical entropy production due to the dissipative drift $d^{\nu}(q)$. Entropy is here increased or decreased due to an increase or decrease of the invariant volume element in q-space

$$dV(q) = (g(q))^{-1/2}\, dq \tag{4.17}$$

carried along by the dissipative drift $d^{\nu}(q)$. This change is irreversible, since the dissipative drift $d^{\nu}(q)$ is irreversible.

The second part, σ^{diff}_{dyn} contains $g(q)$ and $Q^{\nu\mu}(q)$ in a complicated way. The simplest appearance of this term, which then becomes accessible to physical interpretation, is obtained in the special coordinates $*q$, for which all first order derivatives of $Q^{\nu\mu}$ vanish at a given point, q_o say. Such coordinates (Riemann normal coordinates with respect to the metric $Q^{\nu\mu}(q_o)$) can always be found [27]. In these coordinates σ^{diff}_{dyn} at $q=q_o$ takes the form

$$*\sigma^{diff}_{dyn}(q_o) = (*g(q_o))^{1/4}\; *Q^{\nu\mu}(q_o)\; \left(\frac{\partial^2 (*g(*q))^{-1/4}}{\partial *q^{\nu}\, \partial *q^{\mu}}\right)_{*q=q_o} \tag{4.18}$$

We have indicated the special choice of coordinates by marking with $*$ all quantities depending on this choice. The general form of σ^{diff}_{dyn} is fixed by eq. (4.18) and our knowledge that σ^{diff}_{dyn} is a scalar. σ^{diff}_{dyn} describes an irreversible entropy production by an increase or decrease of the invariant volume element in q-space due to diffusion. In particular, for $g(q)=Q(q)$, we have

$$\sigma^{diff}_{dyn} = \frac{1}{6} R(q) \tag{4.19}$$

It should be noted, that σ_{dyn} need not be positive, i.e. entropy may be produced or destroyed by the macroscopic dynamics. The special role of σ^{drift}_{dyn} in systems with strange attractors has recently been pointed out by Shaw [28].
The term P_{dyn} is the total increase or decrease of the invariant volume element. In arbitrary coordinates it is given by

$$P_{dyn} = \sqrt{g}\; \dot{q}^{\nu}\, \frac{\partial}{\partial q^{\nu}} \frac{1}{\sqrt{g}} \tag{4.20}$$

While σ_{dyn} is a scalar, P_{dyn} is not.
If combined with the (nonscalar) measure $D\mu$, the nonscalar term P_{dyn} just serves to make the combined expression

$$\sqrt[4]{\frac{g(q(\tau_{i-1}))}{g(q(\tau_i))}}\ \sqrt{\mathrm{Det}\left(-\frac{\partial^2 S_o(q(\tau_i),q(\tau_{i-1}))}{\partial q^\nu(\tau_i)\,\partial q^\mu(\tau_{i-1})}\right)} \tag{4.21}$$

a scalar density of weight -1.

The physical meaning of $\mathcal{O}$ remains the same as in the linear theory, except that the entropy production along any given trajectory in q-space must now include the dynamical parts due to drift and diffusion.

The total rate of entropy change $P(q,\frac{\partial\Phi}{\partial q})+P_{dyn}$ is still a total differential and can be integrated out in the formula for $W(\{q\})$. We obtain

$$W(\{q\})\ Dq \sim \exp\left[-\frac{1}{2}\int_{-\infty}^{+\infty}(\psi_1+\psi_2+\sigma_{dyn})\,d\tau\right]D\mu(\{q\}) \tag{4.22}$$

A moment's thought reveals that $P(\dot{q},\frac{\partial\Phi}{\partial q})+P_{dyn}$ also drops out from the expression (4.6) for the measure $D\mu(\{q\})$. Thus $W(\{q\})$ may again be expressed entirely in terms of the irreversible entropy production within the subsystem.

The most probable path in q-space (i.e. the path $q(\tau)$ which is at the center of the most probable volume element $D\mu(q)$ in q-space) satisfies the extremum principle

$$\int d\tau\ \mathcal{O}(\dot{q},q) \quad = \quad \min. \tag{4.23}$$

If fluctuations are important $\mathcal{O}(\dot{q},q)$ can no longer be used to calculate the average path.
Instead we have to compute $\Gamma(\{v\})$ from

$$Z(\{\lambda\}) \quad = \quad \int Dq\ W(\{q\})\ \exp\left(\int d\tau\ \lambda_\nu q^\nu\right) \tag{4.24}$$

$$v^\nu \quad = \quad \frac{\delta Z}{\delta\lambda_\nu}\ ; \qquad \Gamma \quad = \quad \int d\tau\ \lambda_\nu q^\nu - \ln Z \tag{4.25}$$

The functional $\Gamma(\{v\})$ now gives the average path by the minimum principle

$$\Gamma(\{<q(\tau)>\}) = \min \qquad (4.26)$$

In order to compute Γ we have to carry out a non-Gaussian path integral. It is well known that this can only be done by reducing the integral to Gaussian path integrals, either perturbatively [23] or by saddle point approximations [26].

5. Linear non-equilibrium thermodynamics

We now take the next generalizing step and allow for non-equilibrium boundary conditions. Thus the system no longer has any detailed balance properties. However, in this section, we will again restrict ourselves to linear equations. The theory we obtain would e.g. be suitable to investigate a system in the linear vicinity of a non-equilibrium steady state [28].

The formal framework is now again similar to section 3. All results of that section, which did not depend on the detailed balance assumption, can immediately be taken over. This covers eqs. (3.1), (3.6)-(3.11).

In order to push the connection with the case of equilibrium boundary conditions even further [5], it is usefull to split $K^{\nu}(q)$ again into two linear parts

$$K^{\nu}(q) = \tilde{r}^{\nu}(q) + \tilde{d}^{\nu}(q) \qquad (5.1)$$

with the properties

$$\tilde{d}^{\nu}(q) = -\frac{1}{2} Q^{\nu\mu} \frac{\partial\Phi}{\partial q^{\mu}} \qquad (5.2)$$

$$\tilde{r}^{\nu}(q)\frac{\partial\Phi}{\partial q^{\nu}} - \frac{\partial\tilde{r}^{\nu}}{\partial q^{\nu}} = 0 \qquad (5.3)$$

The potential Φ is defined via the steady state probability distribution

$$W(q) \sim \exp(-\Phi(q)) \qquad (5.4)$$

The only (but essential) difference between these equations and their counterparts in the case of equilibrium boundary conditions is the fact, that $\tilde{r}^{\nu}$, $\tilde{d}^{\nu}$ and $\Phi(q)$ have not a simple behaviour under time reversal. In particular, $\tilde{r}^{\nu}$ and $\tilde{d}^{\nu}$ are not known independently but are <u>defined</u> by the above equations.

It turns out that $\tilde{r}^{\nu}(q)$ automatically satisfies, besides eq. (5.3), the even stronger conditions

$$\tilde{r}^{\nu} \frac{\partial \Phi}{\partial q^{\nu}} = 0; \quad \frac{\partial \tilde{r}^{\nu}}{\partial q^{\nu}} = 0 \tag{5.5}$$

which are the counterparts of eq. (3.5).

In terms of the quantities $\tilde{r}^{\nu}$, $\tilde{d}^{\nu}$ and Φ the results of the Onsager Machlup theory in the present case are now simply stated:

All results of section 3, except for time reversal properties, still apply also here, if stated in terms of $\tilde{r}^{\nu}$, $\tilde{d}^{\nu}$ instead of r^{ν}, d^{ν}.
It is clear that $\Phi(q)$ in the present case is not one of the usual equilibrium thermodynamic potentials. However, except for time reversal properties, it still plays the same role and has therefore been called a generalized thermodynamic potential.
Under the present assumptions the average $<q>$ in the steady state satisfies the minimum principle, Φ=min.

The average path of approach to the steady state satisfies a 'minimum production of $(-\Phi)$ principle' if we define the production rate of $(-\Phi)$ by the sum $\psi_1+\psi_2$.

Explicitely, the minimum principle reads

$$\int_{q(0)=q}^{t=\infty} d\tau\ (\psi_1+\psi_2) = \min$$

$$\Phi(q) = \text{const} + \min \int_{q(0)=q}^{t=\infty} (\psi_1+\psi_2)\,d\tau \tag{5.6}$$

For the investigation of the building up of a fluctuation we can no longer use known time reversal properties. However, the steady state distribution $\exp(-\Phi(q))$ is still given by extremizing the Gaussian $W(\{q(\tau)\})$ under the constraint $q(0)=q$, thus

$$\min_{(q(0)=q)} \frac{1}{2} \int_{-\infty}^{+\infty} d\tau\ (\psi_1+\psi_2) = \Phi(q) - \text{const}' \tag{5.7}$$

As a result

$$\Phi(q) = \text{const}'' + \min \int_{-\infty}^{q(0)=q} d\tau\ (\psi_1+\psi_2) \tag{5.8}$$

still holds despite the absence of detailed balance. Moreover, the minimizing path for the building up of the fluctuation $q(0)=q$ coincides with the average path which thus still satisfies the 'minimum production of $-\Phi(q)$ principle'.
The same conclusion can be drawn for the average path connecting any two given points in q-space.

6. Nonlinear non-equilibrium thermodynamics

Now the two generalizations, nonlinearity and absence of detailed balance, are combined and considered together. All results of section 4 which did not depend on detailed balance can be taken over.
This applies to eqs. (4.1), (4.5) - (4.10)

We now define again $\tilde{d}^\nu$ and $\tilde{r}^\nu$ by

$$h_g^\nu = \tilde{r}^\nu + \tilde{d}^\nu \tag{6.1}$$

with

$$\tilde{d}^\nu(q) = -\frac{1}{2} Q^{\nu\mu}(q) \frac{\partial\Phi}{\partial q^\mu} \tag{6.2}$$

$$\sqrt{g(q)} \frac{\partial}{\partial q^\nu} \frac{\tilde{r}^\nu(q)}{\sqrt{g(q)}} - \tilde{r}^\nu(q) \frac{\partial\Phi}{\partial q^\nu} = 0 \tag{6.3}$$

The potential Φ is defined by the steady state distribution

$$W(q) \sim (g(q))^{-1/2} \exp(-\Phi(q)) \tag{6.4}$$

Except for the time reversal properties of $\tilde{d}^\nu$ and $\tilde{r}^\nu$, all results of section 4 now apply also in the present case, if d^ν and r^ν of section 4 are replaced by $\tilde{d}^\nu$ and $\tilde{r}^\nu$.
Unfortunately, there is no way to determine $\tilde{d}^\nu$ and $\tilde{r}^\nu$, short of solving the time independent Fokker Planck equation.

Therefore, there is little practical value, in the present case, in expressing O in terms of ψ_1, ψ_2, σ_{dyn}, P, P_{dyn}.
In other words, a thermodynamic interpretation of O is still possible but only from hindsight, after the generalized thermodynamic potential Φ corresponding to the non-equilibrium boundary conditions has been determined explicitely. In practice, therefore, eq. (4.8) is the only explicit expression for O which is available.

7. Conclusions

Let us summarize briefly the main resulting conclusions.

i) Including nonlinearities in the statistical dynamics we find:

- The probability density functional of paths may still be expressed entirely in terms of a single function, the Onsager Machlup function. However, the volume element in the space of trajectories also depends on the Onsager Machlup function.
- Physically, the Onsager Machlup function is one half of the difference of the 'entropy' produced irreversibly within the subsystem per unit time along any given path and the total entropy change along that same path.
- The production rates include dynamical terms due to the change of the invariant volume element along a given path. The invariant volume element changes irreversibly due to dissipative drift and diffusion. Its total change is given by a total differential.
- The Onsager Machlup function no longer determines the average path by an extremum principle. Rather, it is a dynamical coarse grained potential.

ii) Allowing for non-equilibrium boundary conditions, i.e. the absence of detailed balance we find:

- The probability density is still entirely expressed by the Onsager Machlup function $\mathcal{O}$
- The thermodynamic interpretation of $\mathcal{O}$ requires that one first determines the steady distribution $W(q)$ and the generalized thermodynamic potential $\Phi=-\ln W(q)\sqrt{g(q)}$. In other words, it is first necessary to find the thermodynamic interpretation of the steady state. Then two quantities $\tilde{d}^{\nu}$ and $\tilde{r}^{\nu}$ can be defined, which satisfy the same relations as the dissipative drift d^{ν} and the reversible drift r^{ν} in systems with detailed drift balance, without necessarily sharing their time reversal properties.
- A generalized thermodynamic interpretation of $\mathcal{O}(\dot{q},q)$ can then be given. It is one half of the difference of the production rate of the generalized thermodynamic potential $-\Phi$ along any given path, and the total change of $-\Phi$ along the same path.
- However, the practical value of the thermodynamic interpretation of $\mathcal{O}$ is very limited, as long as there is no way to determine Φ or, equivalently, $\tilde{d}^{\nu}$ and $\tilde{r}^{\nu}$ a priori in the absence of detailed balance.

References

[1] L. Onsager, Phys. Rev. 37, 405 (1931); 38, 2265 (1931)
[2] L. Onsager, S. Machlup, Phys. Rev. 91, 1505 (1953); 91, 1512 (1953)
[3] N. Hashitsume, Progr. Theor. Phys. 8, 461 (1952); 15, 369 (1956); L. Tisza, I. Manning, Phys. Rev. 105, 1695 (1957); I. Gyarmati, Nonequilibrium Thermodynamics; Berlin, Springer 1978

[4] R.L. Stratonovich, Sel. Transl. Math. Stat. Prob. 10, 273 (1971)
[5] R. Graham, Springer Tracts in Mod. Phys., 66, 1 (1973)
[6] W. Horsthemke, A. Bach, Z. Physik B22, 189 (1975)
[7] R. Graham, Phys. Rev. Lett. 38, 51 (1977); Z. Physik B26, 281 (1977)
[8] R. Graham, Ann. Isr. Phys. Soc. 2, 948 (1978); U. Deininghaus, R. Graham, Z. Physik B34, 211 (1979)
[9] H. Grabert, M.S. Green, Phys. Rev. A19, 1747 (1979)
[10] H. Grabert, R. Graham, M.S. Green, to be published
[11] R. Kubo, K. Matsuo, K. Kitahara, J. Stat. Phys. 9, 53 (1973)
[12] H. Haken, Z. Physik B24, 321 (1976)
[13] H. Leschke, M. Schmutz, Z. Physik B27, 85 (1977); cf. also this volume
[14] U. Weiß, Z. Physik B30, 429 (1978); cf. also this volume
[15] F. Langouche, D.Roekaerts, E. Tirapegui, Phys. Rev. D20, 419 (1979); cf. also this volume
[16] H. Dekker, Phys. Lett. 69A, 241 (1978); cf. also this volume
[17] L. Garrido, cf. this volume
[18] H.K. Janssen, Z. Physik B23, 377 (1976); R. Bausch, H.K. Janssen, H. Wagner, Z. Physik B24, 113 (1976)
[19] C. De Dominicis, J. Phys. (Paris) 37, Colloque C-247 (1976); C. De Dominicis, L. Peliti, Phys. Rev. Lett. 38, 505 (1977); Phys. Rev. B18, 353 (1978)
[20] L.D. Landau, E.M. Lifschitz, Statistical Physics, Oxford Pergamon 1958
[21] R.L. Stratonovich, Conditional Markov Processes and their Application to the Theory of Optimal Controll, New York, Elsevier 1968
[22] R. Graham, H. Haken, Z. Physik 243, 289 (1971)
[23] R.P Feynman, A.R. Hibbs, Quantum Mechanics and Path Integrals, New York, Mc Graw Hill 1965
[24] I. Prigogine, Ac. Roy, Belg. Bull. Sc. 31, 600 (1945)
[25] R. Graham, Z. Physik B26, 397 (1977)
[26] C. Morette, Phys. Rev. 81, 848 (1951)
[27] O. Veblen, Invariants of Quadratic Differential Forms, Cambridge, Cambridge University Press 1962
[28] R. Shaw, to be published
[29] R. Graham, in Lecture Notes in Physics, ed. L. Garrido, P. Seglar, P.J. Shepherd, Berlin, Springer 1978

THE ONSAGER-MACHLUP LAGRANGIAN AND THE OPTIMAL CONTROL FOR DIFFUSION PROCESSES

Kunio Yasue

Département de Physique Théorique
Université de Genève
CH-1211 Genève 4, Switzerland

CONTENTS

ABSTRACT

A basic role of the Onsager-Machlup Lagrangian as the cost functional for the stochastic control problem is clarified. It is found that any n-dimensional nonlinear diffusion process described by a class of stochastic differential equation of Itô type can be regarded as if it were controlled optimally by the Onsager-Machlup Lagrangian. It is shown that the deterministic path of the diffusion process in the small fluctuation (infinite volume) limit coincides with the most probable path. An outlook on the stochastic control theoretical formulation of the vacuum tunneling phenomena in non-Abelian gauge theory is also presented hoping that it will help us to understand the quantum vacuum structure in quantum chromodynamics profoundly.

1. INTRODUCTION

Since Feynman gave a concept of path integrals or functional integrations in the literature of theoretical physics,[1] it has been applied successfully in many fields. Mathematical foundation of the path integral was investigated by Nelson[2], by Itô[3] and quite recently by Hida[4,5].

The present status of our interests on the path integral is as follows. In quantum mechanics and in quantum field theory where we know at least explicit expressions of Lagrangians, we make an effort to give calculable meaning to path integrals by perturbative or nonperturbative methods. In nonequilibrium statistical mechanics where we know only stochastic differential equations, we try to obtain suitable expressions of Lagrangians as integrands for the path integrals.[6-13] In the latter case different discretization techniques give us different expressions of Lagrangians and there are some confusions in deriving the concept of most probable paths and that of deterministic paths for stochastic differential equations. We are not free from those confusions as long as we use the path integral in the analysis of stochastic differential equations. So it seems not so meaningless to clarify the basic role of Lagrangians in investigating stochastic differential equations not in the framework of the path integral but in that of probability theory. This will help us to make the conventional path integral analysis of stochastic differential equations more refined.

The present paper is devoted to showing the role of Lagrangians as cost functionals for stochastic control problems which characterize original stochastic differential equations completely.

Prior to the analysis of the problem I want to emphasize that the present approach from the stochastic control theoretical point of view will provide us a profound way of understanding the quantum vacuum structure of non-Abelian gauge theory and the instanton effect.[14,15]

2. DIFFUSION PROCESSES AND STOCHASTIC DIFFERENTIAL EQUATIONS

By the notion of an n-dimensional nonlinear diffusion process, I denote an $\mathbb{R}^n$-valued Markov process $X(t) = (X^1(t),\dots,X^n(t))$, $t \in [0,\infty)$, described by a stochastic differential equation of Itô type

$$dX^i = a^i(X)\,dt + dB^i, \quad X(0) = x_0 \in \mathbb{R}^n. \tag{2.1}$$

Here $a = (a^1,\ldots,a^n)$ is a smooth drift vector of gradient type and $B(t) = (B^1(t),\ldots,B^n(t))$ is an n-dimensional Wiener process with a diffusion constant equal to unity. It is a Markov process with an infinitesimal generator

$$G = a^i(x) \frac{\partial}{\partial x^i} + \frac{\partial^2}{\partial x^i \partial x^i} \tag{2.2}$$

and an invariant measure $\mu(d^n x)$.

Before I rewrite the stochastic differential equation (2.1) in terms of the stochastic control problem, it is convenient to introduce the notion of mean derivative. Let $\{\mathcal{F}_t\}_{t\in[0,\infty)}$ be an increasing family of σ-algebras of measurable events generated by $X(t)$, $t\in[0,\infty)$. Then I define the mean derivative of $X(t)$ by

$$DX(t) = \lim_{h\downarrow 0} h^{-1} E\left[X(t+h) - X(t) \,\middle|\, \mathcal{F}_t \right], \tag{2.3}$$

where $E[\cdot|\mathcal{F}_t]$ means to take a conditional expectation with respect to the σ-algebra.[16,17] A straightforward calculation gives

$$DX(t) = a(X(t)). \tag{2.4}$$

Similarly the mean derivative of $f(X(t))$, where f is a smooth function of position, is defined by

$$Df(X(t)) = \lim_{h\downarrow 0} h^{-1} E\left[f(X(t+h)) - f(X(t)) \,\middle|\, \mathcal{F}_t \right], \tag{2.5}$$

obtaining

$$Df(X(t)) = (Gf)(X(t)). \tag{2.6}$$

The probability distribution of $X(t)$, $p^t(d^n x) = \mathrm{Prob}\{X(t) \in d^n x\}$, solves the Fokker-Planck equation

$$\frac{\partial}{\partial t} p^t = - \mathrm{div}\,(a p^t) + \mathrm{div}\,\mathrm{grad}\, p^t \tag{2.7}$$

weakly, and it has an asymptote $\lim_{t\to\infty} p^t = \mu$ in $L_\infty(\mathbb{R}^n)$.

By the notion of a reduced Onsager-Machlup (OM) Lagrangian, I denote a function

$$L'_{OM}(z(t),\dot z(t)) = \tfrac{1}{2}|\dot z(t)|^2 - V_{OM}(z(t)), \tag{2.8}$$

where

$$V_{OM} = -\tfrac{1}{2}|a|^2 - \mathrm{div}\, a \tag{2.9}$$

is a dynamical potential,[18] $z(t)$, $t\in[0,\infty)$, is a differentiable path in $\mathbb{R}^n$ and $\dot{z}(t) = dz(t)/dt$. The following theorem allows us to characterize the diffusion process $X(t)$ globally in terms of the stochastic control theory.

Theorem 1. The diffusion process $X(t)$, $t\in[0,\infty)$, described by Eq. (2.1) is a solution to the stochastic control problem

$$dZ^i = \underline{a}^i(Z)\,dt + dB^i, \quad Z(0) = x_0, \tag{2.10}$$

where the drift vector $\underline{a}$ of class L (Lipschitz functions) is controlled to minimize a cost functional

$$\mathrm{Cost}(\underline{a}) = E\left[\overline{\lim_{T\to\infty}}\, T^{-1} \int_0^T L'_{OM}(Z(t),DZ(t))\,dt\right], \tag{2.11}$$

and $E[\cdot]$ denotes the expectation.

The proof of this theorem is given in Ref. 19.

Theorem 1 gives us a global characterization of the original diffusion process $X(t)$ because the cost functional contains a long-time average. However it is also possible to obtain a local version of Theorem 1 in a sense that for each $t\in[0,\infty)$ the original diffusion process $X(s)$, $s\in[0,t]$, minimizes a t-dependent cost functional as it will be shown in what follows.

In the previous paper[20] I found that the probability distribution of the diffusion process (2.1) was given approximately in the form

$$p^t \sim \exp\left[-\int_0^t L_{OM}(z(s),\dot{z}(s))\,ds\right]_{max} d^n x, \tag{2.12}$$

where

$$L_{OM}(z(t),\dot{z}(t)) = \tfrac{1}{2}\left|\dot{z}(t) - a(z(t))\right|^2 + \mathrm{div}\, a(z(t)) \tag{2.13}$$

is the OM Lagrangian and $[\ \ ]_{max}$ means to take a maximum value over continuous paths $z(t)$'s connecting x_0 and $x\in d^n x$. Equation (2.12) allows us to conclude that a variational problem

$$\int_0^t L_{OM}(z(s),\dot{z}(s))\,ds = \text{minimum}, \tag{2.14}$$

determines a most probable path.

Let us introduce a notion of OM action form

$$dI_{OM}(z(t),\dot{z}(t),dt,dz(t))$$

$$= L_{OM}(z(t),\dot{z}(t))\, dt = L'_{OM}(z(t),\dot{z}(t))\, dt - a(z(t))\cdot dz(t). \quad (2.15)$$

Then I have

Theorem 2. The statement of Theorem 1 is also valid with respect to a local cost functional

$$\mathrm{Cost}^t(\underline{a}) = E\left[\int_0^t dI_{OM}(Z(s),DZ(s),ds,dZ(s))\right]$$
$$= E\left[\int_0^t L'_{OM}(Z(s),DZ(s))\, ds - \int_0^t a(Z(s)) \circ dZ(s)\right], \quad (2.16)$$

where $\circ$ means to take the stochastic integral of the Fisk-Stratonovich type.[21]

The proof of this theorem is also given in Ref. 19.

Thus I have found a basic role of the OM Lagrangian as a cost functional for a stochastic control problem. The original diffusion process $X(t)$, $t\in[0,\infty)$, is completely characterized by the OM Lagrangians (2.8) and (2.13). It is optimally controlled to keep the mean OM action integral minimum.

3. THE ONSAGER-MACHLUP PROBLEM

One of the main interests in recent nonequilibrium statistical mechanics is put on the analysis of the limit behavior of physical random processes in the infinite volume limit. Mathematically this corresponds to studying the limit behavior of an n-dimensional nonlinear diffusion process $X_\varepsilon(t)$, $t\in[0,\infty)$, described by a stochastic differential equation

$$dX^i_\varepsilon = a^i(X_\varepsilon)\, dt + \varepsilon\, dB^i, \quad X_\varepsilon(0) = x_0, \quad (3.1)$$

in the limit[22] $\varepsilon \to 0$, where $\varepsilon = \Omega^{-1} > 0$ and Ω is a system size parameter. This I call the OM problem.

In this section I shall approach the OM problem from a stochastic control theoretical point of view developed in the previous section. I have seen that the diffusion process $X_\varepsilon(t)$, $t\in[0,\infty)$, is a solution to the stochastic control problem

$$dZ^i_\varepsilon = \underline{a}^i(Z_\varepsilon)\, dt + \varepsilon\, dB^i, \quad Z_\varepsilon(0) = x_0, \quad (3.2)$$

with respect to the control condition

$$\mathrm{Cost}_{\varepsilon}^{t}(\underline{a}) = E\left[\int_0^t dI_{OM}(Z_{\varepsilon}(s), DZ_{\varepsilon}(s), ds, dZ_{\varepsilon}(s))\right] = \text{minimum.} \tag{3.3}$$

Therefore, to illustrate the nature of such a limit behavior of $X_{\varepsilon}(t)$, it is convenient to investigate a limit behavior of the corresponding stochastic control problem.

A standard technique to study such a limit behavior will be the asymptotic expansion. I assume $Z_{\varepsilon}(t) = z(t) + \varepsilon Y(t) + O(\varepsilon^2)$ for sufficiently small ε. As the randomness disappears in the limit $\varepsilon \to 0$, the zeroth order term $z(t)$ is not a random process but an ordinary function of time. I also assume the differentiability of $z(t)$. The mean derivative of $Z_{\varepsilon}(t)$ has also an asymptotic expansion $DZ_{\varepsilon}(t) = \dot{z}(t) + \varepsilon DY(t) + O(\varepsilon^2)$. With the help of Taylor expansions for $a(Z_{\varepsilon}(t))$ and dI_{OM}, I obtain an asymptotic expansion of the cost functional

$$\begin{aligned}\mathrm{Cost}_{\varepsilon}^{t}(\underline{a}) &= E\left[\int_0^t L_{OM}(z(s),\dot{z}(s))\, ds + O(\varepsilon)\right] \\ &= \int_0^t L_{OM}(z(s),\dot{z}(s))\, ds + O(\varepsilon). \end{aligned}\tag{3.4}$$

Then I can conclude that in the limit ε goes to zero the stochastic control problem (3.2) and (3.3) tends to an ordinary (non-random) control problem

$$\dot{z}(t) = \underline{a}(z(t)), \tag{3.5}$$

where the drift vector $\underline{a}$ is controlled to minimize a cost functional

$$\mathrm{Cost}_{0}^{t}(\underline{a}) = \int_0^t L_{OM}(z(s),\dot{z}(s))\, ds. \tag{3.6}$$

The limit behavior of the diffusion process $X_{\varepsilon}(t)$, $t \in [0,\infty)$, is thus found as a solution to the ordinary control problem (3.5) and (3.6). This should be given by solving the Euler-Lagrange equation

$$\frac{d}{dt}\left(\frac{\partial L_{OM}}{\partial \dot{z}(t)}\right) - \frac{\partial L_{OM}}{\partial z(t)} = 0. \tag{3.7}$$

The OM Lagrangian has also a basic role as a Lagrangian which characterizes the limit behavior of the diffusion process in the infinite volume limit. By the notion of a deterministic path of the diffusion process (3.1), I denote such a limit behavior as is described by Eq. (3.7). Evidently it coincides with the most probable path (2.14).

4. STOCHASTIC CONTROL PROBLEM IN QCD

Now, before closing the paper, I shall give an outlook on the problem of the quantum vacuum structure of non-Abelian gauge theory. Consider the pure SU(2) Yang-Mills theory defined by the Lagrangian

$$L = \frac{1}{2} \sum_{i,a=1}^{3} \int \left\{ (\dot{A}_i^a)^2 + (B_i^a)^2 \right\} d^3x, \tag{4.1}$$

in the temporal gauge $A_0 \equiv 0$. Here $B_i^a = \frac{1}{2}\sum_{k,j=1}^{3} \varepsilon_{ijk} F_{jk}^a$ and $F_{jk}^a = \partial_j A_k^a - \partial_k A_j^a + \sum_{b,c=1}^{3} \varepsilon^{abc} A_j^b A_k^c$ is an SU(2) electromagnetic field. (Latin letters a,b,c denote SU(2) indices and i,j,k space indices.) A quantum vacuum state of the SU(2) Yang-Mills theory is represented by a functional $\Omega(A)$ which satisfies the Schrödinger equation

$$\sum_{i,a=1}^{3} \int d^3x \left(-\frac{1}{2} \hbar^2 \frac{\delta^2}{\delta A_i^a \, \delta A_i^a} + \frac{1}{2} (B_i^a)^2 \right) \Omega(A) = E_0\, \Omega(A), \tag{4.2}$$

where E_0 is the smallest energy eigenvalue of the quantized SU(2) Yang-Mills field A_i^a.

In classical field theory, vacuum states of the SU(2) Yang-Mills theory are classical field configurations $'A_i^a$'s with zero potential energy. They are pure gauge fields $'A_i^a \equiv ('g^{-1}\partial_i 'g)^a$, where the 'g's are unitary matrices such that $g(\infty) = I$. One can illustrate the classical vacua as continuous mappings from $\dot{\mathbb{R}}^3 \simeq S^3$ to $SU(2) \simeq S^3$, where $\dot{\mathbb{R}}^3$ is a one-point compactification of space and S^3 is a three dimensional sphere. They consist of an infinite number of homotopy classes $\pi_3(S^3) \simeq Z$ classified by an integer $q \in Z$ (the topological charge): $\{[{}^qA_i^a = ({}^qg^{-1}\partial_i {}^qg)^a]\}_{q\in Z}$, where $[\cdot]$ denotes a homotopy class to which the pure gauge field inside the bracket belongs.

In quantum field theory, the classical vacua are rendered unstable by the tunnel effect. To investigate the vacuum tunneling phenomena between classical vacua ${}^qA$'s within the realm of the WKB approximation, the notion of the instanton was introduced.[23-26] Classical Euclidean Yang-Mills fields which minimize the Euclidean action integral are called instantons, and were introduced as an indication of tunneling phenomena between classical vacua. They manifest the most probable tunneling paths between classical vacua ${}^qA$'s and so the real quantum vacuum structure of the SU(2) Yang-Mills theory in the WKB approximation.[15] In the conventional framework, this can be shown in utilizing the Euclidean path integral technique. However if we want to calculate the quantum correction to the instanton with the help of the semiclassical expansion we are not free from the so-called zero mode difficulty.[26] So, as was mentioned by Jona-Lasinio,[27] we need an alternative

method of summing the whole quantum correction to the instanton.

Here I can not forbid at least myself to reconsider the instanton analysis of the quantum vacuum structure of the SU(2) Yang-Mills theory from the optimal control theoretical point of view. Namely I dare to say that the instanton (or the most probable tunneling path) behaves as if it were controlled to minimize the Euclidean action integral; a cost functional! This is clearly an ordinary (nonrandom) control problem. Then I can easily suppose that somewhat the stochastic control problem developed in the previous sections will help us to reconsider the quantum correction to the instanton and to illustrate the real quantum vacuum structure of SU(2) Yang-Mills theory.

Correctness of this supposition is understood in the realm of Nelson's stochastic quantization.[16,17,28,29] There the behavior of the quantized SU(2) Yang-Mills field in the vacuum state $\Omega(A)$ is known to be a diffusion process $A_i^a(x,t)$, $(x,t)\in\mathbb{R}^4$, in a function space.[15] It is described by a stochastic differential equation of the white noise type

$$\partial_t A_i^a(x,t) = U_i^a(A)(x,t) + \hbar^{\frac{1}{2}} Z_i^a(x,t), \tag{4.3}$$

where $U_i^a(A) = \delta \log \Omega(A)/\delta A_i^a$ and $Z_i^a(x,t)$, $(x,t)\in\mathbb{R}^4$, denotes a white noise[30,31] with mean 0 and variance $\delta^{ab}\delta_{ij}\delta^4(x-y)$. This represents the whole quantum tunneling phenomena between the classical vacua in terms of the diffusion process in the function space. Like the OM problem I can rewrite Eq. (4.3) in terms of the stochastic control problem. Namely the quantized SU(2) Yang-Mills field in the vacuum state $A_i^a(x,t)$, $(x,t)\in\mathbb{R}^4$, is a solution to the stochastic control problem in the function space

$$\partial_t A_i^a(x,t) = \underline{U}_i^a(A)(x,t) + \hbar^{\frac{1}{2}} Z_i^a(x,t), \tag{4.4}$$

with the control condition

$$\begin{aligned} \mathrm{Cost}(\underline{U}) &= E\Big[\sum_{i,a=1}^{3} \tfrac{1}{2}\int\{(DA_i^a)^2 + (B_i^a)^2\}\, d^4x\Big] \\ &= E\big[\text{Euclidean action integral}\big] \\ &= \text{minimum}. \end{aligned} \tag{4.5}$$

Now I can generalize the concept of instanton. The instanton with the whole quantum corrections is defined as a diffusion process in the function space which minimizes the mean Euclidean action integral (4.5). This illustrates the quantum vacuum structure of non-Abelian gauge theory in terms of the instanton with the whole quantum

corrections. In the WKB limit ($h \to 0$) the stochastic control problem (4.4) and (4.5) tends evidently to the ordinary control problem for the instanton.

NOTE ADDED AFTER THE CONFERENCE

It was a great pleasure for me to know the recent work of Etim on the instanton analysis of QCD based on the probability theoretical formulation which I explained in my talk only briefly. I think everybody can find the "esprit" of the probability theoretical approach to the QCD vacuum structure in the fine talk of Etim.[32]

ACKNOWLEDGEMENT

I would like to express my sincerest thanks to Professor C. P. Enz for valuable discussions, encouragement and support. I am also grateful to Professors T. Takabayasi and T. Toyoda for their continuous encouragements. I enjoyed helpful discussions with T. Nakagomi, J.-C. Zambrini and M. O. Hongler. Last but not least I am really indebted to Professor E. Etim for his valuable comments and encouragement.

REFERENCES

1. R. P. Feynman, Rev. Mod. Phys. 20, 368 (1948).
2. E. Nelson, J. Math. Phys. 5, 332 (1964).
3. K. Itô, "Proceedings of the Fifth Berkeley Symposium on Mathematical Statistics and Probability," 145 (1966).
4. T. Hida, "Causal Analysis in terms of White Noise," talk given at the conference "Bielefeld Encounters in Physics and Mathematics II," December, 1978.
5. L. Streit, in this volume.
6. H. Haken, "Synergetics," Springer-Verlag, Berlin (1977).
7. R. Graham, in this volume.
8. C. P. Enz, Physica A89, 1 (1977).
9. T. Gotô, Prog. Theor. Phys. 60, 1298 (1978).
10. W. Horsthemke and A. Bach, Z. Physik B22, 189 (1975).
11. H. Dekker, in this volume.
12. F. Langouche, D. Roekaerts and E. Tirapegui, in this volume.
13. L. Garrido, in this volume.
14. K. Yasue, Phys. Rev. Lett. 40, 665 (1978).
15. K. Yasue, Phys. Rev. D18, 532 (1978).
16. E. Nelson, Phys. Rev. 150, 1079 (1966).

17. E. Nelson, "Dynamical Theories of Brownian Motion," Princeton University Press, Princeton (1967).
18. D. Dürr and A. Bach, Z. Physik B32, 413 (1979).
19. K. Yasue, J. Math. Phys. 20, 1861 (1979).
20. K. Yasue, J. Math. Phys. 19, 1671 (1978).
21. K. Itô and S. Watanabe, "Introduction to Stochastic Differential Equations," in: "Proceedings of the International Symposium on Stochastic Differential Equations," K. Itô, ed., John Wiley & Sons, New York (1978).
22. R. Kubo, Lecture Notes in Physics 25, 274, Springer-Verlag, Berlin (1973).
23. A. M. Polyakov, Phys. Lett. 59B, 82 (1975).
24. G. 't Hooft, Phys. Rev. Lett. 37, 8 (1976).
25. R. Jackiw, Rev. Mod. Phys. 49, 681 (1977).
26. S. Coleman, Phys. Rev. D15, 2929 (1977).
27. G. Jona-Lasinio, "Stochastic Dynamics and the Semiclassical Limit of Quantum Mechanics," talk given at the Bielefeld Encounters in Physics and Mathematics II, December, 1978.
28. E. Nelson, Bull. Amer. Math. Soc. 84, 121 (1978).
29. E. Nelson, "Connection between Brownian Motion and Quantum Mechanics," talk given at the Einstein Symposium in Berlin, March, 1979.
30. T. Hida, "Stationary Stochastic Processes," Princeton University Press, Princeton (1970).
31. T. Hida, "Analysis of Brownian Functionals," Carleton University Press, Ottawa (1975).
32. E. Etim, in this volume.

FEYNMAN'S APPROACH TO THE POLARON PROBLEM GENERALIZED TO ARBITRARY QUADRATIC ACTIONS

J. Adamowski*, B. Gerlach and H. Leschke**

Institut für Physik der Universität
D-4600 Dortmund 50, West Germany

INTRODUCTION

The polaron is an elementary excitation in a crystal. It can be understood as an electron dressed by a cloud of phonons, i.e. by the quanta associated with lattice vibrations. In ionic materials the polaron is usually described by the Fröhlich Hamiltonian

$$H := \frac{\vec{p}^2}{2m} + \sum_{\vec{k}} \hbar\omega_{\vec{k}} a^+_{\vec{k}} a_{\vec{k}} + \frac{1}{\sqrt{V}} \sum_{\vec{k}} \left[g(\vec{k}) e^{i\vec{k}\cdot\vec{r}} a_{\vec{k}} + \text{h.c.} \right]. \tag{1}$$

Here $\vec{p}$ and $\vec{r}$ denote the momentum and the position operator of the electron, m is its band mass. The Bose operators $a_{\vec{k}}$ and $a^+_{\vec{k}}$ annihilate and create a longitudinal optical phonon with wave vector $\vec{k}$ and energy $\hbar\omega_{\vec{k}}$, V is the quantization volume. The electron-phonon interaction is characterized by a coupling matrix element $g(\vec{k})$ which in the case of an Einstein spectrum $\omega_{\vec{k}} \tilde{=} \text{const} =: \omega$ takes the form

$$g(\vec{k}) := g/|\vec{k}| \;,\; g := -i\hbar\omega(\hbar/2m\omega)^{1/4}(4\pi\alpha)^{1/2} \tag{2}$$

with α being the dimensionless Fröhlich coupling constant.

Various methods have been used to discuss the properties and consequences of the Fröhlich Hamiltonian (1)-(2), in

*Permanent address: Solid State Physics Department, Academy of Mining and Metallurgy - AGH, 30-059 Kraków, Poland.
**Present address: Institut für Theoretische Physik der Universität Düsseldorf, D-4000 Düsseldorf 1, West Germany

particular, to estimate its spectrum[1]. Here we are especially interested in its ground state energy E_0 as a function of the coupling α. For weak coupling ordinary perturbation theory up to fourth order[2] in α and Rayleigh-Ritz type variational upper bounds[3,4,5,6] have provided trustworthy results the latter of which are often believed to reach the intermediate coupling region. Pekar's estimate[7] is by far the lowest known upper bound for strong coupling. In fact it can be proved that this estimate coincides asymptotically with the exact E_0 in the limit $\alpha \to \infty$. This result is strongly motivated by adiabatic perturbation theory[8], a nonperturbative proof has been given recently[9].

While the above methods have provided reasonable results only for limited regions of the coupling constant, Feynman's[10] functional integral approach has given good results over the entire range of α in a unified way. The present work is concerned with the question if Feynman's approach to the polaron problem can be improved by generalizing his variational ansatz.

Accordingly, we start by defining a (formal) free energy F of the Fröhlich Hamiltonian as a function of a (formal) positive inverse temperature β via

$$e^{-\beta F} := \mathrm{tr}\, e^{-\beta H} = \mathrm{tr}_{ph}\, \mathrm{tr}_{\ell\ell}\, e^{-\beta H}. \tag{3}$$

The functional integral representation of the electronic partial trace $\mathrm{tr}_{\ell\ell}$ enables one to perform the phonon partial trace tr_{ph} leading to the exact result

$$e^{-\beta F} = e^{-\beta F^0_{ph}} \oint \delta^3 R \; e^{-S[\vec{R}]} \; . \tag{4}$$

Here F^0_{ph} is the free energy of the noninteracting phonons and the second factor is a Wiener-type functional integral (path integral) written in the symbolic way used by many physicists. The symbol $\oint \delta^3 R$ is a shorthand notation for two successive integrations symbolized as

$$\int d^3x \int_{\vec{R}(o)=\vec{R}(\beta)=\vec{x}} \delta^3 R$$

which indicates in a first step (Wiener) integration over all closed paths $\vec{R}(\tau)$ in 3-dimensional Euclidean space with the same start and end point $\vec{x}$ and in a second step ordinary (Lebesgue) integration over $\vec{x}$. The integrand in (4) contains the (imaginary-time) noninstantaneous exact action functional

$$S[\vec{R}] := \frac{m}{2\hbar^2} \int_0^\beta d\tau \; |\dot{\vec{R}}(\tau)|^2 - \frac{|g|^2}{4\pi} \int_0^\beta d\tau \int_0^\beta d\tau' \; \frac{G_{\hbar\omega}(\tau-\tau')}{|\vec{R}(\tau)-\vec{R}(\tau')|} \tag{5}$$

where

$$G_{\hbar\omega}(\tau) := \frac{e^{|\tau|\hbar\omega} + e^{(\beta-|\tau|)\hbar\omega}}{2(e^{\beta\hbar\omega} - 1)} \tag{6}$$

is the phonon Green's function and the dot denotes differentiation with respect to τ.

Strictly speaking, the above and some of the following equations can be derived in a mathematically rigorous way only by first dividing out the volume in relevant places and/or by introducing a cut-off in $\vec{k}$-space. Since in the appropiate limits the final answer will be the same, we will not dwell on this point which we consider in the present work to be more technical than physical. The reader who is interested in these questions can find useful information in an article by Ginibre[11].

VARIATIONAL PRINCIPLE

Up to now the functional integral in (4) with S given by (5) and (6) has not been evaluated exactly. Instead, only approximate methods have been applied. Feynman applied Jensen's inequality

$$F \leq F^{0}_{ph} + F_{\tilde{S}} + \frac{1}{\beta} \langle S - \tilde{S} \rangle_{\tilde{S}} \tag{7}$$

valid for any action $\tilde{S}$ for which an associated free energy $F_{\tilde{S}}$ defined by

$$e^{-\beta F_{\tilde{S}}} := \oint \delta^3 R \, e^{-\tilde{S}[\vec{R}]} \tag{8}$$

and the mean value $\langle S-\tilde{S} \rangle_{\tilde{S}}$ exist. Here we have used the notation

$$\langle A \rangle_{\tilde{S}} := e^{\beta F_{\tilde{S}}} \oint \delta^3 R \, A[\vec{R}] \, e^{-\tilde{S}[\vec{R}]} \tag{9}$$

for the mean value of a general functional A with respect to the positive weight functional $e^{-\tilde{S}}$. By minimizing the right hand side of (7) with respect to an appropriate class of trial actions $\tilde{S}$ one gets a variational upper bound on the free energy and, letting $\beta\to\infty$, on the ground state energy of the Fröhlich Hamiltonian (1)-(2).

As is well known from similar variational principles, the actual choice of an optimal $\tilde{S}$ is dictated by two competing criteria. On the one hand $\tilde{S}$ should embody as much of the physics of S as possible, on the other hand $\tilde{S}$ has to be simple enough to allow one the explicit calculation of the corresponding functional averages. Until now the latter restricts the class of trial actions to those quadratic in the path $\vec{R}(\tau)$. Feynman obtained his results by the choice

$$\tilde{S}[\vec{R}] = \frac{m}{2\hbar^2} \int_0^\beta d\tau |\dot{\vec{R}}(\tau)|^2 + C \int_0^\beta d\tau \int_0^\beta d\tau' \, G_W(\tau-\tau') \, |\vec{R}(\tau)-\vec{R}(\tau')|^2 \qquad (10)$$

with the two variational parameters C and W. Abe and Okamoto[12] generalized this choice by using two harmonic terms of the type (10). Therefore, having four parameters C_1, C_2, W_1, W_2 at their disposal, they got a slight improvement of the Feynman results.

GENERAL QUADRATIC TRIAL ACTION

The present work is based on the trial action

$$\tilde{S}[\vec{R}] = \frac{m}{2\hbar^2} \int_0^\beta d\tau |\dot{\vec{R}}(\tau)|^2 + \lambda \int_0^\beta d\tau \int_0^\beta d\tau' \, f(\tau-\tau') \, \vec{R}(\tau) \cdot \vec{R}(\tau') \qquad (11)$$

which is essentially the most general quadratic, isotropic two--time action. Here $f(\tau)$ is a real, continuous function defined for $|\tau| \leq \beta$, assumed, without loss of generality, to be symmetric; i.e. $f(\tau) = f(-\tau)$. The real variable λ is splitted off from f for a later computational convenience. The trial action (11) has been previously proposed, e.g. by Platzman [13] and Thornber[14], but the resulting bounds have not been computed explicitly.

If the function f fulfills the requirement

$$\int_0^\beta d\tau' \, f(\tau-\tau') = 0 \text{ for any } \tau \text{ within } 0 \leq \tau \leq \beta , \qquad (12)$$

the action (11) is translationally invariant. Since this property holds true for the exact action, it is a natural one for the trial action though not necessary for our calculations. An immediate consequence of (12) is the β-periodicity of f

$$f(\tau-\beta) = f(\tau) \quad \text{for any } \tau \text{ within } \quad 0 \leq \tau \leq \beta . \qquad (13)$$

In the following we will generally assume (13) but not always (12).

For the trial action (11) the resulting upper bound on the free energy as given by the right hand side of Jensen's inequality (7) becomes a certain functional of λf. To compute this functional

we introduce the generating functional

$$I\,[\vec{\eta}] := \langle \exp \left[\int_0^\beta d\tau\, \vec{\eta}(\tau)\cdot\vec{R}(\tau)\right]\rangle_{\tilde{S}} \,. \tag{14}$$

If this is known for an arbitrary source function $\vec{\eta}(\tau)$, one can calculate both $\langle S-\tilde{S}\rangle_{\tilde{S}}$ and $F_{\tilde{S}}$. The easiest way to find $I[\vec{\eta}]$ explicitly, is to realize that $\langle\cdot\rangle_{\tilde{S}}$ indicates averaging with respect to an isotropic Gaussian stochastic process $\vec{R}(\tau)$ with mean zero, which therefore is uniquely determined by its covariance $\langle\vec{R}(\tau)\cdot\vec{R}(\tau')\rangle_{\tilde{S}}$. Hence, we have

$$I\,[\vec{\eta}]=\exp\left[\frac{1}{6}\int_0^\beta d\tau \int_0^\beta d\tau' \,\langle\vec{R}(\tau)\cdot\vec{R}(\tau)\rangle_{\tilde{S}}\, \vec{\eta}(\tau)\cdot\vec{\eta}(\tau')\right]. \tag{15}$$

The covariance is determined as an appropriate inverse of the integral kernel of the trial action. Under the assumption of condition (13) and

$$\int_0^\beta d\tau\, f(\tau) \neq 0 \tag{16}$$

the precise reciprocity relation reads

$$\int_0^\beta d\tau'' \,\frac{1}{3}\langle\vec{R}(\tau)\cdot\vec{R}(\tau'')\rangle_{\tilde{S}} \left[-\frac{m}{\hbar^2}\ddot{\delta}(\tau''-\tau') + 2\lambda f(\tau''-\tau')\right]=\delta(\tau-\tau'), \tag{17}$$

where $\delta(\tau):=\frac{1}{\beta}\sum\limits_{n=-\infty}^{\infty} e^{i\nu_n\tau}$ and $\nu_n := 2n\pi/\beta$

denote the periodic delta function and the "even" Matsubara frequencies, respectively. The solution of (17) reads in Fourier analyzed form as follows

$$\langle \vec{R}(\tau)\cdot\vec{R}(\tau')\rangle_{\tilde{S}} = \frac{3\hbar^2}{\beta m}\sum_{n=-\infty}^{\infty}\frac{e^{i\nu_n(\tau-\tau')}}{\frac{2\hbar^2\beta\lambda}{m}f_n-(i\nu_n)^2} \tag{18}$$

where

$$f_n := \frac{1}{\beta}\int_0^\beta d\tau\, f(\tau)\, e^{-i\nu_n\tau} = f_{-n} \tag{19}$$

denotes the n-th Fourier coefficient of f. If in contrast to (16) $f_0=0$, but (13) still holds (which implies that the translational invariance condition (12) is satisfied), the formula (18) remains valid with the understanding that the term corresponding to n=0 has

to be omitted.

With the help of (14), (15) and (18) we can compute all the averages on the right hand side of inequality (7). For example, choosing

$$\vec{\eta}(\tau) = i\vec{k}\left[\delta(\tau-\tau_1) - \delta(\tau-\tau_2)\right] =: \vec{\eta}_{\vec{k},\tau_1,\tau_2}(\tau) \quad , \tag{20}$$

we find by using the Fourier representation

$$\left< \frac{1}{|\vec{R}(\tau_1)-\vec{R}(\tau_2)|} \right>_{\tilde{S}} = \frac{1}{2\pi^2} \int \frac{d^3k}{k^2} \, I[\vec{\eta}_{\vec{k},\tau_1,\tau_2}] \tag{21}$$

the result

$$\left< \frac{1}{|\vec{R}(\tau_1)-\vec{R}(\tau_2)|} \right>_{\tilde{S}} = \left(\frac{6}{\pi}\right)^{1/2} \frac{1}{\left<|\vec{R}(\tau_1)-\vec{R}(\tau_2)|^2\right>_{\tilde{S}}^{1/2}} \quad . \tag{22}$$

The free energy $F_{\tilde{S}}$ associated with $\tilde{S}$ can be calculated by a "coupling constant" integration. In the case of translational invariance it reads

$$F_{\tilde{S}} = F_{\tilde{S}}\Big|_{\lambda=0} + \int_0^{\lambda} d\lambda' \, \frac{\partial F_{\tilde{S}}}{\partial \lambda'} \quad . \tag{23}$$

Here the derivative is expressed by the known average

$$\frac{\partial F_{\tilde{S}}}{\partial \lambda} = \frac{1}{\beta} \int_0^{\beta} d\tau \int_0^{\beta} d\tau' \; f(\tau-\tau') \; \left<\vec{R}(\tau)\cdot \vec{R}(\tau')\right>_{\tilde{S}} \quad , \tag{24}$$

as implied by (8), (9) and (11). Furthermore, we have

$$F_{\tilde{S}}\Big|_{\lambda=0} = -\frac{1}{\beta} \ell n\left\{\left(\frac{m}{2\pi\hbar^2\beta}\right)^{3/2} V\right\} =: F^{o}_{e\ell} \quad . \tag{25}$$

for the free electron.

UPPER BOUNDS INDUCED BY THE GENERAL QUADRATIC TRIAL ACTION

With the use of eqs. (22)-(25) in combination with (18), Jensen's inequality (7) for the general quadratic action (11) can be explicitly given. In the case of translational invariance (12)

it reads

$$F \leq F^{o}_{ph} + F^{o}_{e\ell} + \frac{3}{\beta} \sum_{n=1}^{\infty} \left[\ell n\left(1 + \frac{h_n}{\mu_n^2}\right) - \frac{h_n}{h_n + \mu_n^2} \right] - \sqrt{2}\, \alpha\hbar\omega \int_0^{\beta\hbar\omega} dt \left(1 - \frac{t}{\beta\hbar\omega}\right) \frac{G_{\hbar\omega}\left(\frac{t}{\hbar\omega}\right)}{\Delta(t)} , \tag{26}$$

where we have introduced the dimensionless mean square increment

$$\Delta^2(t) := \frac{\pi m\omega}{6\hbar} \langle |\vec{R}(0) - \vec{R}(\tfrac{t}{\hbar\omega})|^2 \rangle_{\tilde{S}} = \frac{2\pi}{\beta\hbar\omega} \sum_{n=1}^{\infty} \frac{1 - \cos\mu_n t}{h_n + \mu_n^2} \tag{27}$$

and the dimensionless frequencies and Fourier coefficients

$$\mu_n := \frac{\nu_n}{\hbar\omega} \qquad \text{and} \qquad h_n := \frac{2\beta\lambda f_n}{m\omega^2} .$$

The inequality (26) provides an upper bound on the free energy of the Fröhlich Hamiltonian for any set of values, which the h_n can take. This is true for all values of the coupling constant α and the inverse temperature β. The h_n are therefore to be considered as flexible variational parameters. A necessary condition for the upper bound to take its minimum is the stationarity condition

$$h_n = \frac{\alpha\pi\sqrt{2}}{3} \int_0^{\beta\hbar\omega} dt \left(1 - \frac{t}{\beta\hbar\omega}\right) \frac{G_{\hbar\omega}\left(\frac{t}{\hbar\omega}\right)}{\Delta^3(t)} (1 - \cos\mu_n t) . \tag{28}$$

Eqs. (27) and (28) represent a system of highly nonlinear equations for the optimal values of the h_n. Unfortunately, these equations seem to admit no analytical solution.

Let us now consider the limit $\beta \to \infty$ in more detail. Because of $\mu_{n+1} - \mu_n = 2\pi/\beta\hbar\omega$, eqs. (26)-(28) turn into

$$\frac{E_o}{\hbar\omega} \leq \frac{3}{2\pi} \int_0^{\infty} d\mu \left\{ \ell n\left[1 + \frac{h(\mu)}{\mu^2}\right] - \frac{h(\mu)}{h(\mu) + \mu^2} \right\} - \frac{\alpha}{\sqrt{2}} \int_0^{\infty} dt \frac{e^{-t}}{\Delta(t)} , \tag{29}$$

$$\Delta^2(t) = \int_0^{\infty} d\mu \frac{1 - \cos\mu t}{h(\mu) + \mu^2} \tag{30}$$

$$h(\mu) = \frac{\alpha\pi\sqrt{2}}{6}\int_0^\infty dt\, \frac{e^{-t}(1-\cos\mu t)}{\Delta^3(t)} \qquad (31)$$

These equations are valid whether translational invariance holds or not. The solution of the two coupled integral equations (30) and (31) gives the optimal upper bound on the ground state energy of the Fröhlich Hamiltonian according to (29).

Nevertheless, any $h(\mu)$ inserted into (29) provides a more or less restrictive bound. For example, Feynman's approach (compare eq. (10)) can be recovered from (29) by choosing

$$h(\mu) = \frac{4C}{Wm\omega^2}\, \frac{\mu^2}{\mu^2+(W/\hbar\omega)^2} \; . \qquad (32)$$

However, it can be shown that (32) is not a solution of (30) and (31).

For small α one can construct a solution of eqs. (30) and (31) by iteration, starting with $h(\mu)=0$. This gives

$$\frac{E_o}{\hbar\omega} \leq - \left[\alpha + \frac{1}{6}\left(\frac{1}{2} - \frac{4}{3\pi}\right)\alpha^2 + O(\alpha^3)\right] \qquad (33)$$

which up to α^2 agrees exactly with the result of Haga[3]. For large α it can be proved that for $\mu <$ const

$$h(\mu) = \left(\frac{2}{3\sqrt{\pi}}\right)^4 \alpha^4\, \frac{\mu^2}{\mu^2+1} \qquad (34)$$

is a solution of eqs. (30) and (31) to leading order of α. Inserting (34) into (29) one finds

$$\frac{E_o}{\hbar\omega} \leq - \frac{\alpha^2}{3\pi}\left[1 + O\left(\frac{1}{\alpha^2}\right)\right] , \qquad (35)$$

which is the result of Feynman for large α. However, this bound is worse than Pekar's result[7,15]

$$\frac{E_o}{\hbar\omega} \leq - 0.108513\,\alpha^2 \left[1 + O\left(\frac{1}{\alpha^2}\right)\right] , \qquad (36)$$

which can be derived by a Rayleigh-Ritz argument.

NUMERICAL RESULTS

We have solved the system of integral equations (30) and (31) by means of an iterative procedure with Feynman's choice (32) as the first approximation to $h(\mu)$ in (30). The necessary integrations were performed numerically. The results are shown in Table 1. The upper bound obtained from the solution of (30) and (31) is lower than that of Feynman for all values of the coupling constant α. The relative difference between these two bounds reaches 1% for $\alpha \gtrsim 10$. For very small and very large α this difference tends to zero. Table 1 shows that for $\alpha \gtrsim 3.5$ our estimate is lower than the variational bound obtained by Larsen[5]. In the limit $\alpha \to 0$ our bound approaches from below the result obtained from perturbation theory. On the other hand our estimate is very close to that of Pekar[7] for very large α.

Table 1. Comparison of various upper bounds on the polaron ground state energy for several values of the coupling constant α in units of the phonon energy $\hbar\omega$. We have listed the results of Pekar[7], Larsen[5], Feynman[10], Abe and Okamoto[12] and ours. The results labelled as "oscillator potential" correspond to the simple ansatz $h(\mu)=\Omega^2$.

α	Pekar	oscillator potential	Larsen	Feynman	Abe-Okamoto	present results
0.5	-0.0271	-0.5	-0.5040	-0.5032	-0.5032	-0.5035
1.0	-0.1085	-1.0	-1.0160	-1.0130	-1.0133	-1.0139
1.5	-0.2442	-1.5	-1.5361	-1.5302	-1.5308	-1.5317
2.0	-0.4341	-2.0	-2.0640	-2.0554	-2.0564	-2.0577
2.5	-0.6782	-2.5	-2.5995	-2.5894	-2.5911	-2.5928
3.0	-0.9766	-3.0	-3.1422	-3.1333	-3.1358	-3.1379
3.5	-1.3293	-3.5	-3.6915	-3.6885	-3.6919	-3.6946
4.0	-1.7362	-4.0	-4.2476	-4.2565	-4.2610	-4.2644
5.0	-2.7128	-5.0	-5.3755	-5.4401	-5.4472	-5.4524
7.0	-5.3171	-7.3563		-8.1127		-8.1374
9.0	-8.7896	-10.716		-11.486		-11.538
11.	-13.130	-14.944	-12.432	-15.710		-15.827
20.	-43.405	-44.530		-45.283		-45.334
30.	-97.662	-97.580		-98.328		-98.524
40.	-173.62	-171.85		-172.60		-173.37

Table 1 shows also the estimate obtained with the use of a constant trial function $h(\mu)=\Omega^2$, where Ω is a variational parameter. In this case all the integrals can be calculated analytically, what gives us a simple test for the more complicated iterative procedure. Physically, this choice corresponds to a single-time quadratic trial action, i.e. to an instantaneous potential of a harmonic oscillator with frequency proportional to Ω.

CONCLUSIONS

The polaron problem has been considered within the method of functional integration by generalizing Feynman's method to an arbitrary Gaussian approximation. All resulting functional integrals have been calculated in closed form leading to an explicit upper bound on the free energy and the ground state energy of the polaron. The minimum condition for this bound has led to nonlinear equations which have been solved numerically in the zero temperature limit. The resulting upper bound on the ground state energy as a function of the coupling constant is lower than those obtained by other authors for the intermediate coupling region, but admittedly the improvement is not significant. However, the general Gaussian approximation may provide greater deviations for the polaron mass.

ACKNOWLEDGEMENT

We gratefully acknowledge the financial support of the Deutsche Forschungsgemeinschaft. We are grateful to Professor J.T. Devreese and Mr. F. Peeters for valuable discussions during the conference.

REFERENCES

1. J.T. Devreese, Path integrals and continuum Fröhlich polarons, in: "Path Integrals and their Applications in Quantum, Statistical, and Solid State Physics," G.J. Papadopoulos and J.T. Devreese, eds., Plenum Press, New York and London (1978).
2. G. Höhler and A. Müllensiefen, Störungstheoretische Berechnung der Selbstenergie und der Masse des Polarons, Z. Physik 157:159 (1959).
3. E. Haga, Note on the slow electrons in a polar crystal, Progr. Theor. Phys. 11:449 (1954).
4. J.D. Lee, F.E. Low and D. Pines, The motion of slow electrons in a polar crystal, Phys. Rev. 90: 297 (1959).
5. D.M. Larsen, Upper and lower bounds for the intermediate-coupling polaron ground-state energy, Phys. Rev. 172:967 (1968), and, Polaron energy levels in magnetic and Coulomb fields, in: "Polarons in Ionic Crystals and Polar

Semiconductors", J. T. Devreese, ed., North Holland, Amsterdam and London (1972).
6. K. Dichtel, Ein neuer Variationsansatz für das Polaron, Z.Physik 190: 414 (1966)
7. S.I. Pekar, "Untersuchungen über die Elektronentheorie der Kristalle", Akademie-Verlag, Berlin (1954).
8. E.P. Gross, Strong coupling polaron theory and translational invariance, Ann. Physics 99:1 (1976).
9. J. Adamowski, B. Gerlach and H. Leschke, Strong-coupling limit of polaron energy, revisited, January 1980, submitted for publication.
10. R.P. Feynman, Slow electrons in a polar crystal, Phys. Rev. 97:660 (1955), and "Statistical Mechanics", Benjamin, New York (1972).
11. J. Ginibre, Some applications of functional integration in statistical mechanics, in "Statistical Mechanics and Quantum Field Theory", C.De Witt and R. Stora, eds., Gordon and Breach, New York (1971).
12. R. Abe and K. Okamoto, An improvement of the Feynman action in the theory of polaron. I, J. Phys. Soc. Japan 31:1337 (1971), and, K. Okamoto and R. Abe, An improvement of the Feynman action in the theory of polaron. II, J. Phys. Soc. Japan 33:343 (1972).
13. P.M. Platzman, The electrical transport properties of polarons, in: "Polarons and Excitons", C.G. Kuper and G.D. Whitfield, eds., Oliver and Boyd, Edinburgh and London (1963).
14. K.K. Thornber, Linear and nonlinear electronic transport in electron-phonon systems: self-consistent approach within the path-integral formalism, Phys. Rev. B3: 1929 (1971).
15. S.J. Miyake, Strong-coupling limit of the polaron ground state, J.Phys.Soc. Japan 38:181 (1975).

NONLINEAR D.C.-CONDUCTIVITY IN POLAR SEMICONDUCTORS†

F. Peeters★ and J. T. Devreese★★.

Universitaire Instelling Antwerpen, Departement Natuurkunde, Universiteitsplein 1, B-2610 Wilrijk

1. INTRODUCTION.

Although a vast amount of research has been performed on non-linear conductivity problems[1] they still constitute a challenging subject for the theoretical and experimental physicist. E.g. for the design of modern small-scale devices it is necessary to understand the behavior of electrons subjected to relatively high electric fields.

The problem which will be discussed in the present contribution is the conductivity of an electron(or hole) in a polar semiconductor. It is generally accepted that in polar semiconductors dissipation due to the interaction of the electrons with the longitudinal-optical (L.O.) phonons is quite important and can be dominant for high fields. As is well-known an electron which is surrounded by a cloud of virtual L.O.-phonons is called a polaron.

Feynman path-integral methods have been very successful in calculating the energy[2,3,4], the effective mass and the frequency dependant impedance[5,6] of the polaron for all values of the temperature and the electron-phonon coupling constant. Thornber and Feynman[7] have applied the same technique to the dc response(i.e. linear and nonlinear) of a polaron. Apart from some difficulties in the zero frequency limit for the impedance the Feynman model for the polaron(as elaborated in Ref. [2], [5], [7]) presumably provides accurate results for all coupling strength, external field

† Supported by the project E.S.I.S. and a CDC-grant.

★ Aspirant of the N.F.W.O.

★★ Also RUCA and T.H.Eindhoven

values and temperature.

In the present contribution two things are done:

i) a rather simple rederivation of the Thornber-Feynman approximation is presented. The purpose is to elucidate the physical approximations involved and to recognize the Thornber-Feynman approximations in a different language (using operator techniques).

ii) Furthermore it is shown that the Thornber-Feynman approximation relies on a drifted-Maxwellian distribution of the electron momentum for all values of the electric field, the electron-phonon interaction and the temperature. This is a generalization to all coupling of a similar statement made recently by N. N. Bogolubov[8] and F. Beleznay et al.[9].

2. FORMULATION OF THE PROBLEM.

A static and spatially uniform electric field is applied across an ionic crystal, which itself is in thermal equilibrium. At $t=t_o$ an electron is injected into the crystal. It is assumed that after an infinite time duration a steady-state is reached, this means: $\lim_{t\to+\infty} \langle \vec{p}(t)\rangle = 0$ ($\vec{p}(t)$ is the electron momentum operator). In this steady-state the gain of electron momentum by the electric field is compensated by the loss of electron momentum due to scattering with the phonons. The electron average velocity: $\langle \dot{\vec{x}}(t)\rangle = \vec{v}$ is then a constant.

An electron moving in a polar crystal under the influence of an static electric field is described by the Hamiltonian[10,6]:

$$H = H_o + H_I + e\vec{E}\cdot\vec{r} \tag{1}$$

with H_o the Hamiltonian of the free electron and phonon system:

$$H_o = \frac{\vec{p}^2}{2m} + \sum_{\vec{k}} \hbar\omega_{\vec{k}}\, a^+_{\vec{k}}\, a_{\vec{k}} \tag{2}$$

and H_I the interaction term between the electron and the phonons:

$$H_I = \sum_{\vec{k}} (V_{\vec{k}}\, a_{\vec{k}}\, e^{i\vec{k}\cdot\vec{r}} + V^{\star}_{\vec{k}}\, a^+_{\vec{k}}\, e^{-i\vec{k}\cdot\vec{r}}). \tag{3}$$

The net rate of electron momentum gain is given by the operator equation:

$$\dot{\vec{p}} = -e\vec{E} + \frac{i}{\hbar}[H_I, \vec{p}]. \tag{4}$$

If one supposes that at $t=+\infty$ a steady-state is reached, the rate of electron momentum change must be zero. One obtains the equation:

$$e\vec{E} = \lim_{t\to+\infty} \langle [H_I, \vec{p}]\rangle. \tag{5}$$

which expresses conservation of momentum.

In [7] the expectation value of the RHS of Eq.(5) is calculated using path-integral methods. This makes it possible to formulate the problem in terms of electron coordinates alone (for details we refer to [7]). In the next section the RHS of Eq.(5) is calculated using simple operator algebra.

3. THE NONLINEAR RELATION BETWEEN THE ELECTRIC FIELD AND THE ELECTRON AVERAGE VELOCITY.

Starting from the operator equation:

$$\dot{\vec{p}} = -e\vec{E} + \frac{i}{\hbar}[H_I, \vec{p}] \tag{4}$$

the momentum operator in the RHS of this equation is replaced by the identity:

$$\vec{p}(t) = \vec{p}(t_o) + \int_{t_o}^{t} d\tau \, \frac{d\vec{p}(\tau)}{d\tau} \, . \tag{6}$$

The resulting operator equation is transformed in a scalar equation by taking the expectation value in the limit of $t\to+\infty$, one finds:

$$e\vec{E} = \frac{i}{\hbar} \lim_{t\to\infty} \langle [H_I(t), \vec{p}(t_o)] \rangle + \frac{1}{\hbar^2} \lim_{t\to\infty} \int_{t_o}^{t} d\tau \, \langle [H_I(t), [H_I(\tau), \vec{p}(\tau)]] \rangle \tag{7}$$

where it is assumed that a steady-state is reached at $t=+\infty$. For the Fröhlich interaction Hamiltonian H_I, given by Eq.(3), this becomes:

$$e\vec{E} = \frac{i}{\hbar} \lim_{t\to\infty} \sum_{\vec{k}} \langle [(V_{\vec{k}} b_{\vec{k}}(t) + V^{\star}_{\vec{k}} b^{+}_{\vec{k}}(t)), \vec{p}(t_o)] \rangle$$

$$+ 2\sum\sum_{\vec{k}\vec{k}'} \vec{k} \, \frac{V_{\vec{k}} V_{\vec{k}'}}{\hbar} \lim_{t\to\infty} \int_{t_o}^{t} d\tau \, \mathrm{Re}\{\langle [b_{\vec{k}}(t), b_{\vec{k}'}(\tau)] + [b_{\vec{k}}(t), b_{\vec{k}'}(\tau)] \rangle\} \tag{8}$$

with the notation: $b_{\vec{k}} = a_{\vec{k}} \, e^{i\vec{k}\cdot\vec{r}}$.

In calculating the correlation functions on the RHS of Eq.(8) we make the same approximations as in Ref.[7]. The electron coordinate will be described in a reference system in which the electron average velocity is equal to zero. This is obtained by translating the electron position coordinate by $\vec{v}t$. First, one supposes, as in [7] that the resulting correlation function is independent of the electric field and the electron mean velocity. Secondly, the Hamiltonian H_o+H_I is replaced by H_f+H_F, with H_f the free phonon

field Hamiltonian and H_F the Hamiltonian describing Feynman's polaron model[2,3]. Finally one supposes that at time $t(t\to\infty)$ the system is in thermal equilibrium. As an example we consider the correlation function:

$$\langle b_{\vec{k}'}(t)b^{+}_{\vec{k}}(\tau)\rangle = \langle a_{\vec{k}'}(t)a^{+}_{\vec{k}}(\tau)\rangle\langle e^{i\vec{k}'\cdot\vec{r}(t)}\, e^{-i\vec{k}\cdot\vec{r}(\tau)}\rangle \times e^{i(\vec{k}'\cdot\vec{v}t-\vec{k}\cdot\vec{v}\tau)}. \tag{9a}$$

where the first two assumptions have been used. The time evolution of the electron coordinate is governed by H_F, explicitly:

$$\vec{r}(\tau) = \vec{R}(t) + \frac{\vec{P}}{M}(t-\tau) + a\{\vec{c}_{\vec{k}}(t)e^{-i\Omega(t-\tau)} + \vec{c}^{\,+}_{\vec{k}}(t)e^{i\Omega(t-\tau)}\} \tag{9b}$$

while the time evolution of the phonon coordinate is simply:

$$a^{+}_{\vec{k}}(\tau) = a^{+}_{\vec{k}}(t)\ \exp(i\omega_{\vec{k}}(\tau-t)) \tag{9c}$$

with $(\vec{R},\vec{P})$ and $(\vec{c},\vec{c}^{\,+})$ the canonical variables of the diagonalized Feynman model. The significance of these operators is as follows: $(\vec{R},\vec{P})$ describe the centre of mass motion of the polaron while $(\vec{c},\vec{c}^{\,+})$ describe the fluctuations of the electron around this average motion. In Feynman's polaron model the fluctutation of the electron coordinate[Eq.(9b)] is described by one mode, while in Ref.[11] an infinite number of modes have been used.

The relation between the parameters of Feynman's model (v_o,w_o) and the parameters in Eq.(9b) are:

$$\Omega = v_o\omega\ ;\quad M = m(v_o/w_o)^2;\quad a^2 = R(w_o/v_o)^2(\hbar/2m\omega)$$
$$R = (v_o^2-w_o^2)/(v_ow_o^2) \tag{10}$$

with ω the L.O.-phonon frequency.

Inserting (9b) and (9c) into (9a) and taking the average over the canonical ensemble with Hamiltonian H_F+H_f results in:

$$\langle b_{\vec{k}'}(t)b^{+}_{\vec{k}}(\tau)\rangle = \delta_{\vec{k},\vec{k}'}\,(1+n(\omega_{\vec{k}}))\ \exp\{i(\omega_{\vec{k}}-\vec{k}\cdot\vec{v})\sigma - k^2D(\sigma)\} \tag{11a}$$

The other correlation functions can be found in the same way:

$$\langle b^{+}_{\vec{k}}(\tau)b_{\vec{k}'}(t)\rangle = \delta_{\vec{k},\vec{k}'}\,n(\omega_{\vec{k}})\ \exp\{i(\omega_{\vec{k}}-\vec{k}\cdot\vec{v})\sigma - k^2D(\sigma)\} \tag{11b}$$

$$\langle b_{\vec{k}}(t)b_{\vec{k}'}(\tau)\rangle = 0 \tag{11c}$$

$$\langle b_{\vec{k}}(t)\vec{p}(t_o)\rangle = 0 \tag{11d}$$

with $\sigma=\tau-t$ and:

$$D(\sigma) = \frac{\hbar}{2M}(-i\sigma + \frac{\sigma^2}{\beta\hbar}) + a^2(1 - e^{i\Omega\sigma} + 4n(\Omega)\sin^2\frac{\Omega\sigma}{2}) \tag{12a}$$

$$n(\omega) = \{e^{\beta\hbar\omega} - 1\}^{-1}. \tag{12b}$$

Inserting the correlation functions (11) into Eq.(8) leads to:

$$-e\vec{E} = \sum_{\vec{k}} \vec{k}\frac{|V_k|^2}{\hbar} \int_{-\infty}^{+\infty} d\tau \, \{(1+n(\omega_{\vec{k}})) \exp[i(\omega_{\vec{k}} - \vec{k}\cdot\vec{v})\tau] - n(\omega_{\vec{k}}) \exp[-i(\omega_{\vec{k}} - \vec{k}\cdot\vec{v})\tau]\}\exp[-k^2D(\tau)]. \tag{13}$$

This equation, which expresses the nonlinear relation between the electric field and the electron average velocity, is identical with Eq.(13a) of Ref.[7] . (The correspondence between our notation and that of Ref.[7] is: $-eE\to E$, $\hbar=1$, $V_{\vec{k}}\to C_{\vec{k}}$).

4. PHYSICAL INTERPRETATION OF Eq.[13] AND RELATION TO THE DRIFTED-MAXWELLIAN DISTRIBUTION.

In this section it is shown that in Thornber-Feynman's theory the electron velocity distribution function is given by a drifted-Maxwellian, for all temperature, electron-phonon coupling and electric field strength. But first we make an analysis of the physical processes which have been taken into account in Eq.(13). For that purpose the last exponential in Eq.(13) will be expanded such that the time integral can be performed. Therefore write Eq.(12a) in a slightly different form:

$$D(\sigma) = a^2\coth\frac{\hbar\beta\Omega}{2} - \frac{i\hbar\sigma}{2M} + \frac{\sigma^2}{2M\beta} - a^2(1+n(\Omega))e^{-i\Omega\sigma} - a^2n(\Omega)e^{i\Omega\sigma} \tag{14}$$

after exponentiating $-k^2D(\sigma)$, one can expand the terms $\exp\{-a^2k^2(1+n(\Omega))\exp(-i\Omega\sigma)\}$ and $\exp\{-a^2k^2n(\Omega)\exp(i\Omega\sigma)\}$ in a Taylor series. The exponent of the third term in Eq.(14) can be written as an integral:

$$\exp\{-\frac{k^2\sigma^2}{2M\beta}\} = \int d\vec{p}\, f(\vec{p}) \exp\{\pm i\frac{\vec{p}\cdot\vec{k}}{M}\sigma\} \tag{15}$$

where the Maxwellian distribution function then appears:

$$f(\vec{p}) = \{\frac{\beta}{2\pi M}\}^{3/2}\exp\{-\beta\frac{\vec{p}^2}{2M}\} . \tag{16}$$

With the foregoing expansions the time integral in Eq.(13) can be performed, it gives a Dirac delta function. Considering only L.O.-phonon scattering, i.e. $\omega_{\vec{k}}=\omega$ and $V_k=(i\hbar\omega/k)(\hbar/2m\omega)^{1/4}(4\pi\alpha/V)^{1/2}$, Eq.(13) becomes:

$$-e\vec{E} = \lambda \sum_{n=0,n'=0}^{\infty} \sum^{\infty} \int d\vec{p} \int d\vec{k}\, B(\beta,n,n')\, k^{2(n+n')}\, e^{-k^2 a^2(\beta)}$$

$$\times f(\vec{p})\, \vec{k}\, \{(1+n(\omega))\cdot\delta(\omega-\vec{k}\cdot(\vec{v}+\vec{p}/M)+\hbar k^2/2M+(n-n')\Omega)$$

$$- n(\omega)\cdot\delta(-\omega+\vec{k}\cdot(\vec{v}+\vec{p}/M)+\hbar k^2/2M+(n-n')\Omega)\} \tag{17}$$

with:

$$a^2(\beta) = a^2\coth(\hbar\beta\Omega/2) \tag{18a}$$

$$B(\beta,n,n') = [\{a^2(1+n(\Omega))\}^n/n!]\cdot[\{a^2 n(\Omega)\}^{n'}/n'!] \tag{18b}$$

$$\lambda = (\alpha/\pi)(\hbar\omega)^2(\hbar/2m\omega)^{1/2}. \tag{18c}$$

It should be emphasized that expression (17) results automatically from the result of Ref.[7] which is given by Eq.(13).

Writing the result for $\vec{E}(\vec{v})$, of [7], as Eq.(17) facilitates the physical interpretation of it. The first part of the RHS of Eq.(17), the part with the term $(1+n(\omega))$, describes the following process: a polaron with momentum $\vec{p}+M\vec{v}$ emits a phonon with energy $\hbar\omega$ and momentum $\hbar\vec{k}$, while the electron virtual internal state changes from n' to n. In such a process the electron momentum is diminished by $\hbar\vec{k}$. The delta-function ensures conservation of energy, while the population factor $(1+n(\omega))$ appears because a phonon with frequency ω is emitted. For non zero temperature the process in which a phonon is absorbed is also possible. The contribution of such a process is given by the second part of the RHS of Eq.(17), the part with the term $n(\omega)$.

In both types of scattering processes the polaron initial velocity is given by $\vec{p}+M\vec{v}$. In formula (17) an integration has to be carried out, with a weight factor $f(\vec{p})$, over the variable $\vec{p}$. $f(\vec{p})$ plays the role of a distribution function for the deviation of the polaron velocity $(\vec{p}/M)$ from its average value $\vec{v}$ (remark that the average electron velocity is equal to the average polaron velocity). Specifically, $f(\vec{p})$ turns out the probability to find the polaron in a state with momentum $\vec{p}+M\vec{v}$, or with other words, the polaron velocity distribution function $g(\vec{p})=f(\vec{p}-M\vec{v})$ is approximated by a drifted-Maxwellian distribution function. This function is centered around the average velocity $\vec{v}$ and its spreading is determined by the lattice temperature. The electron velocity distribution function is also given by a drifted-Maxwellian, because the internal fluctuations of the electron, which are harmonic and isotropic[Eq.(9b)], can only change the width and temperature of this distribution function.

Indeed an explicit calculation of the electron velocity distribution function (using the foregoing approximations) shows that it is given by:

$$f(\vec{p}_\circ) = \langle\delta(\vec{p}-\vec{p}_\circ)\rangle = \{\frac{\beta_e}{2\pi m}\}^{3/2} \exp\{-\frac{\beta_e}{2m}(\vec{p}-m\vec{v})^2\} \tag{19}$$

with the electron temperature β_e (remember that β=1/kT) given by:

$$\beta_e = \beta\,\frac{M}{m}\,\{1 + a^2\Omega^2\cdot\frac{M\beta}{m^2}\cdot\coth(\frac{\beta\hbar\Omega}{2})\}^{-1} \tag{20}$$

which is thus equal to the lattice temperature β modified by a factor which depends *only* on the effective electron-phonon interaction (characterized by the parameters $v_\circ,w_\circ$) and is *independent* of the electron velocity.

5. DISCUSSION.

Although Thornber-Feynman's theory leads to the expected physical trend between the electron velocity and the electric field there are still several difficulties which have to be solved[7,12]:

1) Because Eq.(5) (and thus also the final result Eq.(13)) expresses only conservation of momentum, it is not necessarily guaranteed that there is also energy conservation. Indeed, as pointed out in Ref.[7] there is no energy conservation at low temperature.
2) For small temperature the small-field conductivity differs with a factor $\frac{3}{2}kT/(\hbar\omega)$ with the result of other theories on polaron conductivity.

It is hoped that the rederivation of Thornber-Feynman's theory presented above and in Ref.[13] , will contribute to a clarification of the problems mentioned under 1 and 2.

For small electron-phonon coupling, another approach to the nonlinear conductivity problem is possible using the Boltzmann equation which is valid in this limit.(for analytic work on this Boltzmann equation see J.Devreese et al.[14] and for a numerical analysis see W.Fawcett et al.[15]). The difficulties 1 and 2 do not appear in this approach. The price to be paid is that now an integro-differential equation has to be solved. The Boltzmann equation is limited to the small coupling region because no interference effects between successive collisions(contrary to the theory of [7]) are taken into account. These effects are important in the intermediate and high coupling region.

The calculations of [14] and[15] shown that, for low temperature and small electron-phonon coupling, the electron velocity distribution deviates markedly from a drifted-Maxwellian. The discrepancy with the result of [7] (see also Eq.(19)) is possibly the reason for the above two difficulties.

REFERENCES

1. See for example: G. Bauer, in: "Springer Tracts in Modern Physics" 74,(1974) and J. T. Devreese and V. E. Van Doren (editors), "Linear and Nonlinear Electron Transport in Solids", Plenum Press(1976).
2. R. P. Feynman, Phys. Rev. 97, 660 (1955).
3. Y. Osaka, Progr. Theor. Phys. 22, 437 (1959).
4. T. D. Schultz, Phys. Rev. 116, 526 (1959).
5. R. P. Feynman, R. W. Hellwarth, C. K. Iddings and P. M. Platzman, Phys. Rev. 127, 1004 (1962).
6. J. Devreese, J. De Sitter and M. Goovaerts, Phys. Rev. B5, 2367 (1972).
7. K. K. Thornber and R. P. Feynman, Phys. Rev. B1, 4099 (1970).
8. N. N. Bogolubov, JNIR E17-11822(1978).
9. F. Beleznay, J. Van Royen and J. T. Devreese, (to be published).
10. H. Fröhlich, Advances in Physics 3, 325 (1954).
11. J. T. Devreese, R. Evrard and E. Kartheuser, Phys. Rev. B12, 3353 (1975).
12. J. T. Devreese, in: "Path-integrals", Eds. G. T. Papadopoulos and J. T. Devreese, Plenum Publishing Corp. (1978), p.315.
13. For more details see: F. Peeters and J. T. Devreese, (to be published).
14. J. T. Devreese and R. Evrard. Phys. Stat. Sol.(b)78, 85 (1976).
15. W. Fawcett, A. D. Boardman and S. Swain, J. Phys. Chem. Solids 31, 1963 (1970).

THE USES OF INSTANTONS FOR DIFFUSION IN BISTABLE POTENTIALS+

U. Weiss and W. Häffner

Institut für Theoretische Physik
Universität Stuttgart
D-7000 Stuttgart 80, Pfaffenwaldring 57

1. INTRODUCTION

The fundamental role of bistable macrosystems in many fields of physics, chemistry, biology and also sociology has become clear in recent years. Of the extensive literature we can only mention a few: tunnel diodes[1], optical bistability[2], autocatalytic chemical reactions[3] and interacting social groups[4].

Here we are interested in the complete time behaviour of fluctuation and relaxation of the stochastic phenomena mentioned above. Especially we are concerned with the following three subjects which decisively depend on the strongly nonlinear character of the problem.

1. Relaxation from the instability point
2. Relaxation from nearly the instability point and occupation probabilites of both sites
3. Escape problem (Determination of the renormalized drift)

These subjects are of fundamental importance, because their control will open the way to a correct statistical-mechanical description of metastable and unstable states.

Among the theoretical efforts to describe such decay processes within the Fokker-Planck equation method we mention the study of explicitly soluble models[5-9], the recent quasideterministic approach of Haake[10], the Liouville projection operator method of Grabert and Weidlich[11] and the scaling theory of Suzuki[12], which has been

---
+presented by U. Weiss

extended to models with an infinite number of degrees of freedom[13].

Suzuki attempted to overcome the divergent variance which was observed[14] in the asymptotic ε-expansion method[15] in the case where the system is initially at the instability point. Here, ε denotes the diffusion constant, which is proportional to the inverse size of the macrosystem. In Suzuki's treatment[12] the whole range of time is divided into three regions: the initial region, in which the linear approximation is assumed to hold, the scaling region, in which the diffusion is neglected and the nonlinearity is taken into account, and the final region, in which the approach to equilibrium is considered again in a linear approximation. Although this procedure gives agreement with experimental data in a number of cases[16], it contains two severe shortcomings on the theoretical side. First, the transition times between the various time regions are fitting parameters and, secondly, it may happen that the various approximation schemes have no overlapping domains of validity, as was made explicit in van Kampen's model[5].

Here we show that the separate treatment of three time regions with different approximation schemes is unnecessary. Rather it is possible to set up a "renormalized" ε-expansion method which yields well behaved expressions for the moments of observables at all stages of the decay of an unstable initial state. As we will discuss below, the failure of the usual ε-expansion method, both in the treatment of Kubo et al.[14] and in the corresponding Hamilton-Jacobi method, is attributable to the degeneracy of the instability point and the stable points in the deterministic problem. In our treatment the annoying degeneracy is broken by an "effective" ε-dependent potential. Thus, the lowest order problem, which amounts to the solution of a Hamilton-Jacobi equation, is intrinsically ε-dependent. The corresponding fluctuation corrections are considered in the next higher order.

Our method works for finite and infinite dimensional multistable systems. Quite generally, the corresponding Euler-Lagrange equations admit solutions where the particle leaves the instability point with velocity of order $\sqrt{\varepsilon}$ and attains a stability point at times infinity. In common with the diction in quantum mechanics and field theory[17] we call these solutions instantons. As will be shown below, the instantons govern the relaxation behaviour of the system for the three processes mentioned above.

In order to represent our method in its simpliest form we consider a onedimensional bistable model. In Section 2 we set up the basic equations and explain our approximation scheme, whereas in Section 3 we give explicit results for two specifically chosen drift functions. The relaxation from nearly the instability point and the escape problem are discussed in Sections 4 and 5, respectively.

2. BASIC EQUATIONS AND GENERAL METHOD

As a stochastic description of a onedimensional bistable system we use the Fokker-Planck equation

$$\frac{\partial P(x,t)}{\partial t} = - \frac{\partial}{\partial x}k(x)P(x,t) + \frac{1}{2}\varepsilon\frac{\partial^2 P(x,t)}{\partial x^2} \tag{2.1}$$

where the diffusion constant ε, time t and macrovariable x are scaled and dimensionless. The nonlinear drift function $k(x)$ of a bistable system is sketched in Fig. 1 and is conveniently expressed as the negative derivative $k(x) = - U'(x)$ of a symmetrical potential function $U(x)$ with two degenerate minima.

In the limit $\varepsilon \to o$ the system moves deterministically according to $\dot{x} = k(x)$. The stable points are $x = \pm 1$, as indicated by the arrows in Fig. 1, and $x = o$ is the instability point of the system. The solution of Eq.(2.1) will approach, as $t \to \infty$, the stationary distribution

$$P_o(x) \sim \exp\{ - \frac{2}{\varepsilon}U(x)\}, \tag{2.2}$$

which for small ε is sharply peaked at $x = \pm 1$.

A well-known approach to solve Eq.(2.1) consists in transforming it into a self-adjoint eigenvalue problem[5,18]. When the system is initially sharp at $x = y$, $P(x,t = o;y) = \delta(x - y)$, one obtains

$$P(x,t;y) = \phi_o(x)\sum_{n=o}^{\infty} \frac{\phi_n(y)}{\phi_o(y)}\phi_n(x)\exp(- \lambda_n t), \tag{2.3}$$

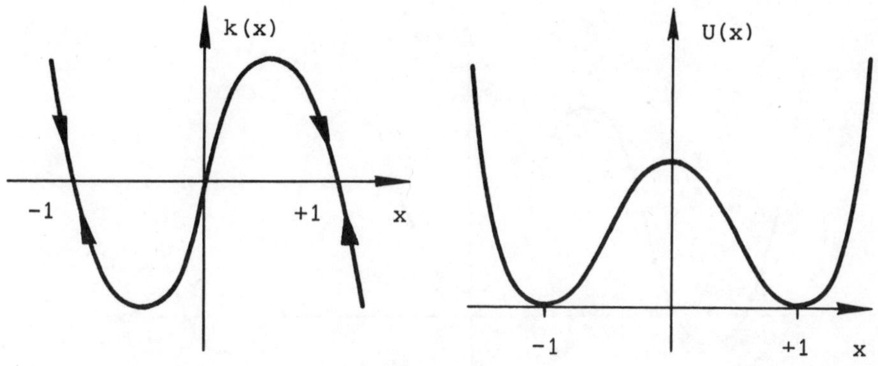

Fig. 1. Drift function k(x) and potential U(x) of a bistable system

where λ_n and $\phi_n(x)$ are the eigenvalues and normalized eigenfunctions of a Schrödinger-type eigenvalue problem ($\varepsilon \hat{=} \hbar$)

$$\{-\frac{\varepsilon^2}{2}\frac{\partial^2}{\partial x^2} + V(x,\varepsilon) - \varepsilon\lambda_n\}\,\phi_n(x) = 0 \tag{2.4}$$

The potential $V(x,\varepsilon)$ is given by

$$V(x,\varepsilon) = \frac{1}{2}k^2 + \frac{1}{2}\varepsilon\frac{\partial k}{\partial x} \tag{2.5}$$

and is sketched in Fig. 2. There holds exactly $\lambda_0 = 0$. The next eigenvalue λ_1 is different from zero by barrier-penetration, whereas $\lambda_2 \simeq \sqrt{V''(0)}$ and hence large compared to λ_1.

The starting point of our approach is the WKB-like ansatz

$$P(x,t;y) \sim \exp\{-\frac{1}{\varepsilon}S(x,t;y;\varepsilon)\} \tag{2.6}$$

By Eq.(2.6) the Fokker-Planck equation is transformed into the non-linear partial differential equation

$$\frac{\partial S}{\partial t} + k\frac{\partial S}{\partial x} + \frac{1}{2}(\frac{\partial S}{\partial x})^2 = \frac{\varepsilon}{2}\frac{\partial^2 S}{\partial x^2} + \varepsilon\frac{\partial k}{\partial x} \tag{2.7}$$

In analogy to the semiclassical expansion method in quantum mechanics, one is tempted to expand $S(x,t;y;\varepsilon)$ in a power series expansion in ε and to solve the hierarchy of equations obtained from (2.7). In lowest order, which we denote by $S^{(0)}$, the right hand side in Eq.(2.7) is neglected.

As we shall now demonstrate, this procedure breaks down, if y is at the instability point.

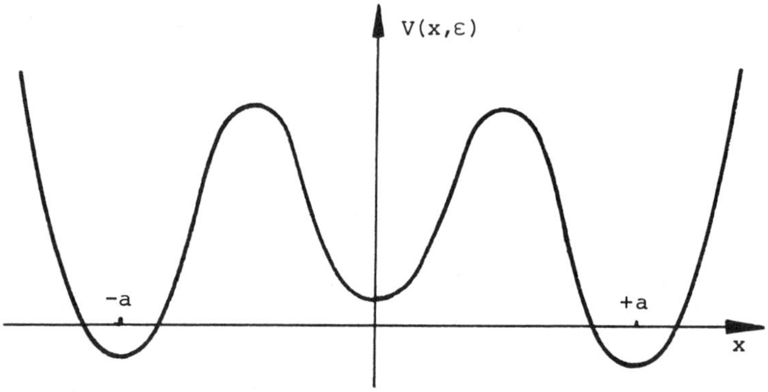

Fig. 2. Potential of the eigenvalue problem Eq.(2.4)

$S^{(0)}$ is conveniently obtained by calculating the motion of a particle in the potential $W(z) = - k^2(z)/2$, which is sketched in Fig. 3. In terms of the Lagrangian

$$L_o(\dot{z},z) = \frac{1}{2}(\dot{z} - k(z))^2 \tag{2.8}$$

the action $S^{(0)}$ is given by the expression

$$S^{(0)}(x,t;y) = \int_o^t d\tau L_o(\dot{z}(\tau),z(\tau)), \tag{2.9}$$

where the path $z(\tau)$ is a solution of the boundary value problem

$$\ddot{z} = - \frac{\partial}{\partial z}W(z) \; ; \; z(o) = y \; , \; z(t) = x \tag{2.10}$$

It is convenient to classify the various path solutions $z(\tau)$ of Eq.(2.10) according to their final direction of motion. We denote by $z_+(\tau)$ a path which has at x the direction of motion as indicated by the arrows in Fig. 1 and by $z_-(\tau)$ a path which has at x the reversed direction of motion. For example, if $0<y<x<1$, $z_+(\tau)$ approaches x from the left. Accordingly, the direct path from initial to final x belongs to this class. The path $z_-(\tau)$ approaches x from the right. Hence it is a path having a turning point near the right maximum of W(z). By the asymptotic property

$$\lim(t \to \infty) \; \dot{z}_\pm(t) = \pm \, k(x) \tag{2.11}$$

and the well-known general expression

$$\frac{\partial S^{(0)}(x,t;y)}{\partial x} = \dot{z}(t) - k(x) \tag{2.12}$$

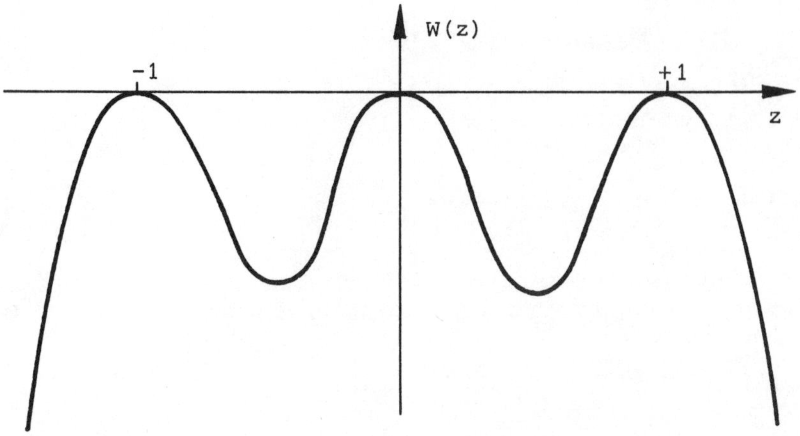

Fig. 3. The potential W(z)

the action $S_{\pm}^{(0)}(x,t;y)$ corresponding to a path $z_{\pm}(\tau)$ goes to the stationary expression $S_{0\pm}(x)$ as t goes to infinity,

$$\frac{\partial S_{0+}}{\partial x} = 0 \quad , \quad \frac{\partial S_{0-}}{\partial x} = -\,2k \tag{2.13}$$

Hence, by Eqs.(2.2) and (2.6), $S_{-}^{(0)}(x,t;y)$ will mainly determine the relaxation to the nearest stability point.

Now observing that $z = 0$ and $z = \pm 1$ are degenerate in the potential $W(z)$ we can draw our conclusions.

In the method of Kubo et al.[14] the variance is calculated by linearising the drift in the moving frame of the deterministic path $\dot{z} = k(z)$. This path, however, remains infinitely long at the instability point $y = 0$. Hence, a divergent variance for the decay of an unstable state is obtained by this method.

As to the Hamilton-Jacobi method, Eqs.(2.9) and (2.10), the action term $S_{-}^{(0)}(x,t;y)$ is absent for $1>x>y = 0$ because in this case there are no turning points. Hence, this method cannot describe the last stage of the decay process in which the fluctuations are reduced to their stationary value.

Thus, our analysis confirms the old result that a strict ε-expansion method breaks down for $y = 0$. Moreover, it exhibits that this failure may be cured by breaking the degeneracy of the peaks of $W(z)$.

Let us elaborate this idea in detail. We now abandon a strict ε-expansion of $S(x,t;y;\varepsilon)$ but rather consider a "renormalized" expansion

$$S(\varepsilon) = S^{(0)}(\varepsilon) + \varepsilon S^{(1)}(\varepsilon) + O(\varepsilon^2), \tag{2.14}$$

where $S^{(0)}$ and $S^{(1)}$ are supposed to contain the relevant nonexpandable behaviour of $S(\varepsilon)$. We choose $S^{(0)}(\varepsilon)$ to be a solution of the Hamilton-Jacobi equation

$$\frac{\partial S^{(0)}}{\partial t} + (k + \frac{1}{2}\frac{\partial S^{(0)}}{\partial x})\frac{\partial S^{(0)}}{\partial x} - \varepsilon v = 0 \tag{2.15}$$

The yet undetermined potential term $\varepsilon v(z)$ is intended to break the annoying degeneracy of the potential $W(z)$ mentioned above. $S^{(1)}(\varepsilon)$ solves the linear equation

$$\frac{\partial S^{(1)}}{\partial t} + (k + \frac{\partial S^{(0)}}{\partial x})\frac{\partial S^{(1)}}{\partial x} - \frac{1}{2}\frac{\partial^2 S^{(0)}}{\partial x^2} - \frac{1}{2}\frac{\partial k}{\partial x} - (\frac{1}{2}\frac{\partial k}{\partial x} - v) = 0 \tag{2.16}$$

A comment should be made about what we have done so far. Inserting

Eq.(2.14) in Eq.(2.7) only gives the sum of Eqs.(2.15) and ε times (2.16) as a result. However, we assume that Eqs.(2.15) and (2.16) are separately valid. In principle, the potential $\varepsilon v(z)$ should be determined by the requirement that this assumption is true. Here we are not concerned with the explicit calculation of $v(z)$. We rather make the simple ansatz

$$v(z) = \frac{1}{2}\,\alpha\,\frac{\partial k}{\partial z} \tag{2.17}$$

where α is a yet undetermined positive parameter.

The solution of Eq.(2.15) is given by the action

$$S^{(0)}(x,t;y) = \int_{0}^{t} d\tau L(\dot{z}(\tau),\, z(\tau);\alpha\varepsilon) \tag{2.18}$$

with the Lagrangian

$$L(\dot{z},z;\alpha\varepsilon) = \frac{1}{2}\dot{z}^2 - k(z)\dot{z} - W(z;\alpha\varepsilon) \tag{2.19}$$

$$W(z;\alpha\varepsilon) = -\frac{1}{2}k^2(z) - \frac{1}{2}\alpha\varepsilon\,\frac{\partial k(z)}{\partial z} \tag{2.20}$$

The potential $W(z;\alpha\varepsilon)$ is sketched in Fig. 4. The path $z(\tau)$ is a solution of the Euler-Lagrange boundary problem

$$\ddot{z} = -\frac{\partial}{\partial z}\,W(z;\alpha\varepsilon)\ ;\ z(0) = y\ ;\ z(t) = x. \tag{2.21}$$

In view of the mode decomposition method, Eq.(2.4), the choice $\alpha = 1$ in $W(z;\alpha\varepsilon)$ seems to be natural. The same result, $\alpha = 1$, is obtained if the Lagrangian (2.19) is identified with the covariant Onsager-Machlup Lagrangian occuring in the path integral representation method[19,20].

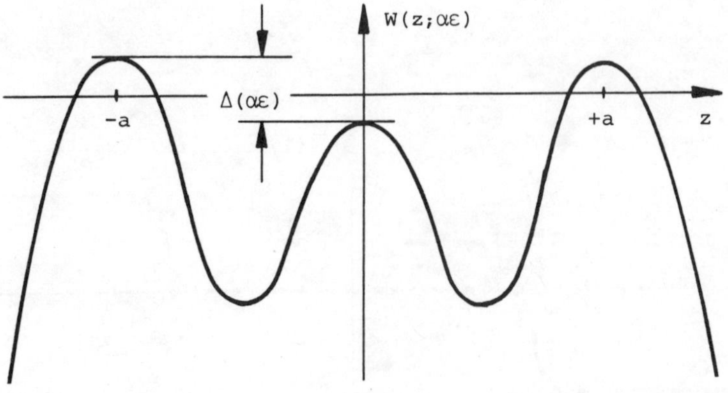

Fig. 4. The potential $W(z;\alpha\varepsilon)$

However, in our treatment the choice $\alpha = 1$ is not favoured. Below we shall determine α by the normalization condition of $P(x,t;y = 0)$ at short times and at time infinity.

The boundary problem (2.21) permits a solution $\bar{z}(\tau)$ where the particle attains the tops of the hills $z = \pm a$ at times plus and minus infinity and crawls over the central hill at $t = t_0$ with a very small velocity

$$\dot{\bar{z}}(t_0) = \sqrt{2\Delta(\alpha\varepsilon)} \; ; \; \Delta(\alpha\varepsilon) = \frac{\alpha\varepsilon}{2}(k'(o) - k'(a)) \tag{2.22}$$

The particle quickly passes through the valleys at times $t_0 \pm t_1$, where $t_1 = - \ln(c\Delta)/2$. The constant c is of order unity and depends on the details of the model.

The particular solution $\bar{z}(\tau)$ is generally called an instanton[17]. It has two distinct correlated structures in time, as is sketched in Fig. 5. Accordingly it is a two-instanton solution with centres at $t_0 \pm t_1$. Note that in the limit $\alpha\varepsilon \to 0$ $\bar{z}(\tau)$ decays into two independent, infinitely separated one-instanton solutions. It turns out below that the instanton $\bar{z}(\tau)$ governs the various relaxation phenomena of our model.

The two-instanton solution $\bar{z}(\tau)$ is very similar to a class of non-classical solitons occuring in some quantum field theoretical models[21,22]. These solitons are due to quantum effects and do not appear in a classical theory. Quite similarly the two-instanton solution is due to diffusion effects and vanishes in the deterministic limit $\varepsilon \to 0$.

Now we turn to the solution of Eq.(2.16). By Eqs.(2.12) and (2.15) we immediately get

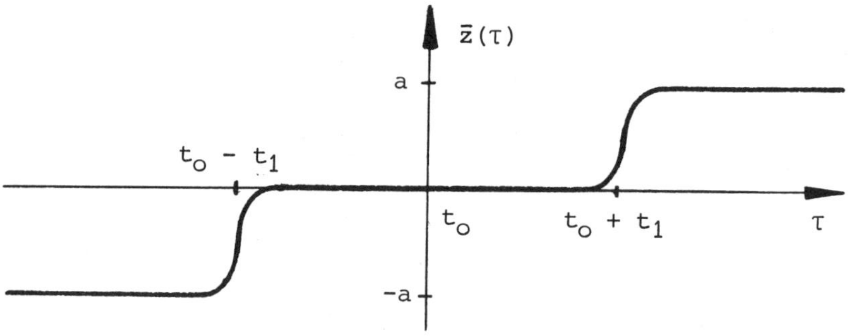

Fig. 5. Two-instanton solution of the potential $W(z,\alpha\varepsilon)$

$$S^{(1)}(x,t;y) = -\frac{1}{2}\ln\frac{1}{2}\left|\frac{\partial^2 S^{(0)}(x,t;y)}{\partial x\ \partial y}\right| + \frac{(1-\alpha)}{2}\int_0^t d\tau k'(z(\tau)) \tag{2.23}$$

and by standard calculation (see e.g. Ref.[23])

$$\frac{\partial^2 S^{(0)}(x,t;y)}{\partial x\ \partial y} = -\left\{ \dot{z}(0)\dot{z}(t)\int_0^t \frac{d\tau}{\dot{z}^2(\tau)} \right\}^{-1} \tag{2.24}$$

The first term on the right hand side of Eq.(2.23) is due to the fluctuations around the path $z(\tau)$. The second term represents the contribution of the additional inhomogeneity in Eq.(2.16).

In the following we deal with the conditional probability distribution in the approximation

$$P(x,t;y) = \sum_{\text{different paths}} \sqrt{\frac{1}{\pi\varepsilon}}\ \exp\{-\frac{1}{\varepsilon}S(x,t;y)\} \tag{2.25}$$

$$S(x,t;y) = S^{(0)}(x,t;y) + \varepsilon S^{(1)}(x,t;y). \tag{2.26}$$

$S^{(0)}$ and $S^{(1)}$ are given by Eqs.(2.18) and (2.23). The prefactor arises from the normalization condition of P at short times.

Finally, the temporal conservation of the total probability is exploited in order to determine the parameter α. Here we calculate α from the normalization condition of the symmetrical distribution $P(x,t;y = 0)$ at time infinity. Since at large times the probability is sharply peaked at the stability points we may restrict ourselves to a Gaussian approximation around the endpoints $x = \pm a$ of the instanton path $\bar{z}(\tau)$. Then there holds

$$\lim_{t\to\infty} S(x,t;y = 0) = \bar{S}(\alpha\varepsilon) + \omega\{\theta(x)(x-a)^2 + \theta(-x)(x+a)^2\} \tag{2.27}$$

where $\omega^2 = V''(a)$. The minimum, $\bar{S}(\alpha\varepsilon)$, is the contribution of the instanton path $\bar{z}(\tau)$ from $y = 0$ to $x = \pm a$. Note that, due to the simple choice (2.17), the stability points are slightly shifted from $x = \pm 1$ to $x = \pm a$, where $a = 1 + O(\varepsilon)$. Using Eqs.(2.27) and (2.25) the normalization condition yields

$$\bar{S}(\alpha\varepsilon) = \frac{\varepsilon}{2}\ln\frac{4}{\omega} \tag{2.28}$$

which fixes α. This concludes the general discussion of our method.

3. RELAXATION FROM THE INSTABILITY POINT

It will be instructive to apply our method to a definite bistable system. In the following we consider the models

$$\text{Model A} \qquad k_A(z) = z - z^3 \tag{3.1}$$

$$\text{Model B} \qquad k_B(z) = \begin{cases} 2(1-z) & z \geq z_r = \frac{2}{3} \\ z & |z| \leq z_r \\ -2(1+z) & z \leq -z_r \end{cases} \tag{3.2}$$

Model B is obtained by linearizing the drift function $k_A(z)$ around the stability points $z = \pm 1$ and around the instability point $z = 0$. The drift function $k(z)$ is shown in Fig. 6 both for models A and B. In a way, it is easier to evaluate Model B than Model A. The Euler Lagrange equation (2.21) of Model A is solved by elliptic functions, which depend on the total energy of the path. However, the special boundary value problem (2.21) is generally not soluble in an analytical way for Model A. As to Model B, the paths $z_B(\tau)$ are given by hyperbolic functions and the joining conditions at $z = \pm z_r$ can be solved algebraically.

The regions where $W_A(z,\alpha\varepsilon)$ and $W_B(z,\alpha\varepsilon)$ differ appreciably are passed very quickly. Thus we expect that both models yield nearly the same results for the relaxation from the instability point. On the other hand, we expect quite different results for the escape problem, since in this case the different potential barriers of $V(x,\varepsilon)$, Eq.(2.5), of model A and B are important.

We now consider the relaxation from the instability point $y = 0$ for the Models A and B.

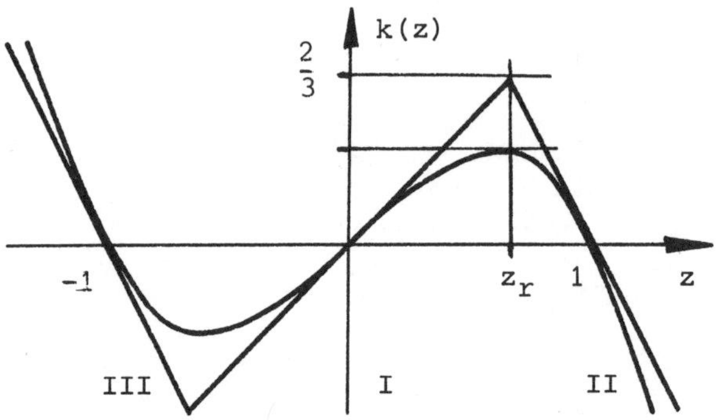

Fig. 6. The drift function k(z) for Model A and B

Instanton

First we give the explicit expressions for the instantons of Model A and B

$$\bar{z}_A(t) = \frac{ab\,\sinh T}{\sqrt{a^2+b^2+b^2\sinh^2 T}} \quad ; \quad T = a\sqrt{a^2+b^2}\;t$$

$$a^2 = \frac{1}{3}\{2+\sqrt{1+9\alpha\varepsilon}\} \simeq 1 + O(\varepsilon) \tag{3.3}$$

$$b^2 = \frac{2}{3}\{\sqrt{1+9\alpha\varepsilon} - 1\} \simeq 3\alpha\varepsilon$$

$$\bar{z}_B(t) = \begin{cases} \sqrt{3\alpha\varepsilon}\;\sinh t & t<\bar{T}_1 = -\frac{1}{2}\ln\frac{27}{16}\alpha\varepsilon \\ 1 - \frac{16}{81}\frac{e^{-2t}}{\alpha\varepsilon} & t>\bar{T}_1 \end{cases} \tag{3.4}$$

Observe that both paths have initial velocity $\sqrt{3\alpha\varepsilon}$. However, in course of time, $\bar{z}_B(t)$ precedes $\bar{z}_A(t)$ and keeps the narrow lead up to time infinity. This follows from Eq.(3.4) and the asymptotic behaviour of Eq.(3.3) with $a = 1$,

$$\lim_{t\to\infty} \bar{z}_A(t) = 1 - \frac{2}{3}\frac{e^{-2t}}{\alpha\varepsilon} \tag{3.5}$$

The calculation of the instanton contribution of Eq.(2.27) gives

$$\bar{S}_A(\alpha\varepsilon) = \bar{S}_B(\alpha\varepsilon) = \frac{3}{4}\alpha\varepsilon \tag{3.6}$$

Thus we obtain from Eq.(2.28) with $\omega = 2$

$$\alpha = \frac{2}{3}\ln 2 \simeq 0.46 \tag{3.7}$$

both for Models A and B. Note that this result is approximately half of the Onsager-Machlup value $\alpha = 1$.

For later convenience we remark that the instantons (3.3) and (3.4) define definite mappings of the total time region $0<t<\infty$ onto the interval $0<\bar{z}<1$

$$0<t<\infty \xleftrightarrow{\text{mapping by instanton}} 0<\bar{z}<1 \tag{3.8}$$

General solution for Model B

The expression (2.26) can be calculated for Model B without difficulty. We get in the interesting region $x>z_r$

$$S(x,t;y=0) = \frac{4}{9}\exp(-2\tau_1) + 2\,\frac{\{x-1+\frac{1}{3}\exp(-2(t-\tau_1))\}^2}{1-\exp(-4(t-\tau_1))}$$
$$-\,\varepsilon(t-2\tau_1) - \frac{\varepsilon}{2}\ln\left|\frac{2}{3}\frac{\partial\tau_1}{\partial x}\right| \qquad (3.9)$$

where $\tau_1 = \tau_1(x,t)$ is the transit time at $z = z_r$ of the path $z(\tau)$ which has boundary conditions $z(0) = 0$, $z(t) = x > z_r$. The transit time τ_1 is given in terms of the total energy E by

$$\tau_1 = -\frac{1}{2}\ln\{\frac{9}{16}(\alpha\varepsilon+2E)\}. \qquad (3.10)$$

E is a solution of an algebraic equation of third order

$$2(E-\alpha\varepsilon)(\alpha\varepsilon+2E)^2 + 48(1-x)(\alpha\varepsilon+2E)u\alpha\varepsilon - 144\,u^2\alpha^2\varepsilon^2 = 0 \qquad (3.11)$$

where $u = u(\bar{z}(t))$ is given by

$$u = \frac{16}{27}\{\bar{z} + \sqrt{\bar{z}^2+3\alpha\varepsilon}\}^{-2} \qquad t<\tau_1$$
$$u = 1 - \bar{z} \qquad t>\tau_1 \qquad (3.12)$$

and $\bar{z}$ is defined in Eq.(3.4). For times given by $1 - \bar{z} > \sqrt{\alpha\varepsilon}/6$ there are no turning points. For times given by $1 - \bar{z} < \sqrt{\alpha\varepsilon}/6$ there are two turning points z_1 and z_2, $z_1 < z_2$. Thus for $x < z_1$ and sufficient large times three paths contribute to $P(x,t;y = 0)$. We have sketched these paths in Fig. 7. Path I is the direct path and paths II and III have the turning points z_1 and z_2, respectively. When t is very large path II spends most of its time near $z = 0$, whereas path III spends most of its time near $z = 1$ and gets close to the instanton in the limit $t \to \infty$. There follows from Eqs.(3.9) - (3.12)

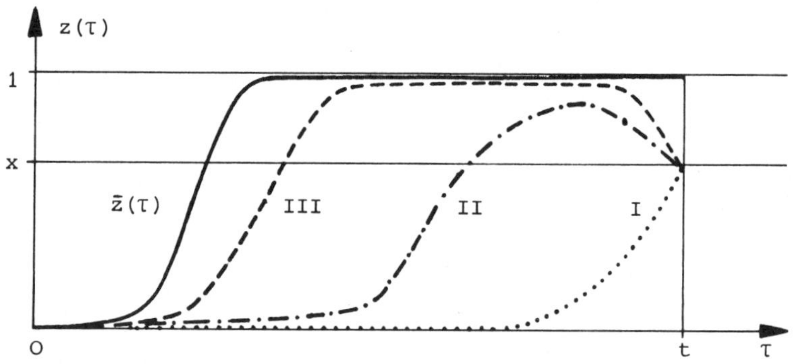

Fig. 7. Different paths I, II and III contributing to $S(x,t;y = 0)$ for large t and $0<x<z_1$.

$$\text{path I:} \quad \lim_{t \to \infty} S_I(x,t;y = 0) \to \varepsilon t \to \infty$$

$$\text{path II:} \quad \lim_{t \to \infty} S_{II}(x,t;y = 0) \to 2(1-x)^2 + \varepsilon t \to \infty \qquad (3.13)$$

$$\text{path III:} \quad \lim_{t \to \infty} S_{III}(x,t;y = 0) \to 2(1-x)^2 + \frac{3}{4}\alpha\varepsilon.$$

Thus, at large times the probability distribution is predominantly determined by path III.

Of course, further path solutions exist at large times. For example, the particle may move first into the region $z<0$ and then may roll back into the region $z>0$ via a turning point near $z = -1$. These path solutions are negligible in the problem considered in this section. However, they are important in the escape problem which will be discussed below.

In Fig. 8 we sketch the time behaviour of $P(x,t;y = 0)$ as given by Eqs.(2.25) and (3.9) - (3.12).

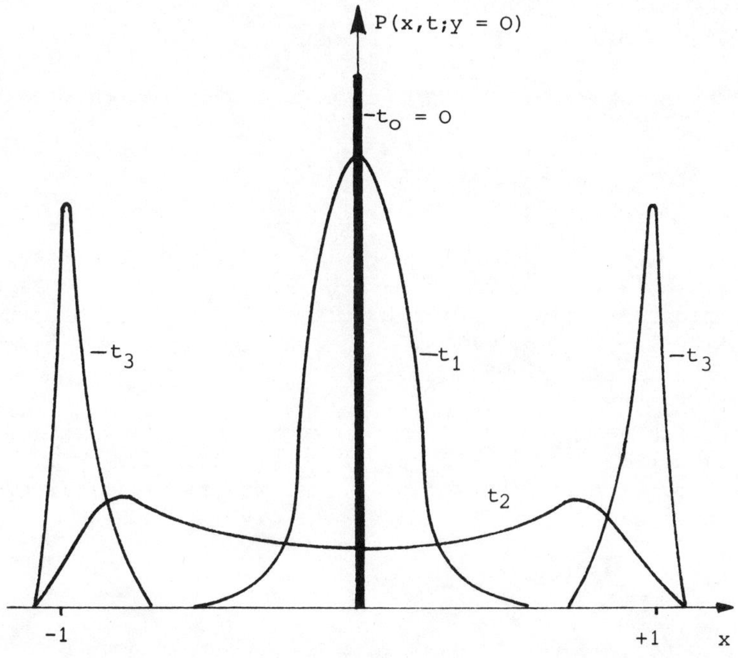

Fig. 8. Change of the distribution function in the course of time ($t_0<t_1<t_2<t_3$).

The total time region $0<t<\infty$ is conveniently divided into three characteristic regions. In the initial region the probability distribution is spreading by diffusion. The fluctuations grow from zero to $O(1)$. In the middle region the probability changes rapidly from a single peak distribution into a double peak distribution. However, the fluctuations stay at $O(1)$. In the final region the distribution changes into the stationary solution and the fluctuations are reduced from $O(1)$ to $O(\varepsilon)$. Accordingly, we call these regions fluctuation enhancement region, transition region and fluctuation reduction region.

It is convenient to mark out the various time regions by the position of the instanton. There follows, quite generally, from our calculation and by use of the instanton mapping (3.8):

$0\le\bar{z}\le O(\sqrt{\varepsilon})$	fluctuation enhancement region
$O(\sqrt{\varepsilon})\ll\bar{z}\ ;\ O(\sqrt{\varepsilon})\ll 1-\bar{z}$	transition region
$0\le 1-\bar{z}< O(\sqrt{\varepsilon})$	fluctuation reduction region

Transition Region

We obtain quite simple expressions in the transition time region for Model B. For the range $0\le x\le 2/3$ there generally holds

$$S(x,t;y=0) = \frac{81}{16}\alpha\varepsilon x^2 u - \frac{\varepsilon}{2}\ln(\frac{81}{16}\alpha\varepsilon u). \tag{3.14}$$

and for the range $O(\sqrt{\varepsilon})\ll 1-x\le 1/3$ there follows from Eqs.(3.9)-(3.11)

$$S(x,t;y=0) = \frac{3}{4}\alpha\varepsilon\frac{u}{1-x} - \frac{\varepsilon}{2}\ln(\frac{3}{16}\alpha\varepsilon\frac{u}{(1-x)^3}) \tag{3.15}$$

where $u = u(\bar{z}(t))$ is given by Eqs.(3.12) and (3.4). The detailed behaviour of $S(x,t;0)$ is shown in Fig. 9. Time t is expressed by the instanton path $\bar{z}(t)$. A minimum of $S(x,t;0)$ corresponds to a maximum of $P(x,t;0)$. Thus Fig. 9 exhibits the formation of the double peaks in the course of time.

The double peaks begin to appear at $x = \pm 2/3$ at a time being defined by $\bar{z}(t) = \sqrt{2\alpha}/3 \simeq 0.32$ and start to move to $x = \pm 1$. In the range of time $\bar{z}(t)>2/3$ the motion of the maxima $\pm x_m(t)$ is given by the simple expression

$$1 - x_m(t) = \frac{\alpha}{2}(1-\bar{z}(t)) \tag{3.16}$$

Quite generally the transition region corresponds to the scaling regime of Suzuki[12]. Note that in our treatment the various time scales are completely settled by the basic equations.

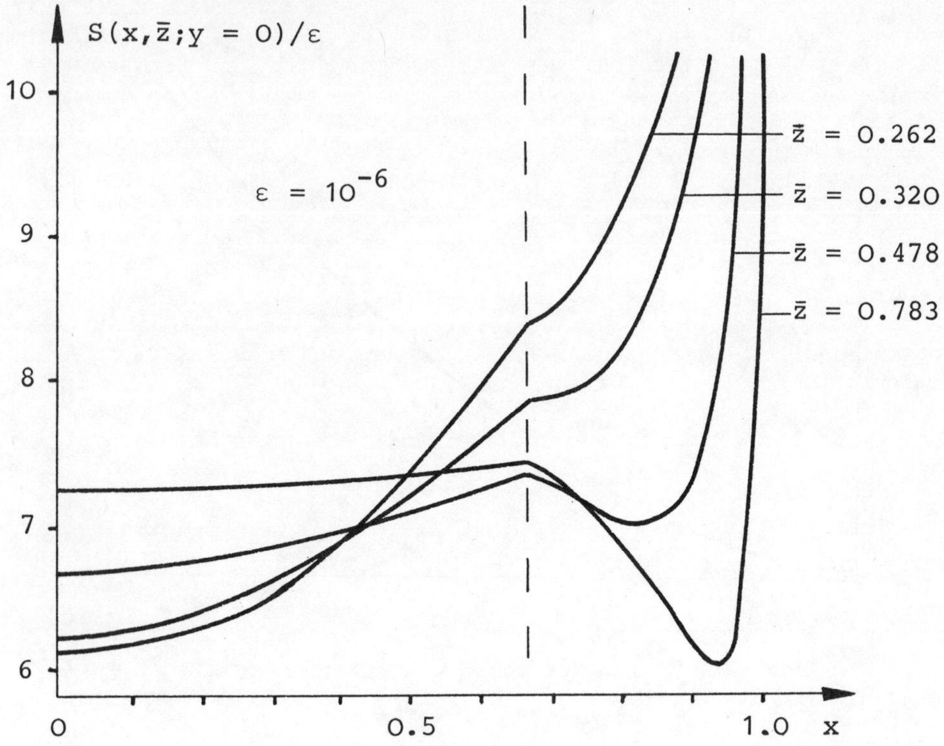

Fig. 9. Behaviour of $S(x,t;y = 0)$ for Model B in the transition region

Fluctuation Reduction Region

In the last stage of the decay process of unstable initial-state the fluctuations are reduced to their stationary value. It is calculated from Eqs. (3.9) - (3.12) that in the time region $1-\bar{z} \lesssim O(\sqrt{\varepsilon})$ the function $S(x,t;y = 0)$ already has curvature of $O(1)$ in the range of its minima $\pm x_m$. Accordingly, the calculation of moments by the saddle point method is appropriate. This yields for the Gaussian variance of Model B (see Fig. 10)

$$\sigma(t) = \sigma_o \quad \{1 + \frac{16}{3} \frac{(1-\bar{z})^2}{\alpha\varepsilon}\}^2 \qquad 1 - \bar{z} \leq O(\sqrt{\varepsilon}) \qquad (3.17)$$

where $\bar{\bar{z}}(t)$ is given by Eq. (3.4), $t > \bar{\tau}_1$. By inspection, Eq. (3.17) also holds for the reduction of fluctuations in Model A, except for the fact that $\bar{z}$ is given by Eq. (3.5). As was discussed above, the instanton path $\bar{z}_B(t)$ precedes $\bar{z}_A(t)$. Thus, the fluctuations of Model B are reduced slightly before those of Model A.

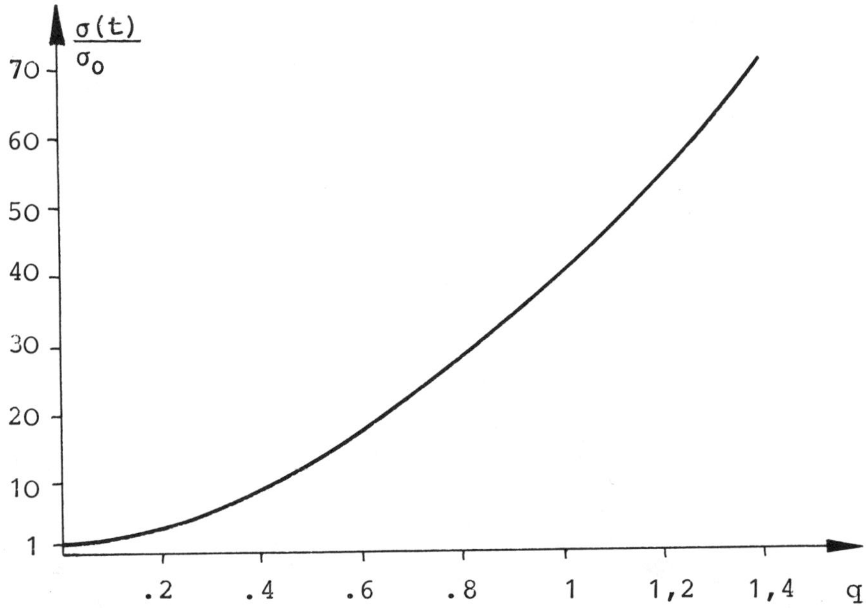

Fig. 10. Reduction of fluctuations as a function of $q = (1-\bar{z})/\sqrt{\varepsilon\alpha}$

4. RELAXATION FROM NEARLY THE INSTABILITY POINT

We now consider the relaxation of the system for a sharp initial state $y \neq 0$. For $y>0$ most of the probability flows towards the stability point $x = +1$. However, the exchange of probability across the instability point $x = 0$ is still appreciable if $y=O(\sqrt{\varepsilon})$. As distinguished from the symmetrical case treated in Section 3, the various time regions of the decay process are covered at slightly different times in the ranges $x>0$ and $x<0$. A somewhat extreme behaviour of $P(x,t;y \neq 0)$ is sketched in Fig. 11. It is simply explained by the instanton solution of Fig. 12 and can be substantiated by our method. At time t_1, where the velocity $\dot{\bar{z}}(t_1)$ is large, the distribution $P(x,t_1;y)$ is broad both in the range $x>0$ and $x<0$. At time t_2 the instanton position $\bar{z}(t_2)$ is close to the stability point +1, whereas $\bar{z}(-t_2)$ is still far away from the stability point -1. Thus, the distribution $P(x,t_2;y)$ is already peaked at $x = +1$, whereas it is still broad in the range $x<0$. Only starting at time t_3, at which $\bar{z}(-t_3)$ is close to -1, the distribution $P(x,t;y)$ is also peaked at $x = -1$.

At times $t \gg t_3$ the contribution of the eigenfunctions $\phi_n(x)$, $n>1$, in Eq.(2.3) has been damped out. Accordingly, in this stage the probability to be to the right or to the left of the instability point is given by

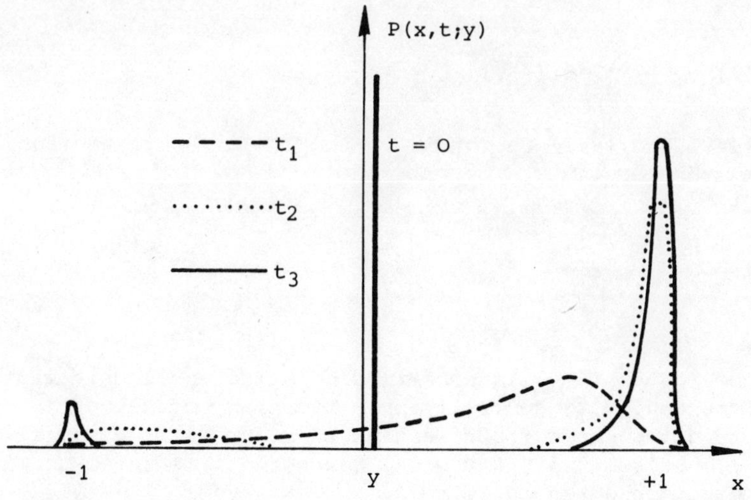

Fig. 11. Behaviour of $P(x,t;y \neq 0)$ at the characteristic times of the instanton solution sketched in Fig. 12

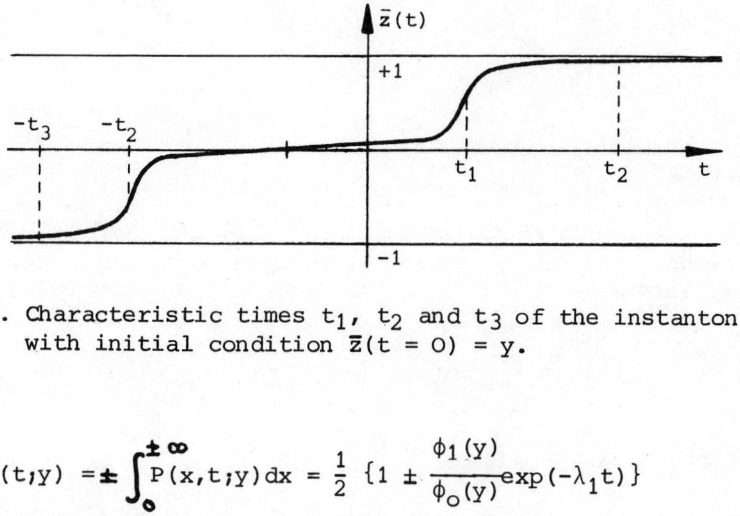

Fig. 12. Characteristic times t_1, t_2 and t_3 of the instanton path with initial condition $\bar{z}(t = 0) = y$.

$$p_\pm(t;y) = \pm \int_0^{\pm\infty} P(x,t;y)\,dx = \frac{1}{2}\,\{1 \pm \frac{\phi_1(y)}{\phi_0(y)}\exp(-\lambda_1 t)\} \qquad (4.1)$$

This yields for $t \ll 1/\lambda_1$ the simple expression

$$p_\pm(y) = \frac{1}{2}\,\{1 \pm \frac{\phi_1(y)}{\phi_0(y)}\} \qquad (4.2)$$

The occupation probability $p_\pm(y)$ can be calculated explicitly for a linear drift model[5].

There follows for $k(x) = cx$, $c>0$,

$$p_{\pm}(y) = \frac{1}{2}\{1 \pm \mathrm{erf}(\sqrt{\tfrac{c}{\varepsilon}}y)\} \tag{4.3}$$

By Eqs.(4.2) and (4.3) we obtain in the linear approximation of Models A and B

$$\kappa \equiv \frac{\phi_1'(0)}{\phi_0(0)} = \frac{2}{\sqrt{\varepsilon\pi}} \tag{4.4}$$

Below, the result (4.4) is confirmed by different considerations. It can be shown quite generally by a rescaling of x that the linearized theory gives the correct leading term for κ, if $c = O(1)$. In van Kampen's model[5], $c = O(\varepsilon)$. Hence the failure of the linearization method observed there.

5. ESCAPE PROBLEM

By Eq.(4.1) the occupation probabilities $p_{\pm}(t;y)$ tend to their equilibrium value 1/2 according to the rate equations

$$\frac{dp_{\pm}}{dt} = -\frac{1}{2\lambda_1}(p_{\pm} - p_{\mp}). \tag{5.1}$$

Thus the probability per unit time to escape over the barrier at $x = 0$ is given by $1/2\lambda_1$.

We now sketch the determination of λ_1 by the functional integration method. The basic object of our consideration is the functional integral

$$P(a,t;-a,-t) = \int_{-a}^{a} Dz(\tau)\exp\{-\frac{1}{\varepsilon}S^{(0)}(a,t;-a,-t) - \frac{(1-\alpha)}{2}\int_{-t}^{t} d\tau\, k'(z(\tau))\} \tag{5.2}$$

where $S^{(0)}$ is the action corresponding to the Lagrangian (2.19). Note that both terms in the exponent of Eq.(5.2) add up to the Onsager-Machlup function. However, in accordance with our discussion in Section 2, we evaluate (5.2) by considering trajectories for which $S^{(0)}$ is stationary. Our task is to evaluate Eq.(5.2) for very large t and compare with the mode decomposition result

$$P(a,t;\ -a,\ -t) = 2\,\phi_0^2(a)\exp\{-(\lambda_0+\lambda_1)t\}\sinh\{(\lambda_1-\lambda_0)t\} \tag{5.3}$$

The functional integration method has been considered in detail by Coleman[17] and Gildener and Patrascioiu[24]. In order to obtain the hyperbolic function in Eq.(5.3) besides the instanton, Fig. 5, also configurations with an instanton and any number of widely separated, non-interacting instanton-anti-instanton pairs must be taken into account. This method is called the dilute-instanton-gas approximation.

The instanton configurations break the time translation symmetry which the action has in the limit $t \to \infty$. However, the symmetry is restored by a zero eigenvalue in the expansion around the instanton configuration. In the standard method[24], the annoying zero eigenvalue is avoided by the introduction of collective coordinates[25] and the Faddeev-Popov technique[26]. In Coleman's treatment[17] the zero eigenvalue is directly eliminated.

The dilute-instanton-gas method leads to the result

$$\lambda_1 = \frac{2}{\sqrt{\pi\varepsilon\omega}}\,\dot{z}(0)\exp(-\tfrac{3}{2}\alpha)\exp\{-\tfrac{2}{\varepsilon}(U(0)-U(a))\} \tag{5.4}$$

where $\dot{z}(0)$ is defined in Eq.(2.22). On substituting Eq.(3.7) we obtain for Models A and B

$$\lambda_{1A} = \sqrt{\frac{\ln 2}{\pi}}\,\exp(-\frac{1}{2\varepsilon})\ ;\ \lambda_{1B} = \sqrt{\frac{\ln 2}{\pi}}\,\exp(-\frac{2}{3\varepsilon}). \tag{5.5}$$

The eigenvalue λ_1 can also be evaluated by the standard WKB method[27]

$$\lambda_1 = \frac{\omega}{\pi}\exp\{-\frac{1}{\varepsilon}\int_{-b}^{b}dx\,p(x)\} \tag{5.6}$$

where $p(x)$ is the classical momentum

$$p^2(x) = 2V(x,\varepsilon) \tag{5.7}$$

$V(x,\varepsilon)$ is defined in Eq.(2.5) and b is the classical turning point. For Model A we have to evaluate elliptic integrals. We obtain

$$\lambda_{1A} = \frac{\sqrt{2}}{\pi}\exp(-\frac{1}{2\varepsilon})\quad ;\quad \lambda_{1B} = \frac{\sqrt{2}}{\pi}\exp(-\frac{2}{3\varepsilon}). \tag{5.8}$$

The WKB results are identical to those obtained by the method of Kramers[28,5]. Recently the same results were derived by quite different methods. We especially mention the Ritz variational method of Larson and Kostin[29] and the Liouville projection operator method of Weidlich and Grabert[11] (in Ref.[11] a factor 2 is misprinted and hence the same result as Eq.(5.8)). Therefore we believe that the prefactors in Eq.(5.8) are correct in order ε^0 for Models A and B.

Note that the choice $\alpha = 1$ in Eq.(5.4) gives a worse result than the choice (3.7). The instanton values (5.5) differ from the WKB results (5.8) only by a factor 1.04. It may be conjectured that the still existing small discrepancy between Eqs.(5.5) and (5.8) is attributable to the rather simple ansatz (2.17).

Finally we come back to the determination of κ being defined in Eq.(4.4). By simple calculation one obtains from Eq.(2.4) the exact expression

$$\lambda_1 = \frac{1}{2}\varepsilon\kappa \frac{\phi_0^2(o)}{\int_0^\infty dx\phi_0(x)\phi_1(x)} \tag{5.9}$$

On evaluating Eq.(5.9) by the saddle point method with $\phi_1(x) \simeq \phi_0(x)$ and comparing with (5.8) there follows

$$\kappa = \frac{2}{\sqrt{\varepsilon\pi}}$$

and hence the result (4.4).

We would like to acknowledge valuable discussions with H. Grabert and P. Talkner.

REFERENCES

1. R.Landauer and J.A.Swanson, Phys. Rev. 121:1668(1961); J.W.F.Woo and R.Landauer, IEEE J. Quantum Electronics 7:435(1971); R.Landauer, J. Phys. Soc. Japan 41:695(1976)
2. R.Bonifacio and L.A.Lugiato, Opt. Commun. 19:172(1976), Phys. Rev. Lett. 40:1023(1978); C.R.Willis, Opt. Commun. 26:62(1978)
3. F.Schlögl, Z. Phys. 253:147(1972); A.Nikan, P.Ortoleva, J.Deutsch and J.Ross, J. Chem. Phys. 61:1056(1971); I.Matheson, D.F.Walls and C.W.Gardiner, J. Stat. Phys. 12:21(1975)
4. W.Weidlich, Collective Phenomena 1:51(1972); W.Weidlich, "Progress in Synergetics" (Erice Summer School, 1974), H.Haken, ed. (North-Holland, Amsterdam, 1974)
5. N.G.van Kampen, Journ. Stat. Phys. 17:71(1977)
6. H. Brand and A.Schenzle, Phys. Lett. 68A:427(1978)

7. M.Mörsch, H.Risken and H.D.Vollmer, Z. Physik B32:245(1979)
8. M.Razavy, Phys. Lett. 72A:89(1979)
9. M.O.Hongler, preprint Université de Genève, UGVA-DPT 12-228(1979)
10. F.Haake, Phys. Rev. Lett. 41:1685(1978)
11. W.Weidlich and H.Grabert, Z. Physik B36:283(1980)
12. M.Suzuki, Progr. Theor. Phys. 56:77, 477(1976), Journ. Stat. Phys. 16:11(1977), Phys. Lett. 67A:339(1978)
13. K.Kawasaki, M.C.Yalabik and J.D.Gunton, Phys. Rev. A17:455(1978)
14. R.Kubo, K.Matsuo and K.Kitahara, Journ. Stat. Phys. 9:51(1973)
15. N.G. van Kampen, Can. Journ. Phys. 39:551(1961); also in "Fluctuation Phenomena in Solids", R.E.Burgess, ed. (Academic Press, New York, 1965)
16. T.Arimitsu and M.Suzuki, Physica 86A:622(1977), 90A:303(1978)
17. S.Coleman, "The Uses of Instantons", Lectures delivered at the 1977 International School of Subnuclear Physics, Ettore Majorana
18. H.Tomita, A.Ito and H.Kidachi, Progr. of Theor. Phys. 56:786(1976)
19. R.Graham, Z. Physik B26:281(1977)
20. U.Weiss, Z. Physik B30:429(1978)
21. H.Pagels in "Proceedings of Orbis Scientiae 1978 on New Frontiers in High-Energy-Physics" ed. by B.Kursunoglu, A.Perlmutter and L.Scott (Plenum Press, New York, 1978)
22. H.Flyvbjerg, preprint Niels Bohr Institute, Copenhagen NBI-HE-79-33(1979)
23. F.Langouche, D.Roekaerts and E.Tirapegui Physica 97A:195(1979)
24. E.Gildener and A.Patrascioiu, Phys. Rev. D16:423(1977; erratum D16:3616(1977)
25. J.L.Gervais and B.Sakita, Phys. Rev. D11:2943(1975)
26. L.D.Faddeev and V.N.Popov:Phys. Lett. 25B:29(1967)
27. L.D.Landau and E.M.Lifschitz, "Quantenmechanik", Akademie Verlag Berlin
28. H.A.Kramers, Physica 7:284(1940)
29. R.S.Larson and M.D.Kostin, J. Chem. Phys. 69:4821(1978)

METASTABLE PHASES AND PERTURBATION EXPANSIONS

Miguel Calvo

Centro de Física
Instituto Venezolano de Investigaciones
Científicas, Caracas, Venezuela

I. INTRODUCTION

Let us consider a statistical mechanical homogeneous system in d dimensions which undergoes a continuous phase transition at some critical temperature T_c and such that in the neighbourhood of T_c the partition function can be approximated by an Euclidean field functional integral possessing a O(2) symmetry.[1]

The typical systems which we have in mind are (1) HeII, (2) Type I (clean) superconductors and (3) X-Y ferromagnets. Each of these three systems have the property of undergoing a second order phase transition at some critical temperature which is characterized by a drastic change in some of their physical properties [2]. In this lecture we shall not attempt to describe all of them, but rather we shall focus our attention on some specific property which is common to them, in spite of their different physical nature. The property of interest is the following :

(1) HeII superfluid : below T_c the liquid can flow with negligible viscosity. The flux current I is, however, restricted by some maximal flux $I_{max.}$ (i.e. $I<I_{max}$). If one attemps to increase I beyond this value the superfluid becomes unstable as dissipative effects set in.

(2) Superconductor : below T_c an electrical current can flow across the superconductor with negligible resistance. Again this current cannot exceed some maximal value for dissipative effects begin to appear.

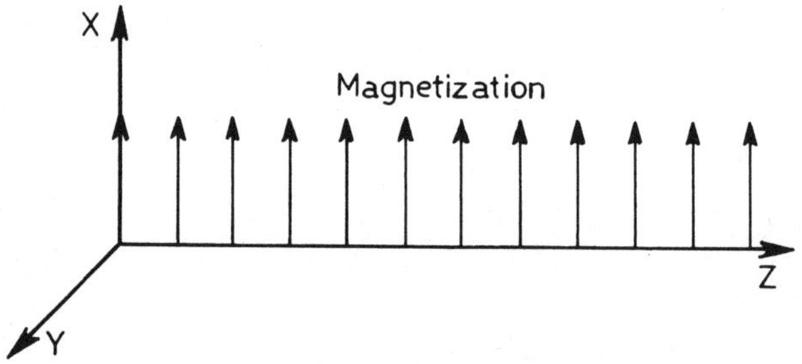

Fig. 1. X-Y ferromagnets

(3) X-Y ferromagnets : these anisotropic ferromagnets with two easy axes of magnetization (the x and y axes) become ferromagnetic below T_c (see fig. 1). There exist, however, other possible magnetic structures of helical form (see fig. 2), which also represent stable configurations of the system. The pitch of the magnetic helix, Λ, cannot be smaller than some minimum pitch Λ_{min}, for otherwise the helix becomes unstable.

In the following we shall see that this particular property of these systems can be described theoretically in a simple and unified way by employing the functional integral mentioned at the beginning.

II. THE LANDAU-GINZBURG-WILSON THEORY

This phenomenological theory postulates that in the vicinity of the critical temperature the partition function is given by the following functional integral :

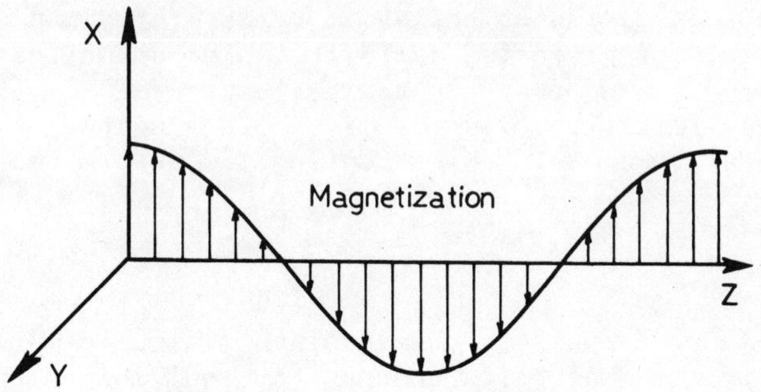

Fig. 2. Magnetic structures of helical form

$$Z = \int \mathcal{D}\, \Phi(x) \exp \{- H [\Phi]/_{kT}\} \tag{1}$$

where

$$H[\Phi] = \int h(\Phi)\, d^d x = \int d^d x \{\frac{1}{2}(\nabla\vec{\Phi})^2 + \frac{\mu}{2} \vec{\Phi}^2 + \frac{\lambda}{4} (\vec{\Phi}^2)^2\} \tag{2}$$

and $\vec{\Phi}$ is a two component real vector function, the so called order parameter of the system. The coefficients μ and λ are analytic functions of the temperature T with the property that for T close to T_c,

$$\mu(T) = \alpha(T - T_c) + \ldots\ldots \quad , (\alpha>0), \tag{3}$$

and

$$\lambda(T) \simeq \lambda(T_c)>0,$$

where the dotted terms are of order $(T-T_c)^2$ or higher.

If we assume that the system is enclosed in a d-dimensional box, then the proper boundary condition on $\vec{\Phi}(\vec{x})$ is that it must be a periodic function on the box.

The above functional integral cannot be evaluated exactly [3] and consequently one must resort to approximations.

The standard technique is the stationary phase method together with a loop expansion. The idea is to search for minima of the functional $H[\Phi]$ and expand $H[\Phi]$ about these minimal configurations. Then decomposing H into quadratic and interaction terms one is lead to the usual loop expansion series in terms of Feymman diagrams[4].

For systems of dimension d = 3 it can be shown that only one minimum of $H[\Phi]$ is important in the evaluation of Eq. (1) in the thermodynamic limit (i.e. V = volume $\to\infty$, N = number of particles $\to\infty$, but N/V finite). For $T<T_c$ this minimum is determined by

$$|\vec{\Phi}_{min}| = \text{constant} = -\frac{3!\mu}{\lambda} \tag{4}$$

which clearly corresponds to the absolute minimum of $H[\Phi]$. Once a particular direction of $\vec{\Phi}_m$ is chosen, the equilibrium properties of the system can be calculated by the procedure described above.

In this lecture we shall address ourselves to a different problem, that is we will consider other (relative) minima of $H[\Phi]$ and investigate their physical significance. Later on we shall develop a perturbative approach along similar lines.

The condition for an extreme of $H[\Phi]$ is the following :

$$\frac{\delta H[\Phi]}{\delta\vec{\Phi}(\vec{x})} = 0 \tag{5}$$

which leads to

$$\nabla^2\vec{\Phi} = (\mu + \frac{\lambda}{3!}\vec{\Phi}^2)\,\vec{\Phi} \quad . \tag{6}$$

Let us restrict ourselves to solutions of Eq. (6) which only depend on one coordinate (say x) : $\vec{\Phi}(\vec{x}) = \vec{\Phi}(x)$. Then Eq. (6) becomes an ordinary non-linear differential equation

$$\frac{d^2\vec{\Phi}}{dx^2} = (\mu + \frac{\lambda}{3!}\vec{\Phi}^2)\,\vec{\Phi} \quad . \tag{7}$$

To solve this equation it is convenient to identify $\vec{\phi}$ with $\vec{r}$, a two component real vector, and x with τ a ficticious time variable, then Eq. (7) represents Newton's equation of motion of a point particle of unit mass moving in a plane under the action of the following central potential :

$$V(\vec{r}) = -\left(\frac{\mu}{2}\vec{r}^2 + \frac{\lambda}{4!}(\vec{r}^2)^2\right) . \tag{8}$$

By introducing polar coordinates $r = |\vec{r}|$ and Θ , we can immediately write the first integrals of Eq. (7) :

$$\ell = r^2 \dot{\theta}$$

$$\varepsilon = \frac{1}{2} [\dot{r}^2 + (r\dot{\theta})^2] - \frac{\mu r^2}{2} - \frac{\lambda}{4!} r^4 = \frac{\dot{r}^2}{2} + W_{eff.}(r) \tag{9}$$

Where ℓ and ε are the conserved angular momentum and energy respectively and $W_{eff.}$ is the effective potential

$$W_{eff.}(r) = \frac{\ell^2}{2r^2} - \frac{\mu}{2} r^2 - \frac{\lambda}{4!} r^4 \tag{10}$$

On physical grounds we can see that we are only interested in bounded solutions $\vec{\Phi}(x)$. This means that we must only search for bounded trajectories of the mechanical problem. This condition will only occur for certain values of ℓ and ε. We can visualize this fact by looking at the curve of $W_{eff.}$ for different values of ℓ (see fig. 3).

Clearly the necessary condition for bounded orbits is that

$$\frac{dW_{eff.}}{dr} = 0 \tag{11}$$

for some value of r. This condition leads after some simple algebraic manipulations to the following cubic equation :

$$Z^3 - a^2 Z^2 + \frac{6\ell^2}{\lambda} = 0 \tag{12}$$

where $Z = r^2$ and $a^2 = -3!\mu/\lambda$.

By analysing the discriminant of Eq. (12) we can determine the condition for the existence of positive real roots. The result is the following :

i) Two positive distinct real roots exist if

$$\ell^2 < \ell^2_{max} = \frac{2\lambda a^6}{81} \text{ and } a^2 > 0$$

This last condition can only be fulfilled for $T < T_c$; above the critical temperature there are no solutions of this kind.

ii) Two positive equal roots exist for $\ell^2 = \ell^2_{max}$ and $a^2 > 0$.

iii) No positive real solution exist if $\ell^2 > \ell^2_{max}$.

An explicit analytic form of these roots can be given in terms of simple radicals by the standard formulae . We shall not bother to do so, but we will call r_o and r_1 the corresponding roots with $r_o < r_1$ (see fig. 4).

By assuming that condition i) is fulfilled we can easily convince ourselves that a family of bounded orbit solutions can exist if the energy ε is within the range indicated in fig. 4. Except for r_o and r_1, which correspond to circular orbit solutions, there will be a monoparametric family of orbits of pulsating radius. Their analytic form can be "readily" found by integration of Eq. (9).

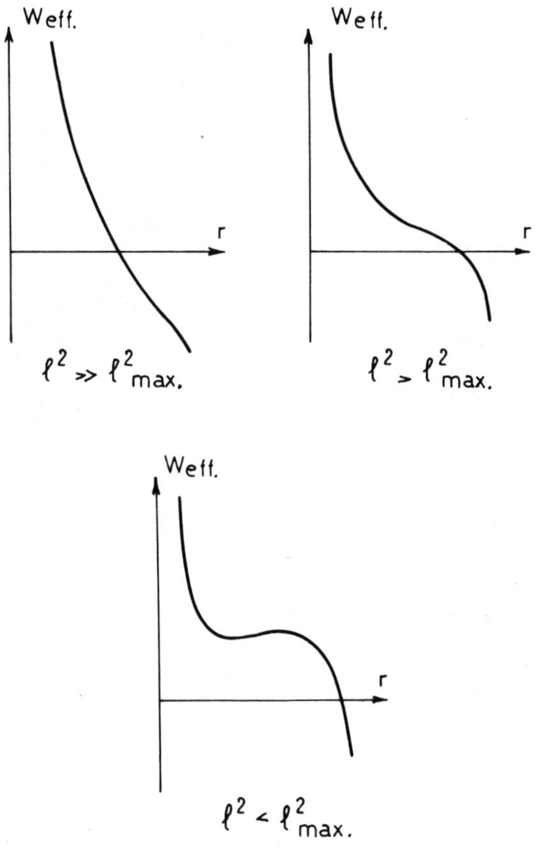

Fig. 3. Effective potential $W_{eff.}$ for different values of ℓ

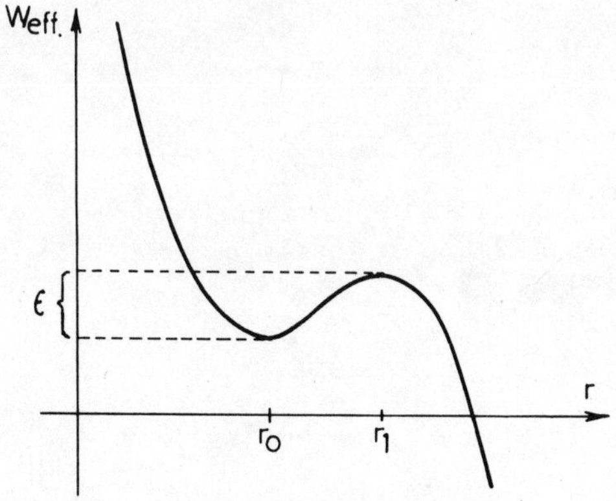

Fig. 4. Admissible range of energy ε for bounded orbit solutions

We must now translate back these solutions of the mechanical problem into our fields variables. It is clear that the correspondence is as follows :

$$\vec{r}(\tau) \longrightarrow \vec{\phi}_s(x) = r(x)\begin{cases}\sin\,(\theta(x)+\delta)\\ \cos\,(\theta(x)+\delta)\end{cases}, \tag{13}$$

where δ is a constant of integration and $\theta(x)$, $r(x)$ are the resulting angular and radial functions of the particle trajectory (with τ exchanged for x).

So far we have constructed a family of extremal solutions satisfying Eq. (5). We must now investigate whether they represent minima of $H[\phi]$ or not. Clearly if $\vec{\phi}_s(x)$ is a minimum of $H[\phi]$ and $\vec{\eta}(\vec{x})$ is any two components real bounded function[5]

$$H[\vec{\phi}_s + \vec{\eta}(\vec{x})] \geqslant H[\vec{\phi}_s] \tag{14}$$

This condition will be satisfied provided the following eigenvalue equation

$$\mathcal{H}\,[\vec{\phi}_s]\;\psi\,(\vec{x}) = E\,\psi(\vec{x}) \tag{15}$$

with

$$\psi(\vec{x}) = \begin{bmatrix} \psi_1(\vec{x}) \\ \psi_2(\vec{x}) \end{bmatrix}$$

and

$$H\,[\vec{\phi}_s(x)] = -\nabla^2 + \frac{\lambda}{3!}\,(\vec{\phi}_s^{\,2} - a^2) + \frac{\lambda}{3}\,(\phi_s(x)\phi_s^{\dagger}(x)), \tag{16}$$

has a non-negative spectrum.[6]

It is interesting to note that the operator $H[\phi_s(x)]$ represents a Pauli-Schrödinger hamiltonian of a quantum mechanical spin 1/2 particle of mass $m = \hbar/2$ and magnetic moment $\lambda/3$, moving in an external scalar potential

$$\frac{\lambda}{3!}\,(2\vec{\phi}_s^{\,2} - a^2)$$

and with its magnetic moment interacting with the periodic magnetic field :

$$\vec{B}(x) = r(x)\begin{bmatrix} \sin\ 2\theta(x) \\ \cos\ 2\theta(x) \end{bmatrix}$$

In order to prove the positivity $H[\phi_s]$ for each solution $\vec{\phi}_s(x)$ of Eq. (7), we have to first obtain its analytic expression by integrating Eq. (9) then substitute it in Eq. (16) and finally derive the spectrum in Eq. (15). This procedure is simple in principle but too difficult to carry out in practice. The integration of Eq. (9) leads in general to elliptic functions and obviously the corresponding $H[\vec{\phi}_s]$ operator will not be easily diagonalized. There is, however, a simpler criteria for determining the positiviness of $H[\vec{\phi}_s]$. It consists of applying the standard variational (Raleigh-Ritz) technique to obtain an upper bound of the ground state energy , frequently used in elementary quantum mechanics. In this case, if for some given $\vec{\phi}_s(x)$, we succeed in constructing a trial wave function whose energy expectation value is negative then obviously the corresponding $H[\vec{\phi}_s]$ will have at least one negative eigenvalue and consequently this $\vec{\phi}_s$ will not be a minimum of $H[\phi]$. It turns out that by this simple criteria, we can easily determine that among all bounded solutions of Eq. (7) only the circular orbit solution of radius r_1, has a non-negative spectrum (see appendix A.1).

Physical interpretation

Let us proceed to investigate the physical meaning of this minimal solution described above. Clearly its analytic expression has the following form :

$$\vec{\phi}\,(x) = r_1(\ell) = \begin{bmatrix} \sin\ \ell x/r_1^2(\ell) \\ \cos\ \ell x/r_1^2(\ell) \end{bmatrix} \tag{17}$$

where $r_1(\ell)$ is determined by Eq. (12) and where the arbitrary phase δ in Eq. (13) has been set equal to zero.[7]

In the case of a X - Y ferromagnet the field $\vec{\phi}(x)$ represents the local magnetization. Thus for each value of the parameter ℓ the above function represents a helical magnetic structure whose pitch is given by

$$\text{pitch of helix} = \frac{2\pi r_1^{\,2}(\ell)}{\ell} \, . \tag{18}$$

Moreover, since according to Eq. (12) ℓ is restricted to be smaller than ℓ_{max}, the corresponding pitch of the helix will be restricted to be smaller or equal to the minimal pitch whose value is

$$\frac{2\pi r_1^2(\ell_{max})}{\ell_{max}} \, .$$

Any magnetic configuration of helical form of smaller pitch will not be a minimum of Eq. (5) and consequently it will be unstable under small (thermal) fluctuations. This is exactly the property that we refered to at the beginning of this lecture.

In the case of HeII, the corresponding order parameter is a complex function Ψ, called wave function of the condensate, with the property that $|\Psi(\vec{x})|^2$ is proportional to the density of He atoms in the ground state and

$$\Psi^{\star} \left[- \frac{i\hbar\vec{\nabla}}{m_{He}} \right] \Psi$$

represents the velocity of the fluid (superfluid). In this case our solution becomes

$$\Psi_\ell(x) = r_1(\ell)\varepsilon^{\,i(\ell x/r_1^2(\ell))} \tag{19}$$

which implies that the corresponding superfluid velocity is given by

$$v_\ell = \frac{\hbar \ \ell}{m_{He} \ r_1^{\,2}(\ell)} < v_{max}$$

Again the maximum velocity of the superfluid corresponds to the maximum value that ℓ can attain.

In the case of superconductor one can, in a similar fashion, derive an expression for the critical current. However in this case the solution is incomplete because we have ignored the magnetic field which produces the supercurrent and which must be determined selfconsistently from the so called Landau-Ginzburg equations[8]. For the one dimensional superconductor the field energy can be shown to be negligible and consequently the above results are valid.

Other thermodynamical properties of these states can be derived to lowest order (tree diagram approximation) by approximating "its partition function" by

$$Z \sim \dot{Z}_{\ell} = \exp \{-H[\vec{\phi}_{\ell}]/_{kT} \}$$

as for the standard Landau theory.

III. FLUCTUATIONS, NUCLEATIONS AND PERTURBATION

Strictly speaking these configurations, although stable under small fluctuations, are not stable under arbitrary (large) fluctuations (nucleations) which can induce transitions from a configurations of a given ℓ to another one of smaller ℓ , corresponding to a lower value of the free energy $H[\phi_{\ell}]$, and eventually to the $\ell = 0$ state. Therefore for $\ell \neq 0$, these configurations represent metastables states of the system.

The situation is analagous to that of a classical point particle in a one dimensional potential sketched in fig. 5, and in contact with a heat reservoir at temperature T.

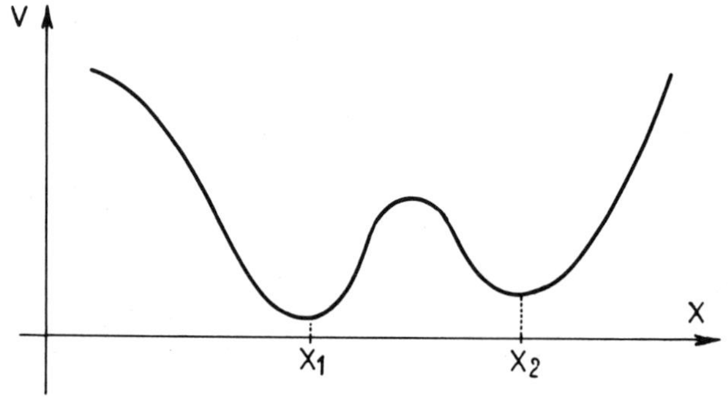

Fig. 5. Classical point particle in a one dimensional potential

If the particle is left stationary at position x_2 it will remain there until thermal fluctuations induce a transition to a lower potential energy step. The point to be stressed here is that if the potential energy barrier separating x_2 from x_1 is large and that the temperature of the reservoir is small (more precisely if : energy barrier /kT << 1), one could expect that the transition rate from x_2 to x_1 is so small that one can ignore the presence of this kind of processes and regard x_2 as the true equilibrium point of the system. One can then compute the thermodynamical properties in the harmonic approximation of the potential and treat the anharmonic terms as perturbations.

In the case of one dimensional superconductors this transition process has been studied in detail (both theoretically and experimentally [9]). The moral one learns from these studies as well as other observations on HeII is that these processes take place at an observable rate only if the systems are very close to T_c. For T not so close to T_c the mean life of the metastable phases can be very long (even years) [10]. It is this circumstance which we will consider in the following and simple ignore fluctuations inducing transitions from one phase to another. Our goal is then to construct the perturbation rules for the small fluctuations of a given metastable state and from them derive its thermodynamical properties.

Perturbation theory

Let us suppose that the system is in a metastable phase corresponding to some configuration $\vec{\phi}_\ell(x)$. In order to develop a perturbation expansion about this state we must proceed as indicated in section I, that is we must write

$$H[\phi] = H[\vec{\phi}_\ell(x) + \hat{\phi}(\vec{x})] \tag{20}$$

and expand $H[\phi]$ about $\vec{\phi}_\ell(x)$. The resulting expression is

$$H[\vec{\phi}_\ell + \hat{\phi}] = H[\phi_\ell] + H_o^{(\ell)}[\hat{\phi}] + H_r^{(\ell)}[\hat{\phi}] \tag{21}$$

where

$$H[\phi_\ell] = -\frac{\lambda\, r_1^4(\ell)\, V}{4!} \qquad (V = \text{volume of box}) \tag{22}$$

$$H_o^{(\ell)}[\hat{\phi}] = \int d^3x \,\{\hat{\phi}^\dagger\, \mathcal{H}[\vec{\phi}_\ell]\, \hat{\phi}\} \tag{23}$$

is the quadratic (harmonic) term and

$$H_1^{(\ell)}[\hat{\phi}] = \frac{\lambda}{4!} \int d^3x \,\{4(\vec{\phi}_\ell\cdot\hat{\phi})\hat{\phi}^2 + (\hat{\phi}^2)^2\} \tag{24}$$

are the cubic and quartic (anharmonic) terms.

The following step is then to construct the propagator which is the inverse of the operator $H[\vec{\phi}_\ell]$. To do so we shall first compute the eigenenergies and eigenfunctions of $H[\vec{\phi}_\ell]$ [11].

$$H[\vec{\phi}_\ell]\ \psi(\vec{x}) = E\ \psi(\vec{x}) \tag{25}$$

This problem is greatly simplified by exploiting the symmetries of $H[\vec{\phi}_\ell]$. Clearly $H[\vec{\phi}_\ell]$ is independent of y and z and consequently the eigenfunctions can be written as

$$\psi(\vec{\chi}) = \chi(x)\ \exp\{i\ \vec{k}_\perp . \vec{\chi}\} \tag{26}$$

where $\vec{k}_\perp = (0,k_y,k_z)$ and $\chi(x)$ is an undetermined two component spinor eigenfunction. However $H[\vec{\phi}_\ell]$ is neither invariant under arbitrary translations along the x axis nor under rotations about the same axis. Nevertheless there exists a continuous symmetry consisting of a general displacement along x followed by an appropiate rotation around the x axis, which compensates the effect of the translation. This symmetry, which is manifest in the function $\vec{\phi}_\ell(x)$, correspond to the screw symmetry of a helix (see Eq. (17)). One can easily show that the infinitesimal generator of this symmetry is given by the following hermitian operator :

$$P_\ell = -i\ \left(\frac{\partial}{\partial x} + \frac{\ell}{r_1^2(\ell)}\ \sigma_y\right) \tag{27}$$

where σ_y is the Pauli matrix. Furthermore it is easily checked that

$$[P_\ell, H[\vec{\phi}_\ell]] = 0\ . \tag{28}$$

The normalized eigenfunctions of P_ℓ corresponding to the eigenvalue k,

$$P_\ell \chi_k(x) = k\ \chi_k(x) \tag{29}$$

have the following form :

$$\chi_k(x) = \frac{1}{(2\pi)^{3/2}}\ e^{ikx}\ S_\ell(x)\xi(k) \text{ where } S_\ell(x) = \exp\{-i\sigma_y \frac{\ell x}{r_1^2(\ell)}\} \quad (30)\ (31)$$

and where $\xi(k)$ is an arbitrary constant unimodular spinor.

Finally the eigenvalues and eigenfunctions of $H[\vec{\phi}_\ell]$ are easily derived by substituting Eq. (26) and Eq. (30) in Eq. (25). The resulting quantities are

$$E_\pm(k,\vec{k}_\perp) = k^2 + \vec{k}_\perp^2 + \frac{\lambda r_1^2(\ell)}{6} \pm\left[\left(\frac{2\ell k}{r_1^2(\ell)}\right)^2 + \left(\frac{\lambda r_1^2(\ell)}{6}\right)^2\right]^{1/2} \tag{32}$$

and

$$\xi(k) = \xi_\pm(k) = R_\ell(k)\eta_\pm = e^{i\sigma_x P_\ell(k)}\eta_\pm \tag{33}$$

where $\eta_+ = [{}^1_0]$ and $\eta_- = [{}^0_1]$, σ_x is the Pauli matrix and

$$\tan P(k) = \frac{2k\ell/r_1^2(\ell)}{E_+(k,o) - k^2} \tag{34}$$

Moreover it is easily checked that

$$\int d^3x\, \psi^\dagger_{j,\vec{k}}(\vec{x})\, \psi_{j',\vec{k}'}(\vec{x}) = \delta_{j,j'}\, \delta^3(\vec{k} - \vec{k}') \tag{35}$$

where j, j' = ± and $\vec{k} = (k,\vec{k}_\perp)$.

We shall assume that the set $\{\psi_{j,\vec{k}}(\vec{x})\}$ forms, for each value of ℓ, a complete set of functions.
The expression for the propagator in coordinate space can then be easily derived.

$$D_\ell(\vec{x}|\vec{x}') = \sum_{j=\pm} \int \frac{d^3k}{(2\pi)^3} \{S_\ell(x)\, R_\ell(k)\, \eta_j\, \eta_j^\dagger\, R_\ell^\dagger(k)\, S_\ell^\dagger(x)\} \frac{e^{i\vec{k}(\vec{x}-\vec{x}')}}{E_j(\vec{k})} \tag{36}$$

with

$$H[\vec{\phi}_\ell(x)]D_\ell(\vec{X}|\vec{X}') = \delta^3(\vec{X} - \vec{X}') \tag{37}$$

It is convenient to define the propagator in momentum space where it takes a simple form. However, because of the complicated x-dependence of D_ℓ on x and x', the usual Fourier transform will not be a simple function. A great simplification of this expression is obtained by introducing some preliminary mathematical definitions.

We have concluded that the set of eigenfunctions $\{\psi^{(\ell)}_{j,k}(\vec{x})\}$ are, for each value of ℓ, a complete set of functions.
Therefore any two component vector function of x, $\phi(x)$, can be expanded in the following way :

$$\phi(x) = \int dk \,\{\, a_+^{(\ell)}(k)\psi^{(\ell)}_{+,k}(x) + a_-^{(\ell)}(k)\psi^{(\ell)}_{-,k}(x)\} \tag{38}$$

Clearly the scalar functions $a_\pm^{(\ell)}(k)$ completely determine $\phi(x)$.
Using the orthogonality properties of the set

$$\{\psi^{(\ell)}_{j,k}(x)\}$$

one obtains

$$a_j^{(\ell)}(k) = \int \psi^{(\ell)\dagger}_{j,k}(x)\, \phi(x)\, dx = \eta_j^\dagger\, \tilde{\phi}^{(\ell)}(k) \tag{39}$$

with

$$\tilde{\phi}^{(\ell)}(k) = e^{-i\sigma_x \mathcal{P}_\ell(k)} \int dx\, e^{-ikx}\, e^{i\sigma_y \frac{\ell x}{r_1^2(\ell)}}\, \phi(x) \qquad (40)$$

A similar expression for the adjoint function $\phi^\dagger(x)$ can be derived. Let us call the function $\tilde{\phi}^{(\ell)}(k)$ the screw momentum transform of $\phi(x)$.

Having introduced these definitions it is then convenient to define the propagator in k-space by performing a double screw momentum transform with respect to x and x' and the usual Fourier transforms with respect to the remaining variables.

$$\tilde{D}_\ell(\vec{k},\vec{k}') = \iint d^3x d^3x'\, e^{-i\vec{k}\vec{x}}\, e^{+i\vec{k}'\vec{x}'} \{R_\ell(k) S_\ell(x) D_\ell(\vec{x}|\vec{x}') S_\ell^\dagger(x') R_\ell^\dagger(k')\}$$

$$= \delta^3(\vec{k} - \vec{k}')\, \{D_+^\ell(\vec{k}) + D_-^\ell(\vec{k})\} \qquad (41)$$

where

$$D_\pm^{(\ell)}(\vec{k}) = \frac{\eta_\pm \eta_\pm}{\vec{k}^2 + \frac{\lambda r_1^2(\ell)}{6} \pm \left[\left(\frac{2\ell k}{r_1^2(\ell)}\right)^2 + \left(\frac{\lambda r_1^2(\ell)}{6}\right)^2\right]^{1/2}} \qquad (42)$$

We can now develop the perturbation rules for dealing with $H_I^{(\ell)}[\hat{\phi}]$. A crucial point, which makes the resulting Feynman rules simple, is to write $H_I^{(\ell)}[\hat{\phi}]$ in momentum space by performing again a screw momentum transform with respect to the coordinate x.

In this form the momentum will be conserved at each vertex. The underlying reason for this fact is that the function $\vec{\phi}_\ell(x)$, which multiplies the cubic interaction term in Eq. (24), is an eigenfunction of the operator $\mathcal{P}_\ell$ with zero eigenvalue.

Consequently in the momentum transformed expression for the cubic term of Eq. (24), the factor $\vec{\phi}_\ell(x)$ will carry no momentum and therefore momentum will be conserved.

Taking into account these considerations the Feynman rules in momentum space can be easily spelled out from Eq. (24). The resulting expression are given in table I.

As concluding remarks it is interesting to note that in the infrared limit (small k) the propagator contains a singularity

$$\lim_{\vec{k}\to 0} [D_-^{(\ell)}(\vec{k})]^{-1} = 0$$

which corresponds to a Goldstone mode. Finally we end this section by also noting that in the limit $\ell \to 0$ one recovers the familiar version of the Feynman rules for the true equilibrium state of the system.

TABLE 1

Propagator : $D^{(\ell)}(\vec{k}) = D^{(\ell)}_{++}(\vec{k}) + D^{(\ell)}_{--}(\vec{k})$

where

$$D^{(\ell)}_{++}(\vec{k}) = \frac{1}{\varepsilon_+(\vec{k})} \quad , \quad D^{(\ell)}_{--}(\vec{k}) = \frac{1}{\varepsilon_-(\vec{k})}$$

3-point vertex : $\frac{\lambda}{3!} \quad (\phi_\ell^\dagger \boldsymbol{\phi}) \; (\boldsymbol{\phi}^\dagger \boldsymbol{\phi})$:

$$\frac{\lambda}{3} (\delta_{-,a} \quad \delta_{b,c} + \delta_{-,b} \quad \delta_{a,c} \quad + \delta_{-,c} \; \delta_{a,b} \;)$$

where a,b,c, = ±

4-point vertex : $\frac{\lambda}{4!} \; (\boldsymbol{\phi}^2)^2$:

$$\frac{\lambda}{3} (\delta_{a,b} \quad \delta_{c,d} \quad + \delta_{a,c} \quad \delta_{b,d} \quad + \delta_{a,d} \quad \delta_{b,c})$$

where a,b,c,d = ±

At each vertex the total energy and momentum is conserved as well as the total energy momentum.

IV. CONCLUSIONS

We have seen in the previous sections how the Landau-Ginzburg-Wilson theory, which has been so successful in describing the thermodynamic equilibrium properties of these systems, also describes their metastable phases. This is thus a good clue that perturbation theory and renormalization group techniques could also provide a good description of the quasiequilibrium thermodynamical properties of these states.

Having derived the perturbation rules for the metastable phases we could proceed to the evaluation of correlation functions of physical interest. However, for reasons of time, this will not be done here. These results will be published elsewhere.

APPENDIX A-1

Let us show that among all bounded solutions of Eq. (7), only the circular orbit of radius r_1 represents a minimum of the functional $H[\phi]$.
In the case of the circular orbit solution r_0 (see fig. 4), the explicit solution of the eigenvalue Eq. (25) shows the presence of negative eigenvalues. This, then, guarantees that it is not a minimum of $H[\phi]$.
Let us next show that any solution $\vec{\phi}_s(x)$ for which $|\vec{\phi}_s(x)|$ is not a constant, must necessarily lead to a Pauli-Schrödinger equation

$$E\psi(x) = \{-\nabla^2 + \frac{\lambda}{3!}(\vec{\phi}_s{}^2 - a^2) + \frac{\lambda}{3}(\phi_s\phi_s^\dagger)\}\,\psi(\vec{x}) = \mathcal{H}[\vec{\phi}_s]\,\psi(\vec{x}) \tag{a-1}$$

with negative energy eigenvalues. This assertion can be proved from the following facts.
The hamiltonian $\mathcal{H}[\phi_s]$ is periodic and consequently is invariant under displacements over one period of $\vec{\phi}_s(x)$ in x. Therefore the eigenstates satisfy Bloch's theorem and can be written as

$$\psi(\vec{x}) = e^{ikx}\,\overline{\psi}_k(\vec{x}) \tag{a-2}$$

where $\overline{\psi}_k(x)$ is a periodic function and k is the pseudomomentum. The spectrum of $\mathcal{H}[\phi_s]$ must be a continuum (a continuous function of k) with possibly band gaps.
Let us prove that for any $\vec{\phi}_s(x)$ with $|\vec{\phi}_s(x)|$ non-constant, there exist at least two linearly independent functions with zero energy. The first of these functions can be obtained by differentiating Eq.(7) with respect to x, and it is given by $d\vec{\phi}_s/dx$:

$$\mathcal{H}[\phi_s]\,\frac{d\vec{\phi}_s}{dx} = 0 \tag{a-3}$$

The function $\phi_s(x)$ can be expressed in terms of the variables r and θ (see Eq. (13)) as follows :

$$\vec{\phi}_s(x) = r(x) \begin{bmatrix} \cos\theta(x) \\ \sin\theta(x) \end{bmatrix} = r(x)\, S(\theta(x)) \begin{bmatrix} 1 \\ 0 \end{bmatrix} \tag{a-4}$$

with

$$S(\theta(x)) = \begin{bmatrix} \cos\theta(x) & -\sin\theta(x) \\ \sin\theta(x) & \cos\theta(x) \end{bmatrix} . \tag{a-5}$$

Therefore we obtain

$$\frac{d\vec{\phi}_s}{dx} = \left\{\frac{dr}{dx} S(\theta(x)) + r \frac{dS(\theta(x))}{dx}\right\} \begin{bmatrix} 1 \\ 0 \end{bmatrix} . \tag{a-6}$$

Let us construct the other zero energy wavefunction. Consider the following trial function :

$$\gamma(x) = N\, r(x)\, S(\theta(x)) \begin{bmatrix} 0 \\ 1 \end{bmatrix} \tag{a-7}$$

where N is some normalization constant. Clearly if $\frac{dr}{dx} \neq 0$ functions $\gamma(x)$ and $d\vec{\phi}_s/dx$ are linearly independent. The expectation value of $H[\phi_s]$ for $\gamma(x)$ is given by

$$\int dx\, \gamma^\dagger(x)\, H[\phi_s]\gamma(x) = N^2 \int r(x)\{- \frac{d^2}{dx^2} + \dot{\theta}^2 + \frac{\lambda}{3!} (r^2-a^2)\} .$$

$$. \, r(x)\, dx = 0 \tag{a-8}$$

The last steps follow from the fact that

$$\frac{d\varepsilon}{dx} = \frac{d}{dx}\{\frac{1}{2}\dot{r}^2 + W_{eff.}(r)\} = 0 \tag{a-9}$$

Finally, we conclude that because the continuity of the spectrum and the existence of two linearly independent eigenstates of zero energy that there must exist some range of energy in which they are negative. (However we have not excluded the possibility of having a doubly degenerate zero energy ground state.)

REFERENCES

1. For a general review on the motivation and derivation of this approximation the reader should consult the following reviews.
   - M. Fisher : Report of Prog. in Phys. 30, 131 B, (1967)
   - L. Kadanoff et al. : Rev. of Mod. Phys. 39, 395 B, (1967)
   - H.E. Stanley : Phase Transitions and Critical Phenomena. Clarendon Press, Oxford (1971)

2. General elementary discussions of the physical properties of these systems can be found in :
   - M. Tinkham : Introduction to superconductivity, Mc Graw-Hill press, N.Y. (1975)
   - J. Wilks : The properties of liquid and solid helium. Oxford Univ. Press, Oxford (1967)
   - S. Vonsovski : Magnetism II. J. Wiley Press, N.Y. (1974)

3. Except for one dimensional systems, see
   - J. Scalapino et al : Phys. Rev. B 6, 3409, (1972)

4. J. Zinn - Justin : Wilson's theory of critical phenomena and renormalized perturbation theory. 1973 Cargese lectures on physics. Edited by E. Brezin and J. Charap. Gordon and Breach press.

5. Strictly speaking this is only true for sufficiently small functions $\vec{\eta}(\vec{x})$ (i.e. max. $|\vec{\eta}(\vec{x})| < \varepsilon$, for some appropiate value of ε)

6. This is the usual criterium employed in determining the stability of solition solutions of non-linear equations. See also I.
   - Gelfand and S. Fomin : Calculus of Variations, Ch. 5. Prentice Hall P., N.J. (1963)

7. The choice of this phase constant δ is equivalent to the choice in the direction of $\vec{\phi}_m$ in Eq. (4)

8. V. Ginzburg and L. Landau : Zh. Eksperim. i. Teo. Fiz. 20, 1064, (1950)

9. See : V. Ambegaoker and J. Langer : Phys. Rev. 140, A 1889, (1965) and M. Tinkham : Introduction to Supercondictivity, Mc Graw-Hill press, N.Y. (1975)

10. R. Donnelly : Experimental Superfluidity. Chicago Univ. Press, Chicago (1967)

11. M. Calvo : Phys. Rev. B 18, 5073, (1978)

PARTICIPANTS

ADAMOWSKI Janusz (U. Dortmund)
ANTOINE Jean-Pierre (U.C.Louvain)
BACH Alexander (U. Münster)
BERG Heinz Peter (U. Clausthal)
BERTRAND Jacqueline (U. Paris VII)
BLANCHARD Philippe (U. Bielefeld)
BOUCKAERT Louis P.(U.C.Louvain and K.U.Leuven)
BRACHET Marc Etienne (U.Paris VI)
CALVO Miguel (U. Caracas)
COMBE Philippe (CNRS Marseille)
DAUBECHIES Ingrid (V.U. Brussel)
DEBACKER-MATHOT Françoise (U.C. Louvain)
DEININGHAUS Uwe (U. Dortmund)
DEKKER Hans (TNO Den Haag)
DEVREESE Jozef T.(U.I. Antwerpen)
DONEUX Joël (U.C.Louvain)
ELWORTHY David (U.of Warwick, Coventry)
ENZ Charles P. (U. Genève)
ETIM Etim (U. Siegen)
GARCZYNSKI Włodimierz (U. Wrocław)
GARRIDO Luis (U. Barcelona)
GERLACH Bernd (U. Dortmund)
GRAHAM Robert (U. Essen)
GRECOS Alkis (U.L. Bruxelles)
HÄFFNER Walter (U. Stuttgart)
HIRSCHFELD Allen (U. Dortmund)
HORNER Heinz (U. Heidelberg)
HORSTHEMKE Werner (U.L. Bruxelles)
JANCEL Raymond (U. Paris VII)
JANSSENS de BISTHOVEN Olivier (U.C. Louvain)
KIEHM Patrick (U. Liège)
KLAUDER John R. (Bell Labs, Murray Hill)
KREE Paul (U. Paris VI)
KUBO Jisuke (U. Dortmund)
LANGOUCHE Flor (K.U.Leuven)
LESCHKE Hajo (U. Dortmund)
MORAWECK Michael (U.Dortmund)

ONOFRI Enrico (U. Parma)
PEETERS François (U.I. Antwerpen)
RIDEAU Guy (U. Paris VII)
RODRIGUEZ Roger (CNRS Marseille)
ROEKAERTS Dirk (K.U.Leuven)
RONVEAUX André (Fac. U. Namur)
SIMMS David J.(U. Bonn)
SIRUGUE Michel (CNRS Marseille)
SIRUGUE-COLLIN Madeleine (CNRS Marseille)
SPEISER David (U.C.Louvain)
STOLZE Joachim (U. Dortmund)
STREIT Ludwig (U. Bielefeld)
TARSKI Jan (U. Clausthal)
TIRAPEGUI Enrique (U.C.Louvain)
TRUMAN Aubrey (Heriot-Watt U., Edinburgh)
VAUSE Michel (U.C.Louvain)
WEISS Ulrich (U. Stuttgart)
YASUE Kunio (U. Genève)

INDEX